OXFORD CLASSICAL MONOGRAPHS

Published under the supervision of
a Committee of the Faculty of Classics in
the University of Oxford

The aim of the Oxford Classical Monographs series (which replaces the Oxford Classical and Philosophical Monographs) is to publish books based on the best theses on Greek and Latin literature, ancient history, and ancient philosophy examined by the Faculty Board of Classics.

Platonic Dialogue and the Education of the Reader

A. K. COTTON

OXFORD
UNIVERSITY PRESS

OXFORD
UNIVERSITY PRESS

Great Clarendon Street, Oxford, OX2 6DP,
United Kingdom

Oxford University Press is a department of the University of Oxford.
It furthers the University's objective of excellence in research, scholarship,
and education by publishing worldwide. Oxford is a registered trade mark of
Oxford University Press in the UK and in certain other countries

First Edition published in 014

Impression: 2

Published in the United States of America by Oxford University Press
198 Madison Avenue, New York, NY 10016, United States of America

British Library Cataloguing in Publication Data
Data available

ISBN 978-0-19-968405-2

Printed and bound in Great Britain by Clays Ltd, St Ives plc

Contents

Preface

I begin my study, in Part I, by examining the character of the response the dialogues invite in the reader, with careful attention to Plato's presentation of the activity of interlocutors, which I treat as a complex model for the reader. In Part II, against this background, I offer a series of case studies in how the dialogues engage the reader. In chapter 4, I look at Plato's use of characterization, and in chapter 5 I consider the structure of individual passages of argumentation. Chapter 6 looks at larger-scale structural patterns that affect the shape of whole dialogues, while chapter 7 considers Plato's handling of plot. In chapter 8, drawing the strands of my study together, I reflect on the value Plato's dialogues attach to reading and on Plato's engagement with civic frameworks and values.

There are two principal reasons I have chosen the present arrangement, both informed by the idea that Plato, in his dialogues, is carving out an arena for a particular type of learning engagement. First, I am concerned to show how my approach can be applied to dialogues usually regarded as coming from Plato's 'early', 'middle', and 'late' periods of composition. For this reason, I have not wanted to limit my study to a single dialogue or period; and in each chapter I offer brief readings of a dialogue of each type, or at least indicate how my ideas might apply to them. Exploring the engagement of the reader in works of these different types allows me to develop a reading of the receiver's development across the corpus, as well as in individual works, as I explain in chapter 2.

Second, I wish to show that my approach can be applied across a range of features of the dialogues, and to illustrate how these complement each other in the ways they engage the reader. When interpreters focus on one feature, such as argumentation or characterization, it often remains unclear how others would be amenable to similar treatment. In particular, I am keen to show that my approach accounts for both 'philosophical' aspects of the dialogues (primarily argumentation) and 'literary' ones.[1] Traditionally, critics have found

[1] A successful interpretation of the dialogues needs to account for both: while 'literary' interpreters have criticized traditional commentators for focusing exclusively

it difficult to show how these work together, sometimes suggesting, to put it crudely, that they engage the 'intellect' and 'emotions' respectively. Such a view, as I discuss in more detail later, is unattractive for a variety of reasons, not least because it seems to make Plato's views on poetry at odds with his own literary practice; and it is now commonly recognized as overly simplistic. Indeed, the juxtaposition of 'intellect' and 'emotion' is itself increasingly being disputed.[2] However, this still leaves us with the challenge of offering a satisfying account of the different aspects of the dialogues, in which both play a valuable role in engaging the reader but their obvious differences are not ignored. The approach I develop in this study, based on the idea that Plato's dialogues invite a distinctive type of engagement in the reader, will, I hope, offer a plausible way of doing this.

Two alternatives to the present structure would have been to offer a study of a single topic across the dialogues or to undertake a study of a single dialogue. Both of these offer scope for more extended analysis than my present arrangement; and, by way of compromise, there is a core group of dialogues to which I regularly return, including *Republic*, *Phaedrus*, and *Sophist*, though I also draw on a wider selection of works to provide context for my arguments.

My thanks go to all those who have helped shape this study or supported me during its development, and in particular: my family; Tobias Reinhardt, who supervised my D.Phil. thesis; Tim Rood, who oversaw its transformation into its present shape; Richard Rutherford; Lesley Brown; my colleagues at Magdalen College School, and in particular the Master, Dr Tim Hands.

on argumentation, the opposite charge is now being thrown back against them. See e.g. the critique of Gordon in Benson (2003). For the parallel problem of the relationship between poetry and philosophy, intellect and emotion, in Lucretius, see Gale (1994) 1, Volk (2002) 72–3, 95 ff.

[2] See e.g. Nussbaum (2001).

Abbreviations

Abbreviated titles for works of Plato:

Ap.	*Apology*
Chrm.	*Charmides*
Euthd.	*Euthydemus*
Euthphr.	*Euthyphro*
G.Hp.	*Greater Hippias*
Grg.	*Gorgias*
Lch.	*Laches*
Ly.	*Lysis*
M.	*Meno*
Phd.	*Phaedo*
Phdr.	*Phaedrus*
Phlb.	*Philebus*
Plt.	*Politicus*
Prm.	*Parmenides*
Prt.	*Protagoras*
R.	*Republic*
Smp.	*Symposium*
Sph.	*Sophist*
Tht.	*Theaetetus*

Abbreviated titles for works of Aristotle:

Soph. El.	*Sophistical Refutations*
Top.	*Topics*

Other titles are given in full.

Part I

1

Reading Plato's Dialogues

Socrates: Would a sensible farmer, who cares for his seeds and wants them to bear fruit, in seriousness plant them in the gardens of Adonis in summer and take pleasure in watching them become beautiful in eight days, or would he do these things in play and on account of the holiday, when he did it at all? As for the seeds about which he was serious, using his knowledge of farming, wouldn't he plant them at the appropriate time, and be content if the things he had sown reached fruition in the eighth month?

Phaedrus: He would act in this way, Socrates, in the case of those he was serious about, and otherwise, as you say, in the case of the others.

Socrates: And shall we say that the man who has knowledge of what is just and noble and good has less sense with regard to his seeds than the farmer?

Phaedrus: Certainly not.

Socrates: Then he won't, in seriousness, write them in ink, sowing them through a pen, with words that are unable to come to their own defence with an account and unable adequately to teach the truth.

Phaedrus: That isn't likely.

Socrates: It is not. But it is likely that he will sow gardens of letters for play and will write, whenever he writes, treasuring up reminders for himself when reaches the forgetfulness of old age, and for everyone who follows the same path, and he will delight in seeing them putting forth tender growth. And when others engage in different amusements, watering themselves with drinking parties and other things akin to these, then that man, it is likely, will spend his time entertaining himself with the things I have just described.

Phaedrus, 276bd

1.1. CONVERSING AND READING

Plato's dialogues portray people engaged in conversations that play—or at least have the potential to play—a part in their philosophical development. The participants engage in discussion with varying degrees of commitment, productivity, and philosophical sophistication; they have different agendas, and respond in very different ways. But we can always see how the conversations *could* contribute—in however preliminary a fashion—to their philosophical progress. Through its presentation as the preferred philosophical method, and its sheer dominance of Plato's works, conversation becomes, in the dialogues, a paradigm of philosophizing. The works tell us a great deal about how we should (and should not) go about philosophically valuable discussion, and how it can benefit us. At the same time, they encourage us to engage in it for ourselves, pointing towards further active philosophizing beyond the confines of the text. In this regard, the dialogues place central value on conversation—an activity in which, as readers, we are not currently participating.

In the very process of doing this, however, the dialogues engage us in another kind of activity, namely reading; and it is the value of the responses of the *reader* of the dialogues that is my focus in this study. Specifically, I will suggest that it makes sense to see our activity in reading as similar in nature and in value to that of interlocutors—that is, as constituting a kind of learning—and that engaging the reader in a process of learning is a central function of the dialogues.[1] The idea that the reader's relationship with Plato's text is analogous to that of the respondent with the discussion leader, that we engage in a dialogue with the text parallel to theirs,[2] is by no means new—indeed, it is almost a commonplace of Platonic criticism. But it is stated and

[1] For the dialogues' relationship with the reader, rather than the dialogue between interlocutors, as the proper focus of interpretation, see Gifford (2001) 88, Sayre (1995) 26, Kahn (1996) xiv–xv. Cf. Lebeck (1972) 288–9, White (1996) 127. This is an important emphasis in Clay (2000) *passim*.

[2] The notion of 'dialogue' is applied to the relationship between many texts and their readers, yet carries particular significance in the case of Plato because of the analogy it implies between the activity of readers and interlocutors. For the dialogue of Plato's texts with their readers, see e.g. M. Frede (1992a). For the analogy between interlocutor and reader, see e.g. Sayre (1988) 103, Sayre (1995) 21–7 and *passim*, West (1995) 59, Krentz (1983) 37, Hadot (1995) 104–5, 149, Gifford (2001), Ausland (1997) 386.

implied so frequently, usually without clarification, that it is often unclear precisely what the interpreter understands by it. What exactly is the relationship between reader and interlocutor? What does the reader's dialogue with the text consist in? How does the dialogue between interlocutors affect that of the reader? What kind of response is invited in the reader, and how, if at all, is it different from that invited by other types of literature? By exploring the analogy in more detail, I hope to shed light on the question that motivates my study: what value does the reader's dialogue with Plato's texts have within the philosophical process?

These are issues to which the dialogues themselves direct our attention, not least in a well-known, yet still puzzling, passage in Plato's *Phaedrus*, which seems to call into question the value of all written texts, including, apparently, Plato's own dialogues.[3] This rich and complex passage, which concludes with the comparison between dialectician and farmer quoted above, opens when Socrates' discussion partner, Phaedrus, asks him what makes writing valuable. In answer, Socrates tells a story about the ancient Egyptian king Thamus, whom the divinity Theuth once visited. Theuth displays to him various arts in turn; when it comes to writing, he proudly introduces his discovery:

> *O king, this knowledge will make the Egyptians wiser and will improve their memory; for I have discovered a potion for memory and for wisdom.*

Thamus' response, however, is much more guarded:

> *Since you are the father of letters, through your affection you have described their power as the opposite of what it really is. For this will produce forgetfulness in the souls of those who learn it, through not practising their memory, since due to their faith in writing, which is external and based on signs which belong to others, they will not remember for themselves from the inside. You have discovered a potion not for remembering, but for reminding; you provide learners with the appearance of wisdom, not with its reality. For, hearing many things without teaching, they will seem to know a great deal, when for the most part they*

[3] The literature on this passage is extensive. See e.g. Ferrari (1987), Rutherford (1995) 267–71, Kahn (1996) 376–92, Derrida (1981b), Griswold (1986) 202–29, Mackenzie (1982), Nightingale (1995) 133–71, Rowe (1986b), Krentz (1983) 37–44, Burger (1980).

> *are ignorant and hard to associate with, since they appear to be wise rather than being wise.*
>
> *Phaedrus*, 274e–275b

There are two principal concerns about written texts expressed in what Thamus says. The first is that writing appears to offer the receiver knowledge, without in fact doing so; as a result, it is in danger of taking the place of dialectical inquiry, which is the only way of attaining true understanding. The damage caused by the receiver's mistaken *perception* is the point here—writing will make him think he has knowledge and will thereby discourage him from engaging in the type of philosophical activity that can actually foster it. But lurking beneath this appears to be a second concern, that writing cannot contain or convey knowledge at all: writing, says Thamus, does not offer the reality of wisdom (σοφίας δὲ τοῖς μαθηταῖς δόξαν, οὐκ ἀλήθειαν πορίζεις 275a6–7). This same concern is echoed in Socrates' comparison of dialectician and farmer; the dialectician will not, if he is wise, sow the seeds of discourse 'through a pen, with words that are unable to come to their own defence with an account and unable adequately to teach the truth' (276c8–9).

At the end of his tale of Theuth and Thamus, Socrates adds a comment that offers further insight into the thought that writing cannot contain knowledge:

> *Writing, Phaedrus, has this strange feature and is in reality like painting. For the offsprings of painting stand as if they are alive, but if someone should ask them something, they keep solemnly silent. And written words are the same. You might think that they spoke as if they had understanding, but if someone asks them about any of the things that has been said, wishing to learn more, it signals only that one same thing forever. And whenever it has once been written down, every account rolls around everywhere, among those who have understanding and equally among quite unfitting company, and it does not know to whom it should speak and to whom it should not. And when it is ill-treated and abused without justice, it always needs its father's support; for it cannot defend or help itself.*
>
> *Phaedrus*, 275de

In Socrates' image, the figures in a painting, lifelike though they are in their momentary pose, are unable to move or change. Just so, a text may seem to offer insights of intelligence, but it cannot expand upon what it currently says. The nature of the written medium, that is, means that a text cannot develop or refine its ideas in response to scrutiny, or explain the reasoning that supports these ideas. In consequence it is unable to demonstrate the depth of understanding necessary for knowledge: its apparent insights can only be treated as unsupported claims. This also means that a text cannot pass on knowledge to its receiver: without the ability to explain, defend, refine, and respond—none of which the text can offer him—the receiver of a text does not have a true grasp on the ideas he has read. He has not examined the reasoning behind the insights in the text nor how they fit in with the rest of his beliefs, and so those insights may easily be dislodged. It is only by working to supply this further reasoning for himself that the reader can start to develop understanding—and once he has done this, the understanding belongs to him, and not to the text. The danger of a text that appears to offer knowledge, as the comparison with painting makes clear, is that a reader may mistakenly think that he has acquired knowledge, and thereby cease from the further dialogic activity that would in fact enable him to move towards it.

Phaedrus' discussion of writing is puzzling, even paradoxical: it appears to call into question the philosophical value of written texts within a written work that itself purports, along with the rest of Plato's corpus, to have educative intent. Is Plato genuinely undermining the value of all of his written output, and thereby the place of reading within the philosophical project—or are we to understand what his characters say in another way?

Critics have interpreted the comments variously, of course; some claim that they are not to be taken at face value, while others insist that writing may play a role of only secondary value for the philosopher. But beyond doubt is their startling effect. To me at least it seems clear that the passage is designed to strike us as troubling, and to trigger in us a process of reflection about the issues it raises. It challenges us to consider all the more closely the role written texts may play within the philosophical project, and the conditions under which that role may be a productive one. In particular, it encourages us to think about the issues from three distinct perspectives: those of the receiver, the creator, and the text.

To begin with, the passage is concerned with proper and improper *receivership* of written works. Highlighting the tension between the immediacy and directness of conversational dialogue and the ongoing nature of reception, the passage asks us to reflect on what happens to written and spoken discourse once it has been 'released' by its author. Without the support of its author, Socrates suggests, a written work is unable to control its reception. It may fall into the hands of those who lack interest or understanding, and 'roll around' (κυλινδεῖται 275e1), the term suggesting a lack of control, especially when we are told that the text rolls around *everywhere* (πανταχοῦ). Later Socrates talks in ethically charged language of the written account being ill-treated (πλημμελούμενος 275e3) and abused without justice (οὐκ ἐν δίκῃ λοιδορηθεὶς 275e4), terms which indicate that such treatment of a written work is far from ideal from the author's point of view, and will be unresponsive to his intentions. The fact that written discourse, by its nature, cannot help itself by coming to its own defence or explaining itself compounds the situation, of course. But receivers who treat it unjustly are presented as blameworthy too, and the language Socrates uses to describe their treatment of the defenceless text evokes a judicial context.

This image resonates with radical strands within reader-response criticism which insist that meaning is not 'in' the text, but created by the reader at the point of reception, with each text potentially open to a range of competing readings.[4] In presenting the fate of the text in these terms, the dialogue evokes the three-way nature of the interaction between author, text, and receiver in creating meaning, encouraging us to view the process of reception, in the language of Louise Rosenblatt, as a *transaction*.[5] The image reminds us of our own input as readers, as well as the fact that this is not the only locus of meaning: the text, if treated properly, will act as a constraint on competing interpretations. The judicial language in which Plato presents the activity of his wayward receivers invites us to consider how we, as readers, measure up to the expectations that the text lays upon us.

The *Phaedrus* passage forms part of a much broader concern with receivership within the dialogues,[6] in relation to both spoken and written accounts, with characters often employing language of a

[4] An approach often associated with Stanley Fish, e.g. Fish (1970). He does however limit the range of meanings a text can be made to render by appealing to the notion of an interpretative community. For a similar approach to Classical texts, see in particular D. P. Fowler (2000a) and Martindale (1993).

[5] Rosenblatt (1978).

[6] Similar concerns arise in the works of other ancient authors. For instance, Aristotle *Poetics* 1449b27 on the role of pity and fear in tragedy's effect on its

similarly ethical character. For instance, just before setting out his idea that in an ideal state, philosophers would rule (*Republic* 473c–474a), Socrates expresses his fear that, if his account is offered, it will drown him in ridicule and contempt like a wave of laughter. Glaucon's response to his proposal echoes these concerns: Socrates' statement is such, claims Glaucon, that he should expect people to take up weapons and attack him. The references to battle and the law court carry unmistakable resonances of judgement—yet this is a judgement, the descriptions imply, that is hasty and unthinking. From a different standpoint, in *Protagoras*, while walking to the sophist's house, Socrates counsels his companion to be cautious about how he receives the ideas he will hear there (*Protagoras* 313c–314a). He compares the sophist to a merchant or petty dealer, even a rogue (ἔμπορός τε καὶ κάπηλος), who is ignorant about which of his wares is good or bad for the body and commends them all indiscriminately, thereby deceiving people; unless the buyer is well informed, he is playing at dice and taking a risk in relation to the things most precious to him (περὶ τοῖς φιλτάτοις κυβεύῃς τε καὶ κινδυνεύῃς). The unflattering comparison of the sophist to an ignorant and perhaps unscrupulous salesman, who is willing to praise everything he sells, alerts the listener to the perils of being a receiver; if he does not approach his role with care, then he is treating his soul with the disregard of a risk-taking dice player.

Many dialogues show us the responses of inadequate receivers within the dialogue's main discussion—the aggression of a Thrasymachus, the complacency of an Euthyphro, the laziness of a Meno—just as others, such as *Theaetetus* and *Republic*, offer us persevering, inquiring, and good-natured ones. Yet other dialogues highlight the issue by offering us a frame dialogue, in which later receivers, bridging the gap between the interlocutors within the dialogue and our own response to the text, debate the action of the main dialogue. In *Symposium*, the layers of reception and the accumulation of accounts within accounts foreground the issue of reception; and in *Phaedo*, where the account of the death of Socrates and the sorrow of his companions makes it among the most emotionally engaging of Plato's works, the frame dialogue helps us negotiate and review our own responses to the text. Several of Plato's dialogues thematize the issue of receivership even further, through the content of the

audience; Gorgias *Helen* 9 on the effects of persuasion; and, more generally, the rhetoricians' concern with techniques to control their audience's response.

discussion. Besides *Phaedrus*' discussion of writing, one thinks of the examination of the effects of rhapsodic performance and the magnetic chain of response in *Ion*, the criticisms of rhetorical discourse voiced in *Gorgias*, the proposals for the censorship of literature in *Republic*, and the discussions of proportion and true measure in *Politicus*. In all these works, there is a direct engagement with the way in which a spoken or written account communicates with its receiver; and the dialogues' use of image and analogy offers us different ways, from the mathematical to the magical, of thinking about how that relationship works.

A little later in *Phaedrus*, in his image of the wise and foolish farmers quoted at the start, Socrates directs our attention to the role and responsibilities of the *author* in the process of communication. A wise grower, Socrates says, will not plant his seeds in pots at the height of summer and watch them reach their peak within a few days, as people did during the festival of Adonis. Such seeds have only shallow roots, and in the summer heat they wither as fast as they have grown, offering no more than passing pleasure. Instead, he will plant his seeds in appropriate soil, using his knowledge of growing, so that they develop gradually and bear properly formed fruit. Just so, the wise educator will choose a 'proper soul', and plant in it λόγοι—words or discourse—together with knowledge. Once the words have had time to mature fully, they will produce an abundant harvest. They will be capable of generating philosophical development in other people, by themselves producing 'a seed from which other words grow in the characters of others' (277a1–2); and they will make the person who possesses them 'as happy (εὐδαιμονεῖν) as is possible for a human'.

This passage makes it clear that there are choices, informed by understanding, which the dialectician can make to help ensure the value of the λόγοι he produces: in fostering the growth of the seeds he plants, his is an active role, in which he must use his knowledge to ensure the best conditions for growth. And as with the receiver, the creator's role is presented in language with ethical resonance. The grower who achieves the best conditions for growing is 'sensible' or 'possessing reason'; he 'cares earnestly' for his seeds (ἐσπούδακεν), language used elsewhere in connection with Socrates himself, connoting the effort and dedication he puts into the search for the truth;[7] the sensible grower uses his craft or skill; and he sows his seeds at the

[7] E.g. *R.*336e9.

appropriate time. Moreover, when he turns to his description of what the dialectician achieves by sowing 'discourse accompanied by knowledge' in the 'soil' of the learner's mind, the language of growth, immortality, and happiness (276e5–277a4) echoes Socrates' talk of the contentment achieved by those who fulfil their potential within the *Republic*'s ideal city. For sure, as Socrates says, it is naïve to think that writing can yield results that are 'clear and secure' (σαφὲς καὶ βέβαιον 275c6)—this is part of the limitation of the written medium itself. But to maximize the potential for successful and productive communication, resulting in philosophical development, the creator has responsibilities which correspond to those of the receiver. Failure to fulfil these, Socrates tells Phaedrus, is a matter for shame and reproach (277de).

Again, this passage in *Phaedrus* is by no means alone in drawing our attention to the role and responsibilities of the person who creates and puts forward an account. Socrates adds a characteristic qualification before offering his mythical account in *Phaedo* (108ce): he will tell his companions what he *believes* about the form and regions of the earth, but does not undertake to *prove* it. Socrates' precision here ensures that his discussion partners understand the status of the account they are to hear, as *Phaedrus* indicates they should—but less scrupulous authors of accounts are not difficult to find. After offering a lengthy and passionate speech in *Republic* I, Thrasymachus is said to have poured a mass of words into his listeners' ears like a bathman (ὥσπερ βαλανεὺς ἡμῶν καταντλήσας κατὰ τῶν ὤτων ἀθρόον καὶ πολὺν τὸν λόγον 344d1–3); his intention is to leave before engaging in further discussion or subjecting his ideas to further scrutiny, and Socrates makes it clear that he has not adequately taught his listeners (διδάξαι ἱκανῶς 344d7). Like *Protagoras*' image of the petty salesman, Plato's comparison of Thrasymachus to a figure of low social standing suggests that there are social and ethical gradations to authoring an account. *Meno* shows us Socrates offering and Meno responding to three sample definitions in different styles: here, while scholars disagree about the respective merits of the definitions, it is clear that Plato is raising the issue of the style and language in which ideas are couched. Meno responds most positively to the most colourful definition, termed 'majestic' or 'in tragic style' by Socrates (τραγική 76e3)—as he does later to the mystically introduced theory of recollection; and we ask ourselves whether it is the responsibility of *Socrates* to make his account accessible to his listener, or whether it is a failing of Meno that this is the type of account to which he responds most positively. A similar issue arises in *Sophist*: asked whether he would like to carry on the discussion by means of dialogue or exposition, the Eleatic Stranger says that he would be ashamed (αἰδώς τίς μ' ἔχει 217d8) to offer a long speech in the manner of an exhibition; once it has been settled that his interlocutor will be Theaetetus, he advises Theaetetus that, should he become distressed by the length of the discussion, he should not blame the Stranger but his companions (αἰτιᾶσθαι 218a9). Here, the Stranger seems to assume that the giver of the account should take some responsibility at least for the reactions provoked by his account—provided, that is, he has chosen the type of account he will offer.

Passages such as these proclaim the dialogues' concern with issues of reception; they suggest that the receiver deserves particular attention in our approach to interpreting the dialogues, and they invite us to reflect on our role as receivers and the value of our activity in reading, as is my focus in this study. More particularly, the dialogues often prompt us to think about the offering and receiving of accounts through the lens of value and civic responsibility. This is something to which I will return when considering in more detail the process of learning. For now, I note that this language foregrounds the transactional aspect of communication and our role within it. It prompts us to think about this as a process that can be performed more or less successfully, and more or less properly, and as an activity to which praise and blame can be attached. Communication between an account giver and an account receiver does not just *happen*; both author and receiver need to fulfil their responsibilities if communication between them is to be productive. By encouraging us to view our responsibilities as receivers as analogous to other moral responsibilities, or as a subcategory of moral activity, Plato's texts motivate us to take an active role in ensuring that we are good receivers and they empower us to make some difference at least to the success of our engagement with them.[8]

[8] In her interpretation of *Republic* X, Harte (2010) claims that the harmful effects of mimetic art are a kind of joint progeny of artist and audience; and she develops the idea of the 'doxastic responsibility' of the audience, which has the structure of moral responsibility. Similar ideas, I suggest, can be detected in the dialogues' handling of receivership of all types; *Republic* X, like *Phaedrus*, foregrounds the issue in dealing with an especially troubling case. Cf. Baragwanath (2008) 17–20 on the juridicial analogy in connection with the reader's role in Herodotus.

In addition, we can see by now that a concern with the different aspects of successful communication is more than an isolated problem raised in one puzzling passage in *Phaedrus*: anxiety about receivership forms a strong strand running through the dialogues. The dialogues ask us to reflect on the difficulties in relation to a wide range of types of account, including definitions, narratives such as myths which are embedded within a dialogue, and whole dialogues themselves; and they raise parallel concerns in relation to various modes of communication—written and spoken, conversational dialogue, and speaking before a crowd. When viewed against this backdrop, *Phaedrus*' discussion of writing, striking though it may be, is far from an anomaly. Accordingly, when exploring the role that written texts may play in the philosophical project, we need to set them in this broader context, rather than treating them as an entirely distinct type of account.

That said, however, there does seem to be something particularly striking about the discussion of writing in *Phaedrus*. On one level, this may be a device for alerting us to the special difficulties which attend communication through an indirect means such as writing, and in consequence, the additional efforts that need to be made by both author and receiver. The passage presents us with a paradox, that is, to get us to think all the more closely about our own actions as interpreters. But many have felt that the passage has further-reaching implications than this, and that it questions the ability of written texts to play a valuable role in the philosophical project by virtue of their fundamental character, quite apart from their treatment by a particular author or receiver.

In my view, the passage is clear in drawing attention to the limitations of writing as a medium. As we have seen, the exchange between Thamus and Theuth raises concerns both about the damage potentially caused by written texts *appearing* to contain knowledge and their ability to do this at all. However willing the receiver—Socrates talks about the frustration of the person who questions a work *wishing to learn* (275d)—there are basic limitations on the ability of a text to communicate with its reader due to its inability to engage in ongoing, active dialogue. This means that a written work cannot move the learning interaction beyond a certain point: reading a written text will always, due to the intrinsic drawbacks of the medium, be subordinate to a broader philosophical process. Slightly later in the same discussion, when Socrates is comparing the wise and foolish farmers, Socrates talks, by contrast with written communication, about the 'discourse which is written, with knowledge, in the soul of the learner', which Phaedrus in turn refers to as the 'living and breathing discourse' of which the written discourse is an 'image' (276a).

If this is the case, then are we correct in viewing communication through the medium of writing as parallel in some sense to other forms of philosophical communication, as I have been suggesting? Can reading a written text have the same value as engaging in a face-to-face discussion—or is the experience worth much less? Does reading a text even engage us in the same *manner* as having a discussion—or must it play a totally different type of role?

For some critics, Socrates (and with him Plato) is in this part of *Phaedrus* ruling out all but an insubstantial role for writing, instead signalling the value of spoken discourse, the 'living and breathing discourse' of which Socrates speaks. Indeed, it should be no surprise to find him highlighting the value of spoken, face-to-face discourse in a literary genre which has the dialogic exchange of views so firmly embedded in its form. As *Phaedrus* indicates, face-to-face discussion means that questions can be asked and answered, explanations offered and ideas scrutinized, thereby enabling the participants in discussion to move to the next stage of understanding. Equally, spoken discourse makes it possible to take account of the character and preoccupations of his interlocutor—a point that Socrates has elaborated at length, earlier in the dialogue, in explaining that the skilled rhetorician needs to understand not only the forms of rhetoric, but also the different types of soul, so that he can successfully apply the one to the other. This is what we see Socrates doing throughout the dialogues—not least in *Phaedrus* where the poetic form of his second speech is plausibly interpreted as in part a response to Phaedrus' character and his responsiveness to showy displays. All these features make face-to-face dialogue a paradigm of productive philosophizing to which other types of philosophical activity need to align themselves.

The importance of face-to-face dialogue as a paradigm, however, does not mean that the value of spoken discourse is straightforward or that writing is unable to have a positive role to play. The discussion of rhetoric makes it clear that spoken discourse varies in value according to the manner of its use, and raises many of the issues that

Socrates later applies to writing.[9] Similarly, by drawing our attention, as he does shortly afterwards, to the conditions under which writing may be productive and the potential for wise and foolish gardening of souls by the philosopher, Plato suggests that the value of writing may not always be the same: much will depend on the way it is used. For all the inherent limitations of writing, there may be circumstances in which it can play a positive role.[10]

Indeed, Socrates' criticisms of writing are balanced by positive specifications for valuable discourse. The person with knowledge, Socrates says, will not regard or present his writing as constituting knowledge (277d6–e3); and he will be able both to defend his writing when challenged and to make the argument that it is not of great worth (278c4–d1). His discourse will nevertheless be *based on* knowledge: the writer must have an understanding of his subject articulated through division (277b4–8). He will also understand the nature of the soul, so as to be able to adapt his discourse to the soul of his receiver (277b8–c3). If it is like the true discourse, moreover, it will be able to defend itself; it will know to whom it should speak and remain silent (276a5–7); and it will be capable of sowing the seeds of discourse in others (276e4–277a4), guiding them towards further philosophizing.

For all that Socrates allows a positive role for writing, though, he is often taken to limit that role, assigning writing a trivial or secondary place within the philosophical project. Socrates and Phaedrus refer to writing as an image (*εἴδωλον* 276a9) of the living and breathing (*ζῶντα καὶ ἔμψυχον* 276a8) discourse, which is its legitimate brother (*ἀδελφὸν γνήσιον* 276a1–2), and possesses a better and more powerful nature. Moreover, written discourse is described as possessing the silence and stillness of a painting, the image again suggesting a contrast with the 'life' of the true discourse (275d6: a painting looks

[9] Socrates says that the true art of speaking involves a grasp of the truth (259e ff.) and must involve an understanding of its subject articulated through division and collection (264e–266c)—a point which picks up his emphasis on defining the subject of one's speech at its opening (263d1–264b2). A successful speaker also needs an understanding of the soul and of the different types of soul, so that he can adapt his speech to the soul of his listener (269e–272b). These points are reiterated at 277bc, where Socrates addresses speaking and writing together.

[10] That is, the value of written and spoken discourse is not absolute, but depends both on the intrinsic qualities of each type of discourse and on how they are used. For a similar approach see Ferrari (1987) esp. 204–22.

as if alive, ὡς ζῶντα). The person with knowledge will write only for amusement (παιδιᾶς 276d2, cf. 276d8, 277e6) and to store up reminders of what he knows (ὑπομνήματα 276d3, cf. 278a1), terms which may encourage us to think of writing as playing a derivate or secondary role.

As commentators have observed, Socrates' terminology here recalls the language he uses at an earlier focal point within *Phaedrus* in describing the relationship between forms and particulars.[11] The discussion of writing forms the highpoint and close of the second 'half' of the dialogue. In the same position within the first part of the dialogue is Socrates' recantation, with its poetic description of the soul's vision of the Forms before birth, and its account of how the sight of beauty in this world reawakens it. Before birth, the soul's journey offers it a glimpse of what is *real* (248a5, cf. 247e3, 247d3, 247c7, 249c4, 249e5); when it enters human form, a philosopher's soul may see an *image* (250a6, 250b1–5) of what he saw there which serves as a *reminder* of the true realities (249d6, 249c7, 249c2). Within this process, the sight of beauty in this world is particularly effective in awakening the soul to those former sights, setting it on its course towards acquaintance with true beauty (249d–250e). In this passage, we find the same terminology that Socrates uses insistently in his discussion of writing, used also in his description of the soul's awakening to the forms; and it is difficult to escape making a connection between the relationship between a form and its manifestations in our world, and between a text and true discourse. The language of *images* and *reminding*, in particular, used both of instances of beauty and of written texts, is often taken to support the view that the latter may play only an insubstantial philosophical role in learning; yet in this dialogue at least, these are terms overladen with ideas of recollection and the awakening of the slumbering soul. Far from devaluing the role of writing, I suggest, this is a particularly powerful way to describe the potential effect of writing on the soul.

If this is correct, then written texts, like other objects in our world, should be viewed as having the potential to awaken our soul to the existence of the forms and start it on its journey towards an understanding of them. Going further, we might suggest that, just as instances of beauty are particularly effective in awakening the soul

[11] Griswold (1986) 206–7, Ferrari (1987) 207, 223.

towards knowledge, so a written work, in the hands of a careful and purposeful author, may have a special role to play in awakening the souls of its receiver towards knowledge. Things in our world are imperfect; they cannot contain knowledge, and should not be seen as the goal of our philosophical efforts, as we are reminded in many places in the dialogues: our endeavours should be directed towards true realities themselves. The same is true of written texts, if the comparison holds; they have inherent limitations, and our engagement with them is not an end in itself. But at the same time, they may have a valuable role within the wider philosophical process.

It may be, further, that we are too hasty, on the basis of *Phaedrus*' discussion of writing, in elevating the role of spoken discourse, by equating the 'true' discourse of which Socrates speaks with face-to-face discussion. Indeed earlier in *Phaedrus*, he seems to cast doubt on the ability of language, in the hands of humans, to convey the nature of the soul, as opposed to its likeness: the former is a task for gods; the latter is both shorter and within human bounds (*οἷον μέν ἐστι, πάντῃ πάντως θείας εἶναι καὶ μακρᾶς διηγήσεως, ᾧ δὲ ἔοικεν, ἀνθρωπίνης τε καὶ ἐλάττονος* 246a4–6). In addition, we commonly find the dialogues employing the same language of approximation and image to describe *spoken* accounts—for instance, in Socrates' introduction to the image of the Sun in *Republic* and his myth in *Phaedo*. For all its advantages, then, it may be that spoken communication, like engagement with a written text, is only an approximation of the soul's true discourse with reality.

The analogy between the two activities, reading and conversing, is further supported by the fluidity of the boundaries between participants and receivers in the dialogues.[12] Participants in Socratic[13] conversation are both givers and receivers of accounts: they have, in turn, to offer accounts of their own and respond to those put forward by another. Moreover, named or anonymous bystanders are often present, who (like us) are 'receivers' of a whole conversation; yet they too are presented as participants. Onlookers often become fully

[12] Cf. Blondell (2002) 51–2, Klein (1965) 6, Clay (1988) 23–4, Nehamas (1998) 47, Ausland (1997) 387–90.

[13] By this, I intend to include conversations in which Socrates does not take part or is not the discussion leader, as occur in 'late' dialogues; i.e. I do not mean to evoke only those dialogues—'early' ones—which have been thought to reflect the practice of the historical Socrates. Of course, not all conversations represented in the dialogues conform to the Socratic ideal (as captured in Socrates' rules of discussion).

fledged interlocutors, and their interjections and responses characterize them as actively engaged with what is being said. We sometimes find a dialogue within a dialogue, where interlocutors become receivers of a further dialogue: Socrates' interrogation of the slave in *Meno*, for example, his conversation with Diotima in *Symposium*, or the discussion between Theuth and Thamus in *Phaedrus*. And on occasion, primary narrators and narratees in a frame dialogue may engage in philosophical conversation prompted by the Socratic conversation being recounted. All this blurs the boundaries between participants and receivers, those who are inside and outside the dialogues: dialogue seems to generate dialogue in a series of interlocking layers. The reader's relation to Socratic conversations represents a further layer, but one that (it is implied) can again merge into the others.

All this suggests to me that we should not view the reader's activity as different in kind from that of these other participants and receivers, but as a version of the same thing. We do not need to view reading simply as a kind of preparation for or exhortation towards true philosophizing: it can play an important part in learning. This is not to say, of course, that written works can form a substitute for face-to-face discussion; the dialogues are clear, I think, in presenting conversation as a central paradigm of philosophizing, and in suggesting that conversational dialogue is necessary for philosophical progress. But it does mean that the activity of readers is of a similar sort and has a similar value to that of interlocutors.[14]

Accordingly, exploration of the analogy between reader and interlocutor will play an important strand in my study; and I will explore the nature and value of the reader's experience in the context of the experiences and behaviour of the interlocutors, whose activity forms, in some sense, a model for our own. It is well recognized and striking that, in the dialogues' presentation of conversation among interlocutors, a great deal of attention is dedicated to how interlocutors should behave towards each other and each other's views in discussion. These issues are a regular and prominent part of the interlocutors' discourse, and they are often termed Socrates' 'rules of discussion': are the interlocutors saying what they think? Are they speaking at too

[14] Thought, presented at *Tht.*189e–190a and *Sph.*263e as an internal dialogue in the mind of the thinker, may be regarded as a further parallel. Cf. Frede (1992a) 218, Kahn (1996) 388–92, Sedley (2003) 1–2, Long (2007) and (2008). See ch.2 n6.

great a length? Are they interpreting what is said as it was meant or purposely twisting their opponents' words? Through these rules of discussion, the dialogues mark out a discursive space which embodies certain expectations, and which is distinctively different from that of other modes of oral engagement—the teaching of the sophists or the performances of poets, for instance.

Plato was writing on the cusp between orality and literacy,[15] at a time when the increasing prominence of the medium of writing may have engendered debate and anxiety about the impact of the new medium on culture and learning. In more recent times, the increasing dominance of new methods of electronic communication through email, text messaging, and social networking has witnessed such anxieties, raising questions about whether these new media will affect the way people process information, the way they approach knowledge, and their ability to retain and memorize information. In educational contexts, a great deal of research and creativity has gone into generating pedagogical approaches for web-based courses, which tackle the problems caused by the lack of face-to-face contact between teacher and learner, and address the difficulties of expecting teachers and learners to transfer to an online environment the skills and behaviours they have developed in a more 'traditional' face-to-face setting. The characteristics of our most familiar methods of communication have been scrutinized more carefully, alongside the possibilities and pitfalls offered by the emerging methods.

The dialogues' preoccupation with issues of receivership, particularly the reception of written accounts, resonates with the anxieties of transition; at such a time, it may have seemed all the more important to reflect on and establish expectations for engagement with written texts. Just as Plato marks out a distinctive type of 'Socratic' face-to-face engagement within the dialogues, I suggest it makes sense to view him as developing the genre of the dialogue as an analogous arena for a

[15] See Havelock (1963), Robb (1994) esp. 214–51 and (1997), Hershbell (1995), Waugh (1995). Cf. also West (1995) and Tarrant (1996) on reflections of oral discourse in the dialogues. The work of Harris (1989) and Thomas (1992) supports the view that oral ways persisted after the spread of literacy. Havelock defends a controversial version of the idea that Plato promotes the spread of literacy, and has been criticized on various scores, most notably for the view that literacy is necessary for cognitive development. I certainly do not wish to espouse his interpretation in full; in particular, I regard Plato as committed to the value of oral education. For detailed criticism of Havelock, see Nails (1995).

particular type of readerly engagement.[16] Though the dialogues' expectations of the reader have received somewhat less attention, I hope to show that Plato's works are concerned to establish the dialogue between text and receiver as a sphere of discourse with its own distinctive characteristics and qualities, which cultivates a response in the reader that is distinctive, and distinctively philosophical, and which sets the dialogues apart from other types of literary or educational interaction, such as watching a tragedy, listening to an orator's speech, or engaging in sophistic debate. This response, I argue, is one that in itself, quite independently of any specific ideas the reader takes away from the text, can contribute to her philosophical development; and my aim in this study is to illuminate some of the means by which the dialogues invite a response of this type. As I hope to show, it is both the responses invited by the texts that are distinctive and also the literary techniques used to evoke them.

1.2. READING AS LEARNING

The reader, then, and the character and quality of her responses to Plato's texts, form the focal point of my study.[17] These responses, along with those of other receivers, are foregrounded within the dialogues, and the ethical language in which they are presented encourages us to think about more and less appropriate types of reading, reading which may or may not measure up to the expectations laid upon us by the text. But what does successful reading amount to?

I have been assuming, first of all, that reading, in so far as it is parallel with Socratic conversation, is an activity that helps us to learn, even if it cannot itself offer us knowledge. Reading, in the ideal case, becomes learning.[18] Most critics would agree, I think, that the dialogues are in some sense concerned with educating their

16 Cf. Robb (1997).

17 Studies that make the reader/reading central include: Sayre (1995), Arieti (1995), Griswold (1988a), Gordon (1999), Szlezák (1999), and Gonzalez (2003). Cf. Hadot (1995) 101–9.

18 Attributing an ethical slant to the reader's experience is common in reader-response criticism. For example, Booth (1961) is concerned with the values of the implied author and reader which the reader is to adopt during the reading process; Iser and Jauss emphasize how reading a work can challenge a reader's presuppositions;

receivers, rather than just, say, entertaining or amusing them.[19] This was an intention attributed to a range of ancient genres; but Plato's dialogues, by choosing to represent serious philosophical activity, proclaim themselves as concerned with education in a much stronger sense. They were produced by someone who, as a disciple of Socrates and founder of the Academy, existed in an educational context. The genre of *Sokratikoi logoi*,[20] more generally, was produced by people with educational interests. And from their ancient receivers onwards, the dialogues have been treated as possessing educational intent.[21] But there are different conceptions of what educational activity involves. Commemorative, protreptic, and didactic, for example, are labels commonly applied to the dialogues; though all are compatible with educational purpose, they imply very different approaches to learning.[22] Some critics, for instance, would maintain that all the dialogues are able to do is to *point us towards* face-to-face discussion, or to show us what productive philosophical inquiry looks like.

Fish (1967) sees the reader of Milton's *Paradise Lost* being educated by analogy with Adam and Eve. Cf. Tompkins (1980b) xv–xvi.

[19] Even a writer such as Dillon, who proclaims his uncertainty as to what the dialogues are up to, assumes a basic educational intent: see Dillon (1999) 207, 221–2. McCabe (2006) articulates the possibility that the content of the dialogues might correspond to a philosophical genre and their form to a literary genre connected with persuasion; this is an approach often associated with Lucretius' *De Rerum Natura*, whose readers are encouraged to be successful learners; see Mitsis (1993), Clay (1983), D. P. Fowler (1997). As will become clear, I do not wish to draw such a distinction between form and content.

[20] By which I mean the literary works celebrating the life of Socrates written by his followers. On the origins of the genre, mentioned by Aristotle at *Poetics* 1447b11, see Kahn (1996) 1–35, Clay (1994), and Rutherford (1995) 10–15, 44–56. The extent to which it was considered a (strongly) didactic one is an interesting question, as is the extent to which generic expectations were established when Plato was writing, though we do not have sufficient evidence to settle these questions. One could interpret the thematization of issues of education and reception, particularly in the introductory sections of dialogues, as an attempt, on Plato's part, to signal the didactic intentions of the Socratic dialogue in his hands.

[21] See Sluiter (1999) on ancient assumptions of Plato's didactic intent.

[22] Cf. Blondell (2002) 28–9, Sluiter (1999) 173–4. Press (1996) 517 lists various suggested functions of the dialogues: to be morally and politically paideutic, to encourage people to pursue philosophy or enrol in the Academy, to provide examples of dialectical practice for study and imitation, to establish philosophy as a new form of high cultural activity, to provide entertainment and amusement. None of these implies as philosophically substantial a role for reading as I would like.

Phaedrus, as I suggested above, invites us to draw an analogy between written texts and particular objects. Particulars are imperfect: *Phaedo*'s imperfectly equal sticks, for instance, do not embody equality, but they can awaken us to the idea of equality and start us off on the journey towards knowledge of it. If the analogy holds, then written texts, like particular objects, are imperfect and unable to embody or contain knowledge—as Socrates insists in *Phaedrus*' characterization of the good writer. A good author will accordingly not expect to endow his works with knowledge, and a good reader will not expect to find it there. However, written texts can awaken us to, or remind us of, the true objects of knowledge to which we should turn our attention, and start us on the journey towards achieving deeper understanding.

To clarify how I believe a written text may do this, it will be useful to set it in the context of one of the most central debates in current Platonic criticism—the split between doctrinal (also called dogmatic or didactic) and non-doctrinal (or non-dogmatic) approaches to the dialogues.[23] On the doctrinal approach, the dialogues contain their author's views on the subject under discussion, as would a treatise.[24] In a strong version of this approach, the reader is cast as a passive recipient of a more knowledgeable person's wisdom—whether she is

[23] I have found the following overviews of trends in Platonic interpretation particularly helpful: Gill (2006), Griswold (1988b) and (1988c), Gonzalez (1995b), Sayre (1995) 1–32, Press (1996) and (2000b).

[24] Doctrinal interpretation of the dialogues has traditionally been widespread: examples include Vlastos (1991), Irwin (1995), Kraut (1992b). More generally, the approach seems to underlie the activity of those who attempt to determine the correct interpretation of the arguments we find in the dialogues, and who often imply—explicitly or implicitly—that the arguments they are uncovering are Plato's own. For a defence of this position, see Rowe (2002), who suggests that the role of the commentator is to reveal what the argument actually is, and what the author actually meant, since 'there will normally only be one way that the author of the text can reasonably be supposed to have thought he could get to *this* particular conclusion... from *that* particular starting point', 299. But even if we could determine the only correct way of interpreting an argument, this would not give us insight into Plato's views. Quite apart from the question of whether the argument was originally intended by the author in the 'correct' way, the views are those of a character, not Plato, and Plato need not be committed to the conclusion, the premises, or the way in which the former is reached from the latter. Later (314–16), Rowe seems to retreat from this position, conceding that we may only be able to produce a range of possible meanings, a controlled indeterminacy; and that this imprecision is intentional: a position rather closer to the one I am adopting. The approach is also defended by Beversluis (2006), Irwin (1996), Gerson (2000), and Kraut (1992b) 25–30; cf. also Rowe (2006).

willing, or has to be induced by additional persuasive techniques.[25] It is most commonly applied to the 'middle' and 'late' works, though the 'early' works, too, are often regarded as less aporetic than they seem. This approach picks up on important features of the dialogues, which any satisfying interpretation needs to explain.[26] We do often feel that one viewpoint is being presented more positively than another, that one character is made more appealing than another, or that a certain passage is somehow particularly significant; and some works do appear to take a more didactic stance than others. But there are also difficulties for this view. Concern is voiced within the dialogues about receiving ideas on another person's authority, a practice presented as dangerous and inimical to true learning. And similar reservations seem to be built into the form of the dialogues. Many dialogues, including 'later' ones, end without conclusive result. Notoriously, Plato does not speak in his own voice or identify himself with any one character, so we cannot assume that views put forward by any speaker, even Socrates, are his. Even in the case of Plato's 'later' works, which can appear his most didactic, attention has recently been devoted to demonstrating that they are in fact committed to a collaborative view of learning, and that here too we should take the dramatic form seriously—an issue to which I shall return in chapter 5.

Non-doctrinal interpreters, by contrast, reject the idea that Plato's works intend to convey their author's views in this way.[27] They emphasize Plato's choice of the dialogue form and stress that we

[25] For the importance of persuasion, see Rowe (2007) and Silk (2001), who sees the dialogues as trying to compel their readers to adopt certain viewpoints using 'non-rational' techniques. On persuasion in *Republic*, see Burnyeat (1992) and Rowe (2006). The relationship between exposition and persuasion is a complex one—since true arguments clearly set out can rationally persuade us: see e.g. Atherton (1988), Irwin (1986), Wardy (1996).

[26] I deal with the prominence of particular characters (especially Socrates), didactic-style arguments, and the apparent authority of myth in chapters 4, 5, and 8 respectively. In my view, these features do not indicate that the texts intend to impose certain ideas upon us: their appearance of doing so is undercut and they are rather a part of the complex way in which the texts encourage a committed yet critical response in the reader, and prompt her to develop her own ideas for herself.

[27] Particularly helpful contributions to the non-doctrinal approach include: Griswold (1988a), Press (2000a) and (1993a), Gonzalez (1995a), Gill and McCabe (1996), Michelini (2003a), and Klagge and Smith (1992); Ausland (1997), Frede (1992a), Krentz (1983), Blondell (2002), Moes (2000) xi–xiv and 1–24, Sayre (1995), Gonzalez (1998). For the reader as active dialectician, see e.g. Belfiore (1984) 144, Nussbaum (1986) 126–9, Szlezák (1999) 4–5, Moes (2000) especially xi–xiv, 1–24, 174–6.

should take seriously the idea of a dialogical relationship between text or author and reader. Within this position, however, is a range of different approaches. To begin with, there is debate over whether the dialogues really withhold doctrinal content, or whether they simply put forward their ideas in an indirect way, so that the reader's task requires more effort and thought. On the latter view, the dialogues do, despite appearances, contain determinate views held by Plato, which we can detect in ellipses, unexplored avenues of investigation, or particularly important passages (arguments felt to be especially 'Socratic' or 'Platonic', for example, or passages in a more elevated medium such as myth).[28] Plato, that is, is credited with the same expository purpose as on the 'didactic' interpretation, but the reader is made to work harder to ferret out the doctrines; this is what her dialogue with the text consists in. This is a view associated, in extreme form, with those who believe that the dialogues communicate with their reader in a secret way: the idea is that Plato held certain views to be correct, yet did not want to set them out in writing directly for fear of misinterpretation, so pointed discerning readers towards them in indirect ways.[29] But the basic approach is one that is common to many different interpreters, such as constructivist critics who claim to see positive doctrine concealed just beneath the surface of Plato's works;[30] literary-minded interpreters who insist that meaning

[28] Iser (1974) and (1978) seems to put forward a similar interpretation of the reader's role, according to which texts contain gaps or 'blanks' which the reader is left to fill in, thereby creating meaning. However, critics have questioned the extent to which, on Iser's view, the reader does actually play a part in *creating* meaning, suggesting that, in filling in the gaps, she is simply uncovering a determinate meaning already contained in the text. See in particular the critique in Fish (1989); for discussion of the issues, see Suleiman (1980) 23–4. Woodman and Powell (1992b) 213–14 note that this kind of practice was a recognized technique in ancient rhetoric: the orator suppressed information to create 'gaps' which the intelligent reader could then fill in for himself. For the importance of gaps/blanks/silences in the dialogues, see e.g. Clay (1987), Farness (2003), Szlezák (1999), Nehamas (1998). I too think that these are important, but not that they need to be handled within a doctrinal framework.

[29] Szlezák (1999) criticizes such a view, which he attributes foremost to Schleiermacher. Szlezák, as a representative of the Tubingen school, himself thinks that the dialogues point towards hidden views—the unwritten doctrines. They are not however contained in the dialogues, but would have been communicated in oral discussion. This view, of course, itself assumes a doctrinal framework. For a recent and extensive discussion of the Tubingen school, see Mann (2006).

[30] Penner (1992) is a particularly striking example. Similar are apparently non-doctrinal interpreters who think that the dialogues do not contain Plato's views but do

emerges from the conjunction of discursive and dramatic levels[31] of composition (rather than just from the discursive level);[32] and Straussian commentators who view the surface of the text as an ironic façade that conceals contrary hidden meanings.[33]

Other critics, among whom I count myself, are keen to resist this slide back into doctrinal interpretation, insisting that the dialogues do not contain determinate views of Plato's. I shall argue that we are not in any simple way able to extract arguments from the text; the contribution that we as readers are required to make to this process means that those arguments become ours, not the text's.[34] Similarly, the focus on the ongoing, iterative, and revisionary nature of philosophizing in the dialogues encourages us to beware of resting content with particular conclusions. Nevertheless, this does not mean that, as a sceptical interpreter might, we need to deny that the dialogues contain a movement towards determinate doctrine.[35] Nor need we retreat towards the idea that the dialogues merely constitute preparation or protreptic: honing our dialectical skills, showing us what philosophy is like, or exhorting us to engage in it. This is an idea compatible with the dialogic engagement of the reader and commonly espoused by non-doctrinal interpreters, but which (for me at

point towards them. Ferrari (2003a) points out that a proleptic interpretation (such as Kahn's) is essentially doctrinal. A similar charge might be made against 'maieutic' views (e.g. Sayre (1992), (1988)) on which the dialogues point towards certain paths of reflection, if these are not left sufficiently open. Frede (1989), for example, suggests that none of Plato's dialogues is genuinely aporetic because there is always an indication of a path/*poros* that would lead to resolution if pursued. For discussion see C. Gill (1996b) and (2002).

[31] Discursive: what is said in a dialogue; dramatic: the circumstances in which it is said. See e.g. Blondell (2002) 2.

[32] E.g. Desjardins (1988), Klein (1965) 17, O'Brien (1971). For an interesting attack on this type of approach, see Benitez (2000). Cf. also Barker and Warner (1992b), who suggest that Plato uses the medium he does to enable the reader better to perceive realities.

[33] For criticism of Straussian approaches, see Burnyeat (1985). Ferrari (1997) offers an appealing defence of Strauss and his reading of Plato, with which (on Ferrari's interpretation) mine has something in common.

[34] Cf. Annas (1999) 22. This does not mean that 'Plato' emerges any less strongly from the text, as is often implied: see ch.2 n31 with text.

[35] For discussion of sceptical interpretations, see Gonzalez (1995b). For the dialogues' affinities with scepticism, see Annas (1992). If a text withholds meaning, this does not indicate that the author does not believe in objective truth; Cf. Gordon (1999) 57–9, Scolnicov (1976) 56. Versényi (1982) 11–15 launches a vigorous attack on sceptical interpretations of the dialogues, arguing that they are self-refuting.

least) unacceptably diminishes the value of the activity attributed to the reader.[36] Instead, we can recognize that the dialogues are committed to a view of learning according to which open-ended interaction with a text, of the sort the dialogues invite their readers to participate in, can have philosophical value. In other words, we can reject the doctrinal interpretation while still maintaining that the dialogues are committed to education; we just have to adopt a different view of what learning involves—one based on developing the learner's ability to engage *in a certain way*, rather than directing her towards certain views.[37]

To place the emphasis on the development of the learner rather than the development of doctrine is by no means, I should emphasize, to diminish the importance of engaging with the arguments and views expressed in Plato's dialogues. Rather, it is to approach argumentation and expressions of doctrine from a different angle. Christopher Gill describes the philosophical outlook implied by the dialogues as objectivist-participant:[38] the dialogues look towards objective knowledge as the goal and the ultimate outcome of dialectic, as doctrinal interpreters have stressed, but they also recognize that the only effective means of moving towards it is through engaging in increasingly searching forms of dialectic. If this is the case, then the manner in which one engages in dialectic becomes crucial, and one's approach to engaging with ideas and arguments is as important as the conclusions one reaches on any given occasion. An idea may need revising in a new argumentative context; new considerations may prompt a revision of one's ideas; a conclusion may not be applicable to a new case: the learner needs to have the skills and qualities to continue thinking and

[36] I would not want to rule out these approaches, but think that they do not exhaust the functions of the texts. I use 'protreptic' in a narrow sense, as contrasted with actual philosophizing. For the suggestion that protreptic or preparation in this sense is the role of reading the dialogues, see e.g. Hyland (1981) 42, Arieti (1995). The idea is, however, stated or implied in the work of a large number of non-doctrinal critics, even though it is in some tension with the commonly accepted idea that the reader's activity is somehow parallel to interlocutors' activity. It need not be confined to the interpretation of 'early' works: M. Frede (1996), for example, suggests that *Sophist* could be seen as a model of philosophical activity. For discussion of the role in protreptic of the *elenchus*, as it is presented in the dialogues, see Slings (1981) and Gonzalez (2002).

[37] This fits well with the emphasis Plato places, in criticizing other genres, on the character of the response evoked in the receiver as much as on the ideas she takes away from a work.

[38] C. Gill (2006) and (1996b).

reflecting in a movement towards fuller understanding, rather than clinging on to conclusions already reached. By focusing on the skills of the learner and the process of learning, we can to some extent move beyond anxiety about doctrine and the acceptance of views on authority: a self-motivated, reflective, and self-correcting learner who recognizes the importance of her independent perspective can engage productively not passively with the views of others. And if a reader is engaging in learning in the right way, with self-criticism and commitment to ongoing reflection, then it does not matter if at a particular time she comes up with a mistaken idea. Since the process is self-correcting, she will, sooner or later, realize she is mistaken.[39]

Accordingly, this study attempts to examine what the process of learning needs to involve, if it is to be successful; and how the construction of the dialogues engages us in such a way as to promote our development as learning agents. For it is only if the dialogues can help us to develop the right approach to learning that they can ensure the ideas they put forward form part of our learning, as well as of Plato's—and it is our learning, I have suggested, which is central to the dialogues' project. More particularly, I shall argue that the character and quality of our responses as receivers are central to the way in which Plato's texts engage his readers, not least in the areas of argumentation and the presentation of ideas. This is not simply to say that the dialogues withhold determinate views to make the point that we need to think for ourselves and to prompt us to do so, a view that is rooted in a doctrinal approach to philosophizing. Rather, I shall suggest, the dialogues are constructed in such a way as to help us to acquire the skills and dispositions of a productive and independent learner: skills which, ideally, enable us to engage constructively rather than passively with the doctrines contained within the dialogues, and to move beyond them as independent, self-correcting learners. While acknowledging the impulse towards positive doctrine in the dialogues, therefore, this study places more emphasis on the development of the reader and the role that different

[39] The importance of a critical, reflexive, open-ended approach is emphasized by several interpreters: see e.g. Gonzalez (1998) 7 and (1995c), Krentz (1983) 35, Nightingale (1995) 168–71, Gordon (1999) 31–2, Hadot (1995) 92, and the conception of Plato's philosophy as doubly open-ended developed in Nails (1995) 218–31.

aspects of the dialogues, including the presentation of argumentation, play in that development.

The attempt to develop a positive model of philosophizing that can replace the doctrinal conception has been an important constructive strand within the debate between doctrinal and non-doctrinal critics; and I hope that this study will form a contribution to it. My study has at its heart a concern with the *experience* of learning—the interlocutor's experience of engaging in Socratic discussion and the reader's experience of moving through the text. The quality and character of our reaction as we progress through the texts, the feelings and responses generated in us, and the value these have for our philosophical development will be the subject of my analysis of aspects of the dialogues' construction in chapters 4–8. This focus grows out of an interest in the distinctive and striking responses that Plato's works engender in many modern readers, which resonate with the experience of interlocutors we read about in the dialogues—the confusion of reading an argument for the first time, for instance, or frustration with the behaviour of interlocutors, Socrates included. These are responses that readers, perhaps especially inexperienced readers, are inclined to attribute to their own inadequacies, or to inadequacies in the work they are reading. No two readers respond to the same text in the same way, of course, and significant problems attend the construction of a generalized response.[40] But the broad patterns in the responses of readers to Plato's dialogues, and the similarities between these and the responses of interlocutors within the dialogues,[41] suggest that they need to be given a more constructive interpretation, and to be viewed as a positive part of the learning process, rather than a consequence of failings on the part of reader or text.[42]

In constructing a positive model for learning that can apply to the reader's activity in engaging with written texts, I will be treating Plato's presentation of his interlocutors as a commentary on responses appropriate and inappropriate in the reader. As I have already explained, the detail in which the interlocutors' experience is evoked, and the degree

[40] For discussion see e.g. Martindale (1993) 15–16. For helpful discussions pertaining to specific texts, see Slater (1990) 1–23, Mossman (1995) 6–12.

[41] Cf. Rowe (2007) 30. See further chapter 3, sections 3.5–6.

[42] Matthews (1999) 121–30 argues that to see concrete answers underneath the surface of the dialogues obscures the role of perplexity and discomfort in learning.

of attention to what we might term the *ethics* of the interlocutor's response, suggests to me at least that Plato's portrayal of the interlocutors should inform our practices as readers as well as our aspirations as discussion partners. If reading can become learning, then the dialogues' reflection on their central paradigm of learning must be relevant, in some sense, to our case too. I do not intend to single out particular types of interlocutor (Socrates and other 'positively characterized' interlocutors, for instance, or primary narrators, in those dialogues which have them), or particular aspects of interlocutors' activities; nor do I intend to look only at what characters say, rather than what they do, or vice versa. Rather, I believe that *all* aspects of interlocutors' activity are relevant to understanding what may make a reader's response valuable. In other words, the presentation of the activity of interlocutors on the discursive and dramatic levels can function as a kind of model for our activity in reading: one that both guides the way we respond to the texts and provides a reference point for understanding how the responses evoked in reading can contribute to our own process of learning, in ways I shall go on to explain. In considering this, we will look in more detail, in chapters 2 and 3, at the experience the interlocutor goes through in learning and how we are to relate his activity and responses to those of the reader.

1.3. PLATO'S DIALOGUES: READ OR PERFORMED?

In talking, so far, of the reader and her response to the text, I have been implying that it is appropriate to treat modern reading practices as a paradigm for the original reception of the texts—yet if this is not the way receivers would originally have come into contact with the dialogues, the approach adopted in this study might seem to be seriously compromised.[43] Private study of texts, as Phaedrus has performed on Lysias' speech in *Phaedrus*, is envisaged in the dialogues; and it seems plausible that this was one way in which original

[43] For discussion and a survey of the evidence, see Blondell (2002) 22–8. See also Tarrant (1996) 132–5, Miller (1999) 254–6.

receivers came into contact with them.[44] But this is only one possible option: performance of texts in a variety of contexts, both informal and formal, was a pervasive part of life in the ancient world; and it seems likely that the dialogues would have been narrated either in a private context (as is represented in *Theaetetus*) or in a group setting (as is portrayed in the introduction to *Symposium*), at least on occasion. Some interpreters even envisage the dialogues being acted out, with different people playing different characters.[45] Given the range of options available—and indeed represented in the dialogues—it is most likely that dialogues were received in different ways in different settings. In fact, it seems possible that an individual would encounter the same dialogue in different ways: the fact that a dialogue was first witnessed being performed would not prevent someone studying it later in written form and vice versa.[46] But these are questions which, given the evidence available to us, we cannot settle for certain. Equally importantly for my purposes, I do not think that the approach to the dialogues adopted in this study stands or falls with a particular answer. Some of the suggestions I make, particularly about the way the dialogues encourage us to pause as we read and to move backwards and forwards through the text, work better if we think of the texts as read. But much of what I say applies equally well to reception via performance. Indeed, certain of the effects I highlight—the impact of the speed of arguments, sudden shifts in direction, and changes in register—might

[44] For the dialogues as read privately, see e.g. Robb (1994) 236–9, Sayre (1992), Blondell (2002) 25. The ancient practice of reading aloud would allow even this to have a performative aspect.

[45] Oral performance is supported by Ryle (1966) 21–54, Blondell (2002) 22–8, Waugh (1995). I am here using 'performance' in a broad sense, to include the speaking aloud of a work by a single person in the presence of any audience, however small. Cf. Blondell (2002) 23. Ryle appears to envisage performance in a more dramatic style; Blondell (2002) 23 withholds judgement on this.

Blondell, in the discussion cited above, suggests that we regard performance of the dialogues as a way of closing the gap between the activity represented in the works and its representation: by performing a dialogue, one participates in the activity of philosophizing the dialogue represents—a possibility particularly interesting if we think of members of the Academy performing the works for their own benefit. I share Blondell's interest in closing the gap between the activity represented and its representation, but disagree with her analysis of how this occurs, which is based on the idea that the dialogues shape their receivers through a process of mimetic pedagogy. I discuss Blondell's approach further in ch.4.

[46] Cf. Blondell (2002) 24–5.

work even better if the receiver were listening to the dialogues, so could not stop or turn back to reorient herself. Read or performed, in my view, the dialogues invite the receiver to engage in learning of a particular type. For simplicity, I will continue to refer to 'readers' of the dialogues, but do not intend to exclude audiences of other types.

2

Readers and Interlocutors

2.1. THE PRISONER'S ASCENT FROM THE CAVE: A PARADIGM FOR LEARNING

Plato's dialogues, I have argued, encourage us to regard reading, in the ideal case, as learning. They also, I suggested in chapter 1, present the activity of interlocutors as a model, of sorts, for our activity in reading; one that both guides the way we respond to the texts and provides a reference point for understanding how the responses evoked in reading can contribute to our own process of learning. In developing these ideas further, it is necessary to look more closely at the experience the interlocutor goes through in learning; and my starting point is the image of the Cave in *Republic* VII, one of the dialogues' most famous images of learning. This passage follows on from Socrates' description of the relationship between visible and intelligible realms in the Sun and Line images; and much scholarship focuses on establishing its connections with the other two images and debating what all three can tell us about the contrasting realms.[1] But the Cave also has a great deal to tell us about the nature of the educational process and the learner's experience of it. The image, Socrates makes clear, is relevant to himself and his fellow interlocutors,[2] not just to education in the ideal state. The prisoners in the Cave are 'like us', he says, (515a5),[3] and he suggests, in introducing the

[1] E.g. Karasmanis (1988), Strang (1986).

[2] See Smith (1997); also Rutherford (1992) 156 suggesting that imagery of descent and the underworld connects the conversation of *Protagoras* with the Cave image, Rutherford (1995) 216–17 on katabatic imagery connecting the Cave with other parts of *Republic*; Burnyeat (1997a) 5–7; Clay (1992).

[3] With most commentators, I assume that the initial state of the prisoners corresponds to the state of most of us before Socratic education, and that the ascent into the

image, that the passage can be viewed as an image of *all* education, ideal or not: its purpose is to illuminate 'the effect of education (*παιδείας*) and the lack of it (*ἀπαιδευσίας*) upon our human nature' (514a1–2).

The image starts with a description of those imprisoned in the Cave: fettered, they see on a wall in front of them the shadows of objects carried behind them, and hear the echo of words spoken by the men carrying the objects. In the first stage of deliverance, a prisoner is made to turn round, to look at the objects and then the fire casting the shadows. Following this, he is dragged by force up a steep path to the outside world, where, once his eyesight has adjusted, he can see first shadows and reflections of things in the world; then the things themselves, and finally the sky, stars, moon, and sun. At this point, the prisoner realizes the true nature of his previous degraded state, and pities his fellow prisoners. Finally, we are told what such a person would experience were he to descend into the Cave again.

Viewed in its entirety, the prisoner's ascent from the Cave represents the learner's growing awareness of the nature of the world around her, and her gradual perception of the true nature of the objects in her world, as she raises her sights to an understanding of 'true' reality. In its details, the image suggests several characteristics of the experience the learner goes through as she makes the journey towards truer understanding.

First, there is the importance of the prisoner's own input. The prisoner's ascent, though he is prompted—even compelled—by a second person, is nevertheless a product of his own effort. Once freed, he has to stand up, turn his head and walk (515c7). He has to see the different things—the shadows and objects in the Cave, the fire, then the things in the outside world—for himself: the unnamed educator can lead him to them, but cannot look at them for him, or ease the process of becoming accustomed to the progressively brighter light. The prisoner is the most important agent throughout the process; the educator is in a facilitating role. The autonomy of the learner in fact increases as the process continues. By the time we reach the outside world, only he is mentioned, not the educator. By now, he is reflecting and reaching conclusions for himself (e.g. *συλλογίζοιτο*

outside world represents acquaintance with the intelligible realm. For a different interpretation of the lower stages, see Wilberding (2004).

516b9, ἀναμιμνῃσκόμενον 516c4, δοκεῖς ἂν αὐτὸν ἐπιθυμητικῶς αὐτῶν ἔχειν 516d2–3); and when he goes back down into the Cave, he is clearly an independently functioning agent.

Second, the prisoner's experience has both cognitive and affective dimensions. On one hand, the prisoner increases in understanding as he ascends: he becomes better able to see realities (515d2–4), leaving behind his misplaced ideas (515c1–2) and his foolishness (φλυαρίας 515d2). He has to answer questions about what each thing is (515d4–5); and he undergoes *aporia* and is asked to revise his beliefs (515d6–7). At the same time, the process undoubtedly engages him on an affective level, causing anger and pain, pity and happiness. By presenting learning as an individual's journey, the image brings home forcefully its connection with a person's whole self and way of life, on a practical as well as a theoretical level. This is something Socrates underscores in his comments following the image, when he describes education as the turning of the whole soul (ὅλῃ τῇ ψυχῇ 518c8).

More particularly, the prisoner undergoes a range of specific experiences during his ascent.[4] He undergoes pain (ἀλγοῖ 515c8, ἀλγεῖν 515e2, ὀδυνᾶσθαί 515e8) and anger (ἀγανακτεῖν 516a1). He is at a loss (ἀπορεῖν 515d6), troubled in his soul (θορυβουμένην 518a5), and at one point flees back to familiar things (φεύγειν 515e2). He is reluctant, and at several points has to be forced on to the next stage of deliverance (ἀναγκάζοιτο 515c6, ἀναγκάζοι 515d5, ἀναγκάζοι 515e1, ἕλκοι . . . βίᾳ 515e6). He finds it hard to see and his eyes have to become accustomed to the increasingly bright light (515c8–d1, 515e1–4, 516a1–3, 516a5–b2; also 517d4–518b4). Significantly, this adjustment occurs at each stage of the learner's progress—when he first turns to look at the objects in the Cave, when he looks at the fire, when he enters the outside world, when he progresses from looking at shadows to looking at real things there, and later when he returns to the Cave (516e3–517a4). At the earlier stages, distress, struggle, and discomfort are central to his progress. But once he is in the outside world, the pain has faded and we are simply told that it took him time to adjust. It seems that the prisoner's unpleasant experiences are in part due to the nature of the process (the light is bright, the path upwards rough and steep), and to this extent unavoidable. But his reluctance and anger are also based on a misunderstanding of his

[4] Cf. Warren (2010), Schofield (2007), Rowe (2007) 63–4.

original state and, as such, they are ultimately misplaced. This comes out most clearly when Socrates describes the prisoner's return to the Cave, a descent from light into darkness, when his former companions mistakenly think that his eyesight has been spoiled, and try to kill the person who would liberate them (516e8–517a6)—they do not realize, as we and the prisoner now do, how misguided their view of the world is. But once the prisoner has ascended to the real world, he leaves those misplaced responses behind. He is happy with the change and pities his former companions; and no longer wishes to share their opinions (516c4–d7). The language of lightness, deliverance and freeing, reality and order, presents this later stage as delightful; here there is no talk of compulsion. It is hard to think that, by now, desire and aspiration do not play a part in the prisoner's upward movement, as they do in other of the dialogues' images for learning, such as the ascents of *Symposium* and of the *Phaedo* myth.

Finally, the process involves two people. Though I have emphasized the prisoner's personal input, the educator's role is crucial too. The language of compulsion so prominent in the initial stages of the ascent strongly implies that without him, the prisoner would not change at all. The educator provides the stimuli that disturb the prisoner's current state, opening up the possibility of change and bringing about the experiences, both affective and cognitive, which he undergoes. In his comments at the close of the image at 518d, too, where he talks of an art of turning the soul around as easily and effectively as possible, Socrates suggests that the role of a second person—the employer of the art—may be vital. As I noted, though, the nature of this relationship changes as the learner progresses.

My suggestion is that these four features are central to the dialogues' paradigm of learning, not just in this image, but for interlocutors and readers more generally. Some of the features of the Cave image I commented on are well-recognized features of Socratic conversation—though later I hope to show that they can also form part of a rather less familiar picture. It is well established, for instance, that Socratic conversation requires the interlocutor's own effort, involves his life and character, and engages the deep beliefs that are essential to his conception of his self.[5] This is implicit in the dramatic settings

[5] On the connection with life and character, see especially Robinson (1953) 15–17, Vlastos (1983) 35–8, McCabe (2006); also Gifford (2001), Kahn (1983), Nehamas (1998) 1–2, 42–3, 46, and *passim*. For language of the self, see King (1987) 106, Teloh (1986) 15–16

Plato gives the conversations; in the connections made between a person's views and their life; in the idea of dialectic as care for the soul; in Socrates' emphasis on an individual's development of his own ideas and his wariness of wisdom received on authority. Similarly, the idea that learning involves two people is a familiar one.[6] More controversial is my suggestion that learning, if it is properly to engage the self, must have both cognitive and affective dimensions. In the work of many scholars, the focus has been on the cognitive aspects of interlocutors' interactions. Interpreters have seen the consistency of an interlocutor's belief set as the key to his development; they have stressed the role of arguments in revealing inconsistency and establishing alternative ideas; and in examining the validity and implications of those arguments, they have detached them from their contexts. While prominent in the discussion of 'early' dialogues, such an approach may seem even more appropriate to 'later' dialogues, where we find more lengthy exposition of arguments and less focus on the dramatic aspects of dialectical encounters. To simplify, many scholars have approached the dialogues from the standpoint of modern philosophical activity,[7] where the validity of arguments is of central importance and their practical and psychological implications receive less attention.

In recent years, however, interest in these latter aspects of Platonic dialectic has been growing. Attention has been drawn to the role of psychological factors in the effect of arguments on interlocutors, as for example in McKim's influential work on shame,[8] and to the

and (1987), Beversluis (2000) 1 n2, Benson (2000) 88, Hadot (1995). On engaging the interlocutor's deep beliefs, see May (1997), McKim (1988), Teloh (1986) 15–16 and (1987).

[6] See e.g. Roochnik (2003) 144, Sayre (1995) 161–3, Beversluis (2000) 34, Zuckert (2003) 146, C. Gill (1996b). We face here the question of whether learning *necessarily* involves two people, or whether private reflection by a single person counts if this involves dialectical interchange between two parts of the soul: see ch.1 n14. Long (2007) and (2008) argues that Plato does not present interpersonal dialogue as essential to philosophy, and suggests that thought may take the place of interpersonal dialogue should a respondent prove intractable. The dialogues seem to reserve individual thought for a late stage in the learning process—by which point, the learner has, according to the Cave model, developed his own autonomy and motivation, and may be able to develop an internal dialogue without prompting from an external educator. See section 2.3 on how the dialogues encourage the reader to develop a dialectical attitude to her own responses, in the absence of a discussion partner.

[7] Cf. Moes (2000) preface and chapter 1; Sayre (1992) 227.

[8] McKim (1988). Cf. also Teloh (1986) 1–2, King (1987), Belfiore (1980) 132–5, Scolnicov (1976), Rutherford (1995) 79–82, Renaud (2002), Schmid (2002), Gordon (1999), Kahn (1983), Beversluis (2000) 7–8.

importance of the interlocutor's character and virtue in his ability to benefit from Socratic teaching.[9] There has been increased appreciation of the flexible and *ad hominem* nature of dialectic,[10] and its disregard for modern concerns about fallacious reasoning[11]—not as limitations or incidental features of Socrates' practice, but as a crucial part of his method for getting through to individuals, whatever the means required. The role of non-argumentative aspects of dialectic, such as myth and rhetoric, in engaging the interlocutor is also coming in for more attention.[12] All this work suggests that, in the dialogues, learning is not seen in purely cognitive terms, but as bound up with an individual's affective responses: these are crucial if the process is to engage with her most deeply held beliefs, and thereby her self-conception, motivational orientation, and ultimately her actions and the shape of her life. In addition, such work suggests that a valuable response needs to be *at once* affective and cognitive. For an argument can only have an impact on us if it touches the feelings that are integral to ourselves; and the way we respond to argumentation is intimately connected with our sense of self, not just our perception of the logic of what is said. In other words, we should not think of the affective and cognitive as two separate parts of learning, occurring at

Slightly different is the emphasis of Blank (1993), who argues that the intended effect of argumentation (in both interlocutor and reader), throughout Plato's corpus, is emotional. While I find Blank's overall approach attractive, I regard the response evoked in interlocutors and receivers as affective-cognitive, not just emotional: this is crucial for distinguishing the dialogues from other genres. In addition, I do not think, as Blank does, that the effects of conversation on the interlocutors are straightforwardly replicated in receivers; and I do not think that reading dialogues can take the place of oral philosophizing. I have similar objections to the suggestion of Gifford (2001) 108 that the dialogues engage and motivate their readers by evoking the tragic emotion of fear.

[9] Blondell (2002), Teloh (1986), Carone (2004), Szlezák (1999) 6–8, Seeskin (1987) 1–4, 23–4, Wolfsdorf (2004), Rutherford (1992). Seeskin interestingly suggests that the social status of Meno's slave, which makes him willingly and humbly submit to questioning, is an important part of what makes him a model interlocutor.

[10] Teloh (1986), esp. 1–23, Carpenter and Polansky (2002), Brickhouse and Smith (2002), Roochnik (2003) 140, Coventry (1990), Hyland (1995) esp. 13–33.

[11] See e.g. Sichel (1976), Dickoff and James (1976), Hobbs (2000) 117, Sprague (1962), Gonzalez (1998) 102–5, Weiss (2001). Beversluis (2000), esp. 7–8, is sensitive to this characteristic of Socratic dialectic, but regards it as exemplifying Socrates' unfair, bullying, and competitive tactics. I take up this question in ch.5.

[12] On rhetoric, see e.g. Carone (2004), though I would reject her implicit division of dialectic into aspects that appeal to emotions and to reason. On myth, see e.g. Morgan (2000), McCabe (1992).

different times and through different means, but as two aspects of a single *cognitive-affective* response.[13] And if this is so, it makes sense to think of all aspects of Socratic conversations—both argumentative and non-argumentative parts—as geared towards prompting such an engagement.[14]

In chapter 3, I offer support for this interpretation of learning. By examining the presentation of interlocutors in a range of dialogues, I build up a fuller picture of the responses that characterize the learning process, and I address the issue of how the picture can apply to dialogues traditionally termed 'early', 'middle', and 'late'. For now, though, I want to turn back to the reader. What implications does the paradigm I have presented have for our understanding of the reader's response and her engagement with Plato's texts? And in what way can we apply a model of learning built up from the dialogues' dramatic and discursive discourse to the activity of the reader herself?

2.2. A DEMANDING TYPE OF READING

It is clear, I think, that the image of the Cave offers us a demanding picture of learning: though the rewards of the ascent are great, struggle, perseverance, and personal endeavour are involved. In turning back to the reader, this means that we should expect the dialogues to be similarly challenging in the type of reading they require of us.

[13] This fits well with recent work on emotions, which emphasizes their close connections with cognition; e.g. Nussbaum (2001). I do not want to commit myself to a particular account of the relation between the affective or cognitive or of how we should relate them to ideas about motivation, action, and the soul put forward in the dialogues. The position I am arguing for is compatible with viewing the affective as attendant upon the cognitive (the view often attributed to the 'early' dialogues) or viewing it as a separate element in a person's motivation (a view associated with Plato's 'middle' period). For a recent extensive discussion of the dialogues' psychological theory, see Lorenz (2006).

[14] For accounts of learning with similar emphases to mine, see Scolnicov (1976) and Schmid (2002). Mackenzie (1988a) draws attention, like me, to the union of affective and cognitive aspects of *aporia*. Gallop (2003) emphasizes the linking of the emotional and intellectual, though his interpretation of how these are unified in the reader's response, based on Aristotelian notions of catharsis, is different from mine.

First, consider the implication for the reader of the need for personal effort and participation in learning. As I have been stressing, the dialogues refuse to offer the reader ideas she can adopt in any straightforward way. This is not to say that the dialogues do not contain expressions of opinion or of doctrine: they do, of course, in the contributions of characters; and these are essential in providing the stimulus and focus for our reflection.[15] My point is rather that they are handled in a way that prevents us responding to them *as* doctrine. A dialogue may contain no obvious message, for example, or it may be unclear what an idea means exactly; there may be contradictions or unresolved issues that destabilize our interpretation; or there may be silences that we have to negotiate in reaching an interpretation. In consequence, we have to do a lot of work for ourselves in constructing the views that we think emerge from the text,[16] and we are constantly asked to go beyond the ideas expressed by characters, treating them as incomplete and inadequate, provisional and unstable, limited by context, personality, and dialectical strategy.[17] This means that views we find in a dialogue are not extracted from it, but constructed by us on the basis of it—and one reader's construction is likely to differ from another's. The ideas we form in reading, therefore, are in an important sense our own, rather than the text's.[18]

In addition, the reader's engagement needs to have a certain quality or character. So far, I have been talking in terms congenial to the many critics who present—explicitly or implicitly—the reader's dialogue with the text in purely cognitive terms: as a matter of the intellectual contribution she is asked to make and the extent she has

[15] This means that the content and subject matter of those views is important: failing to take proper account of this, and turning all dialogues into exercises in method, is a charge sometimes levelled against interpreters with similar emphases to mine: see e.g. Kosman (1987), Weingartner (1973) 6. For the tension between doctrinal content and sceptical handling as central to the dialogues, see Scott and Welton (2000).

[16] Cf. e.g. Klein (1965) 9, Desjardins (1990) 12–13, Nails (1995) 228–31, Nehamas (1998), Wolfsdorf (2004), Ausland (2000), Nightingale (2003).

[17] Cf. Rowe (1999), Kamtekar (2006), Lane (1998) 36–8 on division, Miller (1980) xvi–xvii.

[18] Cf. Seeskin (1987) 10–13, Cohen and Keyt (1992). This means that those who try to reconstruct Plato's views from the dialogues are responding to the texts in an appropriate way; but we should acknowledge that the interpretations they construct are products of their own process of learning, rather than determinate views of Plato's that can definitively be extracted from the texts. So Versényi (1982) 16–17.

to think for herself rather than being able to adopt views from the text.[19] I want to suggest, on the contrary, that the reader's engagement with the text is not just cognitive: as well as critical detachment and reflectiveness, it also requires the personal involvement of an affective response.[20] For without this, the learner's reflection will not connect with her deep beliefs or her conception of herself, nor have the potential to alter her motivation and actions. As interpreters often comment, the dialogues are concerned, fundamentally, with changing people's lives. To do this, they need to foster a capacity for personal responsibility and choice, with all the cognitive and affective commitment that implies.

Especially important here is attention to our experience of a text as we move through it sequentially, and the manner in which our overall response to it is formed. In exploring this, I draw on reader-response criticism,[21] an approach that has been applied with fruitful results to

[19] It is often implied (e.g. by Frede (1992a), Burnyeat (1990), and Annas (1981) 2) that the reader's dialogue with the text involves being made to engage intellectually with questions without being offered answers to them, as are interlocutors. As will become clear in chapter 3, esp. sections 3.5–3.6, I retain some aspects of this interpretation, while rejecting others. Nussbaum (1986), esp. 130–3, argues that the dialogues—unlike tragedy—encourage an intellectual rather than an emotional response (except for *Phaedrus*: see 226–7). Though I agree with Nussbaum's emphasis on the importance of the form of the dialogues in inviting a certain type of response, I disagree with her analysis of what that response is.

[20] For a similar emphasis on the emotional and intellectual dimension of the reader's engagement, see Press (1995). Blondell (2002) 47 also claims that the dialogues stimulate their readers intellectually and emotionally. For an emphasis on the practical implications of reading, see e.g. Gonzalez (1995c) and (1998), Howland (2003), Nehamas (1998) 42–3, Hadot (1995). Pelling (2000) 1–2 brings out the inextricability of the intellectual and emotional in persuasion: persuasion *that* is close to persuasion *to*. Plato's works are clearly rhetorical in this broad sense. In ch.3, I discuss these issues in relation to the dialogues' conception of learning in general (not just reading). Note that this is different from claiming, as does Gordon (1999), that 'extra-logical' parts of the dialogues are important for the reader's response: I am claiming that both logical and extra-logical parts of the dialogues invite a response that is both affective and cognitive. As will emerge from my approach in later chapters, I think that no such distinction between parts of the dialogues can comfortably be maintained.

[21] Though reader-response critics share some central concerns, the movement encompasses a wide range of approaches. Though Jauss and Iser are sometimes viewed as belonging to a separate movement, reception theory (see Holub (1984)), I follow many critics in treating them as part of the reader-response movement. For useful introductions, which include surveys of different approaches within the movement, see e.g. Suleiman and Crosman (1980), Davis and Womack (2002), Tompkins (1980a), Eagleton (1996). For helpful discussions relating particularly to Classical

various Classical authors,[22] though less commonly to philosophical texts.[23] In particular, I want to draw on the importance that many strands of reader-response criticism attach to the process by which the reader engages with a text and constructs her interpretation of it. Many of their insights about this process are central to my reading of Plato: the importance of the order in which the elements of a text are arranged; the creation and frustration of expectation; the role of rereading and the impulse to move backwards as well as forwards through a text in trying to make sense of it.[24] As will become clear, I see such features as crucial to the way the texts invite the response discussed above; and they come into play in all chapters, though in

texts, see Woodman and Powell (1992b) 204–15, Slater (1990). I will not confine myself to the approach of a single critic, but will draw on a range of complementary approaches in developing the one I find most helpful in interpreting the dialogues. On the value of combining different strands of reader-response criticism, see Suleiman (1980) 7. On the value of an eclectic hermeneutic more generally, see Davis and Womack (2002) 10, Segal (1994) viii, xi.

[22] Works I have found particularly helpful include: Slater (1990), Conte (1994), Martindale (1993), Fowler (2000a), Roberts *et al.* (1997), Baragwanath (2008), Pelling (1997a) and (2000), and contributions in *Arethusa* (1986). The link between modern and ancient concerns is noted by e.g. Rosenblatt (1978) 3, Davis and Womack (2002) 51–2, Holub (1984) 13, Sullivan (1994) 15, 19–20, Martindale (1996), Woodman and Powell (1992a) 204.

[23] Lucretius' *De Rerum Natura* is a notable exception. In Platonic studies, as I noted above, there has been an increase in attention to way the texts engage their readers, often under the banner of uniting philosophical and literary approaches. Many of these works, from different scholarly perspectives and traditions, could be seen as contributing to the development of a reader-response approach to Plato, though they are not generally couched in these terms (on which see Szlezák (1999) 25). These include: Blondell (2002), Nightingale (1995), Gifford (2001), Rutherford (1995), Nussbaum (1986), Morgan (2004), Roochnik (2003), Silk (2001), Ausland (1997), Krentz (1983), Sayre (1995), Gonzalez (1998), Szlezák (1999), Arieti (1995), Hadot (1995), and contributions to Griswold (1988a), Klagge and Smith (1992), Press (1993a) and (2000a), Gill and McCabe (1996), Michelini (2003a), and Gonzalez (1995a). Gordon (1999) brings in reader-response criticism in analysing the way Plato's dialogues turn their readers towards philosophy; however, whereas I am concerned to show how *all* aspects of a dialogue produce a valuable type of response, her main focus is on how 'extralogical' features of the dialogues (e.g. drama, image) help engage the reader in philosophy, by providing an emotional appeal that supplements the logical force of arguments.

[24] Such concerns are important in the work of Rosenblatt, Iser, and Fish: esp. Rosenblatt (1978), Fish (1970), Iser (1978),. Cf. also Suleiman (1980) 22, Slater (1990) 21, Woodman and Powell (1992b) 213–14. Such features are often noted by commentators on Plato, but are rarely placed at the centre of an interpretation; though see Ferrari (1997) and Roochnik (2003), which develops the notion of dialectical reading.

different ways. To some degree, this set of concerns overlaps with those of narratology, particularly the analysis of narrative order, selectivity, and speed, and I have on occasion found it helpful to phrase my analysis in narratological terms.[25]

In exploring such aspects of the reader's response, Louise Rosenblatt introduced the idea of an *aesthetic* approach to a text, which places the experience of reading at the centre of its analysis. By contrast, a *nonaesthetic* approach focuses on what we can learn and take away from a text, and its implications for our concepts and our approach to thinking and acting.[26] An aesthetic reading of a text does not exclude these other applications,[27] but insists that the experiences a text evokes in us as we read are central to the way it engages us. This fits very well with the emphasis I have placed on reading as an activity that has value, not just because it can put us in touch with ideas to reflect on, but because in itself it generates valuable responses. Traditionally, Plato's texts often have been—and in the analytic tradition often still are—approached in a decidedly nonaesthetic way. And though there has been a shift of emphasis more recently, there is still room for a great deal more attention to the way the texts affect the reader and the character of the responses they generate.

The development of an approach to learning centred on *process* of course applies as much to oral as to written discourse; as I have already suggested, I think the dialogues are in fact engaged in the twin project of marking out distinctive forms of oral and written discourse, both of which foster learning of this type, in contrast to the alternative approaches implicit in competing literary and educational genres.[28] But despite the common approach to learning, it is

[25] Fowler and Fowler (1996) 871 point out that narratology is helpfully viewed as a method rather than a theory, and can therefore easily be combined with other approaches; cf. also Doherty (2001) 122. For narratology as a reader-response approach, see e.g. Davis and Womack (2002) 57–8, Tompkins (1980b) xi–xiii, Suleiman (1980) 13–15, Doherty (2001) 125. It should be noted that concern with narrators and narratees need not lead to reflection on the implied reader, a point emphasized by De Jong (2004) 3–4 and Volk (2002); cf. Suleiman (1980) 14–15. Nevertheless, both writers acknowledge that the two projects are often carried out together, and that consideration of narrators and narratees provides helpful insight into the structuring of the reader's response. For illuminating application of narratological ideas to Plato, see Morgan (2004) and (2007); also Morgan (2003), Halperin (1992), Rutherford (2002), and Lowe (2000), who sees himself as rehabilitating the place of plot in narratological theory.

[26] Rosenblatt (1978), esp. 22–47.

[27] Rosenblatt (1978) 24.

[28] See sections 2.4 and 3.6.

important to recognize the differences between oral and written discourse and, consequently, between the ways they need to engage their receivers.[29] Given my emphasis on the combination of critical detachment and personal involvement required in the reader, two opposing dangers are particularly pertinent. The first is that the reader will become too close to the text, ceasing to interact with it critically and becoming immersed in a way that impedes independent reflection. The second is that she will become too detached; the critical distancing will be too effective, and she will stop being personally involved, perhaps cease reading altogether. In consequence, the dialogues have to tread a very careful line between distance and involvement. They do this, as I hope to illustrate in subsequent chapters, not by making certain parts of the texts involving and others distancing, but by fostering a type of involvement that is based on critical distance. Truly constructive involvement, one might say, is dependent on distance, in that a reader cannot expose her own perspective to development unless she is sufficiently distanced from the text to engage with it critically.[30] Accordingly, as I hope to bring out, it is the very techniques by which the texts withhold determinate meaning—their most powerful distancing device—that also draw the reader into genuinely engaged and critical reflection. To put it another way, the apparent absence of determinacy in the dialogues is the very means by which they foster in us the most productive type of response.[31]

It will be clear by now that I believe the dialogues foster a particular—and particularly demanding—form of reading engagement. One important strand of my project, in chapters 4–8, is to illuminate the extent to which the dialogues *require* our involvement in reading.

[29] These issues are discussed by Howland (2003), who (as I do) stresses the importance of self-consciousness in the reader, though I disagree with his suggestion that the dialogues are an improvement upon Socratic speech.

[30] Pelling (1997c) 229 suggests, in discussing Greek tragedy, that distancing and zooming work together in engaging the receiver.

[31] By destabilizing our interpretations of doctrine and inviting us to engage in deeper reflection on the text and the issues it raises, the dialogues may actually strengthen the authority of their implied author (in other words, the authority we attribute to the author); but in doing so, they encourage us to connect that authority with an approach to doctrine as much as doctrine itself. Cf. Baragwanath (2008) 8, 33 on Herodotus. For a similar interpretation of Petronius' *Satyricon*, as maximizing the reader's frustration in such a way as to suggest that there is someone controlling our responses, see Slater (1990) 237.

In fact, I hope to show that they stretch the reader's level of involvement, going beyond the demands made on her in other genres. Now, reader-response critics of course stress the role that the reader plays in constructing the meaning of *every* text: meaning is created by the reader, and within the constraints imposed by a text, readers will reach different interpretations. Nevertheless, some reader-response critics also recognize that certain texts make greater demands on the reader and push the burden of interpretation more fully on to her: texts that are, in Barthes' term, more 'writerly' than others.[32] Plato's dialogues fall, I think, into this category. From the way that information about characters is introduced, to the construction of arguments, the introduction of different plot sequences and the inclusion of ellipses, contradictions, and changes of register, the dialogues constantly maximize the reader's contribution and make it difficult for her to reach a secure point of interpretation. This is central to their ability to invite in her a level of participation that is analogous to that of an interlocutor in conversation.

2.3. READERS AND INTERLOCUTORS

In what sense, then, do interlocutors provide a parallel or model for readers? The first issue here concerns the relationship in which we stand to the interlocutors and the manner in which the presentation of their activity affects ours. Before setting out my own approach, it will be useful to discuss some common alternatives. To begin with, critics sometimes suggest that our responses mirror those of the respondents: just as (for instance) a respondent, subjected to one of Socrates' arguments, succumbs to *aporia*, so, as we read that argument, do we.[33] This position, though intuitively plausible, needs

[32] Barthes (1975). At (1978) 171, Rosenblatt insists that all reading requires 'writerly' activity, though at 92–3 she concedes that some texts require such input from the reader more explicitly than others. Cf. Desjardins (1988) on intentional ambiguity in Plato, and Mansfeld (1994) 23–6 and 150 ff. on intentional ambiguity in ancient texts more generally.

[33] For the idea that readers undergo similar experiences to interlocutors, see Belfiore (1984) 137, Nussbaum (1986) 129, Szlezák (1999) 25–7, Annas (1981) 16, Blank (1993), Gifford (2001) 100–1. At (1984) 144, Belfiore comments that Alcibiades' claim, at *Smp.*215cd, that the effect of Socrates' words is the same whether heard

careful handling. In particular, it is crucial to recognize that our experiences do not replicate those of the interlocutor in a straightforward way. For (to continue with the same example) while it may look as though we experience *aporia* because we are exposed to the same argument as the interlocutor, this is not the case. Our response is produced by the presentation of an argument as an exchange between two people in written form, where the omission of pauses or helpful contextualization (such as facial expressions, reactions of participants and onlookers, tone of voice) have an important effect; the interlocutor, by contrast, experiences *aporia* through exposure to one person asking him a series of questions orally. That is, if the dialogues produce the same responses in us as in interlocutors, they do so through different means.[34] More generally, our response is fashioned by all aspects of the construction of a dialogue, not just the presentation of interlocutors; and it is implausible to think that our experience is meant to replicate theirs in a sustained way. This becomes especially important when we think about ways we are encouraged to move *beyond* the reactions of respondents—as I think most critics would agree that we are. Nevertheless, there is appeal in the idea that we, sometimes at least, go through similar responses to interlocutors, and this will remain an important strand in my account.

This brings us to a second tendency in thinking about the relationship between interlocutors and readers: to see them providing either negative or positive paradigms. Some scholars focus on the failings of respondents, whose deficiencies, they suggest, spur us on to more adequate responses.[35] Others emphasize the role of Socrates and

directly or reported by another, implicitly puts the reader of a dialogue in the same position as an interlocutor; cf. *Phd.*58d, 88c–89a, with discussion in Blank (1993), esp. 436–7. According to the model of the relationship between composer/performer/receiver voiced at *Ion* 533de, based on the transmission of magnetic force from a stone to a series of iron rings, the experience of all three is similar in kind. Though *Ion* discusses the deficient response produced by rhapsodic performances, a structurally similar model could apply to a valuable response, and would fit with my approach. These passages are compatible with recognizing the different means by which conversation and written dialogue produce their effects.

[34] Cf. Hadot (1995) 104–5, 149 who suggests that the dialogues were written with the same pedagogical and methodological aims as informed the practice of spoken dialectic; so also Gifford (2001), Sayre (1988) 103.

[35] This is most commonly presented in intellectualist terms, as a matter of coming up with better answers to the problems raised than interlocutors: e.g. Mackenzie (1982) 69, Gifford (2001) 87–8, Blondell (2002) 105. Miller (1980) and (1986) develops similar ideas in relation to 'late' dialogues. For reservations about an

other respondents in constructive works (most obviously the Eleatic Stranger, but also, for example, Glaucon and Adeimantus in *Republic*) as models for us.[36] Yet others see the juxtaposition of positive and negative models as central to the effect on us: we wish to be (and perhaps see ourselves as being) akin to Socrates, but are brought to realize that we are in fact closer to other interlocutors.[37] Again, such positions need to be handled with care. In particular, I am uncomfortable with the idea that any interlocutor is presented in a wholly positive or negative manner, as I argue in chapter 4: rather, we are encouraged to distance ourselves from all characters. Equally importantly, the interlocutors, in conversing, are engaging in a different activity from us, in reading, so we cannot treat them as direct models. Much of what happens in a conversation could not happen during reading; and the behaviour that makes someone a good learner in a conversational context—providing direct, concise answers to questions, for example—is not always applicable to us. The indirectness of the relationship between readers and interlocutors is an important point in itself: the texts do not provide us with anything like a template for correct reading, but we have to think about what this involves for ourselves. Nevertheless, the idea that the presentation of interlocutors is important in shaping the way we react does, I think, capture an important insight. My own view tries to preserve this,

intellectualist interpretation of the reader's response, see above. Others emphasize the respondents' character flaws: e.g. Teloh (1986), Seeskin (1987).

[36] The idea that the reader learns by modelling herself on interlocutors is central to the mimetic pedagogy view of the dialogues, espoused by Blondell (2002) in particular. For further discussion, see ch.4. Gill (2002) suggests that interlocutors in 'early' dialogues are negative paradigms, and those in 'late' dialogues are positive paradigms. For interesting comments on interlocutors as models for us, see also Belfiore (1984) 137–8, Nightingale (1993), Sayre (1995) esp. 97–129. Also relevant here is the idea that the frames of narrated dialogues present us, in Socrates' followers, with paradigm devotees of philosophy: see Morgan (2004); also Sedley (1999b). We need, however, to be more sceptical about how ideal these followers actually are.

[37] Nehamas (1998), esp. 11–12, 27–32, 43–4, presents a nuanced position of this type, suggesting that we are initially encouraged to identify with Socrates as he demolishes his opponents, before being shown that—in doing so—we are no better than them. Irony, in his view, is central in shaping our response; so also Gifford (2001). Gordon (1999) 52–3 implies a similar view. Like Nehamas, I would emphasize the challenge Plato poses to his readers, and also the distance created between us and both Socrates and his respondents, but I put a more optimistic slant on our relationship with interlocutors.

while attributing a more positive and constructive role to the presentation of interlocutors.

Central to my approach is the idea that the behaviour of interlocutors provides us with insight into what learning, as conceived in the dialogues, involves—insight that helps us understand and manage our own responses as readers. We can see, as I discuss further in later chapters, two levels in the behaviour of interlocutors. First, there are the basic experiences they undergo when subjected to the discussion leader's tactics: confusion, surprise, disorientation, for example. Then there is their second-level response to those experiences. An interlocutor may, for example, refuse to participate in conversation or walk off in anger, or he may reflect upon his own inadequacies and redouble his efforts in discussion. The stimuli to which an interlocutor is exposed in Socratic conversation and the experiences he undergoes are, I shall suggest, designed to challenge and stretch him; they are of such a sort, that is, that a productive response would by no means be automatic in any learner, however virtuous or philosophically developed. Both levels of response are necessary for learning (so, at least, I argue in chapter 2), but it is the second level that distinguishes good learners—those who actually make progress—from bad.[38] The same two levels are also, I think, present in the reader's response, even if they cannot be distinguished easily at the time we are reading. The texts, just like Socratic conversations, are constructed in such a way as to produce basic feelings of confusion, surprise, and so forth in even the most recalcitrant recipients. But we also have the opportunity—even if not all readers take it up—to respond to them in a way that actually enables us to learn. And it is here that the role of the interlocutors is most important.

By confronting us with the behaviour of interlocutors, the dialogues force us to reflect on what learning involves: on the challenges we need to be exposed to, the experiences we have to go through, and the value these have for our development. In doing so, we develop an understanding of the learning process—a model for learning—that we can apply to our own experiences in reading. We become able, that is, to see our experiences as replicating those of interlocutors, even if

[38] For an interpretation of Plato's views on the formation of the self that places emphasis on second-order desires/attitudes, see Hobbs (2000) 57–9. King (1987) 111–12 distinguishes between the parts of a person that recognize and cause self-blame, and sees the need to overcome self-blame as the key problem of the *elenchus*.

only indirectly. This added degree of understanding enables us to see *why* the dialogues engage us as they do—why they are interested in confusing or unsettling us for example—and in consequence it enables us to work though these experiences more productively. In addition to this, though, the presentation of interlocutors helps us to reflect on our responses to the learning process more directly. We see in their behaviour a spectrum of possible second-level responses to the basic learning experiences, and learn to recognize and to appreciate positive and negative ones. These are, of course, similar to the responses that we ourselves, as we read, have the tendency to manifest. The behaviour of interlocutors, therefore, holds up to us a mirror of our own behaviour, helping us to recognize and reflect on the value of our own second-level responses.[39]

By acting, in this complex way, as a model and mirror for the reader's response, the presentation of the behaviour of interlocutors in discussion helps make our engagement with the text as dialogic as it can be, given the medium. One of the key features of learning, as the dialogues present it and as we have already seen in the image of the Cave, is that it involves two parties—discussion leader and respondent. The discussion leader provides the stimuli that force the respondent to engage in learning in the first place; he also provides the commentary, exhortation, criticism, and flexibility that enable the discussions to be as productive as they are.[40] Yet, as *Phaedrus* notoriously brings out, this is impossible in the case of a written text, which cannot interact with its reader. I am not trying to claim that the presentation of interlocutors makes up for this deficiency entirely, but it does go some

[39] Cf. Miller (1980) xiv–xvi, which suggests that the dialogues put us, the audience, on stage before ourselves, presenting us with our failings as well as common ways people find to avoid facing up to them—thus helping us move beyond such a defective response. Cf. also Miller (1986). Though Miller's position is complementary to mine, I place more emphasis on our perception of likeness between ourselves and interlocutors, and the role of *understanding* in helping us reach more adequate responses: he stresses how Plato's presentation of interlocutors encourages us to disassociate ourselves from them. Cf. also Moes (2000) 50–1, for interlocutors as providing a mirror of readers' own ailments, and Gould (1992) 13–14. Miller (1999) 257–8 brings out how we see our own positions under attack in the conversations of the dialogues: an important though slightly different phenomenon.

[40] Even when the discussion ends unproductively, the discussion leader's input has generally been crucial in ensuring that it continues even this long: think of Callicles' repeated attempts to end the discussion in *Gorgias*, Meno's introduction of the paradox of inquiry, or the attitude of Protarchus which earns him the rebuke of trying to shipwreck the discussion (*Phlb.*13c ff.).

way towards alleviating it. The dialogues, in their written form, themselves provide us with stimuli parallel to those we would encounter in discussion. And the presentation of interlocutors, by enabling us to engage in a kind of dialogue with ourselves, in which we monitor and mediate our own responses, allows us to go some way towards fulfilling for ourselves the role of discussion leader. Of course, not all readers will take up the invitation to do this, and the possibility of an unproductive response is constantly prefigured in the dialogues. But the parallelism created between reader and interlocutor provides a means by which the text can challenge us, while preventing the challenge being self-defeatingly severe.

2.4. DEVELOPING A GENERIC IDENTITY

In the approach to the dialogues I have outlined so far, both readers and interlocutors are encouraged to engage in a dialogue of a demanding and distinctive type. The possibilities of this approach, when applied to detailed analysis of the dialogues' construction, will (I hope) become apparent in my later case studies. In addition, it offers an alternative perspective on a long-standing problem of Platonic interpretation: the dialogues' blistering attacks on poetry.

The dialogues' criticism of poetry is notoriously complex; nevertheless, two of the objections, which are treated most extensively in *Republic* X, are often viewed as particularly important.[41] The first is that poetry is based on ignorance; though poets claim knowledge, they put forward false ideas about what is to be valued. In fact, they *cannot* write with knowledge, or even true belief, since they only engage in *mimesis*, which is concerned with the appearance of things. The second is that poetry appeals to the emotions, thus strengthening the lower parts of the soul, so that they are more likely to dominate in life too. In other words, it fosters a response proper to someone controlled by his emotions. The idea that literature is not only worthless, but also harmful, has traditionally been held to pose problems for our attitude to Plato's dialogues, which are of course, for all their philosophical purpose, highly literarily worked creations.

[41] E.g. Janaway (1995) 11, 133–57. Cf. Halliwell (1988) 5.

And this applies not least to my own interpretation of the dialogues, which is based, as will now be clear, on a detailed attention to the experience of reading, and to the stylistic and literary features of the dialogues that invite those responses. If, as I am arguing, reading the dialogues can have positive philosophical value, what should we make of their attacks on poetry?[42] How should we make sense of this apparent contradiction?

One common response runs as follows.[43] Plato, despite his various objections to poetry, recognizes its ability to appeal to the receiver and to mould her soul. He therefore *harnesses* its aesthetic effects—which remain the same in philosophical and non-philosophical literature—to his philosophical purpose. This view is suggested by the use of poetry in the early education of the guardians in *Republic*: poets will be forced to compose works that propagate the ideals of the state and guide children towards the good life. Nevertheless, it encounters serious problems.

One is the prima facie unattractiveness of a view that assimilates Plato's own writing to the 'literature' of the ideal state.[44] It is true that this, through the part it plays in education, has a productive philosophical role of a sort. Nevertheless, it is a basic one: the unconscious inculcation of values and patterns of behaviour. We are not encouraged to regard it as part of the conscious development of a reflective adult, but this is closer to the role that I at least want to attribute to Plato's works. It would, moreover, take us back towards a doctrinal interpretation of the dialogues of the sort which I have offered several reasons for rejecting.

A more compelling objection is that the view fits uncomfortably with Socrates' objections to the emotionality of literature. If literary elements, as this view assumes, always tend to foster an emotional response, then even if this is directed towards worthy objects, the reader will still respond in a way appropriate to a person controlled by their emotions. Yet this does not do justice to the strength of Plato's concern with poetry's emotional effect.[45] Conversely, it is hard to see

[42] This subject has generated a huge literature. Contributions I have found particularly helpful include: Nightingale (1995), Ferrari (1989), Barker and Warner (1992a), Janaway (1995), Annas (1982b), Segal (1978), Halliwell (1988), Nussbaum (1986) 122–36, Asmis (1992).

[43] E.g. Stewart (1905) 53–5, 113–14, Janaway (1995) esp. 159–61, 182–3, Rutherford (1995) 175, 235–7, Edelstein (1949) 479, Ferrari (1989) 107–8, 143–4.

[44] Cf. Morgan (2000) 163–4.

[45] Cf. Sichel (1976) in discussion of sophistic discourse.

how, in philosophical literature, reason could 'control' the aesthetic-emotional response of the reader without removing its essential character, and this leaves Plato open to the charge that he does not *really* appreciate the aesthetic effect of literature, but puts it to work for alien ends.[46] It is, of course, a criticism frequently levelled against the literature of the ideal state, that it is not *real poetry* at all.[47] Calling Plato's dialogues poetical philosophy or philosophical poetry merely evades the question of how they can be good literature if they subordinate the literary in this problematic manner.

The approach I take in this study builds on the dialogues' well-recognized attempts to distance themselves, on both dramatic and discursive levels, from other genres and types of discourse, especially those associated with rhetoric, the sophists, and the poets.[48] My suggestion, as I will set out in more detail in the chapters to come, is that Plato differentiates his work, both in the techniques he uses and the effects they produce, from that of his rivals, not least the poets. As later chapters explore, Plato's literary techniques such as characterization, plot, and structure often *appear* very like those in the genres he criticizes, but on closer inspection, differences emerge. As I will argue, Plato's handling of character fosters critical distance rather than emotional identification; his structures tend towards disunity; his stories move away from classical plot. If this is the case, Plato is not *adopting* the literary techniques of other genres, but using them as a foil for creating his own. And he is doing so in order to produce a distinctive, cognitive-affective response in the reader, which can help her to progress in learning.

Though at first sight, therefore, we may think the dialogues akin to other genres—just as Socrates' initial exchanges can look deceptively like normal conversation—in fact a network of literary techniques differentiates them. And these techniques are so pervasive and fundamental that they are crucial to our whole experience and understanding of the works as a genre. They ensure that Platonic dialogue, by its very nature and generic identity, tends to produce a cognitive-affective response; and in consequence, they serve a similar purpose to Socrates'

[46] Janaway (1995) 177–81.

[47] E.g. Annas (1982b) 22–3, Ferrari (1989) 141, Asmis (1992) 358.

[48] See e.g. De Romilly (1975), Nightingale (1995), Sichel (1976), Wolfsdorf (2004), Morgan (2002), Ferrari (1989) 92, Nehamas (1999b), Nussbaum (1986) 122–35, Ford (2008), Goldhill (2002).

rules of discussion, in that they invite a particular type of philosophical engagement. Plato, in other words, is carving out two parallel and complementary arenas for the practice of cognitive-affective learning—Socratic conversation and Platonic dialogue.

If this is the case, the dialogues are encouraging a response of a fundamentally different kind from the emotional reaction they associate with rival genres. Accordingly, there is no need to question the seriousness of Plato's engagement with literary works and literariness; to worry that he subordinates aesthetic experience to philosophy in a way that threatens its essential character; or to accuse him of adopting the poets' 'emotional' techniques to support his own ideas. Rather, Plato is concerned to create a type of literature whose impact on the reader, since it is of a different kind from that of the literature he criticizes, can directly and through its own characteristic aesthetic effect have a constructive role in her ethical development. Plato's attention to creating the kind of specific literary effects I have discussed illustrates that he regards the reader's aesthetic response as very significant for philosophical progress, and that, far from objecting to aesthetic involvement per se, he is worried about a specific type of response that he connects with a bad direction of ethical development. His criticisms of poetry, therefore, should be seen not as an attempt to banish the aesthetic, but as part of an endeavour to define and create his own distinctive type. By the same token, the dialogues should not be seen as 'versions' of poetry, rhetoric, or sophistic debate from which the problematic bits have been purged; rather they take over some of their features and transform them to create a quite different response in the reader: a distinctively philosophical engagement.

2.5. PLATO'S CORPUS AND THE DEVELOPMENT OF THE READER

The approach I develop in this study can, I hope, contribute in interesting ways to the interpretation of individual texts. But Plato's dialogues do not encourage us to view philosophical progress as something that can be achieved by a single conversation or the reading of a single text; and I will also be concerned with the broader shape of the learner's progress, and with how this may inform our approach to Plato's corpus as a whole.

Plato's dialogues are usually regarded as falling into three groups, belonging to 'early', 'middle', and 'late' periods of composition. The stark differences between the three groups of dialogues have posed a long-standing challenge to interpreters of Plato, with critics struggling to explain the shifts in style and philosophical preoccupation between them. On the prevailing developmentalist paradigm, the tendency has been to emphasize the disjunctions between the three groups, explaining these with reference to changes in the views being espoused, the approach to learning implicit in the works, and their intended audience. More recently, though, this view has been challenged, and critics have sought new ways of understanding the corpus.[49] The basis for chronological division of the dialogues has been contested;[50] and there have been moves towards more unitarian

[49] For the question of how to interpret Plato's corpus as a whole, see Griswold (1988b) xi–xiii and (1999), Kahn (1996) xiv–xvii, Ferrari (2003a), and especially Clay (1987) and Miller (1987). A connected issue concerns whether we see each dialogue as an independent whole, which should be studied individually, or whether we see them as forming a systematic pattern which should be interpreted with close reference to one another. For discussion, see Ferrari (2003a) 244–5, Gill (2002). We should, I think, be wary of juxtaposing these two options too starkly. The dialogues do not present anything like a unified body of doctrine, in my view, but this is not incompatible with them forming a coherent whole of some sort. Similarly, we can regard relationships between dialogues as one way in which they affect our response, without thinking that we have to make the ideas expressed in them compatible with one another.

[50] For extensive discussion, see Nails (1995), who adopts an anti-developmentalist stance; also Thesleff (1982) and Howland (1991). Young (1994), a review of the important stylometric studies by Brandwood (1990) and Ledger (1989), provides a critical evaluation of the possibility of establishing a chronological ordering of the dialogues using computer analysis. Annas (2002) also challenges the traditional chronological groupings. Kahn (2002) offers a defence of the results of stylistic analysis in dividing the dialogues into three chronological groups.

Nails' view is that Plato's dialogues contain a critique of Socrates' oral methods of philosophizing, and can be split into those that represent 'Socratic' and 'Platonic' philosophizing on this score. This is at odds with my emphasis on the continuity between methodologies represented in the different dialogues, and the development of a parallel between oral and written discourse—though I am in agreement with her rejection of a chronological developmentalist interpretation of the differences between dialogues. Blondell (2002) 11 suggests that the different presentations of Socrates (elenctic, constructive) should replace talk of early/middle/late groupings, since these represent different layers in Plato's thinking about philosophical method—a view to which I have similar objections.

interpretations, in relation to both doctrine[51] and composition.[52] In sympathy with this second tendency, one important strand in my study is the suggestion of an alternative to chronological developmentalism—one based on the development of the reader, not of Plato.[53]

My approach is not to deny the importance of the changes in style between dialogues noticed by developmentalist interpreters, but to suggest that underlying continuities—continuities that can point to a more satisfactory explanation of the changes—have been overlooked. As I hope to bring out in chapters 4–8, if we look carefully at the handling of specific aspects of composition across different types of dialogue, we can detect strong threads of consistency in the ways they are used and the effects they create. At the same time, there is always a trend, as we move from 'early' to 'middle' and 'late' dialogues, towards greater challenge and inaccessibility. 'Earlier' dialogues make it easy for the reader to engage with their discussions and, though the task of interpretation is far from straightforward, they are more obvious and unsubtle in the way they guide our response. In 'later' dialogues, less work is done for the reader and the interpretative challenges are greater. As she progresses from 'early' works onwards, things become harder for the reader, and to get anything out of 'later' works, she has to be more philosophically advanced and more self-motivated in her approach. As Annas points out,[54] it is common practice today to reserve 'late' works for more advanced students, while introducing students to the study of Plato through 'early' and 'middle' works. Correspondingly, as I argue in my later case studies, the 'later' texts encourage the reader to develop in ways that are appropriate to a more advanced stage of philosophical development: the demands placed on the reader's dialectical virtue become more taxing and the skills she is encouraged to develop become more sophisticated.

[51] See e.g. Annas (1999), Kahn (1996), Rowe (2006).

[52] See esp. Gill and McCabe (1996).

[53] For an overview of the groupings, see Annas (2002), Sedley (2004) 1–2; there is no universally accepted set of groupings. I shall not attempt to provide a rigid classification of types of dialogue. In my view, this does poor justice to the fluidity of the boundaries between different dialogues, and the subtle and varied ways in which they invite us to react. For convenience, while maintaining that the groupings are best interpreted from the perspective of the reader's development not Plato's, I shall work within the traditional threefold classification of Plato's dialogues.

[54] Annas (2002) 10–11. Cf. Kahn (1996) 380–3.

It seems to me, therefore, that there are grounds for regarding the different groups of dialogues as composed with the same basic ideas in mind about how to stimulate the reader to learn, but with readers at different stages of philosophical development in mind. In other words, the traditional groupings do reflect objective changes in the works, but those changes are best explained not by reference to Plato's career, but by reference to the different *readers* they imply: those at early, intermediate, and advanced stages of philosophical development. The dialogues, I suggest, invite us to engage in a corresponding process of development in learning, as we progress through the dialogues as readers; and the 'early' works, as it were, 'train' their readers to respond productively to the more advanced stimuli of the 'later' works.[55] While I will continue to use the labels 'early', 'middle', and 'late' while discussing the traditional approaches to the dialogues, I find it more helpful to think of these as representing different stages—early-stage, intermediate-stage, and advanced-stage—in the development of the reader.

In applying this interpretation to the dialogues, I have found that it reveals interesting consistencies in different parts of the Platonic corpus, as well as a new explanation for some of the features that have puzzled us about the dialogues, especially those traditionally regarded as 'late'. It cannot of course be demonstrated definitely, given our knowledge of the writing, publication, and original reception of the dialogues,[56] though pedagogical considerations are common in

[55] Compare Sedley (2004) 8 on *Theaetetus*: 'Socrates fails to see the Platonic implications, and instead it is we, as seasoned readers of Plato, who are expected to recognize and exploit them.' We could see some of the dialogues' recurrent motifs as likely to contribute to this training: not taking ideas on authority, saying what one thinks oneself, the importance of repeated and ongoing inquiry, the need to remember and interrogate what was said previously, discussion leaders' disavowal of knowledge.

[56] I do not think that study of the type of reading invited and encouraged by the dialogues should be limited by their actual reception (*Phaedrus* warns us against this), and I would like to distinguish my approach from the idea that Plato wrote different styles of dialogue for different actual audiences: so e.g. Ryle (1966); also Taylor (1961) 9–10, 22, Ryle (1968). We cannot know from the dialogues what their actual intended audience was, but can only talk about the type of receivers they invite. However, stylistic analysis of the dialogues may offer some support for my approach. As Kahn (2002) has brought out, such analysis offers evidence for the division of the dialogues into three groups (which do not in all respects overlap with those adopted by developmentalist interpretations of the kind discussed above): a 'late' group consisting of *Sophist, Politicus, Philebus, Timaeus-Critias,* and *Laws*; a 'transitional' group including *Phaedrus, Republic, Parmenides,* and *Theaetetus*; and an 'early' group comprising the

ancient ideas about the categorization of the dialogues[57] and there is some evidence of an ancient approach with affinities to my own. The second-century Platonist Albinus, in his *Prologue* to his edition of Plato's dialogues, suggests that an ordering should take its starting point from the perspective of the receiver's education: 'for we wish to discover the commencement and arrangement of instruction that is according to wisdom.'[58] Albinus goes on to offer two different suggestions for the order in which to study the dialogues, a shorter version comprising four works, and a longer version based on different types of dialogues. These sequencings, it has been suggested, are offered with students of different types or stages in mind;[59] and in each case, Albinus alludes to principles of pedagogy. In describing the shorter course, Albinus implies that there is a link between the characteristics of the interlocutors portrayed in a dialogue and the type of reader for whom it is best suited: *Alcibiades*, he suggests, offers an ideal starting point for a learner who is well born, initiated in instruction, positively disposed towards philosophy, and of a suitable age—in other words, someone who shares the characteristics of Plato's portrayal of Alcibiades.[60] Later, he outlines the stages of the learner's development and the dialogues appropriate to each stage, suggesting that we should start with dialogues of a tentative character, so as to cast out false opinions, before moving on to dialogues of a maieutic character, in order to bring forth the notions relating to physics, as well as to morals, statesmanship, and the regulation of a household. Following that, he says, we need to move on to dialogues of a logical kind, which help prevent

remainder of the dialogues. If we regard these groups as corresponding to different periods of Plato's output (a move which not all critics accept), then making the attractive connection between 'later' works and the Academy would provide support for my suggestion that these works are written with more advanced learning in mind. Cf. Kahn (1996) xvi, 380–3. It should not necessarily surprise us if different types of dialogue do not correspond neatly to changes in Plato's style.

57 Annas (1999) ch.2, drawing on the ideas of middle Platonists, suggests that the different styles of dialogue are related to the order in which they were meant to be taught. Philip (1970) and Tarrant (1993) discuss the importance of pedagogical ideas in ancient orderings of the dialogues. Cf. also Sedley (2002), Annas (2002), Nehamas (1999a) xv–xvi, Kahn (1996) 58 (with an emphasis on doctrine).

58 Trans. Burges.

59 The relationship between the two orderings is contested; some link the short course with those who will stop at true opinion, and the long one with those who aim at knowledge; others think that the long course is a continuation of the shorter one. For discussion, see Reis (1999).

60 Tarrant (2000b) 120–1.

ideas escaping from us; and finally, so that we are not led astray by sophists, we progress to dialogues of a demonstrative character, which help us to learn how to approach those who conduct themselves inappropriately in matters of reason.

The idea of a progression from tentative to maieutic to logical or exploratory works could make sense when applied to the developmentalist picture of Plato's move from the destructive Socratic practices of the 'early' dialogues, to increasing exposition of his own views in 'middle' works, to the sometimes analytical and critical approach of 'late' works. Yet Albinus puts forward his model in connection with the *receiver's* progress. His starting point, like mine, is that the dialogues are directed towards an educable reader; he suggests that changes in the style and content of the works are to be understood with reference to the reader's stage of development, and he implies that some kind of progression through the works of Plato's corpus is necessary for the different aspects of our development.

As readers of Plato's works, I suggest, we are invited to embark on a progression of the sort Albinus indicates, a journey of increasing philosophical advancement that mirrors the prisoner's gradual ascent from the Cave. The affective and cognitive aspects of our development are inseparable, just as the prisoner's regulation of his responses to the difficulties of his journey at each stage is part of his ascent to the outside world; and Plato's texts are constructed in such a way as to engage us in the appropriate kind of dialogue for each stage of our journey, just as, in the Cave, the liberator provides the prisoner with the stimulus and support he needs at each point in his ascent. The nature of the learner's progression, and the character of the reader's changing dialogue with the text, form the focus of the next chapter.

3

Developing the Virtues of Dialectic: A Model for Reading

3.1. 'MIDDLE' AND 'LATE' WORKS: A PARADIGM SHIFT?

If you put me to death, you will not easily find another person of such a sort, who literally, even if it is rather comical to describe, attaches himself to the city, like a horse that is large and noble, and because of its size is lazy and needing to be woken by a gadfly. It seems that god has attached me to the city as such a thing, which settling everywhere, throughout the whole day, does not cease from rousing and persuading and reproving every one of you. You will not easily find another such person, gentlemen, but if you take my advice, you will spare me. But perhaps you may be irritated, like those who are awakened when napping, and obeying Anytus, slapping me you might easily kill me, and then you will spend the rest of your life sleeping, unless god in his care for you sends to you another such person.

Apology, 30e–31a

Those who associate with me suffer the same experience as women giving birth; for they feel the pains of labour, and night and day are full of difficulty, far greater than the women's; and my art is able to bring on this pain or to cause it to cease . . . I suspect that you, as you yourself also believe, are in labour, pregnant with something inside you. Therefore approach me, the son of a midwife who also himself possesses the midwife's art, and be ready to answer the things I ask as best you are able. And if, examining one of the things you say, I should think it an image and not real, then I will take it away and cast it away—do not then be savage, as women bearing their first child are as concerns their offspring. For already many people, my dear friend, have become so disposed towards me that they are actually ready to bite me, whenever I take away some foolish notion of theirs, and they do not think that I do this out of kindness, since they are far from knowing that no god is ill-disposed towards humans, and that I do not do any such thing out of unkindness, but it is not at all right for me to allow falsehood or to destroy what is true.

Theaetetus, 151ad

These two well-known passages both reflect directly on the nature of learning. They come from dialogues usually assigned to different stages of Plato's output as a writer; and they have been taken to offer different views on how learning may occur and, in particular, the role of Socratic questioning within it.[1] Yet they also tell us about the *process* of learning—the experience that a learner goes through as learning occurs—and here they have a striking amount in common.

Socrates' comparison of himself to a gadfly in *Apology* forms part of his attempt to explain and defend his practice as a teacher, in Plato's account of his speech at his trial. In using this image, Socrates assigns to himself a crucial, yet facilitating role. His aim is to waken the drowsy horse, and to motivate the horse to autonomous and self-propelled movement. Socrates has to stir the horse to life, a horse who wants to sleep on for the rest of its life and seems unlikely, without the sting of the fly, to have roused itself independently. But once awake, the horse will of course provide the energy and power to move himself—the gadfly is only a motivating impulse. Though the image is comical or demeaning, as Socrates himself comments, it conveys the importance of Socrates' role as a catalyst; the gadfly has, after all, been sent by god. It also communicates the means by which Socrates achieves his end: as a gadfly, he bites his victim; he irritates the horse; and he provokes in the Athenian people a desire to slap and kill him, the impulse conveying annoyance and frustration, perhaps also, in the legal context of the speech, anger and violence. The Athenians' reaction to the gadfly is negative and emotional; yet it is not, Plato makes clear, prompted by a single bite, but by repeated and ongoing activity: the fly continuously settles everywhere, reproaching every one of the Athenians.

In *Theaetetus*, the context is rather different. Our passage occurs midway through a dialogue, when the discussion has run into difficulty and the interlocutors are attempting to understand what has happened. Socrates diagnoses that Theaetetus is in labour with an

[1] E.g. Burnyeat (1977).

idea, and explains how he, as a midwife, helps to bring his interlocutors' ideas to birth. As a midwife, Socrates again plays a secondary and facilitating role: it is the birth of the ideas of others, conceived and brought to term by them, that is the goal of Socrates' activity; and he himself cannot bear ideas. The role of the 'parent' of the ideas in giving life to the philosophical process is crucial, and it is the independent future of the idea (some of the ideas born need to be rejected, and some are lost through being brought up badly) together with the welfare of its parent (some respondents react badly to the rejection of their offspring, others are too swift to leave Socrates' company) that is the focus of Socrates' efforts. His good intentions notwithstanding, Socrates' actions provoke sometimes unhappy emotions: he describes the impulse his patients have to quarrel with him and bite him when a false offspring is taken away, and his art has the power to bring on or allay the pains the learner feels when in labour with an idea. The process, Socrates stresses, though productive, is far from painless, nor does it end with the birth: ongoing association with him is necessary for the successful upbringing of the philosophical child.

Each of these images has its own particular focus, born out of its function in the context of its dialogue, yet there are broad parallels. In both images, the learning interaction involves two parties; the learner's personal contribution is indispensable, yet Socrates' facilitating role is also crucial in the early stages of the process. In both images, learning involves repeated or ongoing activity, as well as affective responses, such as irritation and pain. And we can observe similar features in other of the dialogues' images for learning too, from psychic pregnancy in *Symposium* and the ascent to the real world in the *Phaedo* myth, to the taming of the beast in *Republic* and *Sophist*'s notion of purification. *Meno*'s comparison of Socrates to a sting-ray again evokes his facilitating role as well as his almost magical effect over his discussion partner, prompting him to call into doubt his previous ideas about virtue, preventing him from making his customary lengthy speeches, and—it is implied—spurring him to new and more successful accounts. In particular, Meno complains, he has been numbed and rendered speechless by Socrates; and his suggestion that Socrates is lucky not to be thrown into prison evokes the anger and violence of some who come into contact with him.[2]

[2] Such images are often treated as providing theories about how learning can occur: see e.g. Scott (1995) on recollection, Sheffield (2001) on psychic pregnancy,

These are features shared, too, with *Republic*'s image of the Cave, which, in chapter 2, I treated as a paradigm for the experience of interlocutors and of readers. Quite apart from the similarities between the Cave and other of Plato's images for learning, Socrates' claim, in introducing the image, that the prisoners are 'like us', as well as his assertion that it represents an image of 'all education', makes it tempting to treat that image as having wider applicability. And this gains support, I think, from the links between the Cave image and familiar features of interlocutors' conversations. The references to *aporia*, confusion, discomfort, anger, reluctance, and the inclination to flee remind us of the behaviour of many interlocutors. The emphasis on the individual's own effort resonates with Socrates' insistence that an interlocutor should say what he thinks and avoid taking what others say on authority. And the figure of the educator, as is often noted, plays a role similar to that of Socrates in many dialogues; the attempt of the prisoners to kill him seems to allude to Socrates' own death. Nevertheless, if I am going to treat the picture of learning that emerges, dramatically and discursively, from the dialogues as a model for the reader's learning, that picture needs further scrutiny.

In particular, I need to address the idea that Plato's views on education underwent a significant change during the course of his career. The Cave image conjures up most naturally the activity of Socrates in dialogues usually regarded as 'early'—the features I have just noted are most typical of those works. Yet *Republic*, at least on one influential line of interpretation, rejects education of this sort as useless, if not harmful.[3] 'Early' dialogues, the argument goes, show Socrates' (often interpreted as the historical Socrates) methods to be purely destructive in scope, unable to achieve productive results. As often as not, they do not even make interlocutors well-disposed

Burnyeat (1977) on midwifery. But they also tell us about the *process* of learning and development. Sluiter (1999) surveys Plato's images of learning.

[3] E.g. Robinson (1953) 17–19, Ryle (1966) 10–12, Annas (1981) 56–7, Reeve (1988) 22–4, Teloh (1986), Seeskin (1987); cf. Blondell (2002) 209–10, 221–8. Beversluis (2000) and Nussbaum (1980) emphasize the harmfulness of Socratic education. Other discussions place more weight on Plato's confidence in the power of new methods as better suited to producing the constructive results he sought: e.g. Vlastos (1991) 117–18, 123–6, 130–1; also Annas (1981) 289–90. Highlighting an interest in new methods of course does not exclude seeing an implicit criticism of elenctic questioning in Plato's new style. Some critics, e.g. Reeve (1988) 23–4 and Robinson (1953) 18–19, talk of the preservation of the essential character of elenctic questioning in 'later' dialogues, but it is clear that they do nevertheless regard it as having undergone a radical transformation.

towards philosophy. Instead, they produce anger and frustration, and have the potential to corrupt morally, by removing a person's moral convictions without putting anything in their place. By the time he was writing *Republic*, it is said, Plato advocated a shift to a less adversarial, more pedagogical model, to be practised among a more restricted group of already well-disposed pupils. All this is symbolized in the adoption of a new style of dialectic after *Republic* I, and in other 'middle' and 'late' works, and it is made explicit in Socrates' pronouncement at *Republic* 539ad:

> *Socrates*: *So that you do not feel this pity for your thirty-year-olds, mustn't you take every care over how they begin dialectic?*
>
> *Glaucon*: *Yes indeed.*
>
> *Socrates*: *Is not this a lasting precaution, not to let the young have a taste of it? For I do not think it has escaped your notice that youths, when they first taste dialectic, take it as a game, always using it for contradiction, and mimicking those who cross-examine them, they themselves cross-examine others, always rejoicing like puppies to drag and tear to shreds with argument those near them.*
>
> *Glaucon*: *Yes, excessively so.*
>
> *Socrates*: *And when they have themselves cross-examined many people and been cross-examined by many, they fall violently and quickly into believing none of the things they believed before. And because of these things, they themselves and the whole of philosophy are demeaned in the eyes of others.*
>
> *Glaucon*: *Very true.*
>
> *Socrates*: *An older person, I said, would not want to participate in such madness, but he will imitate a person who wishes to converse and to seek for the truth rather than one who is merely playing and making contradictions for amusement, and he will himself be more measured and will make the practice more rather than less honoured.*
>
> *Glaucon*: *You are right.*
>
> *Socrates*: *So, haven't all the things that were said before this been said for the sake of caution, so that people with ordered and stable dispositions are the ones who have a share in dialectic, and not as now, when any one at all, even someone not at all fitting, engages in it?*

In the ideal state, Socrates tells us here, dialectic is to be confined to those who are above the age of 30 and have received pre-dialectical training, for fear of corrupting younger participants. If the young come into contact with dialectic, Socrates explains, they treat it as a sport: they attack all who are near them, refute people and are refuted, and finally come to distrust all their former beliefs, without having anything to replace them. All this of course resonates with Aristophanes' critique of

Socrates in *Clouds*, and Plato has therefore been seen as condemning Socrates' dialectical practice along similar lines.[4] This picture is a bleak one: Socratic methods fail; recognizing this, Plato concentrates on a form of education that is more productive, but which abandons the idea that everyone can be educated.[5] On a more constructive interpretation of the shift, Plato does not reject Socratic education, but confines it to a preliminary stage: the purging that precedes learning proper.[6] Either way, however, Socratic education, as represented in 'early' dialogues, is ousted from centre stage in the vision of productive philosophizing put forward in 'middle' dialogues onwards. How then can Plato, in the Cave image, be putting forward a universal model of education that bears such resemblance to Socratic methods? And can I, with any justification, treat the model of learning that emerges from the Cave as a paradigm for the activity of readers and interlocutors throughout the corpus?[7]

First, I do not think that *Republic* 539bd, discussed above, necessarily lends itself to a developmentalist interpretation of Plato. Two other dialogues raise concerns similar to those voiced in *Republic*. The first is *Philebus* 15d–16a, where Socrates describes the behaviour of young men, who, when they first discover the principle of the many and the one, set every argument in motion, bringing themselves and everyone else into *aporia*, and sparing no one, not even their fathers and mothers. The second is the description of youngsters and late learners at *Sophist* 251bc: on discovering the principle of the many and the one, they think they have discovered great wisdom and they delight in quibbling. In both places, the dialectical practice in question is clearly distanced from Socrates', which suggests to me that in the *Republic* passage too, it is *bad* dialectical practice that is being condemned, not Socrates' own.[8]

[4] See especially Nussbaum (1980) 86–8. See Gonzalez (2002) for a discussion—and rejection—of the idea that *Clitophon* intends a similar critique of Socratic practice.

[5] The pessimistic view is widespread. See for example Scott (1999); also Teloh (1986), Seeskin (1987) 13–16, King (1987) 109–12. Cf. Hobbs (2000) 261. For the implication that Socrates aims to turn even the unwilling to virtue, see *Euthd.*274d–275b.

[6] E.g. Slings (1981), Blondell (2002) 12–14. Such a view is often linked with chronological developmentalism, though, as Matthews (1999) 8–9 notes, it need not be: see also the alternative explanations offered by Blondell and Nails, noted at ch.2 n50.

[7] Cf. the handling of the Cave image in Warren (2010), Gordon (1999).

[8] The behaviour described in these passages bears a striking resemblance to that of Euthydemus and Dionysodorus in *Euthydemus*, strengthening the case that they intend to evoke bad dialectical practice. When Socrates refers to the way people

But even if we assume that, in *Republic*, Socrates is being made to refer to his earlier dialectical practice, the fact that similar concerns surface in relation to methods connected with 'late' dialectic (i.e. non-elenctic questioning) is significant. For it indicates that Plato's concern that dialectic could be harmful or counterproductive was not specific to 'early' dialectic—it was a danger that attended *all* dialectical practice.[9] One aim of the pre-dialectical training in *Republic*'s ideal city seems to be to eliminate this danger as far as possible, making the ascent from the Cave as smooth and safe as it can be. But no such training would have been available to the readers of *Republic*. If they were to ascend from the Cave, learners would have to do this the hard way, exposed to the pitfalls that attend dialectical learning. We cannot therefore apply what is said about learning in the ideal state to learning among the interlocutors about whom Plato is writing: for them, dialectic, despite its dangers, is the only way to ascend from the Cave.

Second, analysis of the responses of interlocutors in 'early', 'middle', and 'late' dialogues suggests to me that interlocutors in all types of dialogue experience learning in a way that shares important similarities with the Cave image. This is a task to which I turn later in this chapter, and it suggests to me that the four features of the Cave image I identified do present a view of what learning fundamentally involves that persists throughout the dialogues, rather than applying to dialogues of just one period or type. That is, interlocutors across the full range of Plato's works can be interpreted as engaging in a process of learning that requires two people, as well as the full participation of the individual learner; that has affective and cognitive dimensions, and also a range of specific experiences, to which the learner may react positively or negatively. There is, that is, an important strand of continuity uniting 'early', 'middle', and 'late' works.[10]

behave now, what he says generally excludes his own practice: see e.g. *M.*89e ff., where he argues that there are no teachers of virtue in Athens, and *Grg.*515c ff. Blank (1993) also connects the *Republic* passage with badly conducted dialectic and adduces *Tht.*167e–168b, *Phd.*89de, and *Ap.*23c as parallels. Cf. also *Tht.*154d–155a.

[9] Cf. the concern that learners will turn away from education too soon at *Tht.*150d–151a.

[10] The view I am advocating, therefore, goes beyond the constructive interpretation, maintaining that the core character of the learning experience remains broadly consistent throughout the different dialogues, and that the positive psychological value of what goes on in elenctic questioning is replicated, albeit in a modified

But while I am rejecting a picture of linear developmentalism, whereby Plato's later ideas are incompatible with and replace his earlier ones, this is not to claim that Plato's ideas about the acquisition of understanding remained wholly unchanged.[11] To me it is plausible that Plato could have retained a commitment about broad features of the learning process, such as the involvement of a second party and the role of affective responses such as discomfort, while developing his theoretical understanding of the nature of that process.

To account for this stand of continuity, we need, I suggest, to consider the development of interlocutors and not exclusively the development of Plato. Just as we noticed a series of developments in the Cave image—the increasing autonomy of the prisoner, the changing role of the educator, the decreasing emphasis on the negative aspects of the learning experience (or at least on negative responses by the learner)—so we can observe parallel developments in the activity of interlocutors as we move from 'early' to 'late' dialogues. The differences between these groups of dialogues, obvious to any reader, are best accounted for, I suggest, by taking the dialogues to represent *different stages of learning*, corresponding to the gradual development of the prisoner—not by postulating changes in Plato's views about learning. In other words, 'early' dialogues represent the initial stages of learning, 'middle' dialogues an intermediate stage, and 'late' dialogues a more advanced stage again.

This reading of learning in the dialogues, if accepted, bears some further implications. To begin with, it involves rejecting the idea, central to the developmentalist line of interpretation sketched above, that the activity of 'early' interlocutors is inferior in value to that represented in 'middle' and 'late' works, at best being viewed by the mature Plato as preparation for learning, if not as harmful and counter-productive. Focusing on the cognitive-affective character of interlocutors' responses in 'early' works, I will argue that their activity in fact plays an important and productive part in the learning process itself.[12]

manner, in 'middle' and 'late' works. For an interpretation of the role of *aporia* along similar lines, see Politis (2006). This is slightly different from maintaining, as Slings (1981) 153–4 does, that Socrates uses the same (elenctic) methods at different stages, but with a different function.

[11] For similar reflections, see Annas (1999) 12, Sedley (2004) 14–15.

[12] For elenctic activity as a positive and constructive part of the learning process (rather than being only preparatory), see Gonzalez (1998) 9, Renaud (2002) 192; also Mackenzie (1988b).

In addition, I attempt to show that the activity of 'middle' and 'late' interlocutors is continuous with that represented in 'early' dialogues. This will, I hope, further discourage us from dismissing the value of the activity of 'early' interlocutors. But it should also help to counter a frequent corollary of the traditional view—the idea that, in 'middle' and 'late' dialogues, although the approach to learning is more constructive and positive, it is also less personal and less involving for interlocutors (and readers too). This, it is suggested, is the cost of abandoning Socrates' elenctic style for a more suitable vehicle of philosophical progress. On the contrary, by revealing the cognitive-affective character of the activity of interlocutors even in these dialogues, I hope to show that no such decline occurs, and that the 'later' dialogues preserve the essential principles underlying education in 'early' works.[13]

Further, my interpretation has a bearing on our approach to the corpus as a whole and the principles underlying its composition. If I am correct that the dialogues, taken together, present a consistent picture of learning, in its broad outline, with differences in style and approach explained by reference to the stage of learning in question, then there is no need to appeal to chronological theses about Plato's development in making sense of them. A dialogue representing an early stage of an interlocutor's development could have been produced at a late stage in Plato's career and vice versa.[14] As I suggest later on, this opens the door to a different way of understanding the construction of the corpus, which has at its centre the reader's development, not Plato's.

In the remainder of this chapter, I offer support for my claim that the essential features of learning I identified in the Cave image apply to the presentation of learning throughout Plato's corpus, notwithstanding changes in style, by analysing the responses of interlocutors in dialogues traditionally termed 'early', 'middle', and 'late'.[15] As I do this, I build up a wider picture of the responses that characterize the learning process, building on the work of critics such as McKim on shame. In this way, I flesh out the conception of learning to which

[13] In ch.5, examining different types of question-and-answer exchange, I develop a further line of attack on this traditional interpretation.

[14] For challenges to chronological developmentalism, see ch.2 n50.

[15] Among studies of the presentation of learning in the dialogues, I have found the following especially helpful: Teloh (1986), Scolnicov (1976), Hyland (1981), Seeskin (1987), Renaud (2002), Schmid (2002).

the work of other interpreters points, providing a more systematic and comprehensive account of how it appears from the dialogues, as well as offering a reading of the significance of changes in the presentation of learning across different types of dialogue.

In doing so, I hope ultimately to make it plausible that the conversations between interlocutors present us with a detailed and extended model of the process a person needs to go through in order to make philosophical and ethical progress—just as the Cave image does, in a telescoped and metaphorical way. The picture is complex, in as much as learning is a lengthy process with many stages; and we are not offered an overview of the whole thing at once. Individual dialogues correspond to different parts of the process, gradually filling in the larger picture: 'early' dialogues present the initial stages, and so forth. But, overall, the entire corpus of dialogues presents a picture of what the learning process looks like that can guide our own progress as learners in the ways suggested in chapter 2.

3.2. INTERLOCUTORS IN 'EARLY' DIALOGUES

Let us begin by surveying characteristic responses to dialectic in 'early' dialogues.[16] Perhaps the most common is *aporia*: the perplexity an interlocutor feels when his position has been undermined, and he no longer knows what to say or think. It is perhaps especially associated with the effect of Socrates' questioning on his respondents, though Socrates claims to experience it too. *Aporia* characteristically occurs at the close of an argument or section of argument, and brings it to a halt. It implies, at root, a lack of resource, being without means to make progress: literally, being *aporos*, without means of making a crossing.[17] But although it is often treated as a single phenomenon, in fact it has many aspects.[18]

[16] I will refer to all Socrates' dialectical activity in 'early' dialogues as elenctic, but without wishing to imply that it conforms to a single pattern. For this controversy, see Tarrant (2002), Carpenter and Polansky (2002), Brickhouse and Smith (1994) 5 and (2002), Benson (2000) 36–7.

[17] For discussion of the meaning of *aporia*, see e.g. Politis (2006) 96, Mackenzie (1988b) 16–17.

[18] Cf. Politis (2006) 96, Clay (2000) 179–80. For a full-length study of *aporia* in the dialogues, see Matthews (1999). There is also discussion of the effects of elenctic

Confusion and a failure to understand are central to *aporia*. An interlocutor in this condition is in difficulty; he feels doubt and perplexity; and is overwhelmed by the argument. All this is captured in Socrates' description of himself and his interlocutors in *Laches* as caught in a storm of argument (χειμαζομένοις ἐν λόγῳ 194c2–3), and in need of help from someone more resourceful (εὐπορώτερός 194b9).[19] These feelings also occur throughout the process of questioning: it is common for an interlocutor to claim that he does not understand what Socrates is saying or cannot follow an argument. In addition, interlocutors often report speechlessness, evoked especially eloquently in Meno's image of the sting-ray to describe the effect of Socrates' questioning upon him:[20]

> *And now, you seem to me to be bewitching me and drugging me and actually casting a spell on me, so that I have become full of perplexity. You seem to me to be completely like . . . the flat sting-ray found in the sea. For this makes numb any person that approaches it and comes into contact with it. And you seem to me to have done such a thing to me now, by numbing me. For I am truly numb in both my mind and my mouth, and I am not able to give you an answer. And yet on numerous occasions I have spoken very many words about virtue in front of many people, and I did so very well, at least so I myself thought.*
>
> *Meno*, 80ab

The image implies, too, a quasi-magical dimension to Socrates' impact on Meno, which undermines Meno's usual self-possession. Socrates has bewitched him with spells and incantations, and in another city might be taken for a magician (γόης *M*.80a2–4, b4–7).[21]

In addition to these core features of *aporia*, interlocutors manifest a range of further responses, both on reaching *aporia* and at other

discussion in Robinson (1953) 9–10, Howland (2003), Mackenzie (1988a) and (1988b). For a survey of responses of 'early' interlocutors, see Rutherford (1995) 79–82, Blondell (2002) 125–6.

19 Cf. the spatial disorientation implied in the image of the moving statues at *Euthphr*.11be.

20 Similarly in *Crito*, Crito, who started by making a speech to persuade Socrates to escape from prison, is gradually reduced to silence. Cf. also *Lch*.194ab, *Euthphr*.11b, *G.Hp*.297de.

21 Cf. also *R*.358b1–3, comparing Socrates to a snake-charmer; *Smp*.215ad on Socrates as a satyr; and *Euthphr*.11be comparing Socrates to Daedalus. On Socrates' appropriation of imagery of magic, especially as associated with Gorgias, see De Romilly (1975) and Belfiore (1980).

points in an argument. In *Apology*, examination results in anger at Socrates (ὀργίζονται 23c8–9, cf. 31a4). Anger is also evident in the abusive language used by Callicles in *Gorgias*, Thrasymachus in *Republic* I, and Anytus in *Meno*.[22] This frequently shades into violence, most obviously in *Apology*, where it is implied in the dramatic situation of the trial and evoked in the description of the Athenians' attempt to slap and kill the gadfly (31a3–6). Likewise, Callicles and Anytus both make thinly veiled allusions to Socrates' death at the hands of the Athenians.[23] Closely connected, too, is a competitive instinct: the desire to attack and defeat the threat to one's own position. This is implicit in the behaviour of all these interlocutors, and is confessed by Laches at *Laches* 194a7–8.[24] Such feelings are often connected with the use of techniques that Socrates considers inappropriate in dialectical discussion, such as the long speeches to which Thrasymachus and Callicles resort.

Desire to avoid questioning is another common response. It is particularly striking in the speedy exit, on what appears a fabricated pretext, of Euthyphro at the close of his dialogue, as well as in the reluctance of Callicles (*Grg.*497ac, 505c–506c, 522e), Thrasymachus (*R.*342cd, 344d–345b, 352b), and Protagoras (*Prt.*333de, 348b, 352ab) to continue participating in the discussion. Ion is ironically accused of wriggling like a Proteus, so as to avoid giving Socrates the display of skill he promised (*Ion* 541e1–542a1).[25]

Distress and disturbance are implicit in many of these experiences; but on occasion they are explicitly highlighted. Socrates' conversations are in *Apology* described as βαρύτεραι and ἐπιφθονώτεραι—painful, burdensome, distressing, hateful, and hard to bear (37d1–2)—features also captured, as we have seen, in the gadfly's stinging of the drowsy horse, in Socrates' image for his own activity (30e–31a). In *Protagoras*, we are told that Protagoras was in distress, even agony, at the progression of the discussion (ἀγωνιᾶν 333e3); and later, Socrates says that the argument has accused and mocked them, as a person

[22] Cf. *Lch.*194a8–b1 ἀγανακτῶ, *Prt.*333e3 τετραχύνθαι, *M.*95a2 χαλεπαίνειν.

[23] *M.*94e3–95a1, *Grg.*486a7–c3. Cf. the portrayal of Thrasymachus as a wild animal leaping towards a fearful Socrates at *R.*336be; also *G.Hp.*292ac.

[24] Cf. also the portrayal of Critias in *Charmides*, and Dionysodorus and Euthydemus in *Euthydemus*.

[25] Cf. also *Smp.*216bc and *Ap.*27c, 37de, 31a: the Athenians are keen to get rid of Socrates so they can carry on slumbering. Socrates interprets Meno's paradox as an attempt to avoid discussion and an indication of laziness: *M.*80e, 81d.

might (κατηγορεῖν and καταγελᾶν 361a3–5).[26] Perhaps most evocatively of all, in *Symposium* Alcibiades describes himself as stricken (πληγείς) and stung (δηχθεὶς) by Socrates' discourse, as though by a snake, dwelling on the pain he has suffered.[27]

More specifically, there are the famous instances of shame alleged to play such an important part in the capitulation of Socrates' respondents in *Gorgias*.[28] We might also bring in here the embarrassment that, in *Lysis*, Hippothales feels on witnessing the encounter between Socrates and his beloved, as well as the response that in *Symposium* Alcibiabes reports he underwent during his initial encounters with Socrates.[29] Rather different, it seems to me, is the emotion implicit in Thrasymachus' famous blush at *Republic* 350d3: unlike the shame of Polus, Gorgias, and Callicles, which seems connected with a recognition that, in their heart of hearts, they believe something at odds with their stated position, Thrasymachus' blush is apparently occasioned by defeat in argument, and is closely connected with resentment and refusal to participate properly in discussion. It is not clear that Socrates has, at this point, succeeded in getting through to him at all.

Another common set of responses involves disbelief. Sometimes we find incredulity, bordering on amusement, at a belief expressed or conclusion reached: Callicles' outrage at the outcome of Socrates' argument with Polus (*Grg.*481b10–c4), for example.[30] At other times, the response implies deep-seated discomfort or doubt about

[26] Cf. *G.Hp.*304d1–3, 304e3–5, 291e5–292a1, 292c3–5; *Ap.*30e7.

[27] *Smp.*218a4; cf. *Smp.*215e6–7: οὐδ' ἐτεθορύβητό μου ἡ ψυχὴ οὐδ' ἠγανάκτει ὡς ἀνδραποδωδῶς διακειμένου. Carone (2004) draws attention to the pain of dialectical discourse in *Gorgias*, termed a kind of punishment at 505c4; cf. 521e–522b. Cf. also *G.Hp.*292ab, where Socrates' questioner will fetch a stick to beat him, upon hearing his answer.

[28] See McKim (1988); cf. also Teloh (1986) 143–9, Renaud (2002), Kahn (1983) and (1996) 138–41, Ross (2005). On the original connection of the term *elenchus* with shame/disgrace, see Lesher (2002) and Renaud (2002) 186, 195 n42. For a more modest account of Socrates' success in the argument with Polus, see Stauffer (2006) 74–6.

[29] *Ly.*210e, *Smp.*216bc; cf. also *G.Hp.*304d, *Chrm.*169c, *Lch.*196ab. It is not made entirely clear what has precipitated this response in Hippothales, but it seems most likely to be connected with Socrates' demonstration that the best way to deal with one's beloved is to humble him, rather than flattering him. See Nightingale (1993). Robinson (1953) 13 draws attention to the role of shame in moral education at *Ap.*29de, 39c ff.

[30] Cf. *Prt.*361ad, *Ion* 536d, *Euthphr.*4b, *G.Hp.*294e.

the conclusion reached, even if its source cannot properly be unravelled. Again, Callicles provides a good example when he comments at *Gorgias* 513c4–6 that, though he cannot refute the argument, he cannot quite believe it either.[31]

Of course, not every interlocutor exhibits all these responses. A Callicles tends towards aggression, a Meno towards inertia. But the above reactions occur frequently enough to be seen as an important part of the way learning is presented in 'early' dialogues. What, then, can we say about the role and value of such experiences?

To begin with, the responses noted above all take a very extreme form. An interlocutor in an 'early' dialogue who feels perplexity is completely at sea and sees no way to continue; anger spills over into veiled threats of violence; discomfort makes interlocutors literally wish to flee. The feelings also affect interlocutors in an all-encompassing way: frequently, a response is not connected with a specific problem or issue, but is felt to engulf the interlocutor and his situation in a more global manner.[32] Interlocutors' responses are generally unproductive—rarely, if ever, does an interlocutor seem to depart with greater understanding of himself and a better attitude towards learning. Indeed, their responses are often severe enough to threaten the continuation of discussion; in some cases, such as *Euthyphro* or *Gorgias*, this is precisely how a discussion does end. Socrates' method, that is, seems routinely to fail.[33] What should we make of this? Why should Plato have written so many dialogues portraying Socrates engaged in a method without valuable effect?

Few, I think, would doubt the potentially positive value of at least some of the responses I have mentioned. The core features of *aporia*—perplexity, speechlessness, confusion—are, as is well recognized, connected with an interlocutor's recognition of his own ignorance, a step the dialogues present as crucial to a person's ability to learn.[34] For unless a person perceives that he lacks knowledge, he will

[31] Cf. *R.*334b, 487bd (where Adeimantus describes the response of interlocutors to Socrates' questioning).

[32] Cf. King (1987) 106–8; also discussion in Politis (2006).

[33] A point emphasized by King (1987) 109–12, Teloh (1986) 20–1, Benson (2000) 30, Seeskin (1987) 14–15, Scott (1999), Beversluis (2000). King (1987) suggests that self-blame is a natural response to the *elenchus*; I would see it rather as an ideal response.

[34] Mackenzie (1988a) and (1988b) effectively brings out the importance of self-consciousness as a response to *aporia*; cf. also Renaud (2002). However, as Politis

not be motivated to improve his state. Socrates' commentary, in *Meno*, on the slave's progress in recollecting his understanding of the square, provides the opportunity for him to articulate this clearly:

> *Socrates: Do you see, Meno, the point which he has now reached on the path of recollection? At first he did not know the side of the square of eight feet, just as he does not yet know it, but then he thought he knew it and answered boldly, like one who knew—and he did not think that he was in perplexity. But now he thinks he is perplexed, and just like one who does not know, he does not think that he knows.*
>
> *Meno: You speak truly.*
>
> *Socrates: Isn't he in a better situation now concerning the matter he did not know?*
>
> *Meno: It seems so to me.*
>
> *Socrates: So, by making him perplexed and numbing him like the sting-ray, have we done him any harm?*
>
> *Meno: I do not think so.*
>
> *Socrates: In fact, we have given him some help it seems, towards finding out how things stand. For now, since he does not know, he will gladly search.*
>
> *Meno*, 84ab

Socrates' allusion here to the numbing effect of the sting-ray refers back to Meno's earlier description of the effect of Socrates' questioning on him, quoted above. At this point in the work, Meno himself has only a burgeoning appreciation of his present sense of numbness; Socrates' commentary on the slave's similar experience clarifies the value of the process from the perspective of an impartial observer—a perspective that one hopes, in time, Meno will himself attain.

In addition, as I noted above, a positive role has been attributed to shame, as potentially prompting a person to recognize his deep beliefs. Even if, in many 'early' dialogues, interlocutors do not yet attain such insight into themselves, we can nevertheless see how the experiences of *aporia* might contribute directly to their development as learners, given time and reflection. Significantly, 'later' dialogues continue to insist on the value of such experiences at an early stage of the learning process. As we have seen, *Theaetetus*' image of Socrates as midwife (148e ff.) emphasizes his role in revealing a learner's false ideas—with all the pain, anger, and confusion this involves—before he can bring forth the true offspring of knowledge. Similarly, in

(2006) 96–7 points out, the connection of *aporia* with self-ignorance is not always explicit.

describing education as purification in *Sophist*, the Eleatic Stranger says that the learner cannot benefit until, through cross-questioning, he is reduced to shame, *αἰσχύνη* (230d2), and made to realize that he knows no more than he does. Indeed, the cooperative interlocutors of 'middle' and 'late' dialogues, humble because they realize that they do not have knowledge, seem to have undergone exactly the transformation that Socrates hopes *aporia* will produce in his 'early' interlocutors.

But what about the other responses—the anger, aggression, laziness, desire to flee, distress, and loss of control? These would seem to hinder the learning process rather than further it.[35] And they are the ones that apparently disappear from 'middle' and 'late' dialogues, along with Socrates' abrasive tactics. Interestingly, the 'early' dialogues are also ambivalent towards them. On the one hand, Socrates often condemns his interlocutors' responses. Meno is constantly upbraided for his laziness. In *Apology*, Socrates comments that the Athenians became angry with him rather than with themselves, as they should have. Interlocutors, such as Callicles and Thrasymachus, who want to break off discussion, are said to lack goodwill and friendship. But at the same time, Socrates is portrayed as inciting such responses in a self-conscious way. Meno, in his comparison of Socrates to a sting-ray and magician, sees his discussion partner as deliberately adopting the tactics responsible for his experiences—and the same is true of Euthyphro, Callicles, and Thrasymachus. And although, as Beversluis points out in his eloquent defence of Socrates' interlocutors, we may be tempted to attribute such accusations to the sore-headedness of respondents who resent Socrates' success, they do nevertheless contain a large kernel of truth.[36] Indeed, in having Socrates describe himself as a gadfly stinging the lazy horse of the

[35] See esp. Robinson (1953) 18–19; cf. also Howland (2003) 95–6, suggesting that emotions such as anger, envy, and obsessiveness impede learning, and are aroused incidentally and unintentionally by Socrates.

[36] Beversluis (2000) 10–12. Beversluis (also esp. Nussbaum (1980)) would also regard the production of extreme confusion or perplexity as counterproductive, especially if directed against ideas that are in fact correct: they are liable to shake the interlocutor's moral convictions without putting anything better in their place. I would account for these feelings in a similar way as the apparently unproductive feelings of anger and distress etc. considered here: as part of the severe shock that needs to be administered to some interlocutors. Cf. e.g. Teloh (1986) 36–7, suggesting that confusion is an intentional effect of Socrates' argument in *Euthyphro* and a necessary remedy for Euthyphro's dogmatism; also 149, 163, 187.

Athenian city, Plato invests his Socrates with self-consciousness about his role: the image suggests that Socrates intentionally and knowingly prompts reactions which are—in that work—responsible for his trial.[37] So at this point we face more pressingly the question: why Plato should have chosen to represent Socrates using methods that are—at the time—characterized as unproductive?

Here, we need to distinguish between the experience an interlocutor undergoes and his response to it. In 'early' dialogues, interlocutors are, for various reasons, disinclined to engage in true learning, as represented by Socratic discussion: they are like the lazy horse or the prisoner in the Cave, who see no reason to change their current state. For learning to occur, they need to be exposed to an external shock,[38] as provided by the sting-ray, or the gadfly, or the prisoner's educator—a shock which will challenge their basic values and sense of self, and compel them to re-evaluate their condition. Socrates' argumentative tactics in 'early' dialogues provide this shock; in doing so, they can be seen as uniquely well suited to interlocutors at an early stage of development (or so at least I shall argue in chapter 5). When interlocutors receive the shock, they initially respond negatively—as does the horse when stung and the prisoner when turned to the light. Yet even if interlocutors do not immediately learn the lessons Socrates hopes they will, their negative responses do have a value, for they show that the discussion is getting through to the respondent at a deep level. At this stage, interlocutors' reactions are unsettling and discomfiting, powerful and extreme; they manifest in different ways the fact that discussion has threatened a person's habitual way of going about things, touched his deep beliefs, and challenged his sense of self. And as such they show that the interlocutor has taken the first step to true learning—that is, engagement of the whole self, affective as well as cognitive. A discussion that did not ruffle the participants at all might not generate any negative reactions, but it would not impinge upon their actual beliefs.[39]

[37] Cf. Teloh (1986) 178–94 on Socrates' employment of the idea of the mystery tormentor in *Greater Hippias*.

[38] Robinson (1953) 18 talks of the 'necessary shock' provided by the *elenchus*.

[39] Scott (1999) 25 concedes that such responses show that discussion has got under an interlocutor's skin, but maintains that this does not mean he has become more receptive to Socrates' viewpoint. Irwin (1996) 348–9, however, in reference to *Gorgias*, emphasizes the effect of Socrates on Callicles, and suggests that we should not

In inciting interlocutors to respond like this, Socrates signals the value of such feelings as steps on the path to learning. They are signs—albeit initially unproductive ones—of an important process within the interlocutor.[40] And, as I discuss later, interlocutors in 'middle' and 'late' dialogues continue to undergo similar experiences. In other words, these responses are an indication that true learning, in which the interlocutor is cognitively-affectively engaged, is occurring—not just initially, but at all stages. Yet for a learner to make true progress, he has to move beyond this negative stage. The responses of 'early' learners are unreasoning, produced instinctively and without reflection. Like the prisoner, a learner must come to respond to the shocks more reflectively and openly, to regard the process of change in a more positive light, to take more responsibility for his own progress, and to behave with more restraint. And this is why Socrates calls for such violent and unhelpful responses to be tempered. In doing this, he is not indicating that these emotions have no role at all. He is rather encouraging interlocutors to progress to a stage where they can participate in discussion positively and productively and where, accordingly, there is no longer any need for the discussion leader to bring abrasive techniques to bear on them. It is this stage that, I suggest, interlocutors like Glaucon and Adeimantus, Simmias and Cebes, should be seen as having reached.

3.3. INTERLOCUTORS IN 'MIDDLE' DIALOGUES

Turning to this group of dialogues—of which *Republic* II–X and *Phaedo* shall be my central examples—we can note, first, that discussion still

overplay the fact that Callicles does not capitulate on the spot: progress has been made. Cf. my emphasis on practice and habituation, sections 3.5–3.6.

[40] This is not to say that every interlocutor must go through a negative phase of this sort: it may be the conditions in which most people are educated that make a radical change of perspective necessary before a person can perceive the true nature of things. It is striking, though, how many of the dialogues' images of the educational process suggest that this initial stage is unsettling and painful: the Cave, the gadfly of *Apology*, midwifery in *Theaetetus*, the taming of the brute in *Republic*, the readjustment of one's perspective in *Politicus*. For interesting comments on the painfulness of the learning process, which tie in well with my approach, see Miller (1980) xiii–xiv. Scott (1995) also argues that the progression from belief to knowledge is revisionary and disorientating; for discussion, cf. also Lane (1998) 64–6, Schofield (2007).

pauses as interlocutors find themselves in *aporia*.[41] At *Republic* 368b3–5, for example, Socrates declares himself at a loss (ἀπορῶ) and incapable (ἀδύνατος) in the face of the challenge formulated by Glaucon and Adeimantus; at 375d3–5, he comments that they have fallen into *aporia* after losing sight of the comparison that was guiding them; and at 457bc and 472a, Socrates talks of being swamped by waves of argument. We find instances of confusion, both at specific steps of an argument (for instance, Glaucon's responses at *R*.412e–413b), and as a more general response to the position being put forward, of the sort Socrates' companions feel at *Phaedo* 88c1–7, when Simmias and Cebes have brought their objections to what Socrates has said.

Concern to avoid questioning is also still present, only now characteristically on the part of the discussion leader, not his respondent. At *Republic* 450a7–b2, for example, Socrates says it was in the hope of avoiding the swarm of arguments connected with the management of women and children that he skipped over the topic, and he is only persuaded to address it when Polemarchus, Glaucon, Adeimantus, and even Thrasymachus interrupt and appeal to him. In a slightly different case, at 506b–507a, Socrates expresses his reluctance to speak about the nature of the Good, since he does not have knowledge of the subject, and would not wish to appear to claim it; he and Glaucon settle for an account of the offspring of the Good, not the Good itself.

Disbelief also recurs. Again, this may border on incredulity, as at *Republic* 509a6–8 and 509c1–2, when Glaucon expresses surprise at what Socrates is saying about the Good, suggesting that the powers attributed to it are too great to be believed.[42] Or it may register a deep-seated doubt. At *Phaedo* 107ab, Simmias reports his ongoing disbelief (ἀπιστία) about the immortality of the soul; earlier on, Cebes' intervention has prompted disbelief, accompanied by discomfort (88c1); and earlier still, at 69e6–70b4, responding to what Socrates has said about the fate of the soul after death, Cebes has challenged Socrates' views with reference to the disbelief which people commonly feel

41 It is sometimes suggested that there is no *aporia* in the 'middle' dialogues: see Matthews (1997) and (1999) 70–1. Andiç (1997) challenges this view. Cf. Gonzalez (2002) 169–71 and Griswold (1999) 393 who argue that the 'middle' dialogues are more aporetic than is commonly allowed; also Press (2000c) 31.

42 Cf. Cebes' indication of how strange he finds Socrates' ideas about death at *Phd*.62a8–9.

about the soul.[43] But here, unlike the cases involving Callicles, the respondents are not using disbelief as a way of dismissing the discussion leader's views and stifling discussion. Straight after Glaucon has expressed disbelief, for instance, he follows on, 'Don't stop explaining the similarity to the sun in case you are leaving something out' (509c5–6). Here, the respondent's disbelief functions as a way of spurring on the discussion leader—to produce a more convincing explanation and to take away the interlocutor's doubt. In many more cases, an incredulous reaction is anticipated in others: at *Republic* 500e1, for example, Socrates expects distrust (ἀπιστήσουσιν) at the idea of philosopher kings.[44] Here, the response is more ambiguous in resonance: it may be possible to overcome such people's disbelief, but if not, their ignorance will be untouched, and they will be a barrier to improving society in the way Socrates envisages for his ideal state.

Similarly, an angry response is in several cases anticipated. In *Republic*, Socrates imagines that the sight-lovers will be angry at the opinions he has expressed about knowledge and opinion (476de, 480a). On several occasions, a hostile response to the need for philosopher kings is foreshadowed, most notably at 473e6–474a4, when Glaucon says that a multitude will grab weapons and rush at Socrates, his phrasing suggesting that he would not regard such a response as wholly unwarranted. Later, Socrates refers back to the fierceness of such people (ἀγριανοῦσι 501e2), which it is agreed will disappear, once they become gentle and in shame agree with the proposal (501e–502a). The anger of interlocutors themselves, too, has disappeared: even Thrasymachus and Socrates, after the hostilities of book I, become friends (498c9–d4).

Here, the first point to note is that we find many of the same responses as we did in 'early' dialogues—*aporia*, confusion, incredulity, anger, violence, distress, desire to avoid questioning—but with some crucial differences. First, experiences of *aporia* and confusion take a less dramatic and disruptive form. They still mark important points in the course of a discussion, but they do not threaten its continuation in the same way as in 'early' dialogues. They are not associated with speechlessness or a quasi-magical effect, and interlocutors are able to work through them more easily. In addition, the focus tends to be on

[43] Sedley (1995) 14 sees a difference between the methodologically motivated doubt of Cebes and Simmias' incipient misology.

[44] Cf. *R*.450cd, 457ab, de.

the problem causing difficulty, rather than on the individual's overwhelming feeling of being at a loss. This enables the problem to be dealt with more constructively, so that these moments focus inquiry rather than paralysing it. Similarly, although interlocutors still on occasion make attempts to avoid discussion, these are overcome one way or another, so that inquiry can continue productively. Such moments, because they are less disruptive, may be less memorable for the reader, but they do indicate that puzzlement and difficulty are still features of the learning process at this more advanced stage.

In addition, negative emotions—anger, violence, incredulity—crop up far less often. When interlocutors experience them, they usually take a productive form, one that contributes to the progression of the discussion. And when negative in resonance, they are more usually anticipated in the reactions of others than experienced by the interlocutors themselves. This inclusion of negative emotions through projection is very important, for it indicates that many people, were they to witness the discussion, would respond in the extreme and unhelpful ways we noted in 'early' interlocutors—and indeed to which interlocutors in 'middle' works sometimes feel inclined themselves. But, importantly, they do not, or at least not so as to affect the conduct of discussion; this is left to other, less reasonable people. This suggests to me that we are to regard the discussions of the 'middle' dialogues as challenging their participants in similar ways to 'early' dialogues, just as, in the Cave image, the prisoner goes through a similar process at each stage of his ascent. The difference is that interlocutors have learned how to engage in discussion more appropriately. They are no longer being forcibly turned away from the wall, but have reached a stage where they require less compulsion to move onwards in learning.[45]

[45] It is also interesting that the progress of productive dialectic is sometimes described in language that—paradoxically—recalls the negative responses of 'early' dialogues. E.g. at *R.*471c–472a, when Glaucon challenges Socrates to explain how his proposals for the ideal state are possible, he is described as making a *καταδρομήν* (472a1)—a violent attack—on Socrates' argument: the violence, competitiveness, and aggression implicit in the description recall the behaviour of a Thrasymachus, but now have a positive significance. This suggests an underlying continuity in the experiences of 'early' and 'middle' interlocutors, and in the role of dialectic, but also underscores how 'middle' interlocutors have moved beyond such negativity to a productive approach to learning. This reappropriation of negative language continues in 'late' dialogues. For competition transformed into cooperation in *Lysis*, see Gonzalez (2003).

In particular, respondents now have more understanding of the experiences they are undergoing and a greater willingness to connect them with their own failings. This is particularly clear in Simmias' doubt about the immortality of the soul, expressed at *Phaedo* 107a8–b3, at the close of the dialectical discussion of the topic: he acknowledges that his concern is not caused by the inadequacy of the discussion, but rather by the greatness of the subject and by his own human weakness—a response which, while unsatisfactory in its way, is more likely to have a positive outcome than the dismissive incredulity or stubborn reservation of some early interlocutors.[46] Participants also take a much more positive and enthusiastic attitude towards discussion. The dramatic settings of both *Phaedo* and *Republic* make it clear that Socrates' respondents are keen to converse with him rather than having discussion thrust upon them, as is often the case in 'early' dialogues. This is borne out in the dynamic of the discussion too, as respondents request to hear Socrates' views, and raise questions and objections that further extend it. It is more frequently the discussion leader who wishes to avoid talking about a particular topic than his respondents. Though their actual contributions to the discussions are overshadowed by those of the discussion leader, the interlocutors are not, when viewed from this angle, the anaemic recipients of Socrates' wisdom they are often portrayed as.

The comparative advancement in dialectic of interlocutors in these dialogues is a crucial point here. This is evident not only in the way they react, but is implicit also in the sophistication and complexity of the discussions, as well as in what we are told of their backgrounds. The interlocutors of *Phaedo* are Socrates' most intimate companions, who have conversed with him many times before. And in *Republic*, Socrates is familiar with Glaucon and Adeimantus, who appear to be seasoned in discussion (358cd). This makes it implausible, I think, to regard this type of dialectic as a replacement for that conducted by Socrates in the 'early' dialogues. Quite apart from anything else, such a view leaves us with no answer to the question of how interlocutors like Glaucon and Adeimantus have become as compliant and helpful

[46] See Sedley (1995) 21–2 for the idea that *Phaedo* presents a constructive role for doubt: doubt is not prior to discovery, but an important part of the process of discovery itself. This fits well with what I am saying, both about 'middle' and 'late' dialogues.

as they are. *Republic* may suggest that, in the ideal world, one's childhood education leaves one ready for dialectic; but in reality, such an education is not available. The Cave image indicates that we all start as prisoners who have to be turned around, in a process that is painful and requires force, before we can see true realities. If we cast aside the 'early' dialogues, we are left without a picture of how—in the world in which Socrates' interlocutors live—this process can occur.

3.4. INTERLOCUTORS IN 'LATE' DIALOGUES

In these dialogues, we find a similar pattern of continuity combined with development. It is evident to any reader that these works demand philosophical acumen and dedication of a level higher again than the 'middle' works. And they are self-consciously advanced too: in *Sophist* and *Politicus*, Socrates is replaced as the main speaker by the Eleatic Stranger, who is a recognized and self-confessed expert, and the same is true of Parmenides and Timaeus in their dialogues: the discussions treat the ideas of other named thinkers in detail; questions of methodology are dealt with more overtly; and respondents are treated as models of good philosophical conduct. If we turn to the experiences they undergo, we shall see that they reflect this increasing advancement, while preserving the core of the learning experience as it emerged from 'early' and 'middle' works.

Most obviously, inquiry is still not without its pitfalls and setbacks. Instances of *aporia* pepper the discussion between the Eleatic Stranger and Theaetetus in *Sophist*, and also occur in *Theaetetus*, *Parmenides*, and *Philebus*.[47] We find references to difficulty in seeing the object of one's search, whether through ignorance or the difficulty of the subject (*Sph*.253e7–254b1, *Plt*.291b4–c7); doubt and discouragement when discussion reaches an impasse (the Eleatic Stranger is ἡττημένον *Sph*.239b2); and speechlessness at ideas put forward (*Phlb*.21d4–5). There are constant requests for explanation and greater clarity, as well as concern that the discussion may have fallen into confusion

[47] On the renewed interest in *aporia* in the 'late' dialogues, see M. Frede (1996). On the prominence of *aporia* in *Parmenides*, see McCabe (1996).

or error (τεταραγμένοι *Sph*.242C1, ταραχὴν *Phlb*.16a8). Socrates and Protarchus are storm-tossed in *Philebus* (29a10–b2 cf. 13d6) and at *Theaetetus* 191a3–5 Socrates says that, if he and Theaetetus do not manage to overcome their perplexity, they will be low-spirited like seasick people—images similar to the description of *aporia* at *Laches* 194c2–3. On occasion, difficulty in discussion produces anger and fear (δυσχεραίνω, δέδοικα *Tht*.195c6), loneliness (διαφυγοῦσα ἔρημον καὶ ἄπορον κατέστησεν *Phlb*.16b6–7), concern and pain (*Tht*.148e5 ἀπαλλαγῆναι, e7 ὠδίνεις). Such passages emphasize that we should not think of discussion in 'late' dialogues as a dry, unengaging exercise. The interlocutors still experience it as challenging and disturbing; and it engages them at a more than intellectual level.

However, as in 'middle' dialogues, these difficulties can now be overcome. Most importantly, the whole character of *aporia* has changed. In 'early' dialogues, its psychological aspect is dominant: feelings of doubt, perplexity, speechlessness, loss of control, paralysis. In 'middle' dialogues, the confusion and perplexity remain, but there is an increasing focus on the dialectical difficulty that has prompted them, allowing a more constructive and focused response. By 'late' dialogues, while the psychological dimension is again present, *aporia* is now linked even more closely with the puzzle or problem encountered—indeed, the word now frequently seems to denote the puzzle itself. At *Sophist* 249d9–11, for example, the Eleatic Stranger exclaims to Theaetetus: 'I think we are now becoming aware of the difficulty of the inquiry about being' (τὴν ἀπορίαν τῆς σκέψεως), and then, after eliciting Theaetetus' response, explains what he means: 'consider more closely if, by now agreeing to these things, we may not justly be asked the same things which we ourselves asked a while ago of those who said the universe was hot and cold' (249e6–250a2). In this passage, doubt and concern are expressed, but the *aporia* seems to be identified more strongly with the specific difficulty the Eleatic Stranger raises than with the emotions it evokes. Interpreters often regard this development as a progression towards Aristotle's use of puzzles in inquiry, whereby a puzzle is used as a tool for clarifying the problem under discussion and then evaluating the solutions offered.[48]

[48] Defended recently by Matthews (1999); cf. also e.g. Ryle (1966) 144–5. On the other hand, Politis (2006) thinks that we can see both aspects of usage of the word *aporia* (to refer to the puzzle and the psychological state of puzzlement, termed by

But, while fair, this observation underplays the importance of the altered response of interlocutors in facilitating this change. *Aporia* can have this more focused and constructive role in 'late' dialogues *only because* interlocutors are now able to respond to their difficulties in a constructive way, rather than going into psychological shock.[49] All along, right from 'early' dialogues, interlocutors *could* have responded to *aporia* by identifying the difficulty and treating it as a puzzle, but only now are they sufficiently developed to do this. The change in the use of the word *aporia*, therefore, reflects interlocutors' increasing development as much as Plato's altered views on how to conduct discussion.

In fact, *aporia* is now a spur to discussion, rather than a disaster that threatens to halt it. In response to the *aporia* at *Sophist* 231b9–c7, the Eleatic Stranger and Theaetetus increase their efforts; at *Theaetetus* 190e5–191a6 Socrates motivates himself and Theaetetus in their search by describing how cast down they will feel should they fail. This fits in with the increasing tendency of interlocutors to voice potential problems with their own position—a shift away from their earlier counterparts' desire to appear superior in discussion (e.g. *Sph.*242ac, 248e–249a, 249d–250a; *Plt.*274e–275a). More generally, interlocutors are well motivated and eager: in *Sophist*, Theaetetus claims that he will not tire in discussion (218b1); and in *Philebus*, Protarchus is pivotal in encouraging Socrates onwards in the search at several points, including at the very close of the dialogue.

Again continuing the trend of the 'middle' dialogues, there are few instances of negative responses to *aporia*. These are sometimes evoked without being manifested by the participating interlocutors, a particularly striking instance being the midwifery passage in *Theaetetus* (148e ff.). Here, Socrates describes the angry and violent responses sometimes produced by his art, but which Theaetetus does not himself give way to, despite feeling labour pains just like them. And later, at 195b9–d3, Socrates expresses anger at himself on

him zetetic and cathartic respectively) throughout Plato's works. Making what seems to be a similar distinction, Hyland (1981) 36–7 detects both epistemological and non-epistemological *aporia* in *Charmides*. Significantly, however, the instances of zetetic/epistemological *aporia* cited all characterize *Socrates*—i.e. the response of a more advanced learner. For the positive/constructive role of *aporia* in 'late' dialogues, see M. Frede (1996), Desjardins (1990) 4–6.

[49] Cf. Politis (2006) 108–9 arguing that 'middle' and 'late' dialogues show the emergence of a dialectical response to puzzlement; also Sedley (1995) 21–2.

account of the *aporia* they have fallen into—precisely the inward looking reaction he earlier recommended to Theaetetus.[50] But even more telling is a pivotal moment a short way into the discussion between Socrates and Protarchus in *Philebus*, where the latter *does* display a negative response. It occurs after Protarchus has repeatedly refused to concede a division between good and bad pleasures, despite agreeing that some pleasures are opposed to others—thus demonstrating that he puts victory in debate above genuine inquiry. In frustration, Socrates says that, if they keep on arguing like this, they will show themselves to be φαυλότατοί and νέοι (most commonplace and juvenile 13d1), and will destroy their argument:

> *Socrates*: *We are being carried back to the same argument again, Protarchus, and we will not say that one pleasure differs from another, but that all are alike; the examples spoken just now do not cause us any damage at all, but we will believe and say the things which the most common place and most juvenile in discussion say.*
>
> *Protarchus*: *What sort of things do you mean?*
>
> *Socrates*: *That if I, imitating you and defending myself, were to dare to say that the most dissimilar thing is very similar to the thing to which it is most dissimilar, I would be able to say the same things as you, and we would be shown to be more than necessarily juvenile, and our discussion would be wrecked and destroyed. Let us make a start again, then, and perhaps, coming together on fair and equal terms, we might reach agreement with one another.*
>
> *Philebus*, 13cd

This is of course a situation familiar from many other dialogues—but here, unusually, it has a positive result. What distinguishes this case from others is, firstly, the directness of Socrates' reaction, which is to point out that they are not arguing as people of their dialectical sophistication should; and, second, the meekness and constructiveness of Protarchus' response. He modifies his behaviour in accordance with Socrates' analysis, and this enables the initial exchange to develop into a lengthy and productive discussion.[51] Even with more advanced interlocutors, the implication is, there is still the inclination

[50] Similar in effect is the discussion of the behaviour of the gods and giants in dialectical debate at *Sph.*246ad.

[51] See D. Frede (1996) on the conversion of Protarchus. Socrates' response to the objection attributed to Protagoras that Socrates has not dealt his position fairly at *Tht.*165e ff. is similar; so too the way that the Eleatic Stranger deals with the impatience felt at the lengthy digression at *Plt.*286b ff.

to respond inappropriately to the challenges of argument, but with developing self-knowledge, methodological understanding, and restraint one can move past these moments to profitable dialectic.[52]

3.5. PROGRESS AND VIRTUE

This survey of the experiences undergone by interlocutors in 'early', 'middle', and 'late' dialogues, though brief, allows us to flesh out our picture of how the dialogues present the process of learning. At all stages, learning is challenging, even unpleasant. This is most evident at the start: initially, *aporia* takes a global and deeply disturbing form; it is accompanied by speechlessness, quasi-magical loss of control, confusion, the desire to avoid questioning, anger, violence, distress, shame, incredulity, doubt, and competitiveness. At this stage, discussion engages the respondent's sense of self in a radical and direct way, prompting reactions that are highly affective, unreflective, and that manifest his gut feelings—both positive and negative—in an unmediated fashion. In 'later' works, inquiry is still unsettling and disturbing—doubt, distress, and confusion remain prominent—but now, interlocutors are able to negotiate their responses more successfully, and they react in a more measured, positive, and constructive manner. In consequence, they experience perplexity in a more focused and problem-centred way, and they are able to work through their difficulties. As I have tried to emphasize, all this is closely linked with interlocutors' increasing understanding and self-consciousness, as well as their deeper commitment to discussion—itself a product of their improved insight into themselves and their deficiencies. At all stages, therefore, discussion involves interlocutors in an individual and personal manner, and on an affective as well as a cognitive level—but there are nevertheless developments. What we have is a picture of an increasingly stable and reasoned disposition to engage in dialectical

[52] C. Gill (1996b) makes a similar point about discussions in 'late' dialogues no longer breaking down, connecting this, as I do, with the improved qualities of the interlocutors. He views this as a matter of Plato's choice of interlocutor, however, rather than as demonstrating the possibility for growth in dialectical virtue. On the significance of the ability to carry on dialectical discussion, though with a different slant, see also McCabe (2000).

discussion in a committed and productive way: a progression towards a kind of dialectical ideal.

Indeed, as we saw in chapter 1, we often find interlocutors' behaviour characterized in overtly ethical terms. Dialectic, as presented in the dialogues, is an undertaking that involves virtue on the part of the interlocutor; only a good person can carry it out satisfactorily; and it enables him to fulfil societal relationships and obligations. For instance, in *Gorgias*, Callicles' refusal to engage in dialectic productively is presented as a lack of friendship, frankness, and generosity; and in *Protagoras*, Socrates likens properly conducted dialectical discussion to respectable symposia, whereas discussion that makes reference to poets is symbolized by the symposia of common folk with their flute girls and dancing girls.[53] The language extends from the apparently casual metaphor—the figuring of giving an account as the repaying of a debt or favour (for instance, *Plt.*267a1–3, *M.*75b1–5, *R.*506e6–507a5)—to some of the most exceptional passages in the corpus: *Republic* 450d8–451b7, for example, where Socrates expresses concern that he may deceive his fellow interlocutors unwillingly, and they absolve him from guilt, as though it were murder; and *Sophist* 241d3–242a3, where Socrates presents his refutation of Parmenides as parricide. As we might expect, moreover, there is a change in the application of such language as we move through different types of dialogue. In 'early' dialogues, interlocutors characteristically lack virtue and fail to fulfil their obligations. As we reach 'middle' and 'late' dialogues, however, interlocutors are better able to meet such expectations. Theaetetus, for example, as well as having the intellectual qualities of being quick to learn, of sharp mind and good memory, also—in contrast to Callicles, say—has the virtuous characteristics of being gentle, brave, bold, and persistent in answering, as a model interlocutor needs to be (*Tht.*144a1–b6, 187b9–c3).

Language of this sort, as I suggested in chapter 1, forms part of the dialogues' concern with receivership and the offering of accounts, and highlights the responsibilities of participants in the learning process, reminding us of the role that we as receivers need to play in successful communication. Yet it has been thought that Plato's appropriation of the language of virtue goes beyond this. Some interpreters, focusing on the greater virtue of interlocutors in 'later' dialogues, think Plato's

[53] *Grg.*499bc, 521a, cf. 486e–488b, 500b, 519e; *Prt.*347c–348a.

intention is to suggest that there is a range of qualities that an interlocutor must possess if he is to participate in dialectic successfully.[54] These include both the intellectual traits and the qualities of character lacked by 'early' interlocutors and increasingly possessed by 'later' interlocutors.[55] Such an interpretation is of course in harmony with the traditional approach to Plato's views on learning, according to which, by the time of writing 'middle' and 'late' dialogues, Plato thought that respondents needed to have developed the qualities of character which make them compliant in dialectic *before* taking part in that activity. This is of course what the pre-dialectical training ordained in *Republic*'s ideal state seems to provide for.

While I agree that the language of virtue strongly suggests the importance of an affective dimension to learning, I differ on the question of *when* virtue is acquired. To my mind, the above view does not do sufficient justice to the ongoing difficulty of dialectic. In 'early' dialogues, the rebukes that Socrates levels at the wayward conduct of his respondents (and which are sometimes directed at him in turn) are a familiar feature of the exchanges. Yet throughout 'middle' and 'late' dialogues, too, we find interlocutors being urged to engage in inquiry with eagerness, gentleness, attention, courage, generosity, and so forth. In *Republic*, for example, Socrates constantly stresses the need for endurance and courage in facing arguments (for example, 368bc, 372a, 445b, 453de, 457e, 472e); and at *Sophist* 261a5–c1, the search is like a siege and the interlocutors have to fight through each set of defences without being discouraged. Such passages reveal that even 'late' interlocutors need to be encouraged and reminded to respond virtuously during discussion; they have the ability to do so, but they do not find it easy and cannot be relied upon to do so automatically and unfailingly. These interlocutors, that

[54] Teloh (1986) 11–12, 131–2 and *passim*, Seeskin (1987) 1–4, 23–5, 135–53, and *passim*, Szlezák (1999) 6–8. Cf. Hobbs (2000) 243 n69. Seeskin's picture of the moral and affective dimension of dialectic is similar to mine; but he seems to see the requisite virtues as to be acquired away from dialectic itself, and views Socrates' method as one that does not ever succeed. For an illuminating discussion, based on *Republic*, of the virtues of the intellect required for successful inquiry, including spiritedness, gentleness, competitiveness, shame, courage, and anger, see Patterson (1987).

[55] Although 'middle' and 'late' interlocutors are closer to dialectical virtue than their early-stage counterparts, we need not regard them as perfect. This is a line developed by Miller (1980) and (1999), who suggests that the failings of 'late' interlocutors, though different from those of 'early' interlocutors, likewise help reveal our own failings.

is, are still in the process of acquiring the virtues necessary for dialectic. And, if this is so, it leaves open an alternative interpretation of Plato's use of the language of virtue, whereby the dialectical virtues are not acquired *before* engaging in dialectic, but gradually *during the course of* participating in Socratic discussions. As interlocutors increase in understanding by participating in Socratic discussion, so, at the same time, they are acquiring dialectical virtue: these movements are not independent of each other, but two aspects of a single process. Accordingly, the role of Socratic discussion, I suggest, is to provide a context in which interlocutors can effectively develop these virtues.[56]

In which ways, then, can Socratic discussion act as a suitable context for the development of dialectical virtue? First, discussion motivates interlocutors to learn, providing them with an internal drive to improve themselves. This is what interlocutors like Euthyphro or Callicles, meeting Socrates for the first time, lack, and what more advanced interlocutors—such as Theaetetus, Protarchus, and most evidently Socrates, with their eagerness and perseverance—have acquired. To some degree, the dialogues (as well as the Cave image) present this as a matter of fostering *desire* for change—think of the personal magnetism of Socrates, illustrated in his effects on Alcibiades, for example, or the visions of Forms incorporated in 'middle' and 'late' dialogues to inspire and guide the participants. But motivation is also a matter of being made to feel uncomfortable with one's current state, of being goaded, even forced, to leave it behind—especially, though by no means exclusively,[57] at the early stages. This, as is often noted, is the function of Socrates' abrasive tactics in 'early' dialectic (as well, we might add, as of the similar effects produced in 'later' dialectic): as Socrates says of the slave at *Meno* 84ac, a desire to change is dependent upon a recognition that one's current state is deficient in some way.[58]

[56] Schmid (2002) draws out the parallels between dialectic and virtue, and emphasizes, as I do, the challenge extended to the interlocutor and the importance of persistence in the process. He does not, however, develop the idea to form an interpretation of the different styles of dialogue; or extend it explicitly to the reader (as I do in section 3.6).

[57] Cf. Matthews (1999) on the importance of puzzlement in all learning; also Sedley (1995) 21–2.

[58] For the connection between the positive and negative aspects of motivation, see e.g. Robinson (1953) 17–18, Griswold (1988d) 157, and (with a different focus) Nussbaum (1986) 160–4. Hyland (1981) 13–17 offers a particularly engaging account of *aporia* as a recognition of incompleteness which is also an impulse towards

Second, the dialogues offer interlocutors ample opportunity for self-scrutiny and reflection. These are crucial if interlocutors are to develop the understanding of themselves and the reasoned negotiation of their impulses necessary if they are to progress from the unreflective and uncontrolled participants of 'early' dialogues to the committed and reasoning learners of 'middle' and 'late' works. This is, of course, another well-noted feature of dialectic in the dialogues, especially Socrates' 'early' dialectic. It is perhaps most obvious in the power of *aporia* to turn an interlocutor in on himself, getting him to examine his reasons for thinking and acting as he does. It is also embedded in Socrates' rules of discussion (such as saying only what you believe, not relying on the authority of others, offering only short answers[59]), which encourage an interlocutor to reflect upon—and receive criticism of—what he himself believes.[60] In later chapters, I hope to expand our understanding of the ways in which the dialogues foster reflection and self-scrutiny, as well as emphasizing that this is an important feature of dialectic in 'middle' and 'late' works, not just 'early' ones.

A third (and perhaps less remarked) role of discussion is to provide an arena for practice, habituation, and the gradual acquisition of the

completeness; such a state involves a 'responsive openness' to new possibilities and is termed by him an 'interrogative stance'. It is something we have to work towards as an achievement. Cf. also Renaud (2002) 194 (*aporia* provides the wonder from which philosophy begins) and 197 (a sense of deficiency creates desire). Teloh (1986) places a dual emphasis on Socrates' parallel methods of *elenchus* and *psychagogia* in creating the two elements of motivation, though I would not want to subscribe to his interpretation of *psychagogia* in all respects. Such analyses are usually applied to 'early' dialogues; I hope have shown that similar issues are important in 'middle' and 'late' works.

[59] For these rules, see e.g. Teloh (1986) 17–18, 131–2, Lloyd (1979) 101, Moes (2000) 6, Moline (1981) 39–41.

[60] E.g. Vlastos (1983) 35–8, Benson (2000) 37–55, 86–90 (on the 'say what you believe' requirement in particular). More generally, the rules of discussion can be seen as designed to promote a type of discussion that engages with a person's fundamental desires and drives, and is therefore cognitive-affective: cf. Seeskin (1987) 1–2, Scott (1999) 16–17. For an opposing view, whereby Socrates' rules form part of his unfair strategy of cramping his interlocutors' style, see e.g. Beversluis (2000) *passim*. Beversluis (2000) 11–12, 40 points out, moreover, that Socrates (like his interlocutors) often breaks his own rules. This, however, should not be seen as a lack of commitment on Socrates' part, rather as an index of the extent to which—as yet—the group of interlocutors in question is unable to participate in discussion properly. Adherence to the dialectical rules, like the instantiation of dialectical virtues, is an ideal to which discussion should aspire.

skills necessary for dialectical virtue. One thing that emerges very clearly from the dialogues is that one cannot expect to succeed in dialectic speedily. Not only is the subject matter huge; the skills one needs to engage in it successfully are only gradually learned. This applies on the intellectual level; it also applies to the character traits one needs to engage in discussion: only with practice, and after being repeatedly challenged, does one learn to be enduring, courageous, even-tempered, and consistently enthusiastic in discussion. A beginner, however eager, will soon be discouraged and fall by the wayside; it will take him time to understand himself and to negotiate his automatic impulses. To achieve this, he needs ongoing exposure to dialectical discussion. The importance of this is frequently stressed in the dialogues. Think, for example, of Socrates' insistence that Meno's slave boy must be exposed to questioning repeatedly before he will recollect properly (*M.*85c9–d1); the number of dialogues that allude to earlier or later discussion, or suggest that interlocutors should engage in further discussion; and Plato's emphasis on Socrates' dedication of his life to philosophizing—represented in his appearance in so many dialogues.[61] This is a crucial element, too, in many of the dialogues' images for learning: in *Theaetetus*, Plato emphasizes the importance of repeated association with Socrates for successful delivery of ideas (150d–151d); in *Apology*, the gadfly repeatedly lands on the horse; the ascent from the Cave is a journey of several stages. It is only by repeated dialectical engagement that interlocutors can move on to the next stage of learning, gradually attaining the virtue of an advanced interlocutor.[62]

Yet if this is the case, one might ask, why do we never see an individual interlocutor progressing through the different stages of learning? In particular, why do we never see 'early'—unsuccessful—interlocutors

[61] Cf. also *Seventh Letter* 341cd. For exhortations to future discussion, see e.g. *M.*100b7–c2, *Phd.*78a3–9, 107b4–9. One could see the emphasis on practice in dialectic as a reinterpretation of the tradition of *sunousia*, of which philosophical companionship, as discussed in *Phaedrus*, could be another dimension. For the importance of *sunousia* in the dialogues, see Krentz (1983) 34, Sayre (1995) 31–2. Robb (1993) suggests that the charges brought against Socrates were based on his undermining of traditional *sunousia*. Closely connected is the emphasis on *μελέτη* in learning: see *Smp.*208a3–7, *Tht.*153b9–c2. This is an important feature of the methodologies used in the dialogues, from the examples of definitions offered in *Meno* (see 75a8–9) to the examples of weaving and angling used in *Politicus* and *Sophist.* Cf. Halperin (1992) 100–6.

[62] Morgan (2007) discusses themes of iteration and repetition in the dialogues.

reach a point where they can participate in dialectic productively?[63] If this indicates that a Euthyphro or a Callicles could never progress to further stages of learning, then, in line with the traditional interpretation, we would seem to have a negative verdict on Socrates' 'early' dialectic.

To begin with, if we were to see such a progression, especially within a single dialogue, it would seem too easy an achievement, undermining the dialogues' emphasis on practice and ongoing application. The repeated failures and near-failures of discussion emphasize the difficulty of the process. And the fact that we only ever see interlocutors making small steps forward—never huge leaps and bounds—underscores how long and drawn out it is, reminding us of the need for continued and dedicated application. Instead, individual dialogues present us with interlocutors in the process of practising for virtue, at a particular stage of habituation and skill acquisition. A second consideration is the effect such a presentation would have on a reader's response. To turn to a point of doctrine, Plato famously never gives us a clear and unambiguous description of the Forms. Various explanations have been put forward for this; to me, the most convincing is that such a description would run counter to the personal achievement of discovering the Forms (as well as diminishing one's desire to search for them, perhaps). One has to see them for oneself, the idea is, and only then can one appreciate what they are really like. It is the same, I suggest, with the presentation of the stages of the learning process. We do not have a continuous depiction, and certain key gaps are left; it is clear roughly what needs to happen at these pivotal points, but the reader needs to undergo that transformation for herself and to experience it as is appropriate for her as an individual.[64] By leaving such gaps in the picture of the experience the learner is to go through, Plato ensures that even in her understanding

[63] I do not find it plausible to see Meno as transformed into a model interlocutor (even in a temporary way), a suggestion made e.g. by Seeskin (1987) 117–34, Gordon (1999) 104–8. Cf. Benson (2000) ch.11.

[64] Cf. the comments at Mann (2006) 359–60. Also, Blondell (2000) 143 with n58 on the difficulty of representing moments of philosophical transition in words; Seeskin (1987) 41–2 on why Socrates does not describe his methods fully; and Rutherford (1992) 155–6 on Plato's avoidance of directly representing ideal dialectic. Notomi (1999) 24–5 has interesting comments on the use of negative paradigms to convey positive insights.

of the learning process itself, quite apart from the objects of dialectical inquiry, the reader has to look for her own answers.

The dialogues' emphasis on practice and gradual habituation is important not just for what it tells us about how the learning process is conceived and the manner in which we should approach discussion, but also for the light it sheds on the changes in dialectical style between 'early', 'middle', and 'late' dialogues. Practice is not only necessary at an individual stage of learning—in reaching the initial insight that one is deficient in knowledge, for example—but is crucial throughout one's development. And this is where the changes in dialectic come in. As a learner develops, he needs to be exposed to different and more strenuous challenges, so that he makes further progress, rather than just stagnating at the level he has reached. The changes in dialectical style, I suggest, are designed to provide these changing stimuli.[65] In the 'early' dialogues, for instance, Socrates' dialectical style attempts to engage his interlocutors in a very overt way. He is portrayed as charismatic and enigmatic, inspiring love and devotion in at least some of those who come into contact with him; and he openly exhorts his respondents to pursue learning and knowledge. He is also aggressive and pushy, making them feel uncomfortable in acute ways. In 'later' dialogues, discussion still aims to motivate the learner, but less overtly and obviously, for by this point, he has developed stronger internal motivation and needs less help from the discussion leader. In other words, the style of discussion through 'early', 'middle', and 'late' dialogues changes because, at their respective stages of development, interlocutors need different stimuli to push them towards dialectical virtue. And—to return to the Cave image—it is the discussion leader's role to adapt the stimulus in the appropriate way.[66] The ability of discussion to provide at each stage the most suitable context for the learner's continued

[65] On the importance of the match between interlocutor and method, see Gill (2002) and Morgan (2002).

[66] In the collaborative model of learning I have outlined, the discussion leader may at the same time be viewed as learning, albeit in a different way and on a different level to his respondent. Different types of dialectic, from the confrontational to the collaborative, may play different but equally important roles in his own development as a learner, alongside that of his discussion partner: I do not, with Long (2008), find the range of types of dialectic in Plato's text problematic when viewed from the perspective of the inquirer. We may, furthermore, trace a development in the discussion leader alongside that of his respondent in the three traditional groups of dialogues, and could regard the different dialectical frameworks the dialogues offer as providing

development in virtue is not automatic: it relies on the input of a senior guiding party, of the sort who, even in dialogues concerned with advanced interlocutors and advanced inquiries, remains a key feature.[67]

3.6. LEARNING AMONG READERS

If the dialogues encourage us to conceptualize interlocutors' learning as virtue-acquisition, what implications does this have for the reader? We have already seen, in discussion of *Phaedrus* in chapter 1, that the reader's activity—like that of other receivers—is also characterized in ethical terms. My suggestion is that our reading of the dialogues provides us with a learning context analogous to that which Socratic discussion provides for interlocutors. Just as dialectical discussion, as orchestrated by the discussion leader, provides an arena in which interlocutors can develop dialectical virtue, so our reading of the dialogues provides us with an arena within which we can develop similar virtues. Like the interlocutors, we have to be personally engaged on both affective and cognitive levels; and the role of the text—which stands in for the discussion leader—is to prompt such

learning contexts that can simultaneously stimulate the learning of interlocutors at different stages of development in different ways.

[67] I have found particularly helpful here Burnyeat (1980a) and Zagzebski (1996); also Bonjour and Sosa (2003) esp. 156–70, 184–5. For intellectual virtues in Plato, see also Patterson (1987). Working in the field of virtue epistemology, Linda Zagzebski has put forward a model for learning based on the acquisition of intellectual virtues (e.g. open-mindedness, wholeheartedness, and enthusiasm, which are acquired in similar ways to moral virtues and, like them, are closely connected with our emotions or feelings) that bears some striking similarities to Plato's.

It is also interesting to compare Stoic ideas about the virtues of dialectic. Long (1996c) 92–3 discusses the Stoics' use of terms such as unhastiness, strong-mindedness, lack of empty-headness to characterize competency in dialectic; also 94, 106 on Diogenes Laertius' claim that there is a connection between behaviour in dialectic and in actual events; and 94, 102–4 for links between dialectic and ethics within Stoic philosophy. In Stoic thinking, only the wise man has true competency in dialectic (97–8), an idea that echoes my emphasis on skill in dialectic as something that can only be acquired with time and practice: it is a part of virtue. This approach to dialectic may be part of the Stoics' reception of Plato (and Socrates), on which see also Sedley (1993), Vander Waerdt (1994), Inwood (2005) esp. chapters 8–11. For the importance of taking seriously the Hellenistic reception of Socrates and Plato in trying to understand their thought, see Long (1996b).

engagement in us by providing us with appropriate stimuli. Like face-to-face discussion, the texts motivate us, both by stimulating our desire for learning and knowledge, and by discomfiting us.[68] They provide us with opportunities for self-scrutiny and reflection. And by posing repeated and ever varied challenges, they provide us with the opportunity for practice, habituation, and the gradual acquisition of the skills necessary for dialectical virtue.[69] As they do this, moreover, they provoke in us many of the same experiences as we see in interlocutors.[70] Confusion, a sense of being out of one's depth, the inclination to stop reading, annoyance, incredulity and doubt, discomfort, and even shame are not, I think, uncommon reactions in readers of the dialogues, particularly on first acquaintance. The place of these works in our cultural and intellectual heritage, and their subjection to continuous, detailed academic scrutiny, has perhaps dampened some of these responses—though some still confess to such reactions, or bear witness to them in their students.[71] But, as I hope will have emerged from this chapter, we should not regard such uncomfortable responses as a sign of inadequacy, either ours or the author's; they are intentionally provoked, as part of the way that the dialogues encourage us to develop as learners.

I have focused for the main part of this chapter on the interlocutor, implying that the sophistication of the conversation occurring within a dialogue and the stage of development of its interlocutors can be used to divide the works (along the lines suggested by the traditional early–middle–late groupings) into categories representing stages of increasing philosophical sophistication.[72] Nevertheless, for the remainder of the study, it is in fact the stage of development invited

[68] Cf. Seeskin (1987) 4–8 and White (1996), who sees the dialogues as leaving the reader in a kind of 'radical distress.'

[69] For the habituation of the reader, see Blank (1993), though his interpretation of the response invited in the reader is different from mine; see ch.2 n8.

[70] For observations of a link between the experiences of interlocutors and readers, see ch.1 n2. Howland (2003), while appearing to see a basic similarity of experience between interlocutors and readers, thinks that we do not feel negative emotions such as anger and envy. Though, as I emphasized in ch.1–2, the dialogues encourage us to be more self-conscious about our responses than interlocutors, I think that we tend towards the same responses as interlocutors before we learn to modify them.

[71] Cf. Hadot (1995) 92, 104–5, 149. With different interpretations: Beversluis (2000) 15–16, Rutherford (1995) 80, Szlezák (1999) 9–11, Seeskin (1987) 11, Matthews (1999) 44. Cf. Gould (1992) 17–18, Annas (1981) 16, Blondell (2002) 180.

[72] Cf. ch.2 n50 with text.

in the *reader* that I will be treating as the basis for the categorization of dialogues as early-stage, intermediate-stage, and advanced-stage, as suggested in chapter 2. For the presentation of interlocutors is not the only guide to the stage of development invited in the reader:[73] it may be that we are invited to take a more sophisticated view of a discussion that appears to present an early stage in learning (as, perhaps, in *Euthydemus*), or it may be that a work appears to be advanced in other respects but not this one (as in *Phaedrus*). And as I pointed out in the last chapter, we are encouraged to move beyond the responses of interlocutors, using their reactions to understand and modify our own.

So, just as we see interlocutors develop, we are also expected to grow in virtue as we read, acquiring the ability to move beyond negative reactions and to overcome the difficulties with which the texts confront us in a productive way. 'Early' texts challenge us in obvious and unsubtle ways; but as we progress to 'middle' and 'late' dialogues, the challenges become more complex and subtle, we are required to be more self-motivated in our approach, and the cognitive and affective skills we are encouraged to develop are more sophisticated.[74] By the time we approach a dialogue like *Sophist*, we have to be further advanced in dialectical virtue, or we will gain very little at all from it. And, conversely, by this stage we do not *need* to be exposed to the same obvious stimuli, because we have already, by reading other dialogues, started to internalize the requirements being made upon us.[75] In fact, as suggested in chapter 2, the corpus as a whole could be seen as presenting a kind of pathway for the reader's study, as she progresses from 'early' dialogues, to 'middle', and then 'late' works, increasing in dialectical virtue and understanding as she does so. Viewed in this way, our philosophical development is closely bound up with our development as readers: we learn through reading, and our ability to read productively is an index of our philosophical development. The dialogues are in fact enabling us, as we move through the different types of work, to become better readers—readers who can take up more nearly the invitation to respond ideally,

[73] As suggested at Clay (2000) 113–14; cf. also Kahn (1996) 381.

[74] Moes (2000) 48 suggests that we could see the dialogues' relationship with their reader as akin either to a physician–patient relationship or to a teacher–medical student relationship, depending on the reader's maturity; also 52–5.

[75] Annas (2002) suggests that aporetic dialogues show us how to read later ones. Cf. Szlezák (1999) 25–7.

rather than ones whose inappropriate responses need constantly to be taken into account and off-set. Some of the ways in which the dialogues help us to do this, thereby fostering our development as learners, form the subject of the following chapters.

The idea of a progression through the corpus resonates with the role of practice in the development of dialectical virtue. Ongoing effort and repeated exposure to challenging stimuli is crucial, as I hope to have brought out, in the presentation of the interlocutor's journey towards virtue, as well as being a key feature in many of the dialogues' images of learning. The same, I have suggested, applies to the reader; but, as a reader, she can only gain such practice by engaging with different texts. Each will expose her to a new challenge, and provide her with a stimulus of a different type. I am not intending to suggest that the dialogues form some sort of a course of study, which the reader must rigidly follow. But I do think that the dialogues point us towards an ongoing process of philosophizing which involves dialogue with a selection of texts, as well as with other learners in a face-to-face context.

These ideas also tie in with the well-documented links between dialogues in setting and character.[76] Timaeus begins with a reference to a conversation of yesterday (17a), and Socrates' summary of the discussion indicates that it is the discussion of *Republic* he has in mind. Cebes' description of recollection at *Phaedo* 73ab, in which he refers to questioning on the basis of diagrams, may be a reference to the interrogation of the slave in *Meno*. *Politicus* opens with a similar backwards glance to the conversation of *Sophist*; *Sophist* in turn begins with a reference to the previous day's conversation, thought to refer to *Theaetetus*, which itself, as Socrates' closing remark indicates, appears to take place on the same day as *Euthyphro*. Ancient readers onwards have seen *Euthyphro*, *Apology*, *Crito*, and *Phaedo* as forming a dramatic sequence; and Griswold sees these four works, together with *Theaetetus*, *Sophist*, and *Politicus*, as forming a larger dramatic unit.[77] More generally, Socrates' presence in so many dialogues, some referencing specific stages in his life, contributes a dramatic unity of sorts; and it is common for a dialogue to allude to a

[76] See e.g. Rutherford (1995) 4–5, Griswold (2002), Gill (2006). These links are not straightforward and require negotiation by the reader: see Long (2007), McCabe (2006).

[77] Griswold (2002) 138.

future meeting or discussion. One of the functions of these links is to evoke a wider world of philosophizing beyond the text, and to suggest that each individual philosophical dialogue is part of a larger and longer philosophical process. We never see an interlocutor reach understanding or virtue in the course of a dialogue, for a single conversation is not by itself able to offer this. Just so, a single dialogue with a text is not enough for our philosophical understanding and development; and the links between the dialogues encourage us to think of continued reading and philosophizing as a natural development, rather than viewing a dialogue as a self-contained unit and our dialogue with it as an isolated event.

The approach adopted here, therefore, assigns the reader a philosophically valuable role at the centre of the dialogues' project; and it encourages her to take a positive and proactive approach to reading and interpreting them. We are invited to view our own philosophical development, not as identical to that of the interlocutors, but as parallel with theirs, in both substance and value; and this parallelism is crucial to the dialogues' strategy in encouraging our productive engagement. For by encouraging us to think of our own learning, like that of the interlocutors, as virtue acquisition, the dialogues give us a model for understanding how we may benefit and improve through reading them. As I suggested in chapter 2, our understanding of the process we are involved in as we read is a crucial part of our ability to analyse and critique our responses, and to react to them in a constructive way. Thinking of learning in the way suggested here encourages us to approach our development from an internal perspective; it places the emphasis on our responsibility for our responses and our ability to modify them; and it helps us to appreciate all the more the importance of reflection on past errors, commitment to improvement, and continually renewed effort, in the gradual progression from inexperience to readerly and dialectical virtue—for virtue is something we can only develop for ourselves.[78]

[78] As regards the protreptic function of Plato's strategy here, it is interesting to compare the Stoic tactic of contrasting the sage and the fool (on which see Inwood (2005) 79, 90–1, 141–2). By pointing towards dialectical virtue, even if it is hard (or impossible) for many people to achieve, Plato provides a goal, and our awareness of it can inform the imperfect and incomplete efforts that we do make to improve. For the argument that the Stoics did not regard even themselves as sages, see Brouwer (2002). For a fascinating account of Plato's psychology, in which his representations of the soul aim to give would-be philosophers an understanding of themselves that will

In addition, the approach allows us to leave behind somewhat the dark and pessimistic view of Plato's work which the traditional approach fosters—whereby, unlike Socrates as depicted in the 'early' dialogues, Plato comes to believe that the majority of us cannot make any progress in learning, and we have to regard the inclusive project of the 'early' dialogues, in retrospect, as doomed to failure.[79] On my view, it is doubtless the case that not all readers will make progress in dialectical virtue. The dialogues present learning as a difficult process, and this is reflected in the way they are written: these are not easy works to get to grips with, and not everyone will persevere in the way needed to make progress.[80] As such the group of learners is self-selecting. But the early-stage dialogues extend the invitation to learn to everyone; they help us in numerous ways to reflect on and modify our response; and they offer us repeated attempts to do so. The intermediate dialogues do not represent a new—and more exclusive—approach to learning, they just address the next stage of the task.

In the following chapters, I consider in more detail how the dialogues engage us, the responses they prompt in us, and the patterns of reading they encourage as they guide us and train us to be better readers and learners. And in doing so, I hope to show how we can better appreciate some of the dialogues' most characteristic, as well as their most striking and puzzling, features.

further their ethical progress, rather than encapsulating firm doctrine (i.e. they are practically and protreptically motivated), see Kamtekar (2006). This fits well with the views expressed in ch.1 on the status of doctrine in the dialogues.

[79] See above n5. [80] Cf. Woodruff (1988) 214.

Part II

4

Characterization: A Route into Interpretation?

4.1. SOCRATES AND ALCIBIADES

Having let fly my bolts, as it were, I thought that he had been wounded. And I got up, and not allowing him to say anything further, I wrapped my own cloak round him—for it was winter—and, lying down under his cloak, and putting both my arms around this truly godlike and extraordinary man, I lay there for the whole night. And you will not say that I lie about these things also, Socrates. And when I had done these things, he showed such superiority, and disdained me, and laughed at my youthful beauty and insulted me, with regards to the very thing on which I rated myself, o men of the jury—for you are jurors of the arrogance of Socrates. For know well, by the gods and by the goddesses, that I rose having no more slept with Socrates than if I had spent the night with my father or elder brother.

After this, what state of mind do you think I was in, thinking that I'd been humiliated, but wondering at the nature and self-control and manly spirit of this man?—for I did not think that I would ever happen to meet a man of such a sort for good sense and patience. And so I was not able to take offence and cut myself off from his society, and I was at a loss for a means of attracting him. For I knew well that he was in all respects less susceptible to money than Ajax was to the spear, and he had escaped me in the one method I thought I had of catching him. So I was at a loss, and went about enslaved by this man as no-one has ever been by another person.

Symposium, 219b3–e5

This well-known passage from Alcibiades' speech in *Symposium* offers us a snapshot of an intersection in the lives of two of Athens' most charismatic figures. The account is invested by Alcibiades with general significance, as providing an exemplary case of manly spirit and self-control, and as encapsulating, in some way, the impact of Socrates' life on his own. Yet it takes its starting point from a particular incident, and purports to give us insight into the actions, values, and thoughts of the interlocutors on that specific occasion. As such, it seems to be a clear case of what we may think of as 'characterization'. Alongside his actions, Alcibiades recounts the thoughts and feelings which accompany them: his misguided suspicion that he has influence with Socrates; his sense of the insolence and arrogance of Socrates' rejection of his charms; and the conflicting feelings of admiration and humiliation which follow the encounter. Just before this passage, he describes his decision to confront Socrates, the words they exchanged, and his hesitancy to share such a story with the company—one, he says, that one might blush to recount. His shame and reluctance to share his experience with his companions gives the receiver the sense that he is offering a confidence; and his self-deprecating framing of his own behaviour encourages us to see his revelations as genuine.[1] The strength of the emotions he describes—his enslavement to Socrates after the event, his outrage at Socrates' arrogant treatment of him—brings his confidence alive; and the imagery he uses both here and in the surrounding passages to describe his feelings—the pain of his love caused by the snake's bite of Socrates' company, for instance—conveys them with powerful immediacy.

But while many readers take from this passage as strong a sense of the character of Socrates as they do of Alcibiades', it is worth pausing to consider how to respond to Alcibiades' revelations about the object of his affections. We are told that Socrates is unmoved by money, that he is immune to Alcibiades' physical beauty, and that his imperviousness to Alcibiades' advances amounts to scorn and jeering insolence. These observations appear to take us to the core of Socrates' motivation and values—yet they are offered through the lens of Alcibiades' perception. This is an issue to which Andrea Wilson Nightingale effectively draws attention in her study of the passage.[2] She points

[1] Cf. Nussbaum (1986) 187–8.

[2] Nightingale (1993); see also Nightingale (2002a) and Belfiore (1984). Prior (2006) draws attention to the need for us to unite the different perspectives on Socrates presented by characters in *Symposium*, though he does not draw out the importance for the reader of the unifying process itself. The importance of Alcibiades' speech as a paradigm of misinterpretation is heightened because he presents an appealing picture of Socrates: we are more inclined to question a negative portrayal.

out that, for all our inclination to treat the speech as providing faithful and illuminating insight into Socrates' character,[3] the dialogue urges caution—for even as Alcibiades makes his revelations, he shows himself a misinterpreter of Socrates' ambiguous exterior. As his interactions with Socrates show, he failed to understand Socrates' words and intentions. And if his account of Socrates—as a repository of knowledge and virtue—is in fact correct, then it makes Socrates a deceiver. The speech powerfully evokes the idea of an ambiguous and off-putting exterior concealing hidden treasures, yet the context warns us to be careful about accepting too easily Alcibiades' own interpretation of Socrates' inner core. And we should extend this caution to Alcibiades' presentation of himself, too. As Alcibiades' speech draws to a close, Socrates questions whether the subtlety of his argument belies the drunkenness he claims; and he suggests that Alcibiades' words have been driven by an ulterior motive, of creating trouble between Socrates and his beloved, Agathon. For all Alcibiades' apparent frankness, the context prompts us to consider whether his sincerity is in fact an aspect of his concern—a concern that is at the heart of his encounter with Socrates—with his persona and external appearance.

It is worth asking, too, just how much insight we gain into Socrates' thoughts and feelings here. Just before the passage with which I began, Alcibiades presents Socrates in his own words, as he rejects Alcibiades' initial approaches:

> *And having heard this, he said in that very dissembling manner which is characteristic and customary for him, 'My dear Alcibiades, you're probably not actually a fool, if the things which you say about me happen to be true, and there is in me some sort of power, through which you might be able to become better; you must see in me an irresistible beauty, quite superior to your beauty. And if, seeing this, you are trying to make an exchange with me and to trade beauty for beauty, you think that you are gaining no small advantage over me—you are attempting to obtain true beauty in exchange for the appearance of it, and are in fact intending to exchange "bronze for gold." But, my dear fellow, look more carefully, in case I escape your notice in being worth nothing. The mind's vision begins to see sharply when the sight of the eyes begins to pass its prime. And you are still far from this.'*

[3] E.g. Prior (2006); cf. also Rutherford (1995) 78.

> *And I, having heard this, said, 'Well, this is what I have to say, and none of what I've said differs from how I feel. But you must now consider what you think is best for you and for me.'*
>
> *'You speak well.' he said. 'For in the time that follows we will consider and do what appears to be best for the two of us concerning these things and concerning other matters.'*
>
> *Symposium*, 218d6–219b2

Socrates' response to Alcibiades expresses an overwhelming commitment to true beauty, in contrast to what he sees as the semblance to which the masses are devoted. In conveying this, in place of Alcibiades' language of self-control and strength of mind, he uses an image of measurement and exchange:[4] Alcibiades has offered him a beauty of sorts, but this would be a poor exchange for the beauty of Socrates' soul. Socrates' words gesture towards an alternative rationale for his actions—rather than struggling in a superhuman way, as Alcibiades supposes, with the desires that ordinary people feel, it may be that he is drawn more powerfully by the attractions of another, more 'real' beauty—and from these hints we could, if we wished, construct a more detailed picture of his thoughts and feelings during his encounter with Alcibiades. But what is lacking from the portrait is exactly this, made more striking by contrast with the insight Alcibiades appears to offer us into himself: we do not gain any kind of detailed understanding of Socrates' decision-making process, his assessment of Alcibiades' actions, or his view, later on, of his own. Alcibiades' speech, then, perhaps offers us less insight into the inner Socrates than we may at first be inclined to think. Earlier on in the dialogue, Alcibiades has likened Socrates to a silenus, a statuette whose exterior conceals what is hidden within, and while Alcibiades' speech purports to offer an account of the real man, his own image is a reminder of just how enigmatic a figure Socrates is. Socrates' central action in this most engaging of passages is, of course, to reject an attempt at closeness.[5]

If we do not gain a sense of inwardness with Socrates, we find instead a clear invitation to judge him against ethical ideals. In our opening passage, Alcibiades treats his audience as jurors at a trial (219c5–6) and tells them that their task is to try Socrates on a charge of arrogance. At the same time, he assimilates Socrates' behaviour to central virtues, acknowledging that Socrates has displayed manly

[4] Nussbaum (1986) 179–80. [5] Cf. Nussbaum (1986) 191–2.

spirit and self-control such as he had never hoped to meet. Socrates is an exemplar, so Alcibiades implies, of these general qualities; qualities which are not tied to any individual. While this may compound our lack of insight into Socrates as an individual, it also resonates with a Greek emphasis in the treatment of character on established patterns of behaviour, motivation, and responsibility: character is the basis from which a person's actions, habits, and way of life spring, and is a suitable focus for praise and blame.[6] Though we lack insight into the process by which he reached his decision to act as he did or the thoughts and feelings which accompanied his words and actions, we are shown Socrates choosing between types of value and beauty as a virtuous person would. Indeed, the stark simplicity of Socrates' presentation of the encounter as a choice between beauties contrasts with the conflicting mass of emotions to which Alcibiades lays claim, and invites us to connect the complexity of Alcibiades' feelings with the quality of his response in comparison with that of Socrates. A suggestive parallel is Thucydides' changing handling of character in his narrative of the Peloponnesian War. Following the restricted presentation of Pericles in the earlier parts of the work, in his later account of the declining fortunes of Athens, the figures of Nicias and Alcibiades are more richly characterized: while the restrained characterization of Pericles reflects his ability to resist personal pressures not in the interests of the city, the individuation of Nicias and Alcibiades as characters with specific traits and the individualism of their values are closely entwined with the fate of their city.[7] In Plato's dialogue, too, Alcibiades' individuation marks him out as falling short of an ethical ideal: despite his philosophical aspirations, he is closer to the complex imperfections of our world than to the realities of true understanding.

The encounter between Alcibiades and Socrates raises in striking form issues I will address in the remainder of this chapter. It asks us to reflect on the nature and extent of the insight we are offered into Plato's characters. It foregrounds the ethical dimension to his treatment of character, and it prompts us to consider the connection between Plato's style of characterization and philosophical development. It also confronts us with the dominance and appeal of Socrates, and its function within the dialogues. The encounter between Socrates and Alcibiades

[6] Halliwell (1990).

[7] Pelling (1990a) 259–61, Rood (1998) 157–8.

presents, centrally, Socrates' ability to exert a powerful attraction on those around him. The impulse driving Alcibiades' actions is his desire to be with Socrates; even after being humiliatingly rejected, his response is complete subjugation. At the heart of Socrates' encounter with his wayward follower are both alienation and a power to attract: Alcibiades is kept at a distance by Socrates, yet continues to be drawn to him. While the association of Socrates and Alcibiades is ultimately ill-fated, it represents the power of Socrates to have an impact on another life, even one so different and strongly upheld as Alcibiades', and it also asks us to reflect on the way in which that power makes itself felt.

In Alcibiades' narrative, his response to Socrates' personality is central to his philosophical engagement; and the contribution of character to the appeal and power of Plato's dialogues for their receivers has long been recognized: like the effect of Socrates on Alcibiades in their direct encounters, Plato's depiction of his interlocutors is a crucial factor in engaging the reader. It gives the philosophical issues he explores concrete settings; it brings out their relevance to everyday life; and it makes them vivid and exciting. Accordingly, it should be central to any account of how the dialogues evoke a productive response in their readers. In this chapter, I do not aim to give anything like a general account of characterization and its uses in the dialogues. Rather, taking up issues raised in Part I, I explore how Plato's handling of character encourages us to respond to his interlocutors, and how this helps the dialogues form a suitable context for our development as learners.

4.2. CHARACTER: A ROUTE INTO INTERPRETATION?

In earlier chapters, I suggested that Plato's presentation of interlocutors is a central way in which the dialogues encourage a response appropriate to the development of dialectical virtues among readers—a process, I argued, that is central to the dialogues' presentation of philosophical progress. More particularly, I suggested that interlocutors function as both models and mirrors for readers. Their activity represents the process of learning that we, in reading, also need to go through; and by recognizing the significance of their experiences, we can better understand and manage our own. At the same time, I suggested, interlocutors show us a range of inappropriate and unhelpful responses to the philosophical process, thus pointing us towards a more productive type of engagement. Central, here, is our ability to understand and analyse interlocutors as a guide to ourselves; our distance from them is crucial in enabling us to become involved in learning with self-consciousness and commitment. In other words, for all that the interlocutors serve as models to aid our development, if we are to become fully engaged learners in our own right, we need to develop an independent perspective and identity, and this requires a critical distance from them—or so, at least, has been my argument. Plato's characters do shape our response, therefore, but only by forcing us to stand on our own feet.

However, a widespread approach to Plato's handling of character emphasizes, by contrast, the *guidance* Plato's characters offer the reader. It is sometimes suggested that Socrates' respondents voice viewpoints that his original readers might have held, thereby providing them with an easy way into the conversation (unlike the inaccessible views of Socrates).[8] But ultimately, most critics agree, these are viewpoints from which the dialogues aim to prise us away. They turn us instead towards Socrates,[9] whose portrayal draws us in and makes us receptive to his outlook and ideas.[10] As John Beversluis brings out in his study of Plato's early interlocutors, a negative approach to their role is endemic in criticism.[11] And the idea that Socrates is a hero—often a tragic hero—designed to replace the figures of myth and

[8] E.g. Rowe (2006) 10, Sayre (1995) 60–1, Wolfsdorf (2004).

[9] As well as productive interlocutors such as Glaucon and Adeimantus, and other discussion leaders such as the Eleatic Stranger. Initially, I focus on Plato's more richly characterized dialogues (these include 'early' and most 'middle' works; however *Republic* II–X, though usually treated as a middle work, is in fact more akin to 'later' works in terms of characterization). For characterization in the 'later' dialogues, see section 4.8.

[10] Kahn (1983) suggests, more strongly, that the portrait of Socrates is designed to reproduce the personal impact he would have had on his original auditors.

[11] Beversluis (2000). *Phaedo* or *Republic* II–X, where we are presented with respondents who possess some dialectical virtue but are deficient in comparison to Socrates, are more complex; but many of the observations I make in this chapter still apply.

literature, a positive role model for readers to admire and emulate, is equally widespread.[12]

This approach, implicit in the work of many interpreters, has in recent years been developed in a sophisticated study by Ruby Blondell.[13] She suggests that Plato is working with ancient ideas about the educational importance of the representation of character, whereby 'the representation of persons... exerts an emotional effect on its consumers... that tends to assimilate them to the characters represented'.[14] This process, which Blondell terms mimetic pedagogy, is an extension of the idea, central in Greek culture, that one learns through imitating persons in everyday life; and other ancient genres, especially epic and tragedy, were thought to function in this way too. The most important means by which it is effected, she tells us, is 'the audience's internalization of the character's feelings, attitudes and beliefs'.[15] We are 'united in an emotional and behavioural sympathy' with our role models, we empathize and identify with them, and we aspire to become like them[16]—ideally, at least. Adopting a term introduced by Gill to characterize a similar sort of engagement, I will refer to this as a *personality* response to figures.[17] Blondell argues that Plato encourages this kind of identification with Socrates by privileging his perspective,

[12] For Socrates as a hero, see e.g. Blundell (1989) 8–9, Blondell (2002) 84–8, 112, Hobbs (2000), C. Gill (1996a) 320 with n316, Irwin (1988b), Clay (1972) and (2000) 51–9, Seeskin (1987) esp. 73–95, Segal (1978). Cf. also Ausland (2000), Morgan (2004). For 'anti-heroic' and comic elements in the portrayal of Socrates, see Clay (2000).

[13] Blondell (2002), esp. 80–112; also Blondell (2000), (2003) and Blundell (1989) 7–11, (1992). The notion of role models is also developed in depth by Hobbs (2000), who sees them as important in the formation of second-order desires which control the lower parts of the soul. Their most crucial role is in early education, before reason is fully formed, though they can also have a role once reason is formed. Because of her emphasis on the importance of role models in pre-rational training, Hobbs' view is even further distanced from mine than is Blondell's—as will become clear.

[14] Blondell (2002) 80.

[15] Blondell (2002) 81.

[16] Blondell (2002) 81, 90, 86.

[17] Gill (1990). A personality viewpoint (contrasted with a character viewpoint) has three components (listed in reverse order), of which only the first is important for my purposes (they may not necessarily be linked; cf. Gill (1990) 3–5): (i) it involves a standpoint which is expressive of a person's subjective viewpoint, is first personal and distinctive to the person in question, as regards perceptions, memories, and emotional responses; (ii) it involves giving evaluative status to the expression of personal individuality; (iii) it involves explaining actions with reference to psychological causes as opposed to conscious motives. The account is modified in C. Gill (1996a): see n20 of this chapter.

appropriating heroic paradigms for him and presenting him as a subject of his admirers' imitation. At the same time, she says, Plato is greatly concerned about our potential identification with bad characters, encouraging us to distance ourselves emotionally from them through a range of techniques, including the use of narrative voice, satire, and poetic justice or historical irony.[18]

This picture of our relationship with Plato's characters is rather different from my own and, if correct, would sit uncomfortably with the account of the reader's response I have been developing. Blondell's emphasis is on *closeness* and emotional affinity in the *nature* of our engagement with characters, rather than distance, and this suggests that our response will not have the critical and reflective dimension, or the self-consciousness and independence, I have argued for. Moreover, this aspect of Blondell's approach runs counter to one of *Republic*'s most searching criticisms of poetry:[19] that poetry appeals to the emotions, thus strengthening the lower parts of the soul, so that they are more likely to dominate in life too. This is the case even if the character we are identifying with is in fact virtuous: it is the very nature of the engagement that is harmful. Yet, on Blondell's interpretation, Plato fosters a response to his characters very close to the one here criticized. Earlier on, I suggested that Blondell's reading of Plato's handling of character bears strong resemblances to Gill's idea of a personality viewpoint—a term he in fact coins to capture the special response we have to tragic and Iliadic characters—and the idea that identification and emotional closeness are central to the effect of tragedy is by no means confined to Gill.[20] By emphasizing emotional

[18] For helpful discussion of Plato's views on imitation and the formation of character, see also Janaway (1995) 80–105.

[19] *R.*605c ff. For the significance of this objection within Plato's critique of poetry, see e.g. Janaway (1995) 11, 133–57. Cf. Halliwell (1988) 5. Plato's critique of the arts is a notoriously complicated subject; for helpful discussions, see ch.2 section 2.4. Plato's characterization of the response evoked by other genres is polemical and exaggerated: as many critics bring out, tragedy does encourage reflective evaluation as well as identification and sympathy (see e.g. Blundell (1989) 7, 14–16, Nussbaum (1986), C. Gill (1996a)). Nevertheless, as I argue in this chapter, I think it makes sense to interpret Plato's handling of character as intending to magnify the reflective and critical element in our response.

[20] Gill (1990) suggests that we develop a closeness to key tragic characters because, at important points in the drama, we are encouraged to adopt a personality viewpoint. C. Gill (1996a) recasts this account in terms of a contrast between subjective-individualist and objective-participant views of character. He thinks that tragedy encourages an objectivist-participant response to character (contrary to the

inwardness, identification, empathy, and sympathy in her account of our response to Plato's Socrates, Blondell seems to be underplaying the contrast between the dialogues and these other genres that Plato—as she acknowledges[21]—is at pains to draw.

Further, Blondell's account implies that the dialogues provide clear guidance about the ideals to which we should aspire. This is by no means to say that figures such as Socrates are Plato's mouthpieces—Blondell is clear in rejecting that position—but it does suggest that the dialogues offer us rather more guidance about how to respond and which ideas to adopt than, in Part I, I argued they do.[22] In addition, such a stance seems at odds with the emphasis placed within so many dialogues on rejecting figures of authority and scrutinizing ideas for oneself.[23] For if readers are being asked to identify with Socrates, then, it would seem, they are also being asked to take his values and views on trust—in a way that is inimical to his views about learning. This suggests to me not that Plato is denying the value of role models, but that he envisages a different function for them.

These are problems of which Blondell is, in fact, well aware. She suggests that Plato is striving to develop a version of mimetic pedagogy that avoids these drawbacks, by encouraging us to identify with positive role models *structurally*, whereby we imitate their essential characteristics, rather than *slavishly*, where we passively assume their emotions and mindlessly mimic their superficial outward behaviour. Structural imitation, since it requires identifying our model's essential

implication of his earlier terminology), and regards the especially close nature of our response to tragic characters as due to the insight we are given into their second-order reasoning about their situation. Despite Gill's altered emphasis here, I still find his (1990) idea that tragedy encourages a personality response involving identification, closeness, and inwardness with its figures helpful: these elements are also emphasized e.g. by Pelling (1990c) 247 (on characterization in general), Nussbaum (1986), Blundell (1989) 7, 14–16. Though C. Gill (1996a) brings out the importance of our engagement with characters' reasons in creating a sense of closeness to them, there are different ways in which we can be encouraged to respond to these: critically and with distance, or sympathetically and empathetically. I would see the later effect as important in tragedy, and the former in Plato.

[21] Blondell (2002) 83–5, 95–101; cf. Blundell (1989) 15–16.

[22] Though the mouthpiece and role model positions are distinct, the two debates have a bearing on one another and there is overlap in the arguments used. For the former theme, see Press (2000a).

[23] See e.g. *Prt.*313c–314c, *Chrm.*162ce, *M.*71cd. The importance of this for our approach to Plato's characters is well brought out by Kosman (1987). Cf. also Belfiore (1984) on *Symposium.*

characteristics, implies analysis and understanding—moreover, to the extent that the character we are imitating is an independent and critical thinker, we should become so too. As a view of the kind of reading the dialogues foster, this picture is not dissimilar from mine. Yet I do not think that mimetic pedagogy, even of a structural kind, can successfully cultivate it. For, according to Blondell's model, the reader is always at risk of falling into two opposing dangers. On one hand, she claims, the dialogues are wary of getting us to identify with Socrates too closely—thus falling into slavish imitation, like that of Apollodorus and Aristodemus in *Symposium*.[24] On the other, they are still concerned to get us to model ourselves upon *Socrates*; and if a reader is too critical of or distanced from her model, then she can no longer be seen to imitate him.[25] Blondell recognizes this tension in her model, but offers no convincing account of how the dialogues achieve a balance between these two impulses, as, on the mimetic pedagogy model, she must.

Equally importantly, a close look at Plato's handling of character does not, I think, support Blondell's analysis. In the following sections, I question whether Plato presents us with *any* straightforwardly positive or negative role models. I ask whether Plato does encourage us to identify and develop an emotional inwardness with certain characters. Going further, I consider whether, as is commonly assumed, the dialogues do even provide clearly depicted characters for us to sympathize and identify with. In a variety of ways, as I hope to show, the dialogues encourage distance, and reflective and thoughtful evaluation, rather than closeness and emotional inwardness. If this is the case, then it suggests to me that we should not regard Plato as working within—even while adapting—a framework of mimetic pedagogy, even if that was the prevailing approach at the time. Just as he rejects so many other aspects of his culture and its approach to education, he may reject this too.

An alternative, I suggest, is to regard Plato as using character in a way that, though on the surface it may look similar, is in fact rather different from the practice of other writers: as a stimulus to thought and

[24] Blondell (2002) 107–9; cf. Nightingale (1993) 122–3.

[25] The element of distance and independence in our response does not concern me as much as Blondell, for as I argued in Part I, what matters is that the reader is encouraged to respond in the correct manner, with self-criticism and commitment to ongoing reflection. If she does this, the process will be self-correcting, and she will not for long retain mistaken ideas.

reflection, and to our development of our own independent perspective; and as a way of fostering a certain type of engagement without providing a definite direction for interpretation. As we shall see, this involves neither abandoning the idea that characters act as models *of a sort*, nor ignoring the affective element in our response to them—but these need to be seen differently, as part of the way the dialogues encourage a cognitive-affective response.

In the following sections, I work towards such a reading of the role of character, first by exploring in more detail my reasons for discomfort with central aspects of the mimetic pedagogy view, and then by setting out what I shall term a *functional* view of Plato's handling of character. At the close of the chapter, I turn to the question of the changed handling of character in 'later' works.

4.3. CHARACTERS AS ROLE MODELS?

According to the mimetic pedagogy approach, the dialogues present some characters for us to imitate—the role models—and others from whom we are to distance ourselves; yet in my view this dichotomy is far too sharp. Euthyphro, for example, is a character upon whom, I think most would agree, we are not encouraged to mould ourselves: he is lazy, self-satisfied, slow, and makes little philosophical progress.[26] Yet not all his traits are straightforwardly negative. Unlike Socrates' accusers, he is goodwilled towards Socrates.[27] He also has firm yet unconventional beliefs, and is prepared to act contrary to the opinions of his family and society. Of course, the dialogue exposes how poorly founded his views are. But the suggestion of McPherran, that Euthyphro possesses, in a defective fashion, many of the traits of Socrates, has some appeal.[28] His goodwill, obstinacy, and idiosyncrasy, as well as his unconventional ideas about the gods, are all traits that *could*, in

[26] For unfavourable verdicts on Euthyphro, see Beversluis (2000) 162–3, himself offering a more positive assessment. His book vigorously challenges the idea that the 'early' Socrates is always right and his respondents wrong.

[27] Emphasized by Burnet (1924) 14.

[28] McPherran (2003). Cf. Reynolds (1988) 36–8. Burnet (1924) suggests that Socrates and Euthyphro are kindred spirits in the invention of new gods; however for a critique, see Furley (1985), arguing that Euthyphro is in fact a representative of traditional religion.

different instantiations, be of value; so for us simply to distance ourselves from him is an inadequate response. We are invited to think about how deep the resemblances are, and what makes a given trait positive or negative; by doing so, we gain a greater sense of what makes a life valuable than by looking to Socrates alone.

Similarly, as is commonly noted, a respondent's view may capture an element of truth or have advantages over the discussion leader's.[29] Euthyphro's claim at 4b8–9 that 'one must take care of this thing only, whether the person who killed killed with justice or not' echoes ideas voiced by Socrates in other dialogues.[30] It is often remarked that elements of Polemarchus' and Cephalus' ideas about justice are incorporated into Socrates' account in *Republic*, and Protarchus/ Philebus' idea that pleasure is the Good constitutes an important qualification to Socrates' focus on intelligence in *Philebus*. Significantly, such insights are not uncommonly voiced just when an interlocutor is being portrayed negatively—thus Euthyphro's claim comes in a speech in which he also seems to flout basic intuitions about right action; and in *Republic* I, Thrasymachus makes powerful criticisms of Socrates' mode of argument at the same time as his aggression and violence threaten the discussion. The point is not only, therefore, that most interlocutors are sometimes good, sometimes bad; but, further, that at any given point, we cannot rely on an interlocutor being *simply* a good or bad model: positive and negative traits intertwine, and we have to disentangle the threads for ourselves.

Conversely, the dialogues do not—for all Socrates' heroic traits—present any wholly sympathetic figures.[31] The 'early' Socrates, though Plato's most obviously charismatic and engaging character, uses argumentative techniques that can err on the manipulative side.[32] His use of irony and humour sometimes seems gratuitous and excessive, and his approach aggressive. His repeated requests for definitions that interlocutors cannot provide, and his constant professions of ignorance, at odds with his confident manipulation of discussions, can be frustrating.[33] The fact that criticism of Socrates, which often

[29] See e.g. Nails (2000) 18–19, Thesleff (2000), Tarrant (2000a) 73 ff., Ausland (2000) 185.

[30] See Beversluis (2000) 164–7.

[31] Cf. Hobbs (2000) 158–62 and Arieti (1993) on Socrates in *Gorgias*.

[32] I consider the 'early' Socrates' argumentative techniques more fully in ch.5.

[33] See esp. Beversluis (2000); also Rutherford (1995) 80–1, Thesleff (2000) 53, Nails (2000) 18–19.

resonates with our own reaction, is voiced by characters within the texts—Euthyphro, Thrasymachus, and Callicles, among others—suggests that the effect is not unconscious or unintentional,[34] but integral to the way Socrates is meant to strike us. In 'later' dialogues, too, though Socrates is a much blander figure, some of this endures. In *Philebus*, for example, Socrates repeatedly comes out with abstract and unclear statements, which then need to be clarified on the request of his interlocutor; and Protarchus and Philebus complain that he does not always make clear to them the relevance of his expositions (17e–18a, 18d). He spends some time at the start of the dialogue, in an extremely difficult passage, elaborating a method for identifying the Good, before happening to recollect an idea that means they no longer have to pursue it (20bc). At 19c–20a, Protarchus remonstrates with Socrates for continuing to ask himself and Philebus questions they cannot answer, while appearing to have a better grasp of the subject than them (cf. 54b), and he is uncharacteristically reluctant to continue the discussion, as Protarchus desires. All this is equally frustrating for the reader. The presentation of the Eleatic Stranger is ambiguous, too. Several commentators have detected darker sides to his character and methods, for all their apparent advancement.[35]

In addition, discussion leaders in all types of dialogues are presented as falling short of true knowledge. This is most obviously a feature of the 'early' Socrates, but is also prominent elsewhere, for instance, in Socrates' presentation of himself in *Theaetetus* as a midwife who brings to birth the ideas of others while lacking knowledge himself, and in his use of images to describe the Forms in *Republic*, resonating as this does with the classification of types of understanding in the Line analogy.[36] The Eleatic Stranger, too, describes himself as engaged in a shared search, and succumbs to hesitation and *aporia*. Of course, it can be objected that this is a pedagogical tool or debating tactic on the part of the discussion leader, who in fact possesses knowledge; however, I do not think that we are encouraged to treat what these figures say as knowledge, *despite* their protestations. Ideas expressed by a discussion leader are scrutinized in other dialogues

[34] As seems to be the suggestion of Blondell (2002) 162–4 and Beversluis (2000) 13.

[35] See e.g. Gonzalez (2000). Scodel (1987) goes so far as to view the presentation of the Eleatic Stranger as parodic. Cf. also Miller (1980). I return to objections to his dialectical methods in ch.5. By others, the Eleatic Stranger is commonly regarded as a mouthpiece for Plato's own views: see e.g. M. Frede (1996), Rowe (1995a), (1996).

[36] Cf. Scott and Welton (2000), and Prior (2006) 147–8 on *Symposium*.

(for instance, the discussion of Forms in *Parmenides*, the idea that virtue is knowledge in *Meno* and *Laches*); and there are plenty of occasions when a discussion leader uses weak or flawed arguments, knowingly as well as unknowingly. As I argue later, moreover, the dialogues deny us secure access to any knowledge the discussion leaders may possess, leaving us to reconstruct it for ourselves. This is not to say that the dialogues deconstruct the wisdom of their discussion leaders; but it encourages us to regard knowledge and the knowledgeable man as ideals that lie beyond the dialogues themselves.

These rough edges to the dialogues' potential role models prevent us, I think, from identifying with them too readily, just as they discourage us from rejecting an Euthyphro or even a Thrasymachus out of hand. None of Plato's characters, that is, is one we should imitate ourselves—even thinkingly: they are too complex and imperfect for that. Instead, we have to evaluate each character's traits, beliefs, and actions on their own merit, and look beyond them in constructing our own ideals of philosophical progress and attainment.[37] If we do ultimately come back to the idea that Socrates (or another discussion leader) represents that ideal, we will have done so by looking beyond him, rather than automatically treating him as an ideal. Of course, this is to make us work rather harder than even Blondell envisages: for in doing this, the dialogues deny us an easy interpretative perspective, prompting us instead to be critically independent and self-conscious about the direction in which we are developing as learners. But despite their slightly ambiguous role, this is not to say that Plato's characters do not function as models *at all*. As I have already suggested, they help us to understand what philosophical progress involves, and, by mirroring our own progress, they help us to analyse and improve upon it. Here, as I tried to bring out in chapter 2, the role of the less philosophically advanced interlocutors—the 'bad characters'—is as important as any. If we write them off as negative paradigms, then we ignore the extent to which the dialogues ask us to see ourselves as going through a similar process to them, and the amount we can learn from that recognition.

[37] Cf. Arieti (1993), Tarrant (2000a) 79–80, Kosman (1987). See also Hobbs (2000) 220–49, who thinks that *Republic* raises questions about the desirability of *any* human role model; cf. also Notomi (1999) 284–6. This fits well with the doubts raised in the dialogues about the possibility of human virtue and wisdom, as well as the contrast between the visible and intelligible worlds.

4.4. CHARACTER, REFLECTION, AND CONSTRUCTION

Equally important is the *mode* in which we are encouraged to respond to characters. For there are various reasons for doubting whether, as the mimetic pedagogy view suggests, the dialogues encourage us to engage with positive role models—especially Socrates—through emotional identification. My point is not, as I shall explain, that the dialogues discourage us from thinking about the inner aspects of a person's character—their emotions and unspoken feelings. We do build up a rich picture of certain characters' inner selves, and I do not wish to suggest that the dialogues aim to prevent us doing this—even were this possible. But they do encourage us to relate to characters' inner lives *reflectively*, with careful, insightful thought and perception, and a consciousness of our own independent perspective. We are not encouraged to internalize a character's emotions and assimilate ourselves to him, in a manner appropriate to a personality response, or to get inside his mind and feel as he does, thereby learning to become like him. The emphasis is on self-consciousness, distance, and critical evaluation, and we are constantly asked to question how much we really know about a character.

To begin with, the dialogues draw attention to the activity of *interpreting* character. This is an issue highlighted in Alcibiades' speech in *Symposium*, with which we started the chapter; and the dialogues frequently present us with characters offering readings—or attempted readings—of Socrates' character. On hearing that Meletus is charging Socrates with innovation in religion, Euthyphro offers his own view of what underlies the charge: Socrates' *daimonion*. In *Gorgias*, Callicles offers his analysis of Socrates' life and the practice of philosophizing: a childish pastime that will leave him unable to defend himself in the real world. At the close of *Euthydemus*, Crito reports an unnamed acquaintance's unfavourable view of Socrates' willingness to engage in debate with Euthydemus and Dionysodorus. Examples could be multiplied.[38] The frequency with which we see

[38] The motif of judgement or evaluation is common in the introductions to conversations, with a similar effect: e.g. Socrates' warning to Hippocrates at the start of *Protagoras*; the court-case scenarios of *Euthyphro* and *Apology*; the choice of lives which introduces discussion in *Republic* II and *Philebus*. For further discussion, see ch.1.

Socrates being evaluated heightens our awareness of our own interpretative activity. More particularly, such passages make us think harder about a range of specific interpretations, to which we may be attracted, while at the same time hinting, through context, at their deficiencies. By watching others fail, we become more determined to reach an adequate reading of his character—or perhaps suspicious of assuming we will be able to do so.[39]

Nor is this problem confined to our interpretation of Socrates, as is effectively illustrated by his own account of how Thrasymachus, in the first book of *Republic*, becomes frustrated at the course of the discussion between Socrates and Polemarchus and bursts aggressively in upon the conversation:

> *And Thrasymachus, even while we were conversing, had often started to lay hold of our discussion, then was prevented by those sitting nearby who wanted to hear the discussion to the end. But when we came to a pause as I said these things, he could no longer hold his peace, but having gathered himself up like a wild beast he launched himself upon us as though he was going to tear us to pieces. And I and Polemarchus, taking fright, were panic stricken. And he, after uttering a sound into the midst of the company, said, 'What nonsense has been gripping you both, Socrates? And why do you play the fool, giving way to each other? But if you really want to know what justice is, do not only ask questions and pride yourself in providing a refutation whenever anyone makes an answer, understanding this, that it is easier to ask than to answer—but you yourself answer and tell us what you say justice is. And don't say that that it is the advantageous, nor that it is the profitable, nor that it is the beneficial, but tell me clearly and accurately what you mean. For I will not accept it if you speak such nonsense.' And I, after hearing this, was frightened out of my senses, and looking at him I was afraid, and I think that if I had not looked at him before he looked at me, I would have become speechless.*
>
> *Republic*, 336b1–d7

Here, in a rare comment as narrator, Socrates evokes the context for Thrasymachus' outburst, telling us that Thrasymachus had to be restrained by other listeners while he and Polemarchus were speaking,

[39] Cf. Clay (2000) 61–2, who suggests that we are provided with a range of paradigms—silenus, satyr, midwife—to help us make sense of Socrates. However, just as in *Republic* Socrates offers us an image of the Form of the Good rather than a description of the thing itself, these paradigms also conceal the real nature of Socrates; and they raise further interpretative problems in themselves: are the images accurate, what do they convey, are they compatible with one another? Cf. Clay (2000) 73.

likening him to a wild beast, and suggesting the noise and movement that accompany Thrasymachus' interjection. Similarly, Socrates follows Thrasymachus' words with a hyperbolic description of his own terror, implying that Thrasymachus' violence threatens the continuation of social and dialectical discourse. Faced with this heavily negative presentation, one option, of course, is to regard it as Plato's way of marking out Thrasymachus as a 'bad character', and forestalling a sympathetic response in us.[40] But the starkness of the portrayal, Socrates' use of colourful imagery, and the rarity of this level of descriptive background for what a character says all raise doubts: is it a faithful representation, or is Socrates exercising his power as narrator?[41]

By drawing attention to the activities of interpretation and representation, Plato adds self-consciousness and a critical edge to our engagement with characters. He signals that relating to characters is no more straightforward in literature than in everyday life, and warns us to be wary of accepting others' assessments of them, or indeed of imagining we understand them ourselves. In doing so, he opens up a further and more fundamental issue, which challenges the mimetic pedagogy view at a deeper level—which is the degree of *insight* into character the dialogues actually allow us. It is quite possible for us to respond positively or negatively to a character with very little depth of understanding of them. But for us to be able to *identify* with someone, to feel as they feel, to understand what makes them the person they are, and to assimilate ourselves to them, we do need a certain degree of insight into them. And this is something the dialogues ask us to question whether we do in fact have.

To begin with, the reliability of a person's words as an indicator of their more private thoughts and feelings is constantly flagged as a concern. It emerges in Socrates' insistence that interlocutors should say what they believe; and certain dialogues, most notably *Gorgias*, explore the pressures—shame, fear, reputation, for example—that may prevent someone doing so.[42] It is also bound up with a feature

[40] Cf. Beversluis (2000) 222–3. On Socrates' use of his role as narrator to distance us from other characters, see Blondell (2002) 43–4.

[41] Cf. Morgan (2004) 362, 364 and Blondell (2000) 138–9 who argues that, by having Glaucon and Adeimantus restate Thrasymachus' position in book 2, Plato is criticizing both Socrates' dialectical tactics and Plato's own prejudicial literary techniques in representing them. On narration complicating the interpretation of character, see also Prior (2006) esp. 140–1, Rutherford (2002) 250–1.

[42] See references in ch.3 n28 and n29.

peculiar to Socrates' character: his ironical stance. Socrates' irony[43] has a variety of implications for our interpretation of the dialogues, and has been the subject of a huge amount of scholarly activity, to which I cannot hope to do justice here. I wish to draw attention to just one of its facets: its role in concealing Socrates' character and preventing us from gaining genuine insight into his thoughts and feelings.[44]

On one line of interpretation, of which Vlastos is a key representative,[45] Socrates' irony does not—or need not—conceal him from us. For his words, though they cannot be taken at face value, nevertheless point towards a deeper meaning. In cases of simple irony, the speaker's words intend to convey the opposite of what he says. In cases of complex irony, the speaker both means and does not mean what he says in different senses. For example, in disclaiming knowledge, Socrates means both that he does not have knowledge (of an infallible and certain kind) and also that he does have knowledge (of an elenctic kind). On this type of reading, Socrates' irony may deceive his interlocutors, but it does not deceive us; it is therefore a powerful mechanism for forging a bond between the reader and Socrates, who, in Vlastos' view, is the main repository of wisdom in the dialogues.[46] However, in a stimulating study, Alexander Nehamas has challenged this interpretation, suggesting that in fact Socrates' irony does serve to conceal his meaning from us.[47] Ironic utterances, he argues, need not point to a different, but definite meaning (the opposite of what was

[43] On Socrates' irony, I have found the following helpful: Vlastos (1991) 21–44, Nehamas (1998), Sedley (2002), Vasiliou (1999), Prior (2006), Mackenzie (1988b) 21, Lane (2006), Booth (1974) 269–77, Sayre (1995) 52–9, Gordon (1999) 117–33, Rutherford (1995) 77–8, Reynolds (1988) 14–20, Clay (2000) 93–9. Much of the debate focuses on Socrates' disavowal of knowledge; however, there are different sorts of irony at work in different contexts, and there is no need to try to reach a single interpretation of all of Socrates' ironic utterances. Lane (2006), Vasiliou (1999), and Sayre (1995) 52 stress the disjunction between Socratic *eironeia*, and the concept of Socratic irony that has developed in modern criticism; cf. also Sedley (2002) 40–1. Like most interpreters, I shall continue to refer to Socrates' 'irony', though without prejudging the issue of what that involves.

[44] Plato's treatment of these concerns intersects with debate in epistemology and the philosophy of mind about the transparency of our mental states and our knowledge of other minds; see e.g. Cassam (1994), Williamson (2000).

[45] Vlastos (1991) 21–44, (1994) 39–66. Cf. Reynolds (1988) (who regards Socrates' ironies, in the terminology of Booth (1974), as 'stable') and Sedley (2002).

[46] Cf. also Reynolds (1988) 16.

[47] Nehamas (1998). For the importance of irony in concealing Socrates, see also Prior (2006) 140–1, Morgan (2004) 362–3, Clay (2000) 75–6, Ausland (2000) 185. For

said, for instance); they may in fact simply hide meaning, leaving it unclear what (if anything) lies beyond the utterance. Socrates' irony, he suggests, makes him a silent and ambiguous presence, whose character we have to construct for ourselves.[48] And if this is the case, then it raises the question of how much insight into Socrates' character we actually have. If we are unsure, at crucial points, if he means what he says, or if the feelings he claims to have are genuine, then to what extent can we really identify with him as a character?

I would not necessarily want to suggest, following Nehamas, that Socrates' irony may conceal an *absence* of meaning, so that there is no thought or feeling behind his utterances—just silence. But I do think, unlike Vlastos, that Socrates' irony, at times at least, conceals any definite meaning from us, not just from his interlocutors.[49] Ironic utterances suggest that Socrates means something different from what he says, but they do not give us secure access to it. We can, of course, put together interpretations of what Socrates' ironic words mean; but the point is that the text does not validate those interpretations. The very fact that so many of the dialogues' characters misinterpret Socrates should make us cautious about assuming that we possess the insight they lack.[50] Indeed, it often *does* seem unclear exactly how to interpret what Socrates says—for instance, his report of Meletus' charges against him in *Euthyphro*, a passage usually regarded as a clear instance of irony.[51]

Lane (2006) and Vasiliou (1999), *eironeia* aims to conceal by feigning rather than to convey what is not said (though, for Vasiliou, conditional irony, which his main focus, is understood by the audience, if not the interlocutor). See also Prior (2006) 159 on irony as shamming in *Symposium*. Vlastos (1991) and (1994) stresses the importance of *interpretation* in understanding Socrates' ironic utterances: his hearers have to work out his meaning for themselves.

[48] Nehamas' portrait is based primarily on the 'early' dialogues. In his view, the constructive content of the 'middle' works represents Plato's attempt to explain and give substance to Socrates' ambiguous character; cf. also Long (1998). I, however, would see the ambiguity and silence of Socrates as persisting throughout the dialogues: as I argue later, the irony of the 'early' Socrates becomes the opacity and reticence of 'later' discussion leaders. Sedley (2002) 43–4 links the decrease in irony in 'later' dialogues with the increasing philosophical maturity of interlocutors—an idea that fits my approach well.

[49] For a similar contrast between sceptical and non-doctrinal interpretations of the dialogues, see ch.1 section 1.2.

[50] Nehamas (1998) esp. 32, 40–4.

[51] E.g. Emlyn-Jones (1991) 47, 50–2, Versényi (1982) 30–1, Reynolds (1988) 34. Cf. also Adam (1890) vii.

> *What sort [of action]? Not a trivial one, it seems to me; for the fact that, whilst young, he has recognised such a great matter is no small thing. For that man, so he says, knows in what manner the young are corrupted and the people who corrupt them. He's no doubt a wise person; and, observing my ignorance, he is coming to denounce me to the city, as to his mother, on the grounds that I am corrupting his contemporaries. And it seems to me that he is the only one of our politicians who is beginning the right way; for it is right to care first for the young, so that they may be excellent, just as a good farmer is likely to care first for the young plants, and afterwards for the others. And so Meletus, perhaps, is first clearing out us who corrupt the young plants, as he says. Then after this, it is clear that he will attend to the older men, and will become responsible for bringing very many of the greatest goods to the city—at least that would be the natural result for a person beginning in such a way.*
>
> *Euthyphro*, 2c2–3a5

Here, Socrates extols Meletus' actions, saying that he is wise, that the matter is a worthy and important one, and that his course of action ought to bring great goods to the state. Socrates' words here have been taken to imply the opposite of what he says[52]—a verdict on Meletus that is voiced by Euthyphro in his reply to Socrates just after this. Yet the passage is not so straightforward. Much of what Socrates says *can* be taken at face value—the significance of the issue Meletus is addressing, the primary importance of caring for the young, the value of identifying those with corrupting influence and exposing their ignorance.[53] And we might have fleeting doubts, too, about where Socrates stands in relation to the charges levelled. After all, the dialogues do apparently show him frequently failing to reform his interlocutors, and concerns about the potential of Socratic dialectic to help and improve its practitioners—including the young—are voiced by him and others. Shortly afterwards, when Socrates touches on the charge of inventing new gods, he calls it strange 'on first hearing' (ὥς οὕτω γ' ἀκοῦσαι 3b1)—and the dialogue does give us grounds for thinking of Socrates as an inventor of new gods, even if not in the ways Meletus or Euthyphro envisage.[54] These different potential resonances of Socrates' words make them hard to evaluate. It is

[52] Emlyn-Jones (1991) 51–2.
[53] Cf. Versényi (1982) 31, Reynolds (1988) 34. The passage bears resemblance to conditional irony, as discussed by Vasiliou (1999).
[54] Cf. Burnyeat (1997b).

difficult to know what exactly he thinks of Meletus and his charges, and of how he stands in relation to them. And this is perhaps the point: for it leaves us to face this most difficult question for ourselves.[55]

Another striking feature of this passage is that Plato gives us very little depth of insight into what Socrates might feel about his indictment. Does he feel angry? Betrayed? Afraid? Bitter? Baffled? Or is his response quite different? The conversation moves swiftly on to Euthyphro's prosecution of his father, where the same is true. Here, we are offered a few hints as to the emotional context to the situation—Euthyphro is aware that his relatives think him mad (μαίνεσθαι 4a1) and are angry with him (ἀγανακτεῖ 4d5), and he dismisses their and Socrates' reactions as based on ignorance of divine matters (4b7–c1, 4e1–3)—but these offer only oblique insight into Euthyphro's feelings. Without stopping to explore this dimension of Euthyphro's response, Socrates uses it to springboard into a more abstract discussion of piety. In fact the dialogues, more generally, contain relatively few[56] sustained passages devoted to evoking a character's subjective viewpoint, their first-personal perceptions and responses, and in particular their emotions, of the sort I associated earlier with a *personality* viewpoint—whether in relation to events in their lives, or the course of the discussion itself. Such material is far outweighed by the time dedicated to discussion of beliefs and ideas in abstract.[57] This is, of course, connected with the nature of the genre: as philosophical works, we should expect the dialogues to focus on abstract discussion, not the inner selves of the participants. But if this is so, it poses problems for Blondell's account. For, on her view, it is

[55] On the importance of irony in stimulating thought, see also Reynolds (1988) 14, 19–20, Sedley (2002) esp. 41, 51; also Gordon (1999) 117–33, with a different interpretation of how it does so.

[56] *Pace* Morgan (2004) 363–4. Cf. Nightingale (2002a) 233, Rutherford (2002) 250–1.

[57] Cf. M. Frede (1992a), Blondell (2002) 38. The dialogue form *could*, had Plato so chosen, have accommodated more of such material. Not only could actions external to the conversation—like Socrates' indictment by Meletus—have been treated differently, but we could be been given a more revealing view of characters' participation in discussion. E.g. in narrated works, we could have been offered more commentary of the sort Socrates offers on Thrasymachus at *R.*336b ff. and 350cd; and characters could have expressed more feelings at each step of the argument. Similarly, the works could have included asides and even monologues, for example at the end of a work when one participant is left alone. For the importance of features such as monologues and laments as fostering a personality response in tragedy, see Gill (1990) 30.

by responding to this kind of subjective insight into characters that we identify with them and assimilate ourselves to them. And so, if insight of this kind is in fact rare, it calls her model into question: the inner aspects of a person are simply not presented, in a direct way, for us to identify with. This is not to say, of course, that we do not read emotions and feelings into a character's expressions of belief; we are naturally inclined to do this.[58] But the absence of direct treatments of the affective dimensions of character steers us away from potentially unreflective emotional identification and assimilation, towards a more thoughtful and distanced reconstruction of a character's emotional life.[59]

Having said that, the dialogues do of course contain moments of subjective and immediate insight into character, and these number among their most vivid and memorable passages. Think, for example, of Thrasymachus' blush at the refutation of his argument in *Republic* I, of Phaedo's evocation of Socrates facing death in *Phaedo*, of Socrates' desire on seeing inside Charmides' cloak, of his recantation after his first speech in *Phaedrus*, or of Theaetetus' 'labour pains' when wrestling with the problem Socrates has posed him in *Theaetetus*. Many of these moments represent significant points in the interlocutors' process of learning, in the way illustrated in chapter 3. But they are also crucial for our understanding of and engagement with characters, offering us tantalizing glimpses into their more immediate thoughts and inner feelings which contrast with and complement what we learn about their beliefs in abstract debate. This might seem to undercut my argument—but before drawing that conclusion, let us look more closely.

First, the relative rarity of these moments is crucial to their effect. They are not sustained or frequent enough to allow us a true sense of inwardness with a character, such that we can understand what they

[58] For the idea that our perception of people under mental descriptions (such as 'angry', 'sullen', 'withdrawn') is immediate, see Malcolm (1971) 91–103. Though he is talking mainly about physical descriptions of human behaviour, similar issues apply here.

[59] I am not intending to imply that Plato fosters a purely intellectual response to characters, or that he endorses a clear-cut distinction between the intellect and emotions. As I explained in Part I, the inseparability of the cognitive and affective elements in our response to the dialogues is central to my account. For the affective dimension in our response to characters, see sections 4.5–4.6. My point is that by privileging expressions of belief rather than expressions of emotion in their *presentation* of characters, the dialogues steer us away from an unreflectively affective response of the sort Plato associates with poetry.

are feeling and experiencing. But by intruding, suddenly and strikingly, into the argument-focused texture of the dialogues, they act as a catalyst to the reader's engagement with characters, and they indicate that thinking about the inner psychological state of characters is appropriate and helpful for understanding both their philosophical outlook and their progression in learning. But in themselves, brief and rare as they are, they do not provide that fuller and deeper picture; they leave us to reflect on it and construct it for ourselves. We are not, therefore, steered away from thinking about—or recognizing the importance of—the inner dimensions of character, as we are naturally inclined to do. The moments of insight in fact act as triggers in getting us to reflect on these. However, they do not foster the closeness and emotional inwardness important for identification.

Second, these moments do not always give us as much insight as we initially think. Much has been made, for example, of Socrates' description of Thrasymachus blushing at *Republic* 350d3. But very little elaboration of what the blush signifies, or what Thrasymachus is feeling, is added. It is usually assumed to indicate shame,[60] but even this leaves a great deal open, perhaps most significantly about the *cause* of the shame (being defeated in argument? Having let himself down in argument? Being shown to hold a mistaken view?): Socrates simply does not tell us. Similarly, Phaedo's depiction of Socrates facing death brings us back to the problems of the interpretation of character raised by Alcibiades' speech; and Socrates' recantation in *Phaedrus* is complicated by issues of irony and playfulness.

Third, the dialogues ask us to look beyond such moments in reaching a deeper and more reflective understanding of characters. Consider, for example, Euthyphro's expression of confusion and frustration at the course of his discussion with Socrates:

> *Euthyphro: But Socrates, I don't know how to express to you what I mean. For whatever we put forward always somehow moves around and refuses to stay where we put it.*
>
> *Socrates: Your statements, Euthyphro, are like the works of my ancestor Daedalus; and if I'd said them and set them down, perhaps you would have laughed at me, on the grounds that due to my relationship with him, the works I make in words run away and refuse to stay where one puts*

[60] Blondell (2002) 182, Annas (1981) 52; cf. Rutherford (1995) 124 n7 ('embarrassment and vexation now that his argument has been overturned').

them. But now—the propositions are yours; so we need another joke. For they refuse to stay still for you, as you yourself see.

Euthyphro: It seems to me, Socrates, that the statements require pretty much this very joke. For I am not the one who is making these statements move around and not stay in the same place, but you seem to me to be the Daedalus; because, as far as I am concerned, they would have stayed as they were.

Euthyphro, 11b6–d2

Euthyphro is unable to say what he means, he complains, because the statements that he and Socrates make keep moving around. This passage follows the carried–carrying argument, the most complex in the dialogue yet, and for all Euthyphro's failings, this is a point at which many readers appreciate his feelings. In reply, Socrates compares their words to the moving statues of Daedalus, and questions which of the two of them (Socrates or Euthyphro) is responsible for moving their statements around. Euthyphro's implication, as he spells out in his rejoinder, is that Socrates was to blame, while Socrates maintains that the statues are Euthyphro's and that he therefore is responsible. As is well recognized, this passage raises interesting questions about the ownership of arguments.[61] But it also makes us think harder, and more analytically, about the feelings Euthyphro has expressed. What *has* caused Euthyphro's feelings? What exactly happened to his beliefs in debate, and to what extent is he responsible? Moreover, there is an implied criticism in what Socrates says. If, as Socrates suggests, Euthyphro is responsible for his statements moving, then, rather than blaming someone else, he should seek to reformulate them so that they stay still. As Socrates goes on to say, Euthyphro is shy of hard work (τρυφᾶν 11e2) and does not want to make progress. And this prompts us to think about how valuable and useful Euthyphro's response is, and what a more productive reaction might be. By juxtaposing Euthyphro's expression of his feelings with Socrates' analysis and criticism, therefore, Plato *contextualizes* the insight we are given into Euthyphro's feelings. Contextualization of this sort is a common pattern in the dialogues,[62] and a powerful mechanism for preventing us from accepting what a character says

[61] See Frede (1992a) and, on this passage in particular, McPherran (2003).

[62] Other striking examples include Socrates' responses to Meno's *aporia* at *M.*80d ff., to Theaetetus' expression of discomfort at *Tht.*148e ff., to the grief of his companions at *Phd.*117ce, and to Alcibiades' speech, considered at the start of the chapter. A similar

at face value, even adopting their perspective ourselves. Instead, Plato's approach encourages us to dissect and understand the feelings of the characters before us, thereby prompting us to deeper and more sustained reflection.

So much for moments of subjective insight: rare and elliptical, they are handled in a way that encourages us to be reflective and critical, and most of the time we are confronted with discussion of a character's beliefs instead. This is by no means to deprive us of material that reveals character; on the contrary, beliefs are central to the ethical dispositions which, in Greek thinking, are closely bound up with a person's character and give rise to his actions.[63] So an interlocutor's contributions to discussion often reveal his deepest intuitions and tendencies, the underlying beliefs and values that are central to him as a person—whether or not they are acknowledged in what he usually says and does, or are even compatible with his other beliefs. And as the responses of readers amply illustrate, we are inclined to view them as indicators of an interlocutor's inner feelings. But it does prompt us to think about what makes interlocutors the people they are, and what is central to them as individuals, from the standpoint of the *beliefs* they express, rather than their more immediate psychological state, and to understand the principles of a viewpoint which gives rise to a certain sort of life, rather than to empathize with a specific action or experience. In short, our mode of engaging with characters is based on belief and understanding, not identification and emotional inwardness—and this is at odds with Blondell's picture of imitation through emotional identification.

Even here, moreover, the dialogues ensure that our response is as reflective as possible. For just as the dialogues frequently deny us a full, satisfying, or easy understanding of characters' feelings—they do the same for their beliefs. Sometimes, as with Socrates' views about piety in *Euthyphro*, we are only offered tantalizing hints.[64] Sometimes

pattern can inform the structure of an entire dialogue or section; e.g. in *Phaedo*, the portraits of Socrates' state of mind as he faces death, which open and close the work, sandwich a lengthy and detailed explanation of his beliefs about death and the soul: this stimulates us to understand what lies beneath his extraordinary composure at death, and prevents us from simply accepting Phaedo's evocation of Socrates at a superficial level, or resting content with admiring and emulating him.

[63] Halliwell (1990).

[64] As the diverse attempts of critics to extract them illustrate: e.g. Taylor (1982), McPherran (1985).

it may be unclear exactly what a belief entails, as with his claim that virtue is knowledge, for instance. His ironic tone sometimes makes it unclear whether he means what he says; on other occasions, we may suspect him of introducing an idea or argument for pedagogical purposes, without believing it himself.[65] Such observations are often treated as points about the handling of doctrine—in chapter 1, I adduced similar points to support a non-doctrinal interpretation.[66] But these observations are also points about character; for when the dialogues leave it unclear what exactly a figure believes, they deny us a full and satisfying understanding of an important aspect of his character. Of course, we can attempt to iron out ambiguity, fill in gaps, and draw together disparate ideas—but the point is that we have to carry out this process for ourselves, self-consciously and reflectively. We cannot just adopt what Socrates thinks, because it is not there ready for us, and we have to *construct* it for ourselves[67]—just as we have to construct a picture of his subjective viewpoint and of how the two fit together. Again, this has an important bearing on the mimetic pedagogy approach. For if in this area too, character is only partially evoked, and we are left to do much of the interpretative work for ourselves, the idea that we learn by imitating positive role models is even less convincing.

4.5. THE CHALLENGE OF CHARACTER: A FUNCTIONAL VIEW

It is time to consider afresh the function of characterization within the dialogues. If, as I have argued, it is not designed to guide our response and shape us through imitation, then what role *does* it play?

[65] For a persuasive interpretation of *Meno* along these lines, see Weiss (2001).

[66] Ch.1 section 1.2.

[67] Of course, the receiver's input in constructing character and meaning is important in all works: see discussion in ch.2; also Easterling (1990) on tragedy. This type of construction is compatible with identification—indeed it may be part of the way identification is achieved. However, Plato, I think, requires a stronger sort of construction, which tends to exclude identification—as has been the thrust of my argument in this section. The dialogues ensure that we cannot make sense of characters properly without a degree of effort, and they go out of their way to underscore our interpretative role, making the process a conscious and reflective one. For some texts as requiring a higher degree of input from the reader than others, see ch.2 section 2.2.

In my view, character is one means Plato uses to foster in the reader an involved and committed, yet reflective response of a cognitive-affective sort. By framing his exploration of philosophical issues as conversations between characters, Plato avoids the abstract and impersonal quality that can belong to a treatise. But by handling character as he does, he prevents the kind of affectively weighted involvement, the surrendering of our individual perspective and of our full analytical engagement, that he associates with genres such as epic and tragedy. In doing so, he mediates the parallel dangers of over-engagement and under-engagement which, as discussed in chapter 2, are particularly pronounced in the case of engagement with a written text; this involves a careful balance.

On the one hand, Plato's characterization draws on the intrinsic and immediate appeal of the presentation of persons. We naturally respond to characters in a way we do not when presented with abstract ideas. They engage our interest and our imagination, inviting us to imagine an inner life lying beneath the exterior we see. As complete persons, with beliefs, desires, emotions, and ideas, they call forth a response from us as whole persons too, not just as embodied intellects. This is closely connected with a second impulse, our desire to understand and make sense of characters. When we meet people in everyday life, however fleetingly, we automatically make some sort of assessment of what they are like, what makes them tick as a person. If only subconsciously, we try to draw together and make sense of the different information we have about them. And the same is true of characters in literature: we have an instinctive desire to understand them and to see them as coherent wholes, and the dialogues magnify this natural tendency by emphasizing the importance of coherence, both for persons and ideas.[68] Together, these two

[68] The coherence of a set of ideas is closely bound up with its truth, as is made clear by the workings of the *elenchus* in the 'early' dialogues, which demonstrates that an interlocutor is ignorant by drawing out contradictions in his ideas, or between his ideas and his actions. Conversely Socrates is presented as someone who, although not *knowing*, has done his best to unify his ideas (see e.g. *Ap.*21b ff., *Grg.*486d–488b). The link remains important in 'later' dialogues too: e.g. *R.*398c, *Sph.*241de. On the importance of order and coherence in the dialogues' conception of knowledge, see esp. Burnyeat (1980b), Fine (1979) and (1990) 109 ff. Moreover, internal order or coherence is presented as the proper and happy state of a person: see especially *Grg.*504a ff., *R.*500b ff., *Chrm.*159b (though cf. Cooper (1999b) for a different interpretation). Conversely, the vicious and ignorant are often presented as riven by internal dissent because of the contradictions within their belief patterns (Callicles

impulses act as a stimulus to the reader: they draw us in and invite us to engage actively and imaginatively with characters.

But simultaneously, as I have been arguing, the dialogues deny us a full or easy understanding of characters—and here lies the real dynamism of Plato's handling of character. The information provided is partial; we are encouraged to be reflective and critical in evaluating it; yet there is no guarantee that we will be able to reach a coherent interpretation of any given character—this is part of the challenge.[69] In this way, the dialogues generate impulses in the reader which they then frustrate, and set us puzzles which they do not allow us to solve fully.[70] Our engagement has the affective commitment evoked by the presentation of persons, but also the reflective and critical edge fostered by Plato's particular handling of character. Invitation is balanced by refusal, providing the combination of desire and discomfort which, we saw in chapter 3, is essential in motivating us to learn. We want to reach more satisfying interpretations of participants' characters and make firmer judgements upon them than the dialogues themselves seem to allow. And in doing so we are in fact going beyond the confines of the text, engaging in an independent process of reflection that is prompted by, though not fully constrained by, the texts.

In trying to capture this effect, I find it helpful to think of character in a *functional* capacity. On my reading, Plato is using character *for the sake of* evoking a productive response in the reader, and this is what determines his approach. This does not imply a lack of attention to characterization, since characters can only engage us if they are effectively evoked—thus the compelling idiosyncrasy of Socrates and others, the attention to detail and setting, the range of personas portrayed. But ultimately, it is the reader's philosophical response,

and the souls of the dead at *Grg.*481c–482c, 524b–525a, the unjust man at *R.*586e–592b; also the descriptions of the different defective persons/constitutions in *Republic* VIII, especially 554de). Because of the emphasis placed on it, coherence also becomes crucial for our evaluation of persons and their views: to the extent that persons cannot be understood as coherent, they are inadequate and undesirable. This ground for judgement takes us beyond initial likeability or similarity to ourselves, and becomes the most important basis for our response to character.

[69] In presenting potentially disunified characters, Plato is unusual: see Pelling (1990b) 235–40 on the ancient tendency towards unified or integrated portraits of character.

[70] Cf. Stauffer (2006) 1–2.

not the portrait itself, which matters. This perhaps, to us, sounds too calculated—we may be inclined to imagine Plato lovingly capturing memories of his master, while also extending his work. But in fact the idea is not so unfamiliar to the ancient mind: in discussing the components of tragedy, Aristotle famously claims that tragedians use character *for the sake of* plot or action, the ultimate end or purpose of tragedy.[71] As such, character is crucial to a play's effect upon us: it must be sufficiently plausible to drive the events of the plot and to generate the emotional involvement aroused by it. But its handling is governed by the overall effect at which the plot aims. The underlying thought here—that character needs to be constructed in such a way as to generate a certain sort of response—is similar to the one I am attributing to the dialogues; it is the specific end, or audience response, to which characterization is put that differs. However, given Plato's distinctive views about what constitutes a productive type of engagement, as explored in Part I, this should come as no surprise. As we shall see in other areas too, Plato is adapting standard techniques for shaping the receiver's response to achieve his own particular effects.

4.6. SOCRATES: A DOMINANT CHARACTER

So much for character in general—what about the prominence of Socrates? I have been emphasizing the reader's interpretative input and critical independence; but we need to balance this against Socrates' overwhelming dominance within the dialogues.[72] He is the only character to appear in so many dialogues; his views are frequently given more space and treated with more respect than those of other characters; he is personally and physically idiosyncratic, and in some respects portrayed in heroic terms. Most readers are drawn to him more than any other character. It may be, as I have emphasized, that he is far from being an unequivocally positive model; nor can we always be sure that we know what he stands for and believes. But if his dominance is not designed to guide the reader's response, how *should* we account for it?

[71] *Poetics* 1450a.
[72] For Socrates as the dialogues' 'dominant character', see Blondell (2002) 42–3.

Here, too, the functional approach offers an alternative. The approach has special relevance to Socrates, because he illustrates the two effects of invitation and refusal in a particularly extreme manner: he is both the most captivating of the dialogues' characters and also, because of his unlikeness to other people—his *atopia*[73]—the hardest to understand and identify with. His whole way of life—his poverty, his single-minded pursuit of philosophy, his way of dressing—marks him out as different from others, as more than one interlocutor scornfully alleges. His views—that we should all look forward to dying, that being tortured is better than torturing, to take just a couple of examples—are frequently counterintuitive; and, as I commented earlier, they are often expressed in ways that seem intentionally provocative and opaque. Our occasional glimpses into his subjective perspective reveal his feelings to be different from those we might expect—as Phaedo comments of the way he faces death, for example, Crito of his refusal to escape death by fleeing Athens, and Alcibiades of his response to his overtures. All this is encapsulated in his odd and off-putting satyr-like appearance, which, conflicting as it does with his pure and restrained way of life, is a further puzzle and paradox.[74]

These two elements in the portrayal of Socrates work well together. The ultimate denial of insight prevents us from thinking we can get too close to this dominant character, straightforwardly treating him as a role model or adopting his views as our own. It ensures that our engagement with him is energetic and reflective, and means we are given no sure guidance as to what we should think.[75] Yet his appeal is needed if the reader is to be drawn into engaging with a perspective that might otherwise appear unappealing, outlandish, or unimportant. Socrates' centrality does not guarantee that his views are correct, but it underscores the importance of his perspective and ensures that it is the one with which we engage in the most extensive dialogue. The result is a fine balance between freedom and control, guidance and

[73] For Socrates' *atopia*, see Clay (2000) 61–2, Vlastos (1991) 1–4, Roochnik (1995) 50–1. Cf. also Blondell (2002) 73, 106–7, Michelini (2003b) 45. On Socrates' *atopia* as an enigma which forces us to look more closely, to see if we can bring him into focus, see Nightingale (2002a).

[74] See Zanker (1995) 34–9.

[75] Chatman (1986) draws the useful distinction between character as focus of interest and as focalizer: Socrates is the focus of interest in many dialogues, but this does not require that we see things from his point of view. Cf. the conception of Socrates as Plato's 'favoured character' in Wolfsdorf (2004).

personal responsibility, which means that any views we reach as a consequence of engaging with Socrates are not adopted from him, but rather developed by us through the reflective activity generated by him. For as I suggested in chapters 1 and 2, even if we do eventually adopt the viewpoint we take to be Socrates', we have in doing so developed our own, because no two interpretations of what he says are exactly the same. We do not learn *from* Socrates, therefore, but by *interacting with* him, and he acts as a stimulus for us in developing our own independent perspective. As we shall see, Socrates' effect on us is, in this regard, a microcosm of the effect of reading a dialogue—or indeed the corpus as a whole.[76]

4.7. CHARACTERIZATION AND THE EXPERIENCE OF READING

In this section, I would like to develop a further aspect of the dialogues' functional handling of character, which relates not so much to the *content* of Plato's portrayals as to the presentation or *placing* of information in the text. Consider, for instance, the way information about Socrates' beliefs is presented in *Euthyphro.* It is not grouped together into a neat, comprehensible package, but split up and offered piecemeal throughout the work. At 4b4–6 Socrates implies that he thinks Euthyphro is wrong to prosecute his father; at 6a7–9 he declares that he thinks the traditional stories about the gods are wrong; at 8c7–e2 that no one would (rightly) maintain that a wrongdoer should not pay the penalty; at 9c1–9 that if Euthyphro were to prove that his father acted wrongfully, it would not bring them any nearer a definition; at 14c1–3, that had Euthyphro said what the gods accomplish through their work, they would have understood about piety. These expressions form a series of clues that allow us to construct an increasingly complex—if radically incomplete—picture of Socrates' views in this area, and therefore of one aspect of his character. But as they stand, they are isolated 'islands' of opinion which we have to draw together for ourselves. Their piecemeal release makes the process both more extended and

[76] Michelini (2003b) on Socrates as a paradigm for our interpretation of the dialogues.

more demanding, since as each new belief emerges, it changes our view of the whole. And the same applies, more generally, to everything the dialogue tells us about Socrates—his relationship with Euthyphro, his responses during the conversation, his approach to discussion.[77]

This takes us back to an issue I raised in chapter 2: the importance of our *aesthetic* response to a text, or the impact it has on us as we read through it. The piecemeal release of information about character is crucial in ensuring a reflective and engaged response in the reader: we cannot rely on a picture presented at the beginning, but have to remain alert until the close of the work; and we are constantly asked to look backwards and forwards through the text in reaching a satisfying union of the different information presented. Yet in discussing Plato's handling of characterization, interpreters rarely pay much attention to this. Much more common is a non-aesthetic approach, focusing on *what* we learn about a character from the text, as is particularly evident in the widespread practice of summarizing an individual's character traits, which can then be analysed and evaluated. Thus Blondell, for example, describes the 'maximal Socrates', the figure who emerges from the dialogues overall; the 'elenctic Socrates', who emerges from the aporetic dialogues and *Apology*; the 'constructive Socrates', associated primarily with the 'middle' dialogues; and the Eleatic Stranger, as he appears in *Sophist* and *Politicus*.[78] Such analyses are valuable; but as a way of approaching the texts, this is not so far removed from the extraction and reconstruction of arguments—a practice whose limitations I discussed in chapter 1. Just as extracting an argument conceals the way its steps are handled in context, so collating information about character obscures the way it emerges throughout a dialogue, and the impact this has on our experience of reading and understanding.[79]

[77] For detailed discussion of authors' exploitation of the placement of expositional material to create engagement and suspense in the reader, see Sternberg (1978). Prior (2006) 163–4 notes the progressive revelation of information about Socrates' character in *Symposium*, though he does not draw out its significance for the reader's response.

[78] Blondell (2002). 'Maximal Socrates': 10, 53, 67–80; 'elenctic Socrates': 10, 115–27; 'constructive Socrates': 10–11; Eleatic Stranger: 318–26.

[79] Goldhill (1990) warns against separating character from the text, though he says that character should not be dissolved into considerations of dramatic effect, in the manner of Wilamowitz-Moellendorff (1917). My intention here has not been to do this, but to draw out the importance of the placing of information *as well as* its content. Cf. also the comments at Pelling (1990c) 261–2.

The gradual emergence of information about a character is, of course, a feature of much literary characterization, particularly dramatic characterization.[80] But it is especially marked and pervasive in the dialogues, and Plato employs various techniques for intensifying the basic effect. One is apparent inconsistency in what a character says or does.[81] A celebrated example is the formal inconsistency between the different versions of his viewpoint offered by Thrasymachus in *Republic* I: critics fiercely debate whether the different passages can be satisfactorily reconciled, and if so, how.[82] Though it is easy to focus on the significance of such contradictions for the speaker—he is confused, or vacillating, or has changed his mind—they are also crucial for the reader's experience. They force her to go backwards and forwards through the text, trying to make sense of an interlocutor's different sayings as the expressions of a single coherent character—and this, of course, is the point. If we reach consistency, it will be through effort and thought of our own—and if we cannot, this is instructive too.[83]

Another such tactic is the displacement or delay of information relevant to our understanding of character. While Euthyphro gives his account of his prosecution of his father at 4ae, for example, it is not until 5d–6a, when he offers his first definition of piety, that he gives his reason for thinking his action correct—the analogous behaviour of Zeus in punishing his father Cronos. This proof is clearly at the forefront of his mind—he says he has offered it to many others—so the point is not that the justification has to be recovered from the depths of his psyche. Rather, the delay leaves us wondering, without much guidance, as to the rationale and motivation for so unintuitive an act. Another type of displacement involves the delayed reporting of an interlocutor's response to the argument in which he is engaged. I have already mentioned one particularly striking example, where it is only at the close of a stretch of argument that Socrates tells us that Thrasymachus agreed to the steps of the argument 'not easily as I am

[80] Cf. e.g. Halliwell (1990).

[81] This is often offered as an argument against the mouthpiece view of the dialogues: see e.g. Press (2000c), Thesleff (2000), Scott and Welton (2000) 147–8, Wolfsdorf (2004). Cf. also Belfiore (1984).

[82] See e.g. Chappell (1993), Annas (1981) 34–57, Everson (1998), Kerferd (1964), Nicholson (1974), Hobbs (2000) 165–8.

[83] Socrates' irony, in so far as it often involves the appearance of inconsistency, can produce a similar effect. Cf. Gordon (1999) 117–33.

now telling it, but reluctantly, being dragged', and that then, sweating, he blushed.[84] In analysing this example of delay, Morgan suggests its function is to make the steps of the argument clearer and the description of Thrasymachus more vivid, because it was withheld.[85] But this is not all. By withholding any guidance as to what Thrasymachus (or indeed Socrates) makes of the argument, Plato forces us to evaluate it for ourselves as we first read it. Then when we do find out what the participants think, this prompts us to take another look: to see how our evaluation of the argument tallies with theirs; to understand their viewpoints; and to locate their concerns.

In such cases, Plato uses the placing of information itself as a way of ensuring that our reading experience is dynamic and reflective. As well as contributing to our overall understanding, a moment of insight into character may have a particular role in its context, of surprising us, upsetting our expectations, or forcing us to revisit an earlier passage—thereby turning us back on ourselves and getting us to re-evaluate our responses. In this sense too, characterization plays a functional role, in that it is handled with a view to heightening our level of involvement, our consciousness of that involvement, and thereby our ability to scrutinize and evaluate it.[86]

4.8. 'LATER' DIALOGUES: THE DISAPPEARANCE OF CHARACTER

So far my focus has mainly been on those 'early' and 'middle' works where the characterization is rich and engaging. Yet in 'late' dialogues (as well as *Republic* II–X), there is a marked change. Attention to character does not disappear,[87] but it becomes much less prominent. The participants are less individualized. Socrates' role declines: in *Parmenides* he is the younger and less experienced partner; in *Sophist*, *Politicus*, and *Timaeus-Critias*, he is for much of the time an observer;

[84] *R.*350c12–d1. [85] Morgan (2004) 363.

[86] See Mansfeld (1995) on how Pre-Socratic writers encourage a similar sort of reading.

[87] See esp. D. Frede (1996) on *Philebus*; also Miller (1980) and Scodel (1987) on *Politicus*, Miller (1986) on *Parmenides*, Welliver (1977) on *Timaeus-Critias*, and, more generally, Blondell (2002).

and in *Laws* he is absent altogether. Conflict and interaction between interlocutors is less important to the progression of the conversations. Less attention is devoted to evoking the wider dramatic contexts for discussions, and the arguments themselves spring less directly from these. Why, then, does Plato alter his technique so radically? What effect does it have on the reader's engagement? And can the account I have offered so far accommodate the changes?

One widespread approach is to view the diminishing importance of character as connected with—even emblematic of—other changes in Plato's approach to philosophizing and the dialogue form.[88] In 'later' dialogues, Plato's interest seems to shift away from the *ad hominem* exploration of individual interlocutors' views towards a more abstract and less context-bound exposition of ideas,[89] for which the subtle and vivid evocation of character is not necessary. Moreover, as I outlined in chapter 2, it is often thought that by this stage in his career Plato is committed to a more didactic model of philosophical interaction, whereby the discussion leader guides a compliant partner towards philosophical enlightenment—avoiding the disruptive influence of individual interlocutors so familiar from 'earlier' works, but also resulting in blander characters and a more monotonous style of conversation. The 'later' works' diminishing interest in character, in other words, marks a departure from the 'early' dialogues: both a decline in literary appeal and, more profoundly, a move away from the emphasis on personal involvement and exchange which, for many, is one of the most positive aspects of the 'early' dialogues' picture of learning.

I address this general picture of the development of Plato's dialectical style and philosophical approach directly in other chapters, especially 3 and 5. Here, more narrowly, I want to challenge the idea that the changed handling of character needs to be understood in this way. True, character now plays a less obvious role; but this need not mean that these works are no longer interested in character.

[88] Blondell (2002) effectively brings out the connection of character with questions of philosophical approach and dialectical style. See also e.g. Miller (1980) ix–x, Long (1998), McCabe (2000) 1–8, Campbell (1973) xix–xxiv, Rowe (1995a) 8–11, Rutherford (1995) 274–81.

[89] Nightingale (2002a) offers a suggestive development of this idea, arguing that the diminishing emphasis on character is connected with a shift towards an increasingly otherworldly perspective in 'late' works. This ties in well with what I say later about the increasing difficulty, for the reader, of 'later' works. I develop the idea of an otherworldly perspective in ch.7.

And it certainly does not mean that they involve the reader in a less personal or active way. To return again to a central theme of chapter 2, the changes need to be understood in terms not of Plato's development, but that of the participants—both interlocutors and readers.[90]

To begin with, the less dramatic and increasingly generic treatment of character in 'later' works is closely connected with the increasing philosophical development of interlocutors.[91] In 'early' dialogues, as I argued in chapter 3, we see a range of respondents responding inadequately to discussion. Yet these moments of dialectical inadequacy are frequently the same ones that give us a strong sense of the character of an interlocutor: they involve dramatic interaction between the participants; they often offer us subjective insight into an interlocutor's thoughts and feelings; and they allow us to conceive of an interlocutor as an individual, with a specific viewpoint and concerns. Thus, for example, Meno's response to the baffling inquiry in which Socrates has embroiled him—to introduce the paradox of inquiry and then to leap upon Socrates' proposed 'solution'—is pivotal in revealing his lazy and superficial approach. In 'middle' and 'late' dialogues, however, interlocutors develop the resources to respond more appropriately to the difficulties of discussion, and no longer possess the distinctive failings so important in differentiating

[90] Blondell (2003) and (2002) offers a different challenge to the traditional interpretation of the 'middle' and 'late' works. Plato, Blondell thinks, came to regard the Socrates of the 'early' and 'middle' dialogues as too individual and idiosyncratic to be successfully imitated. For all his appeal as a role model, that is, he in fact threatens the ability of philosophy to survive him. In the 'later' dialogues, therefore, Plato develops increasingly generic figures, who represent the essentials of the philosophical character, while shedding such personal idiosyncrasies. Cf. also Nightingale (2002a) and Sedley (2002) 40. Blondell's approach accounts well for the disappearance of Socrates in many 'later' works, but is based on the assumption of mimetic pedagogy, which I have argued against above, and which becomes even less plausible in the 'late' dialogues, where we are further discouraged from developing an inwardness with characters, as I argue in this section.

Others point out that Plato starts to use character in new ways in these works. Sedley (1995) suggests that Plato uses choice of character to explore his philosophical heritage; McCabe (2000) argues that by ventriloquizing his opponents' positions, rather than having them present in discussion themselves, Plato is exploring the conditions for personhood and successful participation in discussion, and suggesting that the positions held by certain thinkers mean that they cannot successfully take part in debate as persons. See Moes (2000) 156–7 for the interesting suggestion that in *Philebus*, Philebus, Protarchus, and Socrates represent the personified components of the self.

[91] Cf. Blondell (2002) 224.

'early' interlocutors. The dramatic interruptions become less frequent, and the discussions require less by way of *ad hominem* deflationary tactics, remonstration, or encouragement from the discussion leader. In short, the personalities of interlocutors do not *need* to intrude so much into discussion, for the respondent is more self-motivated and committed to learning: his dialectical virtue allows discussion to proceed more smoothly.

This is by no means to say, however, that these interlocutors are perfect. As I noted above, many interpreters have doubted whether the Eleatic Stranger is a straightforwardly positive model, any more than Socrates is. Moreover, in 'later' works there is continued attention to the problems of representing and interpreting character, prompting us to rethink any assumptions about the worth of central characters and, more generally, warning us to be self-conscious in the way we relate to them. Discussion of absent opponents, common in these works, raises the question of whether their views have been fairly represented—as, in *Theaetetus*, Socrates makes Protagoras object, saying that his arguments have been dealt with ungenerously, without attention to their true significance.[92] Both *Sophist* and *Politicus* consider the impact of distance and perspective on the truth of our perceptions and representations, raising again (though in a more abstract way) the issues connected with Alcibiades' speech in *Symposium*.[93] Discussion of the sophist in *Sophist* at points recalls the practice of Socrates, prompting us to reflect upon how we should evaluate the sophist, and whether the Stranger's classification does him justice. Conversely, Socrates' very presence as an observer in *Sophist* and *Politicus* causes us to wonder how he would evaluate the Eleatic Stranger and his methods, as well as whether Socrates' evaluation would necessarily be the correct one.[94] All this encourages a critical and reflective approach and makes it inappropriate to treat characters in these works—any more than 'early' interlocutors—as straightforward role models. But as models of the more complex type, who can help us to understand what philosophical progress involves and to recognize and remedy our own failings as learners, they are

[92] *Tht.*166a ff; cf. Bostock (1988) 87–9, McCabe (2000) esp. 36–40.

[93] *Plt.*285d–287a; *Sph.*233d–236e. See esp. the discussion at Blondell (2002) 365–77; also Nightingale (2002a) and Burnyeat (1992) on *Republic*.

[94] For discussion of the presentation and role of Socrates in 'late' dialogues, see e.g. McCabe (2000), Miller (1980) 8–10, Gonzalez (2000), D. Frede (1996) 223–6, Long (1998), Blondell (2002) chs.5–6, Rowe (1995a) 8–11, Notomi (1999) 60–8, 274–96.

appropriate for readers who have themselves progressed beyond the failings of 'early' interlocutors, and who now need to be presented with advanced learners grappling with the later stages of philosophical progress. The fact that their individual traits intrude less upon the conversation may be something, in itself, the reader can learn from.

We can find continuity underlying apparent difference, also, in the degree of insight we are offered into the inner thoughts and feelings of characters. In looking at the more richly characterized dialogues, I suggested that the tension between invitation and denial in the presentation of characters is crucial in driving our active involvement with them, especially in the case of Socrates. The less richly characterized dialogues look, at first sight, totally different. The element of invitation has radically diminished: the characters are simply not as attractive or idiosyncratic, and they are not evoked in enough detail for us to be drawn into making sense of them in the same way. The Eleatic Stranger, for example, has no name, no associates, no history; nor do we know what he looks like. Neither *Sophist* nor *Politicus* provides a dramatic context that offers any insight into his life, concerns, or personality. During the course of the discussion, the vast majority of what he says is devoted to developing the argument, and Plato avoids giving us any depth of insight into his feelings as the discussion progresses. Yet this very denial of insight can, I think, be viewed as an extension of the denial we detected in 'earlier' works: it is no longer the case, as there, that the insights we are offered are undercut; we are just offered almost no insight at all.[95] As a character in whose company we remain for quite some time, but about whom we learn almost nothing, the Eleatic Stranger is an even more striking enigma than Socrates.

A further continuity relates to the relationship between character, belief, and argument. In the richly characterized dialogues, it generally makes sense to think of the conversations, even their more abstract portions, as exploring the beliefs held by a particular individual, beliefs which are central to their identity and character. Again, the less richly characterized dialogues initially look completely different. It is not quite so easy to relate Socrates' views about knowledge, as expressed in *Theaetetus*, to the way he lives his life, for example, or the

[95] This helps account for the replacement of Socrates with alternative discussion leaders about whom we know nothing, and whose appearances in other dialogues cannot guide us—as inevitably occurs, to an extent, in the case of Socrates.

Eleatic Stranger's practice of the method of division and collection to his (partly, of course, because we know so little about him). Moreover, the proportion of time devoted to impersonal and abstract discussion—in contrast to other aspects of character—has increased. Yet there is more continuity here than is at first apparent. The 'earlier' dialogues, I argued, create a belief and understanding centred approach to character, by encouraging us to relate to characters via their views expressed in discussion, rather than their more immediate thoughts and feelings. In the less richly characterized works, the discussions are still explorations of the beliefs of individuals, and we are encouraged to make sense of what a person says, if we can, as the coherent viewpoint of a single person. It is just that the emphasis has shifted even further on to a character's beliefs, so that it outweighs anything else we have to go on in understanding them. The emphasis on belief and understanding has been extended, and so also the austerity and difficulty of the reader's interpretative task. The dialogues do not ask us to make a distinction between works where we should see the dialectical discussion as revealing character and those where we should not—and I think it would be extremely hard to do so. In both 'early' and 'later' works, there is a link between person and argument, and we can see the importance of the link in both 'early' and 'late' works, while acknowledging how much further down the path the 'later' works have gone.

These continuities suggest that 'later' dialogues do not depart so completely from Plato's 'early' practice after all. If I am correct, what we see is not the disappearance of character but, first, the decline of those aspects of characterization which, in 'earlier' works, give figures immediate appeal; and, second, the intensification of those techniques for encouraging an independent response and discouraging unreflective identification that are already present there. In consequence, the demands placed on the reader are much greater. 'Later' works do not help the reader to engage with arguments by presenting her with charismatic figures. Instead, they require her to find the energy and motivation to engage fully for herself—even though the material may seem less exciting. Dramatic interaction between interlocutors and evocation of their responses both decline, and so we do not find comments by the discussion leader of the sort that, in 'earlier' works, provide us with encouragement, as well as with the resources to analyse and work upon our own responses. Moreover, because there is less contextualization of the arguments, we have more work to do in relating the discussions to persons and lives[96]—in working out what kind of life a certain set of beliefs implies, and how they relate to our own life and values. Whereas 'earlier' works act upon the reader, generating the appropriate type of involvement by producing a tension between invitation and denial, the less richly characterized dialogues require her to bring the correct type of involvement to the works for herself—something that in turn requires a higher level of dialectical virtue on her part. The changing handling of character thereby becomes a way of challenging the reader, as she progresses, to develop the qualities she needs to move onwards in learning.

The dialogues' treatment of character, therefore, is truly functional—geared as it is towards providing the reader with the stimuli she needs at each stage of the learning process. Characterization in the literary sense is closely bound up with our development into self-conscious and self-motivated agents, 'characters' in the sense in which the dialogues encourage us to regard them, through the lens of ethical responsibility. Just as we are encouraged to evaluate the characters with which Plato presents us—to act as jurors, as Alcibiades puts it, of their actions and dispositions—so, as we read, we are prompted to become better judges of ourselves and our lives. Accordingly, Plato's handling of character bridges the gap between the literary world of the text and the world beyond the text, where what matters is our own ability to act as well-developed characters when faced with the complexities of everyday life. Character, energy, and drama within the dialogues gradually disappear, but they are replaced by the reader's own blossoming independence, activity, and responsibility, as she grows into a philosophically mature and self-motivated agent.[97]

[96] See Desjardins (1988) on the importance of the interaction between words and actions/character in helping us interpret what is said.

[97] Cf. Nehamas (1998) 47, suggesting that Plato's readers almost become characters in his fictions.

5

Argumentation: A Descent into Didactic Dialectic?

5.1. AUTHORITIES ON WISDOM

We must see that the sophist, in praising what he is selling, does not deceive us, my companion, just like the merchant and retailer in the case of food for the body. For these people do not themselves know which of the wares they offer is good or bad for the body, but they praise them all as they sell them, and nor do those who buy from them, unless one happens to be a trainer or a doctor. Thus also, those who take items of knowledge around the cities, selling them and hawking them about to whoever wants them, praise all the things they sell, but perhaps, my excellent fellow, some of these men also are ignorant as to which of the things they sell is good or bad for the soul; and in the same situation are those who buy from them, unless one of them happens to be a physician of the soul. If, therefore, you happen to know which of these things is good or bad, it is safe for you to buy knowledge from Protagoras or from anyone else, but if not, watch out, my good fellow, in case you find yourself playing dice and taking a risk concerning the things dearest to you. For the danger in buying knowledge is much greater than in buying provisions. For when you buy food and drink, it is possible to carry them away from the merchant or retailer in different containers, and before you receive them into your body by eating or drinking, it is possible to set them aside at home and take advice, calling in an expert, as to what should be eaten and drunk and what not, and how much and when; so there is no great danger in the purchase. Yet it is not possible to carry away knowledge in another container, but it is necessary, having handed over the price, to take the knowledge in to one's very soul, and having learned it, to go away either harmed or benefitted.

Protagoras, 313c8–314b4

Woken early from sleep by his young friend Hippocrates, Socrates is assailed by an urgent request to join him in visiting the sophist Protagoras, recently arrived in town. Hippocrates effusively explains his wish to meet this famous figure—Protagoras is wise, most skilled in speaking, and the object of everyone's praises—and urges Socrates to depart with him at once, so as to be sure of finding the great man at home. As they walk in the courtyard until it becomes light, Socrates scrutinizes Hippocrates' apparently unreflective admiration for Protagoras, quizzing him about the nature of sophists and warning him, in the passage quoted above, to be cautious in his approach to the knowledge or lessons (μαθήματα 314b1) offered by the sophist. When purchased, Socrates argues, these lessons are received straight into the soul, where they can cause benefit or harm; the purchaser or recipient, therefore, needs to proceed cautiously: as carefully, or more, as he would examine food when purchasing and eating it. Socrates' striking image of marketplace trading, with its dramatic evocation of the care of the buyer, his potential deception by a roguish seller, and the harmful consequences of eating bad food, provides a comic and sharp-edged counter to Hippocrates' idolizing attitude to the sophist, and a memorable warning to the prospective buyer of knowledge.

Socrates' first concern relates to the character of the figure from whom one buys 'wares'—whether lessons or food. By comparing the sophist to a seller of food, who in ignorance praises all his wares indiscriminately, Socrates casts doubt on the trustworthiness of such self-appointed figures of authority, who have neither the knowledge nor the integrity to advise purchasers with accuracy. If we wish to select the correct 'wares' for soul or body, therefore, we need to ensure that we have our purchases checked by an expert or knowledgeable person (ἐπιστήμων 313e3), such as a trainer or doctor in the case of food. Second, Socrates highlights the need for careful scrutiny of the 'wares', to determine what should be consumed, in what quantities, and at what times. This process, which Socrates itemizes in detail, is central to the role performed by the expert on whom the purchaser is to rely. A third concern is Socrates' idea that lessons, once they have been paid for, are received straight into the soul: there is no opportunity for later scrutiny by an expert, as there is in the case of food. Socrates' point here is not, I think, that one is necessarily damaged simply by *hearing* harmful teachings; rather, the potential for damage seems to be closely connected with the buyer's willing acceptance of the lessons he is offered, as signalled by the payment: so convinced is he that the teachings he is buying are good, that he accepts them without hesitation. Since teachings cannot be transported like food for later examination, if he is to overcome this problem, the learner needs to take on the role of the expert, by scrutinizing the wares he is offered before accepting them.

While this passage takes much of its sting from its focus on Protagoras, a figure who (Plato suggests) is happy to be treated as a repository of wisdom and to take money for conveying it to others, the idea is commonly voiced in the dialogues: in a culture abounding with acclaimed sources of wisdom, from poets and divine interpreters to sophists and orators, Socrates is keen to exhort his interlocutors to think for themselves and to question what they have heard on others' authority. It is also the approach he invites towards his own contributions to discussion: quick to affirm their inadequacy and his own uncertainty, he prompts his discussion partners towards active and critical engagement with the accounts he offers. This, as *Protagoras* brings out, is for the safety of the soul of the person who is to receive that account. In addition, though, it may help the person putting forward ideas. Someone who is ignorant of the value of their opinions, just as *Protagoras*' trader is ignorant of the value of his wares, will not develop the ability to be more discerning without being questioned, even should he have the inclination: this, the recognition of the limits to one's own knowledge, is the familiar first step towards understanding. A related idea is voiced by Socrates, with more self-awareness, in his confrontation with Callicles in *Gorgias,* when he for once is on the receiving end of the argumentative onslaught. In striking counterpart to his assertion in that dialogue that he would suffer wrong rather than harm his soul by committing wrong on someone else, Socrates expresses what must seem counterintuitive satisfaction in Callicles' aggressive attitude:

> *Since you do not wish, Callicles, to help me finish the argument, at least listen and interrupt, if I seem to you to speak wrongly at any point. And if you refute me, I shall not be angry with you as you are with me, but you shall be recorded as my greatest benefactor.*
>
> *Gorgias*, 506b6–c3

Despite his failings, Callicles' combative approach contributes to Socrates' insight into his own beliefs and to his progression towards understanding by allowing Socrates to expose his ideas to the most challenging of examinations; this is the benefaction of which Socrates speaks. It makes Callicles a touchstone and godsend (486d2–e3), in Socrates' eyes, since his critical opposing viewpoint may provide the ultimate test of the truth of Socrates' opinions.[1] From different perspectives, then, a questioning and critical attitude cares for the soul and contributes to philosophical progress. Though his wayward interlocutors do not always take his advice, this is the approach we see Socrates model when faced with the many confident pronouncements of his interlocutors, especially in 'early' dialogues.

If we turn to a 'late' dialogue such as *Sophist*, however, the preferred mode of discussion appears rather different:

> *Socrates: Are you accustomed to prefer to set out what you want to explain to anyone by speaking in a long speech of your own, or to proceed through questions, as for example on that occasion when I was present and Parmenides used that method, and carried on a splendid discussion; I was young, and that man was then very old.*
>
> *Stranger: Discussion with another person, Socrates, is easier when one is conversing with an interlocutor who is docile and gives no trouble; if not, it is easier to proceed by oneself.*
>
> *Sophist*, 217c3–d3

Here, the Eleatic Stranger makes it clear that he prefers acquiescence and compliance to critical challenge; indeed, unless his interlocutor can be relied upon to give no trouble, he would prefer to dispense with the question-and-answer format altogether. To be sure, the Eleatic Stranger is a figure far removed from the 'trader' in knowledge caricatured in *Protagoras*, but his proposal does appear to signal a step away from the critical approach whose value is made central to 'earlier' dialogues; and this is reflected in significant changes in the form of dialectic employed in this and other 'late' works. For many interpreters, there is a movement, in 'middle' and 'late' works, towards a more didactic style, which fundamentally alters the way interlocutors and readers are encouraged to engage. If this is the case, it would pose a serious challenge to the idea that there is, as I have been arguing, a core continuity in the learner's response throughout dialogues of different types.

In Part I, I explored the experiences and responses associated with dialectical discussions in 'early, 'middle', and 'late' dialogues with a

[1] Long (2008) discusses the value, for an inquirer, of discussion with different types of interlocutor, including opponents of the Calliclean type.

view to undermining the traditional developmentalist view that, in these different groups of works, Plato changes his underlying approach to education. In all works, I suggested, learners are invited to respond cognitively-affectively; and, despite appearances, there are continuities in the basic experiences they undergo. The differences, rather, are connected with the learners' different stages of development: early-stage interlocutors need to undergo violent and unsettling experiences; at later stages, learners feel the impulse towards the same responses, but have developed dialectical virtues which enable them better to deal with those impulses. Socratic conversation, I suggested, provides interlocutors with the context or arena for the formation of those virtues, and the different types of conversation supply them with the stimuli appropriate to each stage of their development. A similar progression, I also suggested, is fostered in the reader as she progresses through the different types of text.

My aim in this chapter is to support this picture by tackling the idea that the changes in the form of dialectic in 'early', 'middle', and 'late' dialogues amount to a shift towards a more didactic style, a central pillar of the traditional interpretation with implications for the type of response invited in interlocutors and readers. By looking in detail at the construction of arguments, I hope to show that the different types of dialectic do in fact aim to engage us in a relevantly similar way. In doing so, I refine our understanding of the parallels between interlocutors and readers, and also the differences, demonstrating that although the underlying path of learning is the same, we are helped along it in different ways. Indeed, exposing this gap will be at the centre of my rejection of the didactic interpretation of Plato's 'later' dialectic.

5.2. A DESCENT INTO DIDACTIC DIALECTIC?

Let us, then, review in more detail the traditional interpretation of dialectical developments in Plato's works, which runs something as follows. In 'early' works, dialectic starts from the interlocutor, and purports to interrogate his views. The discussion is conversational in character; lines of attack are *ad hominem*; and the personalities of interlocutors have a vital impact on the course of inquiry. The conversations are largely concerned with scrutinizing and undermining currently held views, rather than developing new ones, and they often end in *aporia*. The discussion leader does not claim superior understanding or put forward his views directly. In 'middle' and 'late' dialogues, on the other hand, the interlocutor's views are only nominally the starting point for debate, and are in fact irrelevant to the overall direction of the conversation. Rather, it is said, the discussion leader is putting across his own views, and the interlocutor's role is to assent to the steps of the argument: the emphasis is constructive, rather than destructive.[2]

Of course such changes, as is often pointed out, have a positive dimension. As I suggested in chapter 3, many interpreters think them a signal of Plato's increasing philosophical maturity and independence. They represent the shift to a more impersonal mode of argumentation, necessary if dialectic is not to remain limited by the *ad hominem* practices of 'early' dialogues and if genuine progress towards understanding is to be made. The accompanying shift to interlocutors of a more compliant type means that inappropriate responses do not derail discussion: collaboration replaces confrontation.[3] This sense of progression and improvement is an important one, which I try to retain in my account. But for many interpreters, the benefits of the new style of dialectic come at considerable cost. On the most extreme view, the 'later' dialogues come close to treatises or monologues, where the question-and-answer format has little role to play. Plato is no longer interested in a dialectical

[2] This is a widespread view. For a clear statement, see e.g. Vlastos (1991) chs. 2 and 4; Ryle (1966) 10–12, 193–4, (1968) 72. I here focus on changes in the dialogue form associated with different periods of Plato's writing; however, these are usually also linked with certain doctrinal shifts (most importantly the development and then criticism of the theory of Forms), as well as various further stylistic changes, usually felt to make the 'later' dialogues less dramatically and literarily interesting. On stylistic changes, see Rutherford (1995) 272–81, Campbell (1973) xix ff., Blondell (2002) 314–96.

[3] The changes in dialectical approach and in characterization are usually linked, as in the sustained treatment in Blondell (2002), esp. 199–228; also Rutherford (1995) 213–14. Some critics place more emphasis on the adoption of impersonal argumentation, e.g. Annas (1981) 56–7, Vlastos (1991) 48–9, 107–31, Scolnicov (1988) 1–2; others on the character of participants e.g. Teloh (1986). With a slightly different approach, C. Gill (1996b) argues that the principles underlying dialectic in 'late' dialogues are not dissimilar from those underlying 'earlier' dialogues, but that the improved type of interlocutor means that discussion does not break down. A positive analysis of the changes is compatible with acknowledging their disadvantages, as among many of these interpreters.

style of philosophizing—even of a reformed kind—and only continues to structure his works in this way as a formality.[4] For such scholars, the interlocutors have become nodders or yes-men whose contributions could, without great loss, be excised.[5] Other interpreters, taking a more positive line, maintain that the question-and-answer format retains a valuable role in 'later' dialogues: it helps to ensure that interlocutors learn productively, and assists the discussion leader in developing his views as he expounds them.[6] Either way, however, dialectic is seen as having undergone a radical transformation. It has shifted from inquiry to exposition, and from genuine participation in the interlocutor to passive receivership. In consequence, it no longer involves the interlocutor in the kind of full personal thought and effort which the early dialogues seem to insist are necessary for learning; and accordingly, the reader is involved in a less demanding and productive manner too. This tendency is usually felt to start in 'middle' works such as *Phaedo* and *Republic*, and to intensify as we reach 'late' works such as *Sophist* and *Politicus*.

Before assessing and evaluating this view, I would like to pin down a little more precisely what is taken to be defective about the interlocutor's involvement in 'middle' and 'late' dialogues, and I will do this by bringing in the classification of question-and-answer *logoi* developed by Aristotle in his *Topics*.[7] Aristotle mentions three types: gymnastic/dialectical, eristic, and demonstrative. A deduction is dialectical, he tells us, when it 'reasons from opinions that are generally

[4] See e.g. Annas (1981) 3–4, Ryle (1966) esp. 193–4, Beversluis (2000) 20, 377–8, M. Frede (1996) 137–9, Robinson (1953) 83–4, Sayre (1992) 227–8. Annas emphasizes the dogmatic and monologic style of *Republic*, but thinks that it nevertheless encourages a critical response, rather than 'ready, unreflective agreement' (p.2) by virtue of the challenging ideas it contains. I agree, but hope to show that the drive towards reflectiveness is embedded in the construction of the arguments themselves too. Frede and Sayre both nevertheless offer accounts of the significance of the continued use of the dialectical form.

[5] 'Yes-men': Vlastos (1991) 117 n47; 'nodders': Ryle (1966) 194, (1968) 72. Cf. e.g. Beversluis (2000) 377–8, M. Frede (1996) 137.

[6] Reeve (1988) 22–4, 39; Rutherford (1995) 213–14; Blondell (2002) 199–210, 337–47; Campbell (1973) xx (the philosopher 'guides his pupil by a path familiar to himself to conclusions which he foreknows'); also Robinson (1953) 18–19.

[7] Others who use Aristotle's discussion of dialectic in analysing Plato's dialectic include: Vlastos (1991) ch.4, Annas (1981) 286–90, Robinson (1953) 18–19, 22, 83–4, Frede (1992a), Blank (1993), Blondell (2002) 338, Ostenfeld (2000) esp. 213, 215. In making use of Aristotle's classifications, I do not mean to imply that Plato was—or could have been—writing with these in mind.

accepted'; it is eristic if it 'starts from opinions that seem to be generally accepted, but are not really such, or again if it merely seems to reason from opinions that are or seem to be generally accepted'; and it is a demonstration (ἀπόδειξις) 'when the premises, from which the reasoning starts are true and primary, or are such that our knowledge of them has originally come through premises which are primary and true'. In *Sophistical Refutations*, he adds an extra class, peirastic arguments, which take their name from the *peira*, trial or test, that they are designed to make of the answerer's opinions. These arguments 'deduce from premises which are accepted by the answerer and which anyone who pretends to possess knowledge of the subject is bound to know'. Aristotle here also refers to another class not mentioned in *Topics*, didactic (διδασκαλικοί) arguments: 'didactic arguments are those that reason from principles appropriate to each subject and not from the opinions held by the answerer (for the learner should take things on trust)'.[8] These seem to be closely connected to the demonstrative arguments mentioned in *Topics*.[9]

Now, categorizing the styles of dialectic that occur in Plato is extremely difficult.[10] The style shifts within a single dialogue, and it is not always easy to draw a clear distinction between types. Following Aristotle's analysis of Socrates' argumentative stance, for example, critics tend to class 'early' dialogues as peirastic.[11] But, as others point out, Socrates frequently uses eristic techniques;[12] and there are also places—such as the discussion of the masses' view of *akrasia* at the

[8] *Top.*1.1; *Soph.El.*2. The translations are by Pickard-Cambridge in Ross (1928).

[9] Indeed, later in the same paragraph of *Sophistical Refutations*, he refers to them as demonstrative (τῶν ἀποδεικτικῶν). It is not necessary for my purposes to enter into the difficult question of the relationship between demonstration and didactic arguments in *Topics* and *Sophistical Refutations*, and demonstration in the *Posterior Analytics*. *Posterior Analytics* are usually taken to represent a later and distinct stage in Aristotle's thought, where he is concerned rather with the formal way in which a body of knowledge should be set out, than with the mode of discourse best suited to teaching and learning, which is our concern here.

[10] Cf. M. Frede (1992a) 213.

[11] Aristotle *Soph.El.*183b7–8. See e.g. Vlastos (1991) 94–5, 111–12, Moreau (1968), though some such interpretation underlies the majority of modern accounts of Socratic elenctic discussion.

[12] See particularly Beversluis (2000). The relationship of Socrates' argumentation to sophistic/eristic techniques is discussed by Benson (2000) 86–90, Sayre (1995) 35–46, Sichel (1976), Sprague (1962), Robinson (1953) 84–8. For a defence of Socrates against the charge of eristic argumentation, see e.g. Vlastos (1994) 135–6 and (1991) 132–56; cf. also Moreau (1968). See also n30 of this chapter and discussion in sections 5.4 and 5.5.

end of *Protagoras*, or Nicias' espousal of the Socratic position that virtue is knowledge in *Laches*—where discussion seems closer to gymnastic. It seems, that is, that Plato is not working with precise categorizations of the sort set out by Aristotle. My reason for bringing them in nonetheless, is that in taking the above approach to Plato's 'middle' and 'late' dialogues, critics seem, whether implicitly or explicitly,[13] to regard their dialectical style as close to Aristotle's didactic. What, then, is special—and different—about didactic dialectic?

Aristotle's characterization of didactic (or demonstrative) dialectic, in the passages quoted earlier, has two main features. First, there is the role of the participants. The starting point for a didactic argument is determined by the subject matter—presumably as decided by the discussion leader—not by the opinions of the answerer. The questioner is cast in the role of an expert, with the respondent conditioned to accept what the questioner says as true. If the function of the exercise is to set out and transmit what the discussion leader already knows, and the respondent regards him as an authority, then the latter's input will be incidental. Even if the interactive format helps him to assimilate the discussion leader's ideas effectively, his role is essentially that of a receiver, whose contributions will have no real impact on the course the discussion takes.[14] Such a form of dialectic is far from the collaborative project, in which the interlocutor is fully and actively participating, with which we are familiar from Plato's 'early' dialogues.

Second, Aristotle's descriptions suggest that, in didactic dialectic, the material being discussed will be set out in a different way, for we are now dealing with a demonstration rather than a search. The questioner already has knowledge, so the focus is on setting out his views comprehensibly, rather than following the difficult and uncertain paths of an undirected inquiry, with its detours and wrong

[13] Language of didacticism, dogma, and doctrine abounds in discussion of Plato's 'middle' and 'late' dialogues. For explicit references to Aristotle's conception of demonstration/didactic dialectic to characterize Plato's 'later' dialectic, see n50 and n62 of this chapter.

[14] Since didactic is treated as a form of dialectic, at least in *Soph.El.*, we tend to assume that it will proceed by question-and-answer. However, for the implication that it does not, see *Soph.El.*171b1–2, 172a15f. Possibly if questions were only asked to ensure that the respondent understood the steps of the demonstration, it was not regarded as *real* question-and-answer debate, and therefore as equivalent to continuous discourse. See Owen (1968b) for the move from question-and-answer to single person exposition in dialectical debate. Cf. *Top.*163a36–b16.

turnings. Nor is the discussion affected by the interlocutor's peculiarities, since it no longer takes its starting point from his views but is rather concerned with the exposition of impersonal truths to which his personal history is irrelevant. The key goal is enabling the respondent to understand the material (rather than convincing him at a superficial level), for which a clear and logical exposition will be essential, more akin to a proof or demonstration in the modern sense. Again, this contrasts strongly with what we are familiar with from 'early' dialogues, where it is often tempting to think that if the aim was to convey a certain idea effectively, the argument would have been better set out in another way.

It is usually thought, I take it, that 'middle' and 'late' dialogues tend towards didactic dialectic on both the above counts. Respondents play a diminishing and increasingly passive role; the arguments look more like demonstrations than inquiries; and in consequence, the experience of being taken through them is quite different. In the following discussion, I want to challenge this view by arguing that 'middle' and 'late' dialogues still engage us in a creative and personal way. But first, let us briefly review some other ways of resisting the traditional picture.

5.3. POSSIBLE SOLUTIONS

First, we can mount a direct challenge to the categorization of 'middle' and 'late' interlocutors as yes-men. In *Republic*, for example, we can point out that interlocutors offer substantive contributions (most obviously their speeches at the start of book II, but also, for example, in the construction of the ideal city) and at points have a decisive impact on the course of the discussion (for instance at the start of books II and V). Indeed, the whole conversation is on an important level responsive to their views—or at least their concerns.[15] Recognizing this provides a corrective to extreme interpretations of 'middle' and 'late' works, which assimilate them to monologues,[16]

[15] Cf. e.g. Blondell (2002) 194–5, 203–9, Rutherford (1995) 210; cf. Scott (1999) 26 and Hyland (1995) 35–57.

[16] In so far as 'late' dialogues seem to minimize the interlocutor's role still further, the approach is less successful here, though we can still point to places where the

and brings out the blurred line between inquiry, teaching, and exposition in many dialogues. Nevertheless, such an approach can only do so much: for there is undeniably a progressive change in the extent and character of the contributions made by respondents as we move from 'early' to 'late' works; and picking out examples of interlocutors' contributions is not enough to undermine this picture.

A related approach is to point to continuities in the way dialectical activity is *conceived* in dialogues of different types.[17] Throughout 'middle' and 'late' works, we find references to the lack of knowledge and uncertainty of the discussion leader; to the shared nature of dialectical activity; and to discussion as a hunt or search. *Aporiai* occur frequently, and the outcome of discussion can seem unclear as we progress. These are features prominent in 'early' dialogues, and suggest that it should be possible to interpret dialectic in 'middle' and 'late' works as similarly collaborative. While such considerations help challenge assumptions about the degeneration of the dialogue form, observations about how dialectical activity is *conceived* need to be backed up by consideration of how the question-and-answer procedure *actually* engages the receiver: for otherwise we remain open to the charge that language such as this, like the question-and-answer form itself, is belied by the dialectical approach actually used.[18]

Alternatively, we can appeal to indirect ways in which 'middle' and 'late' works resist the didactic label. One option is to focus on the *authority* with which views put forward are endowed. In 'early' works, an important role of the dialogue form is to force the reader to reflect and reach answers for herself, preventing her from taking for

interlocutors do make important contributions: e.g. *Phlb.*19c–20a, 37e–38a, 41a, 45de, *Tht.*146cd, 147c–148b, 185c–186a, 199e, 201cd. See Gill (1995) for the idea that *Politicus* does involve the interlocutor's views in a significant way because of its defamiliarization (a process which may involve refutation) then theorized reconstitution of the respondent's beliefs, with criticism by Rowe (1996). Rowe himself argues that we can see a Phaedrean model of dialectic, according to which the teacher is subjected to questioning, underlying dialogues such as *Politicus*, but concedes that the dialogues' practice of Phaedrean dialectic lacks the excitement of Socrates' description of it in *Phaedrus*.

17 See especially C. Gill (1996b); also Blondell (2002) 199–203, 346–8, Gill (1992), Lane (1998) 68–9.

18 See Blondell (2002) 347, also 199–201. Blondell discusses the idea that such features might be a formality or pedagogical tool, calling the Eleatic Stranger's sincerity into question. But his sincerity is not something that we can properly determine; more important is whether his dialectical style is in fact compatible with the stance he adopts.

granted—and attempting to rely on—what Plato himself thinks. And in 'later' dialogues too, we might maintain, the dialogue form still performs this function. This is the line taken by Michael Frede: in an article on *Sophist*, he argues that, though the dialogue is effectively a treatise, Plato uses the question-and-answer form to undercut the apparent authoritativeness of his views.[19] Despite the appeal of this view, however, I wish to challenge the underlying assumption that the character of dialectic in the 'middle' and 'late' dialogues is fundamentally different.

A further option is to argue that, despite the changed nature of the arguments themselves, 'later' works are nevertheless dialectical in a broader sense.[20] To begin with, they engage in dialogue with the positions of other philosophers, such as Heraclitus in *Theaetetus* and Parmenides in *Sophist*, as well as with ideas expressed in other Platonic dialogues, mostly obviously in *Parmenides*' reflection on the Forms.[21] In addition, they encourage us to engage in reflection beyond the confines of the text, thus initiating a dialogue of a different sort—between text and reader. So, for example, Frede argues that *Sophist* invites us to think about the nature of the philosopher, despite focusing overtly on the definition of the sophist.[22] Scodel, interpreting *Politicus*, argues that the status of the Eleatic Stranger as a figure of authority is undermined, and that we are invited to carry on for ourselves a debate between the views he expresses and those of the elder Socrates, expressed in other dialogues.[23] These two views, in their different ways, highlight the importance of inconsistencies and ellipses, both within individual dialogues and between dialogues, and emphasize the work left for the reader to do—and represent a line of

[19] M. Frede (1996); also, more generally, (1992a). See also Guthrie (1975) 64–5, Annas and Waterfield (1995) xxiii. Criticism of the approach is voiced at Rowe (1996) 156–7.

[20] C. Gill (1996b) identifies three kinds of dialogue: the fictional interchange among interlocutors; the dialogue between text and reader; the dialogue of a philosopher with his earlier philosophical positions.

[21] E.g. Brown (1998), Notomi (1999) 211–13, McCabe (2000).

[22] M. Frede (1996). Cf. also Notomi (1999), Sayre (1992), and Schofield (1996). This is an approach in effect adopted by many critics, though it is not always presented as a way of defending the dialogue form.

[23] Scodel (1987). Cf. also Miller (1980), who rejects the idea that *Politicus* lacks dialectical and dramatic power by identifying tensions within the ideas expressed by characters in the dialogue. For commentary on these approaches, see Rowe (1995a) 10 and (1996), Seeskin (1984), Gill (1988).

interpretation with which, as should have emerged from Part I, I am much in sympathy. But we still, I think, need to make a case for the question-and-answer form having this effect in its own right.

5.4. AN ALTERNATIVE APPROACH: ARGUMENTS AND THEIR PRESENTATION

Each of these different interpretations, then, while appealing in its own way, ultimately fails successfully to challenge the picture of a descent into a less engaging and more didactic form of dialectic. The indirect approaches help to present 'later' works as engaging and productive, but they do not adequately address the character of the dialectical argumentation itself. And the direct approaches, which focus on the contributions made by interlocutors, do not persuade us that a change has not taken place. I too want to mount a direct attack on the didactic picture. But whereas those interpretations I have looked at focus primarily on the role of the interlocutor (the first of the features of Aristotle's picture of didactic dialectic discussed above), I will approach this issue via the second feature of didactic: the idea that the arguments themselves now take a more demonstrative form. What I hope to show is that, even though they contain more exposition and less interaction, arguments in 'middle' and 'late' works do not turn into didactic expositions of the sort that give the respondent a diminishing role and assimilate him to a passive receiver: there is still a decided dialectical edge to them. And far from encouraging a lower level of input, the construction of arguments in these works in fact requires increasingly active and full participation on the part of the receiver. Fundamental to my approach is the idea that the actual spoken contributions made by the respondent do not determine the level or quality of engagement of the receiver, whether interlocutor or reader. 'Middle' and 'late' arguments do require less *overt* contribution, but they are not, thereby, equivalent to didactic proofs, and nor do they thereby invite a less active type of engagement. In fact, I shall argue, it is those arguments which appear on the surface to require less from the interlocutor that are the most demanding—precisely because they are less obvious in the way they involve their receiver.

In arguing for this reading, I start from two interconnected aspects of the form arguments take in the different types of dialogue. The first is the way in which the steps of the argument are presented—that is, the space between the argument itself and the way it is put across in the dialogue—and here narratological analysis offers a useful point of comparison. Narratologists examine the relation between the underlying story and the way it is presented in the text's narrative in exploring the response in the reader invited by the text. In a similar way, we can look at the relation between the steps of an argument—the underlying 'story', for our purposes—and the way they are presented to us in the discussion between interlocutors.

The significance of the presentation of material surfaces at various points in Plato's dialogues.[24] In his famous recasting of the opening of Homer's *Iliad* in *Republic* III and the surrounding discussion of poetry, Socrates shows an awareness of the impact of the manner in which the story is narrated for its affective and ethical effect on its receiver;[25] and in noting that Meno prefers the sample definition he has offered in especially elaborate language (τραγική 76e3, 'majestic' or in 'tragic style'), Socrates links the diction of his accounts with their reception by his respondent. In his critical analysis of Lysias' speech during the discussion of rhetoric in *Phaedrus*, these concerns shade into the presentation of arguments. Lysias, Socrates complains, seems to have put his speech together at random (χύδην 264b3), with no compelling reason or 'necessity' (ἀνάγκης 264b4) for the placing of one point after another. He then compares it to the inscription on the tomb of Midas, an epigram made up of four verses that can be arranged in any order, he claims, without changing the meaning (264c7–e2). Socrates' criticism here, that the ordering of the epigram (like Lysias' speech) makes no difference, carries the implication that in a correctly composed work, the parts are so ordered that they could not be rearranged without damaging the overall effect. Instead of presenting, as he does, an accumulation of independent considerations in the hope of overwhelming his listener, then, Lysias would have done better to arrange his points in an overarching argumentative structure, whose progression added to its impact. This would

[24] See especially Morgan (2004) and (2007).

[25] For detailed discussion, see Laird (1999) 46–63.

have given it an order derived from necessity, ἀνάγκη, a term that Socrates often uses to signal the logical 'compulsion', for the receiver, of steps in an argument leading to their conclusion.

Elsewhere, importance is attached to the order in which passages of argument are constructed.[26] The need to discover the nature of something before its properties can be determined is a motif in several works. So, at the end of *Republic* I, Socrates laments the order of their inquiry into justice, a factor in their failure to make progress:

> *I have not dined well, but that was due to my own actions not because of you. But, just as gluttons always taste everything that is carried by, snatching at it, before they have reasonably enjoyed what has gone before, I also seem to have behaved in this way, and before we discovered the object of our first enquiry, what justice is, letting that go I embarked on investigating whether it is vice and ignorance, or wisdom and virtue; and when another argument came upon us, that injustice is more profitable than injustice, I could not abstain from pursuing this and turning away from the other one, with the result now that the outcome of the discussion for me is that I know nothing.*
>
> *Republic*, 354a13–c1

Later in the same work, while setting out the programme of study for the guardians of his ideal city, Socrates chastises himself for failing, in his haste, to include discussion of the dimension of depth after geometry, as he meant to (528de); while in *Politicus*, it is the roundabout definition of weaving, which incorporated more material than it needed to, that prompts the discussion of true measure (283b–287a). At the close of this discussion, Socrates returns to the frustration prompted in himself and his companion by the long-windedness of the argument, and he reflects directly on the importance of the presentation of an argument not just for the receiver's affective response, but also for his understanding: 'if either a full-length account or a briefer one leaves the hearer more able to make discoveries, it is this which must be zealously pursued, and no annoyance must be expressed at its length' (286e1–4). Here, it appears to be the responsibility of the discussion leader to tailor the presentation of his argument to the needs of his respondents.

[26] Cf. Morgan (2007), esp. 362.

Now, in analysing the arguments we find in Plato's dialogues, many critics assume that these have a basic underlying form that we can perceive beneath the dialogical exchanges. Moreover, it is often implied that this corresponds to a proof in which all the premises are available and the steps of the argument are set out in their proper order. This is what interpreters present to us when they extract arguments from Plato's texts and recast them in numbered steps,[27] and when the Socrates of the 'early' dialogues is accused of using eristic techniques, the concern is often that he has somehow obscured the underlying form of the argument (which may or may not be valid) so as unfairly to gain his respondent's assent to it. To return to Aristotle's characterization of didactic dialectic, the suggestion seems to be that a didactic argument will be set out in a way that corresponds as closely as possible to its underlying form—for this is what will be most conducive to clarity and comprehensibility. One of my main concerns, therefore, will be the extent to which arguments in dialogues of different types are in fact presented in their basic form (when understood like this), the ways in which they diverge from it, and the effect on the receiver's response if they do.

In *Topics* 8, Aristotle turns his attention to techniques for presenting an argument in dialectical/gymnastic discourse (as opposed to didactic), and gives a range of suggestions for enhancing the effect of an argument on its receiver:[28]

A. Do not propound the propositions through which a deduction is effected directly, since the coming conclusion is less easily discerned at greater distance.
B. Induction should proceed from individual cases to the universal and from the familiar to the unknown; and the objects of perception are more familiar either without qualification or to most people.
C. Do not state the conclusions but deduce them later all together.

[27] A conspicuous feature of the work of many prominent interpreters of Plato, including Irwin and Vlastos. I set out general reservations to doctrinal approaches to the dialogues, of which such practices often form a part, in ch.1.

[28] *Top.*8.1, paraphrased. I have included only those points in Aristotle's discussion relevant to my analysis of Plato. Though Aristotle is here concerned mainly with gymnastic dialectic, he also comments on how these features might play a part in eristic argumentation; and, as I point out later in this section, they are familiar from peirastic discourse as found in Plato.

D. Do not secure the axioms on which deductions are based in their proper order, but alternately those that conduce to one conclusion and those that conduce to another, for if the appropriate ones are set side by side, the conclusion that will result from them is more obvious in advance.[29]

E. Leave it as far as possible doubtful whether one wishes to secure an admission of the proposition or its opposite; for if it is uncertain what the argument requires, people are more ready to say what they themselves think.

F. Try to secure admissions by likeness, for such admissions are plausible and the universal involved is less patent.

G. Occasionally bring an objection against oneself.

H. Add that a view is commonly held, for people are shy about upsetting the received opinion.

I. Formulate your premise as an illustration, for people admit more readily a proposition made to serve some other purpose and not required on its own account.

J. Do not formulate the very proposition needed, but rather something from which it necessarily follows.

K. Put last the point that one most wishes to have conceded, for people are especially inclined to deny the first questions put to them.

L. Expand the argument and insert things it does not require, for in the mass of material the whereabouts of the falsity is obscured.

We can also add similar points made in *Sophistical Refutations*:[30]

M. The importance of length: it is difficult to keep several things in view at once.

N. The importance of speed: when people are left behind they look ahead less.

[29] Compare the narratological term *interlace technique*, referring to the interweaving of different storylines or scenes; see De Jong (2001) xiv.

[30] *Soph.El.*15. Aristotle is here concerned with contentious arguments, but envisages a close relationship between the techniques used by contentious and dialectical questioners (e.g. 174a; 175a) and at 174a26–8 seems to refer to the discussion of these issues at *Top.*8.1. For the overlap between *Soph.El.*15 and *Top.*8, and dialectic and eristic generally, see Dorion (1995) esp. 63–9. See also n12 in this chapter, and section 5.5.

O. The role of anger and contentiousness: when a person is angry he is less able to take care of himself.

P. Do not put the universal as a question, but assume it, when a person has granted the particular case.

Q. Place contraries side by side when asking a question (e.g. 'should one always obey one's parents or never obey one's parents?').

R. State one's conclusion as though one has deduced it, rather than putting it as a question.

S. Place one's opponent on the horns of a dilemma, so that either a paradox or a refutation results.

T. Bring out contradictions in what a person says, whether between his own statements, or between his statements and the view of someone he admires.

U. Draw distinctions in the way one is using a term, e.g. saying one's conclusion is directed against one use of a term but not another.

V. Argue against other positions than the main one in question.

In discussing these tactics, Aristotle testifies to the importance of an argument's presentation for its effect on its receiver. The techniques centre on concealment, and work by creating a gap between the argument and its presentation that confuses and unsettles the receiver.[31] Many of them, moreover, are familiar from the Platonic dialogues; in fact, they include some of the very features often regarded as characteristic of 'early' Platonic dialectic.[32] A didactic argument, on the other hand, constructed with a view to clarity and order, would not, one might think, have need for such tactics. Indeed, we might wish to question the aims of the discussion leader who used such techniques, and their appropriateness—given their likely effect on the interlocutor—for achieving genuine understanding. One of my lines of attack on the traditional interpretation, therefore, will be to demonstrate that features of the sort Aristotle discusses are still present in the arguments of 'middle' and 'late' works.

The second aspect of Plato's arguments with which I shall be concerned is their underlying complexity: the demands an argument makes on the reader and the input it requires her to make into

[31] Cf. Aristotle *Soph.El.*14–15.

[32] Robinson (1953) 22.

understanding how it works.[33] I will take into account features such as the length and difficulty of an argument, as well as the extent to which a given passage relies on or interacts with others inside or outside the dialogue in question. In doing so, I hope to counteract from another angle the idea that arguments in 'middle' and 'late' dialogues require less input from the receiver because they are expository in form. As we shall see, there are significant changes in the shape of the underlying arguments as we reach 'later' dialogues, but these do not tend to make life easier for the receiver. On the contrary, only a receiver engaging in the fullest way could hope to benefit from them.

In the following discussion, I look at examples of argumentation from 'early, 'middle', and 'late' works in turn, highlighting features of their construction and presentation, and asking how they invite us to respond. I will start by considering an example of elenctic argumentation, since here the personal and involving nature of Platonic dialectic is most apparent and the non-didactic character of the arguments is not in doubt.

5.5. 'EARLY' ARGUMENTS

As an example of argumentation typical of 'early' works, let us look at the 'uselessness' argument brought against Polemarchus at *Republic* I, 332c5–333e2.[34] Polemarchus and Socrates have just been discussing what Simonides means in saying that it is just to give to each what is owed to him. Polemarchus interprets the quotation as meaning that one owes it to one's friends to do good to them, and to one's enemies to harm them; and at this point Socrates starts to interrogate Polemarchus' position. He suggests that individual crafts, such as cooking

[33] These considerations overlap with certain features of gymnastic dialectic considered above—for example, (A) and (D)—in as much as these have a bearing on the apparent complexity of the argument and the extent to which its underlying steps are made plain to us. However, the distinction I am intending to draw is between the argument itself and the way it is presented to us.

[34] Although *Republic* is usually regarded as from Plato's 'middle' period, the style of argumentation contained in book I is commonly regarded as typical of 'early' arguments: see e.g. Irwin (1995) 169. I do not intend to imply that I regard *Republic* I as having at any stage existed as a separate work.

and medicine, each have a specific field of activity; then, by analogy, he tries to induce Polemarchus to specify a field for justice. After this, he points out progressively that the field of justice is taken up by other crafts, until Polemarchus is forced to concede that justice has no substantial field, and is useless.

The argument underlying this set of exchanges is not itself terribly demanding. It is short and self-contained, and does not make use of theoretical assumptions or arguments set out elsewhere in this work or in others (though of course it does resonate with them). It mainly proceeds by reference to commonplace examples familiar to and open to scrutiny by anyone. Its basic structure, whereby, as a kind of *reductio*, possible answers are progressively eliminated until only an unacceptable one remains, is simple. And the main idea it seems to convey—that we run into trouble if we think of justice as a craft with a specific field of application like other crafts—is not difficult to grasp.

In making this point, Socrates could have encouraged Polemarchus to reflect on the similarities and differences between justice and other crafts, thus exploring whether or not it is helpful to regard justice as having a specific field of activity like other crafts—as Socrates' argument implies many people do. This might potentially have helpfully contributed to Polemarchus' understanding both of his own views and of the concept of justice.[35] Yet, notoriously, the argument is far from achieving this. There are many readers who regard the argument as among Plato's worst, and view Socrates' argumentative techniques here as more eristic than dialectical.[36] They think Socrates uses unfair and non-transparent tactics to trick Polemarchus into accepting an argument that refutes him, and believe that if Socrates' main purpose had been to explain a flaw in Polemarchus' position, he could have done so in a more straightforward way. In fact, it seems that his intention in bringing this argument is not to increase clarity or understanding, but to confuse his respondent,[37] and this is borne

[35] For a similar analysis of the point of Socrates' argument, see Joseph (1935) 1–14. Cf. also Annas (1981) 23–34, Reeve (1988) 8, White (1979) 63–4, Beversluis (2000) 205–6. For the argument as bringing home to Polemarchus the inadequacy of his views, see Cornford (1941) 8, Page (1990) 249; also Adam (1938) 18.

[36] See Annas (1981) 23–34, Beversluis (2000) 203, Blondell (2002) 178, Guthrie (1975) 439–41, Cross and Woozley (1964) 4, 10–12, Joseph (1935) 1, Gifford (2001) 85. See also n12 above.

[37] Cf. Teloh (1986) chs. 2, 3, 5, 6 for similar observations about the character of argumentation in 'early' dialogues. Page (1990) 249 thinks that Socrates is here less

out by the effect of the argument upon Polemarchus. During the course of the argument, his responses become increasingly hesitant and non-committal, shifting from 'πάνυ γε' ('certainly') and 'ναί' ('yes') to 'κινδυνεύει' ('it's likely') and 'φαίνεται' ('it seems so').[38] At one point, 332e12, Polemarchus withholds his assent, yet his reservation is not properly dealt with. He is given no comment of agreement at the end of argument, where Socrates moves straight into another attack. Shortly into this next section, at 334b7–9 and 334d7–8, Polemarchus twice emphatically expresses dissent, confusion, uncertainty, and frustration, and it is hard not to think that these are a cumulative product of our argument as well. So Polemarchus may have been shown that there is a problem with his views, but unless he revisits the argument more carefully, he will not understand why.

Socrates' techniques here often resemble the dialectical techniques discussed by Aristotle (which will be noted in brackets). Most importantly, the analogy between justice and other crafts, so crucial to Socrates' strategy, is not directly stated, explained, or argued for; nor is it clear that Polemarchus himself subscribes to such a view of justice (A).[39] Instead, Socrates imports it indirectly through the use of examples from cookery, sailing, and so forth, implying that these are like the case of justice in order to gain congenial responses from Polemarchus (F). The use of specific instances masks the fact that Polemarchus is committing himself to a potentially problematic universal principle—that all crafts work in the same way and that justice is one of them—and in particular, the use of everyday examples makes the analogy seem obvious and straightforward (B).[40] Socrates' use of abundant illustrations introduces what might be thought unnecessary material into the argument and creates the superficial impression of thoroughness in argument, thereby encouraging acceptance (L). The false sense of security is enhanced by

interested in proving Polemarchus incorrect than in upsetting his tendency to assume that his view is 'self-evident and comprehensive'. Gifford (2001) 86–7 sees the 'paradoxical paths of the argument' as a means of showing that Polemarchus has not given much thought to what justice is.

[38] On qualified assent, see Beversluis (2000) 45 and (on this argument in particular) 206–7; also Scott (1999), esp. 18–20.

[39] See Beversluis (2000) 207–11, 219–20, Cross and Woozley (1964) 11. Annas (1981) 24–8 thinks Polemarchus *is* committed to such a picture of justice.

[40] For Socrates' familiar premises as 'compelling' his interlocutors, see Kraut (1983).

repetition, both in the examples used and in the rhythm of the exchanges, where closed questions are followed by an open question relating to justice—and it is heightened on occasion by wordplay, such as πεττῶν/πεττευτικός at 333b2. Socrates regularly turns to justice last in his series of questions, as Aristotle recommends (K). He keeps his conclusions—that justice is only useful when things are in use and that justice is therefore not a very important thing, 333d10–e2—right till the end of the argument (C), which adds to their impact and their finality. He also puts the last conclusion as a statement rather than a question, which further discourages Polemarchus from objecting (R). The paradoxical effect of Socrates' conclusion derives its power at least in part from contradicting the commitment to the usefulness of justice implied in Polemarchus' original definition—that justice is helping one's friends and harming one's enemies (T).

The use of pace, combined with sudden changes in direction, further adds to the argument's effect. In general, the pace is fast (N).[41] The conversation moves forward in a series of short sections, each of which is typically made up of three exchanges leading to a concession by Polemarchus;[42] within these, a swift argumentative pace is maintained by the use of closed—and at times syntactically abbreviated—questions. Moreover, the sections of the argument follow one another in quick and unrelenting succession. There is rarely a pause between them, marked either by a break in conversation altogether or by, for instance, commentary on the respondents' response to the progress of discussion. Instead, Socrates just moves off on to another series of questions, sometimes from an unexpected direction (as when, at 333a13–333b1 for example, he shifts from asking what Polemarchus means by contracts to asking who is a useful associate in a checkers game). This is particularly marked on the occasion when Polemarchus actually disagrees with the conclusion being reached—the idea that justice is useless when one is not fighting a war (332e11–12)—where no time is devoted to getting to the bottom of Polemarchus' hesitation or understanding its deeper relevance. At the very close of the argument, too, there is no pause for

[41] White (1979) 63 comments that the argument is 'too briskly framed to be cogent'. Speed is particularly important in the (sophistic) argument conducted by Euthydemus and Dionysodorus at *Euthd.*275d–277d.

[42] Adam (1938) 15.

reflection or recuperation: Socrates just moves straight on to the next argument. The combination of speed and changes in direction creates a disorientating effect; we are exposed to repeated argumentative assaults, yet left no time to make sense of or repel one before we move on to the next.

In short, the argument is far from didactic in its approach. Many of Socrates' tactics are designed to conceal the outcome of the argument,[43] lulling the answerer into accepting argumentative moves he might not otherwise have done, and thus leaving him open to surprise and confusion; others add disorientation. In achieving this, it is worth noticing the degree of control Socrates exerts over the argument. As a refutation, the passage relies on prior analysis on the part of the discussion leader, who must know from the start what objection he will bring against the definition put forward and where his questions will end up. For the most part, Socrates supplies the substance of the argument, and Polemarchus simply goes along with it. Particularly important here is the use of closed questions, where the respondent must assent or dissent to an idea put forward by the questioner. Although the response technically still belongs to the respondent,[44] it is much easier for him to go along with the direction Socrates suggests than to resist that movement. In other words, the role of the questioner and his state of knowledge *in relation to the argument* is not unlike that attributed to him in didactic dialectic—if he had wished, he could have presented the opposing argument as a proof.[45] Yet controlling the course of the discussion need not produce a 'didactic' response, and does not entail controlling what the respondent thinks. Polemarchus' experience of the argument is akin to that of a person participating in an inquiry, who follows the uncertain and unclear paths of his thought through to its refutation, undergoing confusion and bafflement as he proceeds; and this is a product of the specific way in which Socrates, as director of the discussion, engages him in dialectic.

What, then, might be the purpose of presenting the argument in this way? Why not set it out in a clearer and more didactic manner?

[43] Cf. Robinson (1953) 22. [44] Cf. Frede (1992a).

[45] This line is strengthened if, with Vlastos, one thinks that Socrates takes himself to be proving the conclusions of his arguments: Vlastos (1983). Cf. also Robinson (1953) 16 and Irwin (1988a) 7: 'in the *Protagoras* and *Gorgias*, and in many later dialogues, Plato does explicitly what he does implicitly in the earlier dialogues, using the Socratic method to argue for positive philosophical positions.'

This brings us back to the debate about Plato's attitude towards elenctic dialectic, discussed in chapter 3. One possibility is to regard the portrait of Socrates here as intentionally negative, designed to expose his techniques as unfair, even bordering on the eristic—or at least as inadequate in producing philosophical progress. After all, one might say, their defects are not simply evident to us; they are voiced in the text by Thrasymachus, when he interrupts at 336b, and are borne out by the change in dialectical style after book I. Something of this view underlies traditional developmentalist accounts of the changes in Platonic dialectic from 'early' to 'late' works. By contrast, I offered a more positive interpretation of the dialectical style Socrates employs in 'early' dialogues, based on the picture of the learning process that emerges from the dialogues.[46] At an early stage of philosophical development, interlocutors need to have their ideas and self-conception radically challenged; this produces violent feelings, only some of which are directly helpful in the learning process; but manifesting them is nevertheless a positive thing, for it shows that the learner is involved in a cognitive-affective way—the first step in true learning. The purpose of the dialectical style of 'early' works, I argued, is to produce such a learning experience in the interlocutors—and the argument with Polemarchus is no exception. Here, I have probed the argumentative techniques through which the effects are achieved. The purpose, therefore, of the gap between the underlying argument and its presentation is, if my interpretation is accepted, to produce the responses necessary for the receiver to make her initial steps in learning.

If this is the case, then the arguments we find in 'early' dialogues are educational in intent and in effect, but they shun a *didactic* approach as inappropriate to this stage of a learner's development. In fact, there are a number of ways in which Socrates' style in our argument is particularly well suited to an interlocutor at an initial stage of philosophical development. The argument itself is short and independent of Socrates' other arguments, so does not require the interlocutor to follow lengthy and complex stretches of reasoning. Its underlying form and message are simple, and its methodological approach is not demanding. The *ad hominem* form is crucial in

[46] Besides, the above approaches to the portrayal of Socrates make poor sense of Plato's presentation of such a picture in so many dialogues; cf. the criticisms of Beversluis' approach in Gill (2001).

bringing home *personal* inadequacy to an interlocutor who is not yet convinced of his need to learn. Furthermore, Socrates' tactics are obvious and unsubtle, drastic and abrasive, and so ideal for getting through to complacent interlocutors who need to be exposed to an unsettling shock if they are to see the need to engage in learning. The methods leave Polemarchus with little room to manoeuvre: just by following the argument through, he seems inevitably drawn into confusion and uncertainty. To the extent that he is engaging with what Socrates says at all, the argument will prompt such experiences in him. Moreover, to have a beneficial effect, they do not require the interlocutor to be deeply committed to the learning project, or to be self-conscious about his own progress. He need, at this stage, take no responsibility for his development, but can make progress just by reacting to the stimuli to which the questioner exposes him: for, as I have suggested, just experiencing confusion, discomfort, and the further feelings attendant upon these, is valuable as a first step in learning. Even in cases where the respondent is only participating in the discussion to a minimal extent—failing to manifest the dialectical virtues or to comply with Socrates' rules of discussion, like Thrasymachus, for example—Socrates' methods can still produce such effects. At this stage, the learner is essentially treated as a passive subject, encouraged by the tactics of the discussion leader to respond in a way that will enable him to embark upon the process of learning—though of course his second-order response, on which his further progress depends, is still largely up to him.[47]

[47] This approach also offers us a way of accounting for the eristic elements of such arguments, which have long troubled interpreters and form the basis of the negative interpretation outlined above. If the key purpose of these arguments is to produce certain responses in the receiver—engaging him in a cognitive-affective way and prompting him to further reflection—the use of unfair tactics will not prevent it from doing so, and may even assist it. Ideally, the respondent will come to reflect critically on ideas put to him, so the discussion leader's use of flawed or unfair arguments does not pose a threat to his long-term development—indeed it should make him even more wary of accepting what the discussion leader says. The line, that is, between eristic and other forms of dialectic is not in Plato as clear, or as important, as we are sometimes inclined to think (as is reflected in the overlap between eristic and dialectic in Aristotle's discussion). On the value of fallacious and eristic reasoning, see e.g. Teloh (1986) 50–3, 187, Gonzalez (1998) 102–5, Sichel (1976), Sprague (1962). Blondell (2002) 178 suggests that since Polemarchus 'is already enthusiastic about Socrates and his methods, Socrates has no "excuse", as he does e.g. in the case of Hippias, for using bad arguments deliberately in order to shake up his complacency'. But the depth of Polemarchus' commitment is questionable: see n49.

So far, in an effort to highlight the type of dialectical exchange in question, I have focused on Socrates' argumentative tactics and Polemarchus' responses. But what of the reader? In chapter 2, I warned against assuming that the reader's response, even if it is similar in kind to that of the interlocutors, simply mirrors theirs. In the stretch of argument with which we are dealing, Polemarchus' responses are not in fact directly expressed: they are hinted at in his increasingly qualified answers to Socrates' questions, and we infer them from his later outbursts of frustration and bafflement. It cannot therefore be the case that our responses are dependent upon his. Nevertheless it does, I think, make sense to see ourselves as going through a similar set of experiences. The argumentative tactics which Socrates uses—the lack of clarity about the direction of the argument, the changes in direction, the concealed premises—all confuse and disorientate us as much as they do Polemarchus. Indeed, the way the argument is presented to us in the text arguably intensifies the effect these tactics would have had in conversation.

To begin with, Polemarchus is not at any point made to voice in an extended way the feelings of confusion or uncertainty which the text indicates he is experiencing or to raise any objection to what Socrates says—moments that would have allowed us to reflect on the argument and to diagnose its strategy. More generally, the use of pace enhances the impact of the exchanges upon us. Pace is of course an important factor in a face-to-face situation. But a conspicuous feature of the arguments reported in the dialogues is that, with some notable exceptions, they give us very little sense of how time actually passed during a conversation—whether someone paused before answering or whether a question was delivered ponderously or rapidly. Instead, our perception of pace is governed entirely by the responses given: if they are short, then the exchanges are fast from our perspective; if they are padded out with conversational words, then the pace slackens. Similarly, a comment not directly advancing the argument—on the situation, or on a person's response to the argument—slows the pace further, and occasionally a pause is provided by a comment from the narrator.[48] In this argument, these elements of padding are absent, the conversational style is very taut, and in consequence the pace from the reader's perspective is quick. This is particularly conspicuous at the

[48] Cf. Morgan (2007).

end of each mini-section of argument, and especially after Polemarchus' expression of dissent midway through the argument, at 332e12. In other words, if this conversation had in actual fact taken place, it might have been as swift as we have the impression of it being, but equally it might not. That impression is created through the way Plato presents the argument to us.

Like Polemarchus, therefore, we are confused and frustrated as we follow the argument through. Like him, too, we are left with little choice about how, initially, to respond.[49] As we noted of Socrates' tactics themselves, the argument is unsubtle and ungentle in the way it engages the reader; we cannot just follow the steps of the argument without getting more deeply involved. Plato is not simply showing us what reflection needs to be like if it is to be productive; he is trying to initiate that process in us, and he is doing so in a way suited to someone at an early stage of development, who cannot be relied upon to take responsibility for his own engagement and progress. This will change when we come to other types of dialectic.

5.6. 'MIDDLE' ARGUMENTS

My example of 'middle' dialectic is *Republic* IX, 583b ff., where Socrates argues that the life of the just man is more pleasant than that of the unjust man. Here, Socrates argues that the philosopher's pleasures are the only true ones, and that only in the just man will the reasoning part be able to enjoy the pleasures proper to it—namely true ones. He then goes on to demonstrate, through a notoriously

[49] Though, as I suggested in earlier chapters, a more productive second-order response is open to us, likely to involve revision, rereading, and pause for reflection. The extent to which Polemarchus himself embarks upon this is debated. At the time, he does not appear to reflect in a productive way on the arguments Socrates has involved him in; and in consequence he has been interpreted as a paradigm of the complacent interlocutor, for example by Annas (1981) 18–34. Others have pointed to the more productive role he plays later in *Republic* and want to see him as that rare thing—a Socratic success story: see Blondell (2002) 176–8. True, by the time Thrasymachus interrupts at 336b, Polemarchus does seem reconciled to Socrates' viewpoint. However, I am inclined to see this not as a real conversion, but rather as a further way of intensifying the effect of the sequence of interlocutors on the reader: Polemarchus' capitulation is too easy, and in fact confuses and frustrates us even further, as it is not warranted by Socrates' arguments.

obscure calculation, that the life of the philosopher king is 729 times more pleasant than that of the tyrant.

As I outlined above, in arguments such as this one, Plato is generally held to abandon the dialectical style characteristic of 'early' dialogues in favour of a more constructive and didactic approach, and several features of our passage lend themselves to this view. First, the argument leads to a firm conclusion: that only the pleasure of the man of intellect is true and pure, while that of others is illusory. Moreover, Socrates states that conclusion at the outset, thereby presenting himself as offering a demonstration (at 583b3, Socrates tells his listeners to 'observe'—ἄθρει—the conclusion), rather than as exploring the views of his interlocutors. True, he still portrays himself as engaged in a shared search, saying that he will discover the conclusion as his interlocutor answers (583c1), but Glaucon makes little substantive contribution and Socrates is firmly in charge. His questions frequently make clear the answer he is expecting, and his phrasing sometimes suggests that he has worked through the argument before (e.g. the selection of the pleasure of smell as a sufficiently convincing example of a more general phenomenon at 584b). His explanations of desire (as a kind of emptiness) and of pleasure (as having a below, middle, and above) again suggest an already worked-out view, and so, most emphatically, does the closing calculation comparing the lives of philosopher and tyrant. It looks, in effect, as though Socrates is in his most didactic and persuasive mood, expounding his ideas and trying to ensure that his interlocutors agree with him.[50]

But is the shift to a didactic style really so comprehensive? We can start by noting the presence here, as in the argument with Polemarchus, of many of the dialectical techniques recommended by Aristotle. Socrates begins by securing Glaucon's assent to a series

[50] This argument is markedly more didactic/persuasive than arguments, say, in *Republic* II, which are exploratory and open in structure. For references to Aristotle's didactic dialectic in characterizing the dialectic of 'middle' dialogues, see e.g. Vlastos (1991) 117–18, 123–6, 130–1, who connects the abandonment of the *elenchus* in 'middle' dialogues with a new devotion to mathematical method, which is used as the model for a more demonstrative (in Aristotle's sense) approach to philosophizing. Annas (1981) 289–90 also sees mathematics as the model for the conception of dialectic put forward in *Republic*, and likewise refers to Aristotle's conception of scientific method in this context. Blondell (2002) 200–1 draws attention to language of demonstration and teaching in *Republic*.

of propositions—that pain is the opposite of pleasure (583c3), that there is such a thing as feeling neither pleasure nor pain (583c5), and that this mean state is a calmness of the soul (583c7–8)—to which he returns at the close of this section of the argument, drawing out all the conclusions at once, as Aristotle recommends (583e7–584a11) (C). Here, Glaucon's affirmation that the mid-state between pleasure and pain is itself neither pleasure or pain is used at 583e7–8 to reject the idea that the state could be *both* pleasure and pain, as the view of the masses seems to imply, and his affirmation that the mid-state between pleasure and pain is a kind of calmness is also used for the same end (584a1–5), seeing that he has also agreed (at 583e9–10) that pleasure and pain are both types of movement. In this section of argument, Socrates also uses some of the aspects of the handling of instances and universals on which Aristotle comments. At 583d, Socrates introduces familiar examples—the sick person who says that nothing gives them more pleasure than health, and the person in pain who says that nothing is as pleasurable as cessation from pain—to ease us into accepting the less familiar universal observation that people frequently praise freedom from pain, rather than the feeling of pleasure, as the most pleasant thing (583d6–9) (B). Here, Socrates states the universal, rather than putting it as a question (R), and straight afterwards states the opposing principle—that the cessation of pleasure will be regarded as painful—without any further examples or argument. It is worth noting Glaucon's rather lukewarm response at this point: ἴσως ('perhaps', 583e3). Similar is Socrates' approach in the passage that immediately follows (584b1–c3), in which he supports the conclusion that pleasure is not the absence of pain and vice versa by noting that some pleasures are not preceded by pain. At this point, he introduces the pleasures of smell to exemplify this idea (B), observes that there are many other pleasures like this, and then states the universal principle as his conclusion, with no further argument (P, R).

In the following section of the argument (584c4–586b), Socrates turns to explaining the relationship between true and untrue pleasures.[51] His first approach to the issue involves introducing the idea of

[51] I am inclined to regard the first section of argument as introducing the idea that there are true and untrue pleasures and that we may be mistaken in the pleasures we take to be true; and the second section as exploring what it means for pleasures to be true and untrue. Cf. White (1979) 229. Others, however, regard the two sections of

below-middle-above, and applying it to the concept of pleasure. Since this is, in the context of the argument, a new idea, and different from the conceptions of pleasure used so far, this constitutes a small change of direction. Socrates then, at 585a8, in another change of direction, starts to use the ideas of emptiness and filling to elucidate the realness of the true pleasures. Finally, from 586ab, having concluded the analysis in these terms, he paints a picture of the life of the masses, in which he combines language of emptiness-filling and of below-middle-above, using it to bring out the conclusion that in ascending to the middle, the masses in fact experience pleasures that are less real, and therefore less pleasant, than the true pleasures of wise people. The changes of direction here are rather reminiscent of those we observed in the argument with Polemarchus, and they also illustrate Aristotle's observation about the ordering of questions, as Socrates shifts between different threads of argument (D)[52] before drawing together the conclusions at the close (C). In relying on the power of the images he brings in—below-middle-above, the illustration of white, grey, and black used at 585a to support it, emptiness and filling—Socrates uses likeness as a way of making his analysis plausible (F). Similarly, the picture of the masses and their pleasure at 586ab which forms the conclusion of the argument, with its wealth of colourful details, might be thought an example of expanding the argument with additional material (L); for it seems to be as much the picture that Socrates paints, as his actual argument, that prompts Glaucon's positive response at 586b5–6.

In addition, Socrates here employs unstated assumptions (A), another important feature of the argument with Polemarchus. In using the language of below-middle-above to present the pleasures of the masses as having a smaller share in truth and reality than those of the philosopher, he is relying on the epistemology of the work's middle books, and particularly the Cave image, which his argument here strongly recalls (especially 584d–585a, 586ab).[53] Similarly, the shift from the reality of the things with which one is filled, to the

argument as producing two separate accounts of real pleasures and point out that they do not converge perfectly. See e.g. Cross and Woozley (1964) 266–8, Annas (1981) 311–12.

[52] See Sichel (1976) on the abandonment of logical order in arguments in the dialogues. Cf. also Robinson (1953) 22.

[53] Cross and Woozley (1964) 266.

reality of the pleasure of being filled, at 585ae, again relies on ideas put forward earlier in the work, particularly the idea that Forms exist and have a higher degree of reality than the things of this world.[54]

Further, there is the consideration of speed (N), which was crucial to the effect of the uselessness argument. Here, the pace is slower for the majority of the argument, which contributes to its more cooperative and didactic feel, and allows greater time for the consideration of ideas in a productive way. Socrates takes more time over the introduction of the concepts he uses; his contributions to the conversation are longer, frequently several lines long each; and he introduces the kind of illustrative detail which slows the pace rather than increasing it.[55] However, when Socrates turns to applying the results of the argument to the lives of the appetitive, spirited, and philosophical men (from 586b), the pace rises a notch; it continues to increase progressively, as Socrates whizzes through conclusions about the relationships between the parts of the soul reached earlier in the work, combines them with the conclusions about pleasure, and ends up by speeding through the obscure steps of his proof that the philosopher king's life is 729 times more pleasant than the dictator's. Here, Socrates' contributions are noticeably shorter, and he takes less trouble to ensure that his interlocutor follows each step, as indicated by Glaucon's responses at 587d11 and 587e5–588a2: Glaucon does not display the baffled confusion of Polemarchus, but he makes it

[54] Cf. e.g. White (1979) 229–32, Annas (1981) 312–13, Reeve (1988) 148–9, 110–12. Cross and Woozley (1964) 267 also comment that Plato fails to argue, as he needs to, that pleasure is so inextricably bound up with the activity of filling as to derive its degree of reality from that of the activity.

[55] In narratological terms, a pause occurs when 'the action is suspended to make room for a description' (De Jong (2001) xvii). In narrated dialogues, intrusions by the narrator will count as pauses in the narratological sense. But other features I have pinpointed as characterizing pauses are more difficult. If we treat the events of the conversation—the conversational exchanges—as equivalent to the events of the story, then the features I have identified as slowing the pace do not involve a slow-down in narrative time, since text time is equal to story time (cf. De Jong (2001) xvii, who terms this 'scenic' treatment). If, however, we take the underlying argumentative steps to be parallel to the events of a narrative, as I have been advocating, then the features I have been talking about do in fact constitute pauses, in a sense akin to the narratological one, in as much as they interrupt the flow of the argumentative story. Cohen (2002) views such hiatuses as annoying for the solitary reader, but quotes Robb (1994) 233, who thinks they would have the opposite effect. For discussion of 'slow down' in Plato's dialogues, see Morgan (2007) 362–3.

abundantly clear that the speed of Socrates' demonstration has left him unclear how the conclusion has been reached.

Even more important than speed in this argument, however, is length (M)—at least in the main part of the argument up until 586b. It is not simply that the argument is longer than the typical elenctic argument, making it difficult, as Aristotle comments, to keep several things in view at once. It is also that the threads of reasoning that Socrates uses are more complex in themselves, more numerous, and are interwoven with each other.[56] The argument is also lengthy in another sense, in that it requires us to call upon ideas put forward in the whole of the rest of *Republic*, from the picture of the tripartite soul, to Socrates' ideas about knowledge, opinion, and Forms, to the images of Sun, Line, and Cave. As I said above, references to these are not actually spelled out in the argument itself, but they are necessary for a satisfactory comprehension of the argument; and by requiring us to supply what is missing for ourselves, the argument, in effect, increases hugely in length—as well as in difficulty. In this sense, length shades into the second of my categories for looking at an argument: its underlying complexity. In effect, this passage acts as the culmination of the argument of the whole *Republic*, both because it is the third and final proof that the life of the just man is preferable to that of the unjust man (583b1–3), and also because the proof rests on the argumentative structure built up throughout the rest of the work. It is not a separate, detached proof, but an additional consideration drawn from all that has gone before. As such, the demands it makes on the reader—if we think of the process of rereading or rethinking she has to undertake, the considerations she has to bring in, the connections she has to make—are immense. The style may be more didactic and directional, but there is no way that a receiver can appreciate the significance of this argument without a great deal of her own input—and not just here, since she needs to have been attentive over a much longer period.[57]

The above observations should make us hesitate before dismissing any similarity between arguments like this one and typical 'early'

[56] Cf. Cross and Woozley (1964) 266: the argument 'is extremely complicated; and it is difficult to be confident that one has sorted out all the threads of it'.

[57] See Rutherford (1995) 210–11 on how *Republic* becomes increasingly demanding as it progresses, relying as it does on arguments put forward earlier in the work. A similar movement can be seen in the corpus as a whole, as I suggest later.

arguments. Not only does our passage again contain many of Aristotle's dialectical techniques; at times, the tactics Socrates uses appear somewhat eristic and—especially in the case of unstated assumptions—can look like holes in his thinking. Of course, as commentators show in reconstructing the argument, it is not that we cannot follow his reasoning; it is rather that he does not always spell out the assumptions on which it is based, and some of them we may want to challenge. That Socrates is made to take this approach to 'teaching' or 'persuading' Glaucon is very interesting. It makes it misleading to assimilate their relationship to the sort associated with didactic dialectic, as outlined in sections 5.1–5.2, where the discussion leader, as an expert figure, sets out ideas in as transparent a manner as possible and the respondent is conditioned to accept them as knowledge. There is a decided edge to Socrates' approach, whether we call it persuasive, competitive, or eristic, which makes a passive-receptive attitude in the receiver inappropriate. Indeed, for all his goodwill towards Socrates, Glaucon sometimes reacts with wariness or incredulity: he is open and motivated, but will only accept Socrates' reasoning if he finds it convincing. Accordingly we too have to be fully critical and reflective, asking if we are prepared to accept Socrates' ideas and his reasons for them. In this regard, the character of the responses evoked in us here is not dissimilar from *Republic* I.

At the same time, there are changes. The underlying argument is lengthier and more challenging, requiring the receiver to follow and interpret complex strands of thought. Its greater constructive content itself stimulates the receiver, in as much as it exposes her to a larger range of unfamiliar ideas to evaluate and take on board. The ideas considered, moreover, are more difficult and abstract. The passage includes more impersonal discussion, broadening the philosophical horizon but leaving receivers to relate what is said to their own ideas. The passage also encourages us to take an unfamiliar view of our human condition, regarding our customary pleasures from a detached, ideal perspective.[58] All this means that the argument encourages a more philosophically sophisticated type of engagement: the receiver has to deal with more difficult concepts and less familiar viewpoints, confront a broader spectrum of ideas, bring together a range of different arguments, and locate her own thoughts in relation

[58] On this aspect of the argument, see especially Nussbaum (1986) 136–64.

to the ideas explored in a more self-conscious way. At the same time, the slower pace, longer format, and more expansive style give her more time and space to do so. This is crucial when we come to evaluate whether the argument does represent a shift towards didactic dialectic. On the surface it may look as though the interlocutor is getting an easier time, for the dialectical style is smoother and less aggressive, and the discussion leader contributes most of the substantive material. In fact, though, this type of discussion requires greater philosophical sophistication from the receiver, prompting him to develop towards the next stage of philosophical progress.

Equally importantly, the interlocutor has to take much greater personal responsibility for his involvement in the argument than Polemarchus did. The less interactive style—which is crucial to the appearance of didacticism—means it would be possible for an interlocutor (or reader) to coast along without getting fully involved. So if he does become productively engaged, then this is a consequence of his own commitment, self-motivation, and perseverance. The less interactive style, that is, acts as a challenge to the interlocutor to motivate his own engagement. When he does so, he meets an argument as testing, in its own way, as the one Socrates earlier brought against Polemarchus, and one which leaves him vulnerable—as Glaucon's responses occasionally make clear—to the same sorts of negative responses. But whereas, in 'early' contexts, an interlocutor can profit by participating in an argument with only minimal dialectical virtue, the same is not true here. To benefit, the interlocutor needs to curb his negative responses, and show perseverance in engaging in a positive and committed way. If this style of discussion is to be successful, in other words, it requires the interlocutor to have made some progress in the development of dialectical virtue.

As regards both his intellectual input and his affective responses, therefore, the interlocutor is required to contribute a great deal more for himself than in 'early' works. By this stage, the Cave's educator needs to do less to prompt the learner; and the learner is closer to the stage where he can make progress on his own. Now he has reached this stage, he does not *need* to be exposed to the violent stimuli provided by the elenchus, but will benefit more from the more complex stimuli of 'middle' dialectic, which help him develop as a more sophisticated and independent learner. The learner's stage of development, that is, can account for the change in dialectical style. But if this approach is accepted, we are faced with a significant disjunction between the actual contributions of the interlocutor to the conversation, and his real level of participation. Glaucon's actual contributions are minimal and unsubstantive, as are additional dramatic indicators of the interlocutors' responses. Yet if, as most readers are inclined to, we think of him as engaging productively with the argument,[59] much more—thoughts, feelings, concerns, and so forth—must lie behind these responses. The same is true, I suggest, of the reader's response: if we engage with the argument, we must be more cognitively and affectively involved than Glaucon's spoken contributions would suggest. We should not be fooled into thinking that our response replicates the spoken contributions of interlocutors: here as elsewhere, the way interlocutors are depicted and the type of involvement they are presented as having are means of prompting a certain kind of engagement in the reader.

5.7. 'LATE' ARGUMENTS

In 'late' dialogues, it is usually felt, the move away from Plato's 'early' dialectical style intensifies, and this seems particularly true of *Sophist*, which has been called the most dogmatic of Plato's dialogues.[60] Again, it is the idea that such works establish a didactic or dogmatic relationship with their receivers that I want to challenge; and the passage I will address is *Sophist* 224e6–226a5.[61]

This passage comes from the initial section of the dialogue, in which the Eleatic Stranger and Theaetetus apply the method of division in trying to reach a definition of the sophist. They carry out the process a number of times, each time reaching a description of the sophist, which then turns out to have another aspect they need to

[59] The majority of 'middle' and 'late' interlocutors are usually thought to provide positive exempla of philosophical endeavour. Exceptions, for whom we can account in different ways, include Philebus and perhaps Aristotle in the second part of *Parmenides*, on whose presentation as an imperfect interlocutor see Miller (1986).

[60] M. Frede (1996) 135.

[61] I have chosen this passage because, on the surface, it comes from the most formally uninteresting and undemanding part of the work: e.g. Ryle (1966) 140 claims that the divisions 'presuppose no philosophical sophistication whatsoever'. The later discussion of being and non-being is frequently felt to approximate to a treatise, and is also I think amenable to the approaches I used for *Republic* IX and will be using here.

pursue. Our passage forms one of these attempts; in it, Theaeteus and the Eleatic Stranger approach sophistry as a subsection of the art of fighting. At first glance, the passage seems amply to bear out the traditional idea that, in 'late' dialogues, the question-and-answer mode is merely a formality. It involves a process of classification that is highly systematic and rather resembles, perhaps, the logical exposition of results reached through a prior investigation of the sort we might associate with Aristotle's didactic dialectic.[62] The discussion proceeds smoothly, even mechanically; there are fewer deviations and interruptions than in 'earlier' dialogues; and there is a strong emphasis on the correct order of discussion. The Eleatic Stranger dominates the proceedings: at the start of the passage, he appears to initiate another round of division because he has another aspect of the sophist's nature in mind (224e6–7), and he then conducts the division himself. Theaetetus contributes almost nothing; his responses are minimal and the Eleatic Stranger's questions usually make it clear which answer he is expecting. Theaetetus' role seems to be merely to prompt the Eleatic Stranger to carry on the path of division he is already pursuing (225a5: 'say of what sort they are'; 225b4: 'how?') and to draw the final conclusion, to which the Eleatic Stranger has effectively led him (225e3–5).[63] All this seems to bear out what is said in the introduction to the conversation at the very start of the dialogue, where we are told that the Eleatic Stranger, in the manner of an expert, has worked through the topic in advance (217be).

But things are not quite so straightforward. Most importantly the passage does not take the form of a worked-out proof. The Eleatic Stranger does not set out the conclusion at the start of the argument, but leaves it to be drawn at the close (C). This is crucial to the impact

[62] Blondell (2002) 338 refers directly to Aristotle's conception of didactic dialectic in characterizing the dialectic found in *Sophist*; Taylor (1961) 20–1 likens collection and division to Euclid's *Elements* book X, a work often treated as a model for Aristotle's approach to demonstration. See Cavini (1995) for discussion of the logical form of diaeretic arguments and their relation to Aristotle's theory of the syllogism. For division as presenting the results of prior investigation, cf. Griswold (1986) 185, Mackenzie (1982) 70, Annas and Waterfield (1995) xi (though of course the respondent is being led to see new things); also Bluck (1975) 35–40. The opposing view, that collection and division is about discovery, is voiced e.g. by Rowe (1984) 46. Lane (1998) 18, 68–70 maintains that, even if division is concerned with restructuring understanding, it may still represent a form of inquiry.

[63] See Blondell (2002) for similar points.

of the argument: for even if the discussion leader knows in advance how the conversation will proceed, this is not how he presents things to the receiver. As we noted in section 5.5, Socrates frequently stands in such a relationship to his arguments in 'early' works. The effect is heightened, moreover, by the place of our passage within a series of attempts to define the sophist, each of which destabilizes the previous definition by revealing it to be incomplete, before turning out itself to be inconclusive. This is not dissimilar in its effect to the series of elenctic arguments typically found in an 'early' dialogue. There, repeated argumentative assaults undermine the interlocutor's position from different angles, progressively reducing him to bafflement. Here, though each burst of dialectic appears to work towards providing a constructive new outcome, with each new argument we in fact become less and less sure how to regard the definitions reached so far.[64] And, just as the 'early' interlocutor is left to work out the implications of the different arguments for the views he started off holding, so here we have to work out how the different definitions reached relate to one another. This parallelism in the way the two types of argument engage their receivers is borne out by the *aporiai* which result at 231b9–c6 and 236c9–237a1: Theaetetus' response is not that of someone who is being led through a clear demonstration by an expert whose guidance he trusts, but that of someone who is responding with perplexity to the difficulties of inquiry in progress—and the same applies to us.[65]

Moreover, though the passage is very far from a dialectical exchange, the Eleatic Stranger does nevertheless use several of Aristotle's dialectical techniques in easing through his analysis.[66] To begin with,

[64] Cf. Campbell (1973) lii, lv. Ambiguity over the precise number of divisions carried out—and therefore how we should understand the divisions themselves—may add to the effect; see Dorter (1994) 125.

[65] On *aporiai* in *Sophist*—and how they recall 'early' dialogues—see M. Frede (1992b) 423, (1996) 143–4. The similarities are underscored by the evocation of the elenctic Socrates at *Sph.*230ae, at the close of a series of rounds of division. For a different view, see Sayre (1992) 222, who opposes collection and division to elenctic argument, on the grounds that the latter usually ends in a quandary, but collection and division with positive results. On the inconclusiveness of *Sophist* as a whole, in which it also resembles early dialogues, see ch.7.

[66] Though M. Frede (1996) suggests that the *Sophist* is effectively a treatise, Frede (1992a) 209 suggests that pure didactic dialectic is very rare in Plato. See Robinson (1953) and Davidson (1994) for the idea that, even in 'late' dialogues, Plato retains commitment to the *elenchus* in modified form—the question is, how modified it is, and what role it actually plays in the conversations. Davidson maintains that *Philebus* contains elenctic arguments based on what the respondent takes to be

as I noted above, the Eleatic Stranger initiates the attempt to pin down another aspect of the sophist in this passage, following the definition of sophistry reached at the end of the previous section as part of the acquisitive art (224e1–4). Though he is not precisely formulating an objection to the previous definition he and Theaetetus have reached (G), he is claiming that it is incomplete, and this has much the same effect in practice: the receiver is impressed at the discussion leader's ability to interrogate even his own position, and so more ready to accept his analyses. He often formulates the points of his division as statements not questions (R); he relies on 'what people are accustomed to say' in making his categorizations (H) (εἰθίσμεθα 225b10, 225c9; cf. 225c3–4); and his use of familiar examples helps win acceptance even for some of his unfamiliar divisions (B). The method of classification frequently depends on identifying opposing pairs of classes, which, like placing contraries side by side in a question (Q), implies that the options are comprehensive and exclusive. Moreover, the Eleatic Stranger frequently relies on fine distinctions within a term in drawing out the branches of his classification (U). The speed, as in a typical elenctic argument, is swift (N): the Eleatic Stranger's style is taut and compact, with each contribution often closely syntactically linked with the last, and Theaetetus' responses barely break up the flow of what he says. To compound matters, the Eleatic Stranger offers little reasoning for the divisions he makes—the principles on which his argument proceeds (A). For example, no reasons are given for the initial division of ἀγωνιστική (the art of fighting) into ἁμιλλητικὸν (the competitive part) and μαχητικόν (the pugnacious part) (225a2–8), nor for the division of μαχητικόν into βιαστικόν (the violent part) and ἀμφισβητητικόν (controversy) (225a9–b2). The latter seems to work on the basis of the likeness between physical and verbal altercations (a possible case of F); but neither here nor elsewhere does the Eleatic Stranger explain why he is including this category under this heading, or how division manages so frequently to proceed in neatly contrasting pairs.[67] From the point of view of the interlocutor or first-time reader,

true (e.g. 21e–22b) and represents a return to these as the best way of discovering how we ought to live—though he admits that such arguments form a very small part of the dialogue. Robinson also notes that such arguments gradually cease to appear in the dialogues. Cf. Gill (1995) 293 for *Plt.*291–9 as a classically Socratic refutation and D. Frede (1996) 224, who brings out the applicability of the description of the elenctic Socrates here to the method practised in *Philebus*.

[67] Though not always: see e.g. Ackrill (1997b) 102–3.

the very proliferation of categories, too, can feel overwhelming. Category after category is introduced, and as each new one is brought in, we can feel unsure how absorbed in it to become. Is it going to be the crucial one, or is it a step towards a yet more central one? Although this is not the same as expanding the argument to conceal the progress of one's argument (L), the effect on the receiver is not dissimilar, in as much as she is presented with a wealth of material that is hard for her to make sense of until, reaching the final definition, she can look back and see how the path of division has proceeded. As in the case of the *Republic* IX passage, if we accept too readily the presentation of the Eleatic Stranger as an expert and a teacher, we may be in danger of overlooking the dialectical—even eristic—edge to his argumentative style, which, as ever, requires a critical and alert response from the receiver.

So much for the Eleatic Stranger's presentation of his argument; what of its underlying structure? This is where things become really interesting. Superficially, the argument appears simple: a step-wise process of classification;[68] and this might seem to strengthen the hand of those who maintain that the receiver is cast in a passive and inactive role. Yet, again, things are less simple than they appear. A fundamental point here is that it is misleading to focus, as I have done, on just one of the attempted definitions of the sophist. For these are not really separate, like different arguments brought against a definition, but each is a subsection of the larger project of defining the sophist that takes up the entire dialogue, including the complex section on being and not-being. It is this larger structure to which we must attend if we want to understand the argument—and this

[68] This is not to say that the Eleatic Stranger's method of classification *is* straightforward; on the contrary, it raises many questions. Do the divisions reveal different aspects of the sophist, different types of sophist, or are they competing attempts at definition? Can division successfully identify true similarities and dissimilarities? Can it capture the value of the things it divides? What exactly is division dividing—Forms, particulars, or something else? Does it reveal correct definitions, or does it just formulate definitions to be tested by other means? For discussion, see e.g. Moravcsik (1973b), (1973c), Cohen (1973), Bluck (1975) 34–40, Ackrill (1997b), Campbell (1973) vi–xix, Ryle (1966) 132–44, Guthrie (1978) 124–34, 166–8, Dorter (1994) esp. 13–17, 173–80, Rosen (1983), Cavini (1995), Rowe (1995a) 4–8, Notomi (1999), Miller (1980), Lane (1998) esp. 13–61, Gonzalez (2000), Blondell (2002) esp. 357–65, White (1993) xi–xii. Lane (1998) challenges the standard assumption that *Sophist* uses collection and division, arguing instead for a method of division and example.

certainly undercuts the idea that the receiver has an easy time. For even if the progress of an individual passage of division is easy to comprehend, the argumentative structure of the whole, it is usually acknowledged, is particularly demanding and lengthy. Of course, one can make similar points about the relation of any passage of argumentation in a Platonic dialogue to the whole work. What I want to bring out here is that the individual passage resists being separated from the whole more firmly than before, in as much as the dialogue really presents just one extended argumentative progression. The short passage I have been considering, though on some levels it seems simpler than things we find in 'early' and 'middle' dialogues, in fact requires us to engage with a structure that is more challenging than what we find there.

Further, there is the scope of the material touched on by the argument. The process of division of which our passage forms a part involves, it seems, reviewing and classifying the whole of reality.[69] In 'early' dialogues, one point that emerges from the abortive attempts at answering 'What-is-X?' questions is the magnitude of the attempted project: one cannot reach an account of piety (for example), one comes to realize, without trying to understand all the things to which it is related. In *Sophist*, the discussion does actually go some way towards evoking the vast web of relationships in which the definiendum needs to be located. So many directions for investigation and subjects for scrutiny are presented—many of which touch on discussions in other dialogues[70]—that the effect is almost overwhelming. Yet to make proper sense of the conversation, we have to attempt to understand how the sophist fits into this web of relationships, and how the present discussion fits in with those of other works. As a result, the scope of our reflection is being further widened, and we are being asked to develop an increasing awareness of how each individual inquiry fits into the broader project of acquiring knowledge. The method of division provides us with a more systematic, precise, and methodical way of doing so.

[69] Cf. Blondell (2002) 357–61 and Lane (1998) 35–7 on division 'mapping' reality, an idea going back to Skemp (1942) and (1952).

[70] E.g. Forms in *Republic* and *Phaedo*, the tripartite soul in *Republic*, *techne* in *Protagoras*, the arts of sophistry and rhetoric in *Gorgias* and *Phaedrus*, proportion and disproportion in the soul in *Timaeus*. For comments on such references, see e.g. Bluck (1975), Dorter (1994). Taylor (2006) 159, going further, suggests that the divisions sum up discussions of the sophist in earlier dialogues.

Once we realize the complexity of the argument that is implied by our passage, its presentation becomes even more interesting. For what we notice is its incredible lightness of touch. It alludes to other dialogues but does not help us to relate them to *Sophist*; it presents us with a classification, but does not explore its validity or the principles upon which it is based;[71] it evokes the place of the sophist in the whole of reality, but does not spend time exploring that relationship, nor how the different facets of the sophist fit together. In other words, the text invites us to get involved in an immensely demanding and extensive process of reflection, but it does not do the work for us. And this makes it, I think, crucially different from didactic dialectic. For didactic aims to present ideas to the receiver in such a way that he can understand them and adopt them. Here, the process of reflection we need to undertake is set out, but the dialogue simply does not, in many cases, explore the issues in sufficient detail for us to understand them fully or to adopt the conclusions as our own: it relies on us to do a great deal more independent and constructive thinking. Any Platonic dialogue leaves the receiver with a great deal to do, but here, the very allusiveness of the way the investigation is handled means that our contribution is on a different scale.

Once we recognize how very demanding this argument in fact is, we can begin to appreciate how certain elements in its presentation, even apparently didactic ones, further increase the challenge to the receiver. The greater systematization and order of the discussion need not indicate a didactic exposition of information; it rather fosters greater methodological self-consciousness and a more ordered appreciation of the subjects under investigation. The impersonal approach to the subject matter, unlike an *ad hominem* argument, leaves the interlocutor to relate the material covered in the conversation to his own particular ideas and concerns. The minute and repetitive divisions foster attention to accuracy and detail. The smooth, uninterrupted flow of conversation means that the interlocutor must take responsibility for resolving his concerns and queries for himself. As I suggested in discussing *Republic* IX, a non-interactive style of dialectic—and even more so here than there—though it may appear to ask less of the receiver, is in fact more demanding, precisely

[71] Campbell (1973) xv comments that the process of collection and division seems like an abridgement of Socratic procedure: it would have taken 'a morning of ironical banter' to reach a single generalization or distinction of the sort presented here.

because it is less obvious and less controlling in the way it engages him. For not only does it require him to put more input into making sense of the argument on an intellectual level, it also means that the affective demands on him are greater too: if he is to engage productively, he must take responsibility for his own motivation and perseverance, as a dialectically virtuous and independent agent.

To turn to the most problematic feature of the argument of all, even the greater authority and dominance of the discussion leader does not mean that the receiver is passive. As we saw, the discussion leader is dominant in discussions in all works, even 'early' ones. There, the respondent is in denial about his need for improvement and the discussion leader does not claim superiority overtly. But by 'late' dialogues, as we saw in chapter 3, even though respondents are objectively much more philosophically advanced, they are more humble and realistic about their state of philosophical development. They are more self-conscious about their failings, have a greater understanding of what is required of them, and are more ready to take criticism and advice in a constructive manner. This is exactly what we see here, I suggest, in the increased recognition of the dominance of the discussion leader. It is not that the gap between discussion leader and respondent is actually any larger; rather, the respondent is now sufficiently advanced in dialectical virtue to recognize that he is a learner, to acknowledge another as an expert, and to seek his help. That is, he is just reaching the point where, acknowledging how much he has to learn and eager to embark upon the process, he can start to make real and independent progress.

Contrary to appearances, therefore, 'late' dialectic is not less demanding than 'earlier' dialectic, but more so. Whatever the contribution Theaetetus makes to the argument presented in the text, his role, if he is a committed interlocutor, must be far from that of a passive receiver.[72] Again, the same is true of the response of a committed reader. To benefit from the argument, we must be prepared to put in a great deal ourselves: in our own response, we can realize the affective and intellectual activity that is only hinted at in the text. As such—because 'late' dialectic *seems* even less interactive

[72] Blondell (2002) 123–4 and 393 argues that silence (in a friendly dialectical context) should not be taken to indicate withdrawal, but acquiescence, and as such is compatible with silent reflection and participation rather than passivity.

and demanding—it further widens the gap between the involvement of interlocutor and reader observed in *Republic* IX.[73]

5.8. TOWARDS INDEPENDENT READERS AND LEARNERS

The preceding discussion will, I hope, have gone some way towards undermining the traditional idea that 'middle' and 'late' dialogues descend into didactic dialectic, as well as providing an alternative way of looking at the dialectical changes that undoubtedly do occur. In all types of dialogue, there is a dialectical—sometimes eristic—edge to the arguments which unsettles and discomfits us. It encourages us to react critically, reflectively, and warily, as Socrates counsels in the *Protagoras* passage with which we began; and it ensures that the impulse towards improvement, which in chapter 3 I argued was central to the learner's motivation at all stages, remains alive. Moreover, far from making fewer demands on the receiver, 'middle' and 'late' works are in fact more challenging—in many cases, through precisely those features that strike us as more didactic. On an intellectual level, they require the receiver to approach learning in a more systematic way; to develop a more precise sense of where his individual inquiry fits into the larger project of acquiring knowledge; to deal with more abstract and difficult ideas, and with longer and more complex chains of reasoning; to adopt a more methodological approach to inquiry, as well as a more impersonal attitude towards himself and his concerns. The receiver also needs to possess those dialectical virtues, particularly self-motivation and self-criticism, necessary for engaging in inquiry increasingly independently—more so than in 'early' dialogues, where the *ad hominem* tactics and continual

[73] A similar progression can be seen in some of the key methodologies used in 'early', 'middle', and 'late' dialogues: definition, hypothesis, and collection and division. These are all, I would argue, based on a similar conception of the philosophical task, but they embody increasingly sophisticated and challenging ways of going about it—again promoting development in respondent and reader. For comments on the underlying continuities in these methods, see Moline (1981) 169–70 who suggests that dialectic in 'later' dialogues preserves the 'early' dialectical procedure of looking for contradictions; also Lloyd (1979) 100–2, Nehamas (1999c) 240–1, Kahn (1996) 292–328, Blondell (2003) 258–9, Bluck (1975) 39–40.

interventions of the discussion leader help prod the respondent in the right direction.

What we have, therefore, is not a picture of fundamental change in the dialectical style used or the response it evokes, but of deepening demands within a framework of continuity. It is not a picture of decline, but of development: at each stage, the changes in dialectical style stretch the interlocutor further, providing the context he needs to develop his skills, both intellectual and affective, and to progress to the next stage of dialectical virtue. The dialectical changes are all about *challenging* the interlocutor, not about introducing a mode of philosophizing that makes ever-diminishing demands on him. In this regard, the traditional interpretation is, in my view, almost the opposite of the truth.

But even if this picture of development is accepted, we may still have the nagging feeling that the spirit of drama and excitement, of genuine participation and involvement, so important in 'early' dialogues, is abandoned in 'later' ones. This idea has a superficial appeal, but it is important to realize that it is nevertheless misguided. To begin with, there is the question of the stimulus appropriate to the learner at each stage of development. By the time he reaches 'middle' and 'late' dialogues, a learner *needs* the more demanding yet less obvious challenges provided here, if he is to progress further. But to benefit from them, he also needs to have gone through the earlier—and more turbulent—stages of philosophical development, represented by early-stage and intermediate dialogues. As such, 'late' dialectic does not replace 'earlier' dialectic, or abandon the principles that appear to underlie it; it just represents a subsequent stage.

Perhaps even more importantly, there is the question of the character, depth, and source of a learner's participation and motivation. In 'early' dialogues, interlocutors' participation is generally more vocal and dramatic; but it is also generally superficial—not yet deep, nor necessarily long-lasting. In 'later' dialogues, the input of interlocutors seems to diminish, but in fact, as I have argued, it must increase. Their intellectual contributions must be deeper and more searching, and their affective contribution, though less overt, need be no less personal: in being more internalized, it is also deeper and more enduring. In other words, drama and participation have not disappeared,[74] but

[74] Miller (1980) xi observes that 'late' dialogues only become less dramatic if we equate explicit antagonism with drama: they may contain more subtle hidden conflicts. Cf. also Weingartner (1973) 5–6, 12.

have rather shifted to a less obvious, though deeper, plane: the internal dialogue of the receiver. This is true, I think, of interlocutors, but even more so of the reader. By 'later' dialogues, the most interesting dialectical activity is taking place in the reader's interaction with the dialogue, not among the interlocutors portrayed within it—and it need be no less exciting for being invited by, rather than represented in, the text. In consequence, as I have observed, there is an increasing divergence between the response and activity of interlocutors, as presented in the dialogues, and that of readers. On one level, this is a literary observation about how the dialogues engage us. However, it is also integrally linked to their view of philosophical development and the manner in which they foster it in us. In studying the Cave image, we saw recalcitrant prisoners gradually lose the need for the educator's assistance as they ascended to the brighter and brighter light, becoming self-motivated agents capable of independent progress. The same process is at work in our reading of the dialogues: our response is gradually prised away from that of the interlocutors and we learn to engage and respond responsibly and productively for ourselves, as independent readers and learners who can participate in the silent dialogue of thought with ever-diminishing guidance from Plato's characters. Our literary distancing from the interlocutors is in consequence a part of our developing philosophical independence.

6

Structure and Unity: Challenging the Reader

6.1. SEARCHING FOR UNITY

But come now, and try to fulfil your promise to me, by telling me about virtue as a whole, what it is; and cease making many out of one, as the jokers say each time people break something, but leaving virtue whole and sound, tell me what it is.

Meno, 77a5–9

You [the philosophers] must each in your turn go down to live together with others and grow accustomed to seeing in the dark. For when you have become accustomed to it, you will see vastly better than the people there, and you will recognise what each image is and of what it is an image, through having seen the truth concerning things that are beautiful and just and good.

Republic, 520c1–6

Whenever someone should perceive the unity belonging to many, he should not desist before he sees all the differences, as many as exist within the forms. And again, when he should see the various unlikenesses, whenever they are observed within groups, it is not possible for him to be out of countenance or to cease before he has enclosed all those which naturally fit together within one likeness and has encompassed them with the essence of a type.

Politicus, 285a8–b6

Throughout the dialogues, the quest for unity is at the heart of the journey towards understanding. A learner needs to discern unity in the apparent disunity of the particulars in this world; he must perceive the truth or reality whose existence underlies those many imperfect instantiations, and he needs to present his understanding in a definition which captures the essential unity in many instances.[1] This involves developing a different way of looking at the world around him. The *Republic* passage, in which Socrates describes why philosophers should return to the Cave as rulers, expresses this in terms of light and darkness, image and reality: perceiving true justice, beauty, and goodness allows the philosopher to negotiate the Cave's shadowy images of these things more successfully than those who have never ascended to the light—but only once his eyes have adjusted to the new conditions. In *Politicus*, there is again a process of adjustment, since the philosopher must search for unity amidst apparent disunity and uncover distinctions among apparent likenesses. Meno, asked to explain what virtue is, needs to understand that he is to move beyond the many examples of virtue he sees in the world around him, towards a general account; for him, seeing unity in this plurality involves a no less challenging change of perspective. Yet for all its significance in the process of learning, the character of the unity for which learners must search remains, like the objects of knowledge themselves, an elusive presence within the dialogues. Images and analogies often prompt us to reflect on what it involves—one thinks, for instance, of Meno's 'swarm' of virtues, the 'sacrificial victim' which the Stranger must carve up in carrying out the process of division in *Politicus*, and *Protagoras*' suggestion that the virtues may be connected like parts of a face or parts of a piece of gold—yet true insight into its nature is reserved for those who pursue their search for understanding beyond the confines of the text.

In *Phaedrus*, connections are again made between unity and understanding, this time as part of Socrates' and Phaedrus' discussion of the principles underlying the proper composition of spoken and written discourse, an investigation that also touches on structure and unity of form in composed works. A successful speech[2] on any subject, Socrates insists at the outset, needs to be based on truth (259e4–6), and it involves the pursuit of philosophy (261a3–5). This is because, he suggests, a successful orator is someone who has the capacity to lead his audience away from the truth to its opposite; to do this, he needs to exploit the similarities and differences between things; and this he can carry out successfully only if he grasps their

[1] On the importance of order and coherence in the dialogues' conception of knowledge, see esp. Burnyeat (1980b), Fine (1979) and (1990) 109 ff.

[2] For the inclusiveness of Socrates' view of rhetoric, see *Phdr.*261ab.

true nature, and the similarities and differences between them (261e–262c). Rhetoric, Socrates and Phaedrus continue, has greater power when concerned with those things about which people disagree, for here they are more easily deceived; so the orator must undertake a 'systematic division' to understand the class of things about which we agree and the class about which we disagree (263ac). Socrates implies that every topic of rhetoric will fall into one of these two classes, and Phaedrus' exclamation in response to the idea ('It's a fine thing, Socrates, that the person who grasps this will have understood!' 263c1–2) underscores the magnitude of the task Socrates is proposing: an investigation into the whole of reality. As in our earlier passages, the inquirer (here, the orator) needs to move beyond the varied and mistaken opinions of the masses towards an understanding of the true nature of things. He needs to appreciate the overarching divisions which give order to the myriad topics of rhetoric, and must employ a 'sharp eye' (263c4) to determine to which class the topic of his speech belongs; once he has done this, his knowledge, in Socrates' account, enables him to lead astray his less discerning listeners. Though he is presented rather differently from the philosopher of *Republic or Politicus*, an orator with understanding is again one who sees things differently—and more accurately—than others.

At this point, Socrates returns to the speech of Lysias that Phaedrus has earlier admiringly recounted. Socrates points out that Lysias' speech, which is not based on a systematic division of this sort, did not begin with a definition of its topic, love (263de); nor, as a result, was the remaining material arranged in accordance with that account. In consequence, Socrates comments, the speech appears to have been thrown together at random (χύδην 264b3), without any compelling reason or 'necessity' (ἀνάγκης 264b4) underlying the arrangement of points. In fact, Socrates suggests, it lacks the coherent structure and unity such a work should possess:

> *... every account must be put together like a living thing, having a body of its own, so that it is not without head nor without feet, but it must have a middle and extremities, composed so that they are fitting both to each other and to the whole.*
>
> *Phaedrus*, 264c2–5

Socrates' image stresses the author's choice of material: he must ensure that his work includes the requisite parts, just as a body must not be without head or feet in Socrates' example. In addition, it highlights the importance of arrangement and order: if the parts are to form a living creature, they must be properly fitted together, for their individual arrangement is crucial to the life of the whole. At the heart of Lysias' failure to do this, as Socrates' earlier points make clear, is his lack of understanding of his topic.

Phaedrus' reflections here stress the significance of structure and unity in composed works; yet they are far from straightforward to interpret. They form part of a complex discussion that extends from the structural principles underlying successful composition to the conditions under which spoken and written discourse can be philosophically valuable, and notoriously, although the passage intersects with the concerns of modern critics about unity of form, it is much broader in scope.[3] Nor is it always clear what is meant by a particular structural principle. What, for instance, is the 'necessity' by which the parts of a work should be arranged? And what does it mean for the parts of a work to fit together 'like a living thing'? The earlier parts of the discussion make clear the importance of the creator's knowledge in allowing him to achieve a well-structured and unified work; but what is it that distinguishes true unity of form from the unity possessed by works like the speech of Lysias, which is viewed by others as a fine example of its kind?

These questions become especially pressing when we turn to the unity of Plato's own works. Though there are many works whose unity is not in doubt, there is also a handful whose structure has long struck critics as problematic. Among them is *Republic*, whose first and last books stand somewhat apart from the intervening ones, and whose central books—to many the heart of the work—are presented as a digression.[4] *Parmenides* seems to fall into two separate parts,[5] and *Politicus* is traditionally thought of as poorly constructed, made up of a series of episodes which are not fully integrated, and some of which extend beyond what their significance seems to warrant.[6]

[3] Cf. e.g. Heath (1989c) 18–21.

[4] Rutherford (1995) 208–18 states the concerns clearly; cf. also Notomi (1999) 33–5.

[5] See e.g. McCabe (1996) 5–6, Weingartner (1973) 11, M. L. Gill (1996) 2–3.

[6] See e.g. Annas and Waterfield (1995) x–xii, Scodel (1987) 9, Blondell (2005) 23, (2002) 374–5, Notomi (1999) 35–7. Concerns about unity have been voiced about other dialogues too: see e.g. Rutherford (1995) 121, 131–2 and (1992) on *Protagoras*; Moes (2000) 113–61 on *Philebus*; Notomi (1999) esp. 1–10 on *Sophist*.

Perhaps most challenging of all, though—not least given the dialogue's reflection on the same topic—is *Phaedrus*, whose structure presents a number of problems to the critic.[7] An initial puzzle is the relationship between Socrates' two speeches on love. After listening to Phaedrus recount Lysias' speech (230e–234c), an attempt to persuade a young man that (contrary to normal ideas) he should accept as his admirer someone not in love with him, Socrates produces a competing speech on the same theme, designed to better that of Lysias (237b–241d). At its close, Socrates proposes to leave; but straightaway his divine sign intervenes, warning him of the impiety of his speech, and in a reasonably extended passage (242b–243e), he describes his unease and clarifies the offence he has committed—to have spoken ill of love. He then launches into a recantation, which connects love with the best and most fulfilling life for humans, equivalent to the life of philosophy (244a–257b). Quite apart from the disjointed effect created by Socrates' self-criticism and his subsequent shift in stance, the dialogue leaves it unclear how we should view what he says in his first speech. At the time, we are inclined to think that the second speech trumps and replaces it; yet in the subsequent discussion, the two are presented as parts of a single serious inquiry into the nature of love and madness, each containing one part of a complex definition of love (265c–266b).[8]

More problematic still—the major preoccupation of most critics—is the relationship between the first and second halves of the work. The initial part of the dialogue, up to the end of Socrates' second speech, seems to deal with love, while after that the focus shifts to rhetoric; yet the two themes are not overtly linked. The later part of the work is also rather different in style: no longer dominated by long speeches and a high linguistic register, it is characterized by short question-and-answer exchanges, and is more analytical and technical in approach. Particularly problematic, given this shift, is the place we should attribute to Socrates' second speech within the work as a whole. This is the highpoint of the discussion of love, both stylistically and thematically. It is a lengthy speech, the third in a series, mythical in style, with a rhetorical, poetical, and imagistic emphasis which

[7] See e.g. Rowe (1986a), (1986b), (1989), Rutherford (1995) 261–7, Helmbold and Holter (1952), Heath (1989a), (1989b), (1989c), Hackforth (1952) 8–12, Kahn (1996) 372–6, Griswold (1986) 138–65, De Vries (1969) 22–4, Werner (2007).

[8] Cf. Rowe (1986a) 8.

caps earlier efforts at rhetoric. It also provides the most profound treatment of love so far, and introduces what has struck many readers as the central philosophical material of the dialogue: the fate of the soul after death, reincarnation, and education—themes that are central in several other dialogues.[9] Viewed from this perspective, the speech is central to the 'meaning' of the work and our interpretation of it. Yet Socrates says that the speech was given playfully (προσεπαίσαμεν 265c1, παιδιᾷ πεπαῖσθαι 265c8–9) and may have led them astray (παραφερόμενοι 265b8); there is minimal reflection on it in later parts of the work; its themes are not further developed; and its style is abandoned. All of this suggests that we may be at risk of overemphasizing its significance—while leaving us to puzzle why, if that is the case, the account is offered at a central point in the dialogue, and given such weight.[10]

A further puzzle is posed by the final section of the work, which appears to question the philosophical value of writing, and by implication, therefore, the philosophical value of the dialogue of which it forms a part (and others too).[11] The rest of the work has not directly prepared us for such a development, and many find this concluding twist surprising, even shocking. In response, we can either try to find a way of reading the passage that allows it to be consistent with the thematic development of the rest of the work and with the practice of philosophical writing more generally,[12] or we can see it as a deconstructive epilogue that undercuts what has gone before.[13] Either way, it remains puzzling why Plato introduces the theme in the way he does, as an undeniably unsettling sting in the tail.[14]

These factors combine to give *Phaedrus* a structure that is puzzling, even disunified, something all the more unsettling in the light of the

[9] For links between *Phaedrus* and other Platonic dialogues (with different interpretations) see Kahn (1996) 373–5, Rowe (1986a) 9–10, Nussbaum (1986) 201–2.

[10] Cf. Rowe (1986b) 106–7, Rutherford (1995) 265.

[11] See chapter 1 section 1.1 for a fuller account of this passage.

[12] Cf. Rowe (1986b).

[13] For the passage as an appendix or 'dessert', see Derrida (1981b) 73. Ferrari (1987) 206–7 offers a survey of interpretations of the passage in this light. He regards the passage as an epilogue (p.214), but in a different sense from Derrida, and one that makes the passage part of a consistent thematic development.

[14] Thought-provoking, too, is the striking space devoted to scene setting or topography within the work. This is an important factor in many dialogues, but its prominence in *Phaedrus* is somewhat unusual. For detailed discussion, see Ferrari (1987), Griswold (1986), Rutherford (1988).

significance the dialogue appears to attach to unity.[15] Critics have sought in a number of ways to defuse such problems of structure, in *Phaedrus* and also in other Platonic dialogues; and it will be useful to survey them before turning to the approach I propose.[16]

6.2. STRUCTURE AND UNITY: POSSIBLE APPROACHES

To begin with, one can simply say that, in cases where we think a work disunified, Plato has been artistically unsuccessful.[17] Of course, the thought runs, he was *aiming* to provide a structurally coherent and unified work, as he does in other cases, but for some reason—perhaps his focus was on philosophical exposition rather than literary artistry—he did not succeed. Although this is always a possible approach, I am among those who regard it as an ultimately unsatisfying one, and seek to explain the structural features we notice in other ways.[18]

A second option is to deny that there is a problem with the unity of these works at all. Heath has argued that it is misguided to apply modern notions of coherence and unity to ancient works. He points out that ancient writers and critics appear to set a high aesthetic value on features we find troubling, such as changes in direction and digressions, and tend to prefer *poikilia*, variety, to uniformity. In particular, he points out that Greek tragedies contain abrupt changes in direction and often continue beyond what we might think a natural resting place.[19] These are two central problematic features in *Phaedrus*, and if Heath is right, then we are misguided if we insist that such features

[15] Cf. e.g. Rowe (1986a) 7, Kahn (1986) 372, Werner (2007) 92, 120–1.

[16] For general discussions of unity, which review possible approaches as well as applying the results to Plato, see Heath (1989c) chs.1–2, Rutherford (1995) 260–7. Similar debates exist in relation to other ancient genres, including—perhaps most relevantly—tragedy, as both Heath and Rutherford bring out, though I shall mainly confine my discussion to Plato. Werner (2007) provides an extensive survey of approaches to unity in *Phaedrus*, and develops a reading that is different from, though complementary to, mine. I note major points of intersection below.

[17] E.g. Campbell (1973) introduction to *Politicus* liv, Taylor (1961) 250.

[18] Rowe (1995b) 13–14 defends *Politicus* against this charge. Cf. Heath (1989c) 5, Rowe (1986a) 7, (1986b) 107, De Vries (1969) 22.

[19] Heath (1989a) 161–3.

render a work disunified and artistically unsatisfying: we should instead acknowledge the distance between our aesthetic values and those of Plato's original readers. This is a line of interpretation with which I am in sympathy, not least because it acknowledges the features that worry us and makes them central to a positive interpretation of the works' structure. What I find unconvincing, however, is its normalization of those features: while Heath's arguments persuade me that the structure of, say, *Phaedrus* would not have struck ancient readers as worryingly disunified or incoherent, I still think that, just because of the extreme way in which it instantiates the structural principles Heath highlights, it would still have seemed unusual and striking. A satisfying interpretation needs to accommodate this.[20]

A third approach is to accept that there is some sort of problem with the structure of the works in question, but to minimize it, in effect insisting that the works are unified, despite our initial impressions. Beginning with formal features,[21] we can emphasize dramatic unity: each dialogue takes place in a single location and over a continuous stretch of time, and there is a high degree of continuity in characters present at the conversations.[22] We can bring out strands of language and imagery that run through individual works and that encourage us to see its different parts as an artistic whole. In *Phaedrus*, for instance, references to motion, growth, writing, food, gold, memory/forgetfulness, and sophistication/naïvety perform this function.[23] Further, we can draw attention to structural links between

[20] For a different critique of Heath (whose view he terms the 'debunking approach'), see Werner (2007) 125–9. Heath (1989a) and (1989c) further suggest that the thematic diversity of *Phaedrus* is a reflection of Phaedrus' needs as an interlocutor (possibly chosen as representative of the audience's needs); and argues that we should not try to reduce this diversity by bringing out a single thematic development. In this respect, Heath argues that the dialogue corresponds to the idea (which he finds in other works) that a work is unified if all its parts are philosophically useful. As will become clear, I agree with Heath's emphasis on a work being unified if all its parts are philosophically useful—even if that means it departs from our preconceived notions of unity. I do not feel however, that his interpretation goes far enough in attributing a positive significance to the troubling aspects of the work's structure, as it needs to if it is not to shade into one of the more sophisticated versions of thematic unity (on which more later in this section), to which he opposes his approach.

[21] See Heath (1989a) 160–1 for a clear contrast between formal and material (or thematic) unity; also Werner (2007).

[22] Cf. Rutherford (1995) 261, Heath (1989a) 161.

[23] For the first three themes, see Lebeck (1972); for the others, see Rutherford (1995) 262–4. Cf. Blondell (2005).

different parts of a dialogue. Most notably, the passage on writing occupies a place in the second half of the dialogue which is structurally parallel to that of Socrates' second speech in the first half, and Socrates' designation of his second speech as playfully given at 265bc mirrors his earlier change of direction after his first speech.[24] Such factors do help us to see a work such as *Phaedrus* as a unified whole, but at the same time they do not, I feel, provide a convincing explanation of the dialogue's structural oddities. Other works, after all, are united by dramatic setting and by imagery, but do not seem to present structural difficulties in the same way as *Phaedrus*. Even if we can see, on an abstract level, that *Phaedrus* is unified, that is, our *experience* of it may still be uneasy—and this is something that this kind of approach simply ignores.[25]

In addition, we can argue that thematic unity persists below the surface of an apparently disunified dialogue.[26] For *Phaedrus*, the main strategy of critics has been to bring out links between the discussions of love and rhetoric. We can note the references to the earlier speeches that are made in the discussion of rhetoric, and view Socrates' second speech as an example of the good type of rhetoric discussed in the later part of the work.[27] Going further, we may detect a deeper concern underlying, and thereby unifying, the two discussions: the true nature of philosophy, the proper shape of the philosophical life, or perhaps the correct character of philosophical and rhetorical discourse.[28] These are overarching concerns that can be

[24] Rowe (1986a) 7–8. For further structural links see Rutherford (1995) 261 n37, Lebeck (1972) 284, Griswold (1986) 161–5, 206–7. Helmbold and Holter (1952) suggest that the light and playful tone throughout the work is one means by which it is unified. Cf. Rowe (1986a) 10. Others, though, detect changes in tone throughout the work, and see this as an important aspect of the problem of unity. Cf. Rutherford (1995) 261. These unifying strategies are summarized and discussed by Werner (2007), esp. 114–25.

[25] Cf. Rutherford (1995) 265.

[26] As Notomi (1999) 10–19 brings out, this approach bears affinities to ancient commentators' search for the *skopos* of a dialogue, which he glosses in terms of thematic unity, while noting that the *skopos* may be more apparent in some works than others.

[27] Rowe (1986b). Cf. Griswold (1986) 159 on direct connections between the two themes. Rutherford (1995) 261 notes that there are fewer cross-references than we might anticipate.

[28] For the nature of philosophy/the philosophical life, see Ferrari (1987), esp. 34; also Guthrie (1976), Hackforth (1952) 9–11. Rutherford (1995) 262 sees philosophical art and rhetoric as combined in the figure of Socrates, whose continuous presence unifies the work. For the proper nature of philosophical/rhetorical discourse, see

used to explain the change in subject and also the shifts in dialectical mode throughout the dialogue.[29] This kind of approach is important and often illuminating. Nevertheless, it does encounter problems. First, critics do not agree on the underlying thematic unities they detect, and this calls into question the persuasiveness of individual accounts. More seriously, if the unifying themes lie so deeply beneath the surface and need to be uncovered in this way, then they cannot really do the work we need them to in providing a sense of structural unity.[30] This kind of approach can help us draw out the significance of what is said in the work and its interconnections, therefore, but it does not actually provide a solution to the matter in hand.

Finally, some critics detect subtle connections between the form a dialogue takes and the thematic concerns it addresses. In the case of *Politicus*, with its uncomfortable form, Blondell has suggested that the structure of the dialogue presents a more truthful—and therefore less superficially appealing—view of reality, in line with the ideas expressed in the dialogue on *mimesis* and perspective.[31] Rutherford suggests that that the imperfections of *Phaedrus* mirror the imperfections of Phaedrus himself: the work is complex because Phaedrus is himself complex and divided, and ultimately fails to achieve a truly philosophical life.[32] Along similar lines, Ferrari has interpreted the disjunction between the discussions of love and rhetoric as reflecting the

Rowe (1986b), (1989), De Vries (1969) 23, Szlezák (1985) ch.5, cf. also Griswold (1986) 138–65. For subtle applications of this approach to other dialogues, see Stauffer (2006), Weingartner (1973), Rowe (1995).

[29] For a survey of thematic approaches, see Werner (2007) 94–109. He rejects thematic monism of this sort in favour of thematic pluralism (109–14), whereby a dialogue is unified if it contains one or more themes that are used to tie together the different parts of the text. Cf. Halliwell (1991) 231 who notes, in criticizing Heath (1989c), that thematic unity need not involve singleness of theme; also Guthrie (1975) 120–31 who argues, correctly in my view, that there is no 'real subject' in any dialogue, so we are mistaken if we search for tight thematic unity and then find it wanting. These critics do not, however, offer an account of why some works seem more disunified on this level than others.

[30] Cf. Heath (1989a) 170–3. As I shall explain in sections 6.3–6.5, I think that the reader's contribution in creating unity from apparent disunity is central to the dialogues' handling of structure. On the approach I am rejecting, however, the reader's contribution is not made central: critics tend to suggest that thematic coherence just exists in the work—and it is this I would dispute.

[31] Blondell (2002) 375. Cf. McCabe (1996) 46–7 on *Parmenides*; she unites this kind of approach with attention to thematic coherence.

[32] Rutherford (1995) 266–7. Cf. Griswold (1986) 158–9, Heath (1989a), (1989c) (see n20 above), Werner (2007) 130–1.

difficulty with which the two are integrated into a single life, and in particular the disturbing contingency of love when it enters a life.[33] Taking a different tack, Kahn sees the first part of *Phaedrus* as a farewell to the Socratic dramatic dialogue, with the second part pointing forward to the more didactic compositions of later years.[34] Once we see this kind of connection between the content of a work and its form, the thought runs, then we can see it as a coherent whole—albeit an intentionally misshapen one—because our understanding of the *reason* for the form of the work helps us perceive its underlying unity. This is, again, a line I find appealing (though one may want to question particular readings), not least because it does not try to deny that there is a problem of structure, and it is compatible with the one I advocate. Nevertheless, it again fails to take account of the impact that apparent disunity has on us as we read, or to explain why thematic mirroring takes a problematic form in only some dialogues and not others.

As I hope will have become clear, these approaches do a great deal to further our appreciation of the structure of the dialogues, and to help us discern unity in even the most challenging of them. Tied together by its location, by time frame and characters, by imagery, by connections between the discussions of love and rhetoric, and by underlying thematic continuities, we can, I think, see *Phaedrus* as a coherent unit. But even so, there are two respects in which the approaches considered so far remain unsatisfying. First, none accounts for the fact that, even if we can perceive that a dialogue such as *Phaedrus* is unified, we still *experience* it as structurally challenging when we read. A successful account should, I think, provide a positive account of the effect of the dialogues' structural features on the reader.[35] Second, none explains why we find problematic structural features in some works and not others. If they are simply a part of the Greek aesthetic, why do they not occur more frequently? And if they are an interesting

[33] Ferrari (1987) 230. [34] Kahn (1996) 372–3.

[35] My interpretation is thus, in Rosenblatt's terminology (see ch.2 section 2.2), 'aesthetic' in approach, in that it makes the experience of reading central. Cf. Mossman (1995) and Dunn (1997) who try to account for the troubling structural features of Euripides' *Hecuba* and *Heracles* with reference to the response they evoke in the reader, and pay particular attention to the sequence of elements within the plays. The account of *Phaedrus* I suggest in section 6.5 can be seen as a version of what Werner (2007) calls a 'strategic approach', though he develops the idea in a different way from me.

way of mirroring thematic concerns, why is it one that Plato chooses to employ only occasionally? In this regard, they simply push the problem back a stage further: we are no longer asking why some of Plato's works are disunified, but are still left to wonder why only some of them deal with structure in such an unusual and challenging way.

The approach I develop in the rest of this chapter involves stepping back from problematic works such as *Politicus* and *Phaedrus*, in order to set them in the context of their less structurally challenging counterparts. In the sections that follow, I set out a range of structural features characteristic of the dialogues, analysing the effects they have on our experience in reading and on the way we engage with the texts. For, I suggest, once we understand these common patterns, we are better able to see the continuities between problem cases and more obviously unified dialogues, as well as to understand the significance of the way in which works such as *Phaedrus* are constructed.

6.3. COMMON STRUCTURAL PATTERNS

In this section, I draw predominantly (though not exclusively) on *Meno* to illustrate a range of structural patterns[36] that pervade the dialogues. I have chosen *Meno* since it contains many of the structures I want to comment on, and because the unity and coherence of the work are not in doubt: we may find certain aspects of its construction surprising, but we have no trouble making sense of them in context. As will become clear, in the features of a more obviously unified work like *Meno* we can see the seeds of the extreme structures found in problematic works such as *Phaedrus* and *Politicus*.[37]

[36] I do not provide a comprehensive account of the structural principles typical of the dialogues; in particular, I do not discuss conversational structure and the question-and-answer format, which are basic to the genre.

[37] In exploring the following structural patterns, I have found it illuminating, at points, to draw on narratological analysis of story patterns. If, as suggested in chapter 5, esp. n55, we treat the underlying argumentative material of a dialogue as constituting its story, then some of the structural features I consider can be recognized as standard techniques for shaping a narrative: pauses and unexpected length

6.3.1. Dead ends and pauses

A dead end, as I shall be using the term, involves some sort of crisis in the way the conversation is proceeding. This might be because a definition or solution proposed is found to be inadequate, an avenue of inquiry is abandoned as abortive, or one party is unhappy with the way discussion is being conducted.[38] In consequence, the flow of conversation is arrested, and we come to a halt.

Such stops vary considerably in emphasis. Sometimes they simply involve the statement of the problem that has arisen, before the conversation moves off again. But, frequently, they involve more considerable pauses in the main flow of the conversation. Of course, conversational exchanges of some sort or another continue to occur: a dead end might, in real conversation, be marked by a silence, but this cannot be represented in the dialogues, except by indicating that a character was rendered speechless. Rather, a pause occurs when the exchanges that occur do not further the main line of conversation—say, the inquiry into virtue. On a small scale, there may be more than usual conversational padding: repetition of a conclusion; emphatic statements such as oaths; and reflective or gnomic remarks. On a larger scale, we might find the expression of a party's response to the conversation so far—anger, bafflement, frustration, *aporia*—or methodological reflection on the way it is being conducted. A contribution by the narrator in his own voice may (if the work is narrated) be used to enhance the effect, and it tends to be more marked if we are presented with a long speech, in as much as this interrupts the pattern of question-and-answer exchange. At times, as we shall see, the pause associated with a dead end is so pronounced that it creates a division in the work.

Meno contains a series of dead ends. The first follows Meno's first definition (71e–72a), a list of the virtues of a man, a woman, and so

manipulate narrative speed; the disparate treatment of themes and changes in direction are akin to the manipulation of narrative order; iterative structure can be connected with narrative frequency. Recognizing this brings out the extent to which the construction of the conversation—concealed beneath the illusion of free-flowing discussion—is used to influence the way in which the reader engages with the material presented, my central theme in this chapter.

[38] One common place for dead ends is at the close of elenctic arguments, which typically end in *aporia*.

on, which Socrates challenges, saying that he wants Meno to identify the single quality common to all virtuous things. The argument does not come to a halt immediately, as Meno asks for clarification of what Socrates means (72d2–3) and then expresses the reservation that virtue is not the same as Socrates' other examples (73a4–5). But finally, once Socrates has got Meno to concede that all mankind becomes good through the same qualities, it reaches a standstill with Meno's οὐ δῆτα ('no indeed') at 73c5. Following this, Meno goes straight on to offer his next definition, that *arete* is the ability to rule men.

Socrates' refutation this time is much shorter, and it concludes in a more definite halt: at 74a7–b1, addressing Meno by name, Socrates comments that they have repeated the error of producing many virtues, not one; then Meno, addressing Socrates by name in turn, asserts that he is unable to do what Socrates has requested. This exchange pinpoints the methodological problem, or at least the confusion, that is causing their discussion to founder, and Socrates goes on, in response, to offer three sample definitions, two of shape and one of colour. These can, if we wish, be regarded as an extension of the pause already created: they form a methodological interlude, which aims to clarify the type of definition Socrates is looking for, but does not directly advance the inquiry into the nature of virtue. This second dead end is a step up in scale from the first, and acts as a preparation for the third—the most significant in the work.

This is triggered when Socrates, at the close of his criticism of Meno's third definition (that *arete* is to desire fine things and have the power to obtain them, 77b2–5), points out that it fails in the same way as his previous attempts. This passage lasts from 78e6–79e6, and is given emphasis by the rhetorical spin Socrates gives their dilemma: his image of splitting *arete* up into fragments; his accusation that Meno is trying to make fun of him; and the repeated questions he poses Meno. The effect is to bring out much more forcefully the crisis they have reached, suggesting that they just cannot reach a definition of *arete* this way. At this point (79e7 ff.), in a famous passage, Meno expresses his *aporia* in lengthy and vivid terms, using the image of the sting-ray, as well as the language of enchantment and medication; Socrates in turn expresses his *aporia*; and Meno then introduces the paradox of inquiry. This moves the crisis to a more serious level, potentially undermining the whole basis upon which Socrates and Meno have been proceeding. It leads, of course, into the theory of recollection, which Socrates expounds first with reference to the immortality and reincarnation of the soul, and then by his demonstration with the slave. Finally, at 86c7–d2, a return to the main line of inquiry is signalled by Meno's reiteration of the question with which the dialogue began.

Now, this passage is on one level the philosophical core of the dialogue, and contains, many would maintain, the most substantive and seriously meant ideas of the whole work.[39] But on another, it is a methodological interlude that brings to a halt the primary line of inquiry: the quest for the nature of virtue. In addressing the value of the elenctic method, it is furthering inquiry in a way, but it is also a point of crisis in the conversation, which cannot continue until some sort of resolution has been reached. While acknowledging the importance of the passage, we can also recognize that it interrupts the flow of the main line of inquiry, and represents a pause or fracture within that line.[40]

Following the return to the main line of inquiry at 86c, we find two further dead ends, both accompanied by short pauses: at 89c5–d6, after Socrates expresses doubt about their grounds for concluding that *arete* comes about by education; and at 96d1–e5, at the conclusion of the argument that virtue cannot be taught.[41]

These passages—and particularly the more severe among them—disrupt and challenge our reading of the conversation. Each one comes as something of a shock, which grabs our attention and forces us to reconsider what has gone before, emphasizing the importance of proceeding warily and critically. And, as well as shock, there may be annoyance, bafflement, frustration, or dismay, as we realize that we have been making false assumptions or following a line of inquiry to no effect, and need to start on a new tack. Of course, the impact depends on the seriousness of the dead end, as well as on the cumulative build-up of such features: part of the power of the paradox of inquiry comes from its position as the third in a series of dead ends of increasing importance. This makes the fundamental concerns raised in that episode seem well motivated, and compounds our feelings of

[39] Cf. Cohen (2002) on the central section of *Protagoras*, and Burnyeat (1990) 35 on the digression within *Theaetetus*. McPherran (2003) 10–11 with n30 notes that positive doctrine is often introduced after this kind of dramatic break. For the central ('pedimental') position of many interludes, see Cohen (2002) 4, Brumbaugh (1988).

[40] See ch5 n55.

[41] Cf. also the pause at *M*.94e3–95a6, at the departure of Anytus.

helplessness and disorientation, as we apparently fail to make any progress through the paths of inquiry. The effect is quite different from being offered a demonstration that a certain position is wrong in preparation for the right one: there we know where we are; here, until we reach a dead end, we may not know that we are on the wrong course.

6.3.2. Changes in direction

A change in direction during discussion involves, most obviously, a change of subject. Socrates' introduction of recollection, during the third dead end in *Meno*, is a good example. True, the connection of this episode with what has gone before is evident; but while it lasts, the conversation is concerned with how inquiry is possible, not with how *arete* is to be defined.

The concept is clear enough; more difficult, however, is the question of where exactly we should draw the line between a progression and a change of course. This depends, to some degree, on our sense of the conceptual relationship between two passages. The dead ends after Meno's first and second definitions both result in Meno attempting to offer a different definition of *arete*. In one sense, these are changes in direction: Socrates and Meno do not continue investigating the definition that has been refuted. But we are more inclined, I think, to regard them as a development of the same search. The interlocutors are still trying to answer the same question, using the same methodological approach. Conversely, the switch to discussing rhetoric in the second half of *Phaedrus* seems, to many, an extreme change in direction because, although rhetoric has had an important presence in the first part of the dialogue, Socrates and Phaedrus appear to have been talking about love—and the conceptual connection between the two subjects is not immediately apparent. Such moments—like dead ends—produce shock, surprise, and perhaps perplexity. They disorient us, challenging our assumptions about where in the course of the discussion we are, and where we are heading. And as well as asking us to look afresh at what has gone before, they pose the fresh challenge of how to relate the new subject to the old. In consequence, they foster renewed attention and alertness,[42] indicating that we cannot take for granted the course or

[42] Cf. Dunn (1997) 84.

outcome of the discussion, as we might in the case of a demonstration, but must stay alert to the twists and turns it takes as it progresses.

In many cases, the conceptual relationship between two passages may be rather murky. The myth at the end of *Gorgias* purports to address a question that has been running throughout the work—which life is most beneficial—yet it follows a new tack, talking about life after death: is it therefore a progression or a change in direction? Some readers will say one thing, some another.[43] And of course we may change our minds, perceiving on rereading, perhaps, connections that at first we missed, and that enhance our understanding of the work's unity and coherence. Nevertheless, if we do so, this does not affect the impact the shift has on us when we experience the dialogue for the first time: no matter how close the conceptual relations between two sections of discussion, if they are not apparent to us at the time we are reading, the shift will still strike us as a change in direction. What matters is our *experience* of a change. This introduces a further factor: the way the shift is presented.[44]

To begin with, the shift may be signposted to a greater or lesser extent. If, for example, a change in direction follows a dead end, as Socrates' introduction of the theory of recollection does in *Meno*, then we are already aware that there is a crisis in the conversation, and expect an alteration of course of some sort—though, as perhaps in this case, we may be unprepared for the extent of it. At other times, we may have less warning. For example, the introduction of the hypothetical method and the discussion of whether *arete* is teachable—while of course we can see in retrospect how they are motivated by Meno's failure to take on board the significance of the recollection episode, and Socrates' desire to get him to continue inquiring into the nature of *arete* by any means[45]—are not overtly prepared for.

[43] Annas (1982a) argues that the *Gorgias* myth contradicts what is said earlier in the work; Sedley (2009) offers a more continuous interpretation.

[44] I realize that in saying this, I have simply pushed one stage further back the question of what counts as a change in direction: our decision about what feels like a new departure is as subjective as our evaluation of the conceptual relation between subjects discussed. In fact I doubt whether a clear line between progressions and changes in direction can be drawn: there is a sliding scale; and lesser examples will simply produce the same responses in smaller measure.

[45] Cf. Wilkes (1994) 212–13, Sharples (1985) 10.

Second, a change of subject may be accompanied by an alteration in mode or style. The introduction of recollection (which shifts to a mystical, poetical style) and of the hypothetical method (which is given a mathematical prelude) involves something of this. More radical is the introduction of a myth. At the close of *Gorgias*, as we enter the mythical realm of the underworld, we are immersed in a different level of reality and encouraged to see our place in the world from a different perspective. The poetical style demands a different kind of attention; and in particular Socrates' evocation of the terror the underworld holds for wrongdoers invites a different, and more affectively charged, response. There are also new challenges of interpretation—how seriously to take the mythical narrative, on what level of reality to understand it, how to interpret its relation to our life in this world, and how much significance to read into its details. In short, the shift into the mythical mode disturbs our response on various different levels, and all this contributes to the impression that a change in course is taking place.[46]

Third, a change in method or dialectical style may be involved. This is arguably the key shift involved in the introduction of the hypothetical method following *Meno* 86d. When we look closely, we can see that the hypothetical discussion bears striking resemblances to the inquiry into the nature of *arete* in the earlier part of the work: in a very short space (by 87b), Socrates has brought the discussion back to what *arete* is; the style of questioning is not substantially different from that used earlier; and the actual hypothetical structure of the conversation is rather vague.[47] Nevertheless, the new method does represent a changed approach, and we are left wondering why Socrates has chosen to introduce it, what benefits it offers, and how it is meant to relate to the earlier pursuit of definitions.[48] Particularly strikingly, here, the method seems to abandon a fundamental principle of the earlier inquiry—the need to discover the nature of a thing before investigating its features[49]—and this apparent contradiction enhances the disjunctive effect.

[46] For this aspect of Plato's myths, see Nightingale (2002a).

[47] On hypothesis in *Meno*, see Sternfeld and Zyskind (1976) and (1977), Robinson (1953), Bedu-Addo (1984).

[48] Cf. *Phlb.*20b, when Socrates proposes abandoning the many-over-one method; and the change in dialectical style from *Republic* II onwards and in the second part of *Parmenides*.

[49] Cf. Crombie (1994) 191–2, Sharples (1985) 9–10.

6.3.3. Non-directed structure

As we read a Platonic dialogue, we frequently do not have a clear sense of the overall course of the conversation; rather, it seems to develop as we read.[50] A dialogue does not open with a statement of the conclusion to be reached or the path to be followed, of the sort we might find at the start of a demonstration.[51] Rather, we are presented with undirected discussion, in which new themes emerge in response to questions that are asked, objections raised, interests expressed, or problems reached, and may not be directly integrated with previous episodes. The discussion may progress, or seem to progress, beyond the scope suggested by its opening, and not all the material may be directly relevant to the main thematic development.[52] In consequence, the works frequently have an additive, almost episodic, quality. Of course, Plato's dialogues are not transcripts of real conversations; their apparently free-flowing quality is a product of his crafting: what is striking is that he chooses to present the conversations in this way.[53]

In typical style, *Meno* opens with a question: how *arete* is to be acquired, by teaching, nature, or practice. This gives us a sense of the conceptual terrain that is to be covered within the work, and provides a framework within which to think about the conversational developments that occur. At this point, however, we are given no indication of the conclusion that will be reached, nor any signposting to prepare us for the various surprising turns the conversation will take. Socrates and Meno launch straight into an inquiry about what *arete* is,

[50] Well brought out by Stauffer (2006) 3–6; also O'Brien (1971) and Roochnik (2003). For interesting discussion of intentional ambiguity in Pre-Socratic proems, see Mansfeld (1995). Intriguingly, this is one of Socrates' criticisms of Lysias at *Phdr.*263c–264b: Lysias does not offer a definition at the start of his speech, and starts from the end of the topic not the beginning. But Socrates' treatment of rhetorical tropes at 266d ff. suggests he is not advocating a conventional approach to the structuring of a speech.

[51] Cf. Rowe (2002) 300, Mansfeld (1995).

[52] Cf. Heath (1989a) 162.

[53] Non-directed structure is of course not confined to the dialogues (see e.g. Hardie (1993) and (1997) on Roman epic, Harrison (1999b) on the Roman novel); and in every work we continue to build up meaning as we read, unable to reach a full or final interpretation before the close. Nonetheless, the techniques I highlight show Plato going out of his way to magnify such effects and the consequent need for a high level of reader input.

a necessary prerequisite—they have agreed—to discovering how it is to be acquired.

As the dialogue unfolds, moreover, it is shown to be markedly additive in structure, falling into a number of distinct sections: the opening discussion of what *arete* is; the discussion of recollection; the introduction of hypothesis and the argument that virtue is teachable; the argument that virtue is not teachable; the discussion of right opinion and Socrates' closing suggestion that in fact *arete* comes through divine dispensation. Each is introduced in response to a concern voiced by one of the interlocutors, and each moves the conversation into a new phase that fits with the thematic development so far but for which we have not been directly prepared. Some indeed (most notably the recollection episode) take the discussion well beyond what we might have expected from Meno's opening question. It is also striking that, although the reader can make sense of the episodes as a coherent development, Socrates and Meno do not themselves bring out the connections between them: each is treated as a self-contained unit, left behind as the discussion moves on to a new phase. No attempt is made to explain why the hypothetical method is introduced, for example, or to explain how we should square it with the principles of the earlier elenctic discussion.

All this creates, above all, a sense of uncertainty. The developments surprise us, and also disorient us, challenging our ability to make sense of the course and structure of the discussion as a whole. Unsure about the direction we are being taken in and the endpoint we are going to reach, it becomes harder for us to manage our attention and to make sense of the different parts of the discussion as we reach them: for we have no overall pattern within which to fit them. This sense of uncertainty may be uncomfortable and frustrating for the reader; it also encourages her to look forward, thinking about what may be coming next, because she has not been prepared for it in advance.

6.3.4. Disparate treatment of themes

A closely connected, though nevertheless distinct, upshot of this kind of episodic structure is that we often find discussion of the same or closely connected issues in different parts of a work; yet frequently they are not brought into direct relation to each other. The reader is left to decide how to relate the two passages, to determine which to privilege if there are discrepancies, and to understand what each adds to the other. In *Meno*, this is perhaps most obvious in the two passages which deal explicitly with the theme of knowledge and inquiry: the slave demonstration (82b–86c, esp. 85c9–d8) and the passage about the statues of Daedalus (97d6–98a8). In the former, Socrates says that the boy's opinions will be turned into knowledge if he is asked the same questions many times, a process which it is natural, in the context, to connect with recollection—though Socrates does not clarify how exactly the two are related (is the questioning recollection itself, a part of recollection, or a preparatory process?), nor what precise function the questioning serves. In the later passage, the idea that turning opinions into knowledge is like tying down statues seems to refer back to the earlier idea of confirming opinions by repeated questioning. Yet Socrates also introduces—without elaboration—a new concept, the *αἰτίας λογισμος* ('reasoning out the explanation'), which is what enables the statues to remain stable.[54] Plato seems, therefore, to be inviting us to read the two passages in the light of one another, but does not make it clear exactly how we should do so; and their different conceptual vocabulary compounds the problem. We are left to think about what the *αἰτίας λογισμος* might be, and how it fits in with recollection and with the repeated asking of questions.[55]

My point here is not that the passages are incompatible—most accounts of recollection and inquiry in the dialogue draw close links between them—but that by separating them, Plato leaves open various questions of interpretation, and makes our task more challenging. Nevertheless, when such passages do appear to contradict one another, the effect is even more unsettling.[56] In *Meno*, instances are concentrated in the later part of the dialogue. An argument to the effect that *arete* is not teachable directly follows one apparently showing that it is teachable. The statues of Daedalus passage seems to jar with the ideas just put forward in the argument that there are no teachers of *arete* and in the discussion of the road to Larisa

[54] For discussion, see e.g. Irwin (1995) 132–46. For discussion of the Daedalus image in *Euthyphro*, see McPherran (2003).

[55] Burnyeat (1990) 8–10, 37–9, 45–8, and *passim*, is suggestive on the need to draw connected passages into a coherent whole in *Theaetetus*.

[56] Cf. e.g. Clay (1988) 23–4, White (1996), Krentz (1983) 39, Scott and Welton (2000) 147–8; also Roochnik (2003) 145–6 and *passim*.

(96d5–97d3), where Socrates suggests that right opinion is as valuable as knowledge. Moreover, the view expounded at the very close of the dialogue, that virtue comes by divine dispensation and not by teaching, seems to contradict the emphasis on inquiry that is implicit in much of the dialogue, and especially the discussion of recollection and the Daedalus passage.[57] An even more obvious example is the treatment of *mimesis* in *Republic* X, which seems directly to conflict with the way the term is used in books II/III.[58]

In such cases, the pressure upon us to connect the different treatments—always present when related themes are touched upon in separate places but not integrated—becomes more intense. The contradiction forces us to confront the relationship between the passages, as we attempt to come up with a unified and coherent reading of the work as a whole. And at the same time, it seems to threaten our ability to do so, creating feelings of irresolution, frustration, and discomfort, especially when, as in *Meno* and *Republic*, the contradiction emerges as a twist in the tail of the dialogue. It upsets the reader's expectations right at the close, turning on its head the interpretation of the structure and meaning of the dialogue she has been developing as she reads, and forcing her to re-evaluate her reading of the entire work.

6.3.5. Iterative structure

In the previous two sections, I have highlighted disconnectedness in the structure of the dialogues: the way in which later parts of the works develop from, but also move beyond, what has gone before, leaving the reader to draw together and to connect the different passages. At the same time, however, it is common for a dialogue to revisit an earlier point, producing the effect of repetitiveness or

[57] On these oddities, see e.g. Wilkes (1994). The Larisa passage raises various problems of interpretation; see e.g. Burnyeat (1980b) and Sharples (1985) 10–14.

[58] Of course, contradiction can be generated even when two passages do not directly treat the same theme: as I noted in section 6.3.2, the presuppositions of the hypothetical method seem to contradict those of elenctic questioning. Contradiction may be closely bound up with paradox—a pervasive feature of the dialogues, and a powerful means by which the reader is engaged. See e.g. Vlastos (1991) 2–3; also Mackenzie (1986) and especially (1982) on the significance of the process of solving paradox, as opposed to the solution reached.

circularity.[59] For instance, the question with which Meno opens the dialogue—whether *arete* is acquired by teaching, practice, nature, or in some other way—is repeated at 86c7–d2, when he requests that they return to his original concern,[60] and again at the very close of the work, when Socrates says that their investigation has, if correct, determined that *arete* is acquired neither by teaching nor by nature, but by divine dispensation (99e4–100a1). Similarly, Socrates' and Meno's initial discussion of *arete* contains numerous repetitions. Most obviously, there is Socrates' insistent voicing of the troubling question 'what is *arete*?' (71a5–7, 71c1, 71d5, 73c6–8, 77a5–b1, 79c4, 79e5–6, cf. 86c4–6)—the later cases couched as a return to the beginning of the inquiry, a repetition of their previous attempt, or a discharging of Meno's as yet unfulfilled promise to answer the question, underscoring their continued lack of success. There is also repetition in the problems Socrates detects in their proposed answers. At 72a6–8, using the image of bees, and then again at 74a7–10, he says that they have found many virtues when they were only looking for one; at 77a5–9 he tells Meno to stop producing many from one, as people say when they break something (*παῦσαι*, 77a7, implying that Meno is doing what he has also done in his previous definitions); and at 79a7–c3 Socrates accuses Meno of ignoring his request not to break virtue up into bits, instead doing exactly that. Finally, there is the repeated exasperation expressed by Socrates and Meno as each of their attempts fails.

This kind of structure is akin to ring composition.[61] The encircling allusions allow the reader to see the portion of text in question as a discrete section, giving a sense of closure and completeness, at least on a formal level.[62] Thus, Socrates' allusion to Meno's opening question right at the end of the work signals that the opening dilemma has on some level been resolved. Similarly, the repetitions

[59] On aspects of circular structure in the dialogues, see McPherran (2003) 23, 25 with n63. On the iterative nature of Socratic dialectic, see Morgan (2007) 347–54.

[60] For discussion, see Wilkes (1994). The examples I look at here involve clear verbal repetitions that are acknowledged as such by the characters. The dialogues also contain verbal echoes which are not acknowledged, but which create a sense of iteration.

[61] On ring composition in classical texts, see for example, with further references, Edwards (1991) esp. 44–8, Nimis (1999).

[62] For ring composition as a closural device, see e.g. Roberts *et al.* (1997). Cf. Notomi (1999) 40–1 on *Sophist*.

that accompany the initial discussion of *arete* mark off each definition from the next, encouraging us to view them as separate attempts to solve the problem, with different things to tell us about *arete*, definition, and inquiry.

Simultaneously, though, repetition may create a powerful effect of irresolution, opening up the discussion rather than resolving it. Repeatedly returning to the same question without answering it, as Socrates and Meno do in the initial part of the dialogue, adds a sense of urgency, so that more seems to depend on the solution with each asking. The repetitions create a crescendo effect, as Meno and Socrates become more and more frustrated with their inability to reach a resolution, until the discussion erupts into Meno's extended *aporia* at 80ab and the paradox of inquiry. Their frustration is an index of their affective commitment to resolving the problem, and it encourages a similar response in us, making the question the focus of our emotional as well as our intellectual engagement. At the same time, Socrates' and Meno's repeated failure, despite their intensifying efforts, makes the question seem increasingly difficult, and resolution increasingly remote. At the start of the dialogue, we may have thought the question a straightforward one, as Meno does. By 80ab, we see exactly how hard it will be to answer: the repetition has in fact deepened the problem, and opened up the question in a far more powerful way. Now, Socrates' renewed request to Meno to say what *arete* is triggers a fundamental discussion of the possibility of inquiry and the means by which we can acquire knowledge—as it could not have done when put forward for the first time. By repeating the question, the dialogue has gradually deepened our understanding of its meaning and significance.[63]

[63] Cf. Dodds (1959) 3–5, Miller (1987). Also, Taplin (1971) on the repetition of significant actions in Sophocles' *Philoctetes*, Hardie (1993) 14–18 on Roman epic, and Kraus (1998) on the destabilizing effect of doublets in Livy. Douglas (2007) brings out the exegetical function of ring composition. Similar to the *Meno* examples are the two discussions of whether plausibility is sufficient for rhetorical success at *Phdr.*259e–260e and 272d–274a. These seem to address the same topic, but the second comes to a rather different conclusion: Socrates argues that plausibility derives from truth, so that a truly plausible speaker needs to know the truth about his subject and about the types of people he is addressing. Here, Plato seems to be appropriating and reworking the concept of plausibility as it was treated in rhetorical theory (see e.g. *Rhetoric to Alexander* 7). In such a case, it is tempting to think of a 'false' ring, since the broad similarity of topic can conceal the progression in its handling. The psychological turn of the second passage, in particular its concern with different types of soul, may

The iterative pattern undermines resolution in a further way, moreover, by suggesting that the failed attempts to answer the question form part of an ongoing pattern, and that any apparent resolution is only provisional. Important here is the fact that we do not just have one ring, as in classic ring composition, but several. In *Meno*, this is particularly important at the very close of the work. At 99e4–100a1 Socrates offers an answer to Meno's opening question—that *arete* comes by divine dispensation, not by teaching or by nature—in words that directly recall Meno's. On one level, as I suggested earlier, this indicates that Socrates has (in some sense) solved the puzzle and that the conversation has attained closure (99e4–100a1, 100b2–4). Right beside it, however, comes the assertion that we can only know how *arete* is acquired once we know what it is (100b4–6)—the very question that has been at the heart of Meno's and Socrates' repeated failed attempts at definition. By reiterating it here, Socrates reopens that as yet unfinished investigation, and undercuts any sense of final resolution. The question points towards further iterating rings of inquiry, which may eventually reach resolution, as they touch more and more profound themes, or may reveal knowledge of this sort to be beyond the reach of humans. Either way, the tactic compels us to see the inquiry presented in the text as far from completed, and threatens our ability to make sense of it as a complete and coherent unit in itself, pointing us to further philosophizing beyond the bounds of the text.[64]

6.3.6. Length, proportion, and digression

Our perception of the significance of a passage within a work is conditioned in a range of ways. The extent to which it is *treated* as being significant is one important factor. Thus, for example, if a passage is termed a digression, we tend to think that, while it may be important and interesting, it will be of secondary or incidental relevance to the main concerns of the work. The length of time spent

provide a link with the analysis of the soul in the earlier part of the work: see section 6.1 above.

[64] Cf. Clay (1987) and Miller (1987), Rutherford (1995) 214, Morgan (2007) 347–54.

on an episode is another factor.[65] More significant events tend to be developed at greater length within a narrative, while insignificant ones are skimmed over, perhaps in summary form. Such markers help us to think about the shape of a work and how to make sense of its parts as a coherent whole.

Now, such patterns can of course be disrupted. A crucial event can initially be treated very briefly, or indeed omitted altogether, with great effect when its significance is later revealed, a technique common (for instance) in the detective novel.[66] In Plato, we find mismatches of a different sort: namely places where a passage is accorded a low level of significance within the thematic development, but is treated at greater length than—that being the case—we would expect. This is an issue particularly prominent in Plato's 'late' works, not least *Politicus*.[67] To many readers, the structure of *Politicus* has seemed badly proportioned or 'lumpy', particularly due to the myth and the discussion of weaving. Both are accorded a role in the overall thematic development: the myth will help young Socrates and the Eleatic Stranger to correct errors made in their discussion of the statesman (274e1–3); and weaving is a *παράδειγμα* (example) they can later apply to statesmanship (279a7–b6). Yet the episodes are longer and more detailed than seems necessary, and this is reflected in the comments of the Eleatic Stranger. In introducing the myth, he associates it with play (*παιδιὰν* 268d8), which could imply a break from serious discussion, and he casts some doubt over whether the *whole* of the tale he is about to tell is necessary for the discussion (*συχνῷ γὰρ μέρει δεῖ μεγάλου μύθου προσχρήσασθαι* 268d8–9). At 273e4–6 he duly declares that for their purpose of elucidating the nature of the statesman, they need consider only the first part of the myth. Then at 277a4–b8, and again at 286b6–c2, he says explicitly

[65] Speed is the preferred narratological term; but, especially in *Politicus*, Plato uses the language of length. For discussion of the relation between space devoted to an episode within a narrative and its importance, see Rood (1998) 24–57 (esp. 24–6, 35–6), 89, 133–58, 205–24, 239–44.

[66] Cf. Rood (1998) 35–6 pointing out that our reaction to narrative speed depends upon our expectations, and only when these are not met do variations in speed become interesting; also De Jong (2001), esp. xvii.

[67] On the structure of *Politicus*, see e.g. Campbell (1973), Taylor (1961), Blondell (2002) and (2005), Rowe (1995a) and (1995b). On digression, see Heath (1989a) and (1989c), Brumbaugh (1988) 84–6, Barker (1976), Notomi (1999) 27–42 (with interesting comments on the reader's response to digressions), Roochnik (2003) 145; also Burnyeat (1990) 34–6 on *Theaetetus*.

that the myth was too long. Similar points might be made about the treatment of weaving: at 283b1–c1 the Eleatic Stranger implies that it has gone on longer than necessary, and at 286b6–8 he groups it with the myth as a part of the discussion that lasted too long.

At 283c, the Eleatic Stranger himself raises this very issue. He suggests that we should distinguish between relative and absolute length, and goes on to say that we should not wish for a discussion to be the length most pleasant for us, but rather the length required to increase the understanding of the listeners (286c–287a). Only if this latter objective could have been achieved more briefly should the speaker be criticized. This discussion thematizes the very structural feature I have been describing, and provides a way of accounting for the apparently disproportionate length of certain passages.[68] Yet that disproportion does still have an important impact on the way we make sense of the work. When we come to evaluate the unity and coherence of the work as a whole, we are unsure of the role to attribute to these passages. Should we continue to think of them as secondary, viewing their overly lengthy treatment as a way of unsettling the reader and disrupting her normal patterns of reading? Or should we revise our views about the value of digressions in the dialogues, or at least these digressions: their designation as *exempla* or *paidia* need not indicate that they are less central, and indeed this may be another way of confounding the reader. Our decision will vary from case to case, yet it has important implications for our overall interpretation; Plato's tactic adds to the reflectiveness, and the difficulty, of that interpretative process.

Such structural features also have an important impact on our experience as we read. As the Eleatic Stranger notes at 286bc, excessive length, particularly in a passage that seems to have been designated a secondary role, is annoying or unpleasant (ἕνεκα τῆς δυσχερείας 286b6), and may tempt us to skim read (286e4–287a1). Cases such as the middle-book digression in the *Republic* prompt surprise and disorientation, as we realize that the 'digression' has taken us to some of the most difficult and challenging material in the work. Then again, passages such as the discussion of weaving in *Politicus*, which are no less demanding but which the reader suspects are less central thematically, really challenge her motivation to keep

[68] See Blondell (2002) 366–77, Heath (1989a) and (1989c).

going and her ability to maintain a high level of concentration over a long period. Both cases make it hard for us to know how to manage our attention as we read, and this encourages us to be continuously attentive, scrutinizing all parts of the work for what they can offer us, rather than making easy, unreflective assumptions about what to regard as important.

6.4. STRUCTURAL PATTERNS AND THE READER

The features I commented on in the last section have, of course, been noticed before. But they are generally regarded as unfortunate, perhaps unintentional, facets of the dialogues' conversational format,[69] and explained with reference to the specific dialogue in question: a discussion leader's need to accommodate the dialectical needs of a particular interlocutor,[70] or Plato's desire to expound ideas in a certain way.[71] By contrast, I want to look at such structural features from the point of view of the *reader's* experience, adopting an *aesthetic* approach to the construction of the dialogues, in the terminology introduced in chapter 2.[72] We should not view each instance (as we may be inclined to) as an isolated case whose impact is incidental, but rather as part of an interconnected set of complementary features which pervade the dialogues, together encouraging a certain pattern of reading and a particular type of response. In fact, as I hope is by now becoming clear, these structural features reproduce in the reader—albeit on a larger scale—many of the effects we observed in chapter 5 in the handling of individual arguments.

First, there are the sudden effects of surprise, disorientation, and shock, often complemented by perplexity, bafflement, and annoyance, which disrupt our reading in a dramatic way. These are mainly produced by dead ends and changes in direction, though also by contradiction and inconsistency. They shake us up and grab our attention, arresting our

[69] See e.g. Rutherford (1995) 132 on *Protagoras*, Halliwell (1988) on *Republic* X, Roochnik (2003) 140–9. Cf. Heath (1989c) 14.

[70] See e.g. Heath (1989a) 172–3, (1989c) 25–7, Wilkes (1994) 218, Griswold (1986) 158.

[71] See e.g. Taylor (1961) 250–1 on *Politicus*; also Annas and Waterfield (1995) xxiii–xxiv.

[72] Cf. Ferrari (1987), Mackenzie (1982), Roochnik (2003), Heath (1989a) 173.

progress and challenging the interpretation we have been building up. When we come up to a dead end, for example, it forces us to look again at the path the discussion has been taking, jolting us into a more alert, more critical mindset, and prompting a renewed phase of reflection. It makes us more self-conscious about how we are relating to the discussion—about assumptions we may have been making or lazy habits of acceptance we may have been falling into. It also fosters a more personal, or more affectively charged, response. We are frustrated and baffled by the setback that has occurred, and perhaps annoyed with ourselves too, and this creates an impulse in us to solve the problems with which we are confronted. Because these problems have disturbed us, we want to resolve them satisfactorily: they become, in a sense, our problems. And this is crucial to the fully engaged, yet critical attentiveness that is necessary for productive learning.

More subtle and persistent are the feelings of irresolution and uncertainty produced by certain structural patterns, especially open-ended structure and digression, but also iterative structure and the disparate treatment of themes. These unsettle us by preventing us from feeling that we know how to go about making sense of the work as a whole, making it hard for us to assess which of its parts are central or the direction in which it is heading. They prompt us to reflect on how we *do* usually go about interpreting a work—our critical processes and interpretative assumptions—and they ensure that we remain attentive and open to new developments as we read. We have to read *through* the work,[73] for we cannot, at an early stage, rest comfortable in the assurance that we know its overall structure—as may be the case in works structured as treatises or demonstrations. By challenging us to reach a coherent interpretation of a work without much guidance, the structural patterns prompt us to deeper and more searching reflection on the work. And, as before, there is an important

[73] See Roochnik (2003), esp. 1–9, for the importance of 'dialectical' reading, emphasizing our changing understanding of *Republic* as we read through it. Cf. also Rowe (1989) 176 on the dynamic role of Socrates' palinode in *Phaedrus*, our perception of which changes as we progress through the dialogue; and Ferrari (1987) 34–6 on how the structuring of *Phaedrus*, in particular the attention to orientation, prevents us reading straight through the work to extract its 'message'. Similarly Blondell (2002) 375 n255 on the importance of reading through *Politicus* before getting a complete picture of the statesman. Mansfeld (1995) brings out similar effects in Pre-Socratic writings.

affective edge to our response. The ongoing uncertainty—and the discomfort it causes—create energy and forward momentum, increasing our desire to reach resolution, as well as the effort we are prepared to put into doing so.

Third, there is the impulse towards repetition and revision created primarily by iterative patterns and the disparate treatment of themes, but also by dead ends and changes in direction, in so far as these send us back through the work to try and make sense of the point we have now reached. In part, this is about the way in which the dialogues encourage us to *read*: they make it hard for us to proceed without stopping, and they use a variety of means for getting us to move backwards through the text, perhaps a number of times, rereading and re-evaluating.[74] This means that our engagement with the text is more intensive, critical, and reflective than it might be, as we revisit passages and scrutinize them more carefully, and also that it simply lasts for a longer time. But the impulse towards revision also goes beyond this. As I noted when discussing iterative patterns, the dialogues use repetition to open up problems, by engaging us in ongoing consideration of questions to which they do not provide the answer. The same is true of the other ways in which the dialogues encourage rereading. Inconsistencies and surprise changes of direction send us back through the text, but there are no straightforward clues that, previously overlooked and now uncovered, enable us to make sense of the later passages. In consequence, these features generate a pattern of revision and repetition that extends beyond our reading of the dialogue, into our own self-directed inquiry.

Like the individual passages of argument considered in chapter 5, then, these large-scale structural patterns leave an awful lot for the reader to do, and prompt her to engage in further independent reflection. They also stimulate us in a complex way, encouraging attentiveness and critical activity that are charged with affective intensity and a personal relevance. The effects they produce are less intense than the

[74] Cf. again Roochnik (2003) on dialectical reading; also Blondell (2002) 377, Stauffer (2006) 6–8. See Guthrie (1978) 164–6 on how the 'weaving' structure of *Politicus* enables us to see connections in Plato's thought. Although I here place the emphasis on the importance of rereading and revision for our development in understanding, this need not, in principle, be incompatible with prolepsis as elaborated by Kahn (1996), whereby ideas in earlier works point towards and foreshadow their development in later works, so that we gradually attain a deeper understanding of them.

acute anger, frustration, and perplexity sometimes sparked by smaller stretches of dialectic, particularly in 'early' dialogues, but they are the more powerful for being extended over a whole work. More particularly, the large canvas we have been dealing with allows us to see very clearly how the dialogues are constructed so as to produce the three elements of dialectical virtue I set out in chapter 3: motivation; self-analysis and self-understanding; and practice. Discomfort and desire for resolution, the two central components of motivation, are key upshots of the sudden effects of disruption and the lower-level feelings of uncertainty; the challenge to our normal patterns of reading posed by both these groups of effects prompts us to look more closely and analytically at interpretations of the text we have reached, and also, more profoundly, at the way we are approaching the very process of interpretation; and the role of revision and rereading in fostering practice and ongoing reflection is easily apparent. Far from being incidental features of Plato's works, therefore, these structural patterns are one of the means by which they engage the reader in a way that enables her to learn.

6.5. STRUCTURE, UNITY, AND 'LIVING' DISCOURSE

Returning to our more challenging cases, my hope is that the patterns identified in the previous section can help us reach a positive interpretation of the structure and unity of works such as *Phaedrus*.[75] For the troubling features we find in *Phaedrus* (and other such works) are, I suggest, helpfully viewed as instances—albeit extreme ones—of the structural patterns we observe in more obviously unified works such as *Meno*. To begin with, the passage between Socrates' first and second speeches in *Phaedrus* carries many of the hallmarks of a pause of the sort that characterizes emphatic dead ends. Socrates' attempt to leave creates a closural effect. Moreover, the passage includes gnomic remarks (242c7–d2, cf. 241d1, which brings Socrates' first speech to a clear close) and, with similar effect, allusion to

[75] For the importance of structure in Plato's approach to wholeness, see Harte (2002).

Socrates' poetic predecessors; in addition, there is reflection on the course of the discussion so far and the expression of strong feelings, here primarily discomfort and unease, though also inspiration (particularly in Socrates' self-presentation as a seer, 242c3–4) and agitation (especially in Socrates' repetition of δεινὸν/δεινότερος and his use of questions at 242d3–10). Socrates' second speech, with its contrasting tone and argument, creates the effect of a change in direction, compounded by the element of contradiction with the first speech. Similarly, the shift to discussing rhetoric after Socrates' second speech on love is a clear case of a change of subject—though here it is so extreme that the work effectively falls into two parts—and the change of style at this point makes the shift all the more shocking.[76] If we accept at face value Socrates' hints that the speech is not to be regarded as the vehicle of his central philosophical insights, then it could be read as a case of disproportionate length, which upsets our ability to judge what is of importance both while we are reading and when we come to analyse the work in a more detached way.[77] The discussion of writing, as well as being (in one sense) a change in direction,[78] can also be read as a case of contradiction: although, in this case, the passage does not contradict something that has been explicitly stated, it seems to undercut an assumption embedded in the work up until that point—that writing can have philosophical value. In all these cases, moreover, Plato is making use of the techniques of additive structure and lack of signposting. The dialogue falls into discrete sections that emerge as the conversation progresses and are not fully integrated with one another. And a large part of the impact of Socrates' second speech, the shift to discussing rhetoric, and the passage on writing, comes from lack of preparation: they are surprising and unexpected developments, which take us into areas that we were not (given our progress so far) anticipating.

These parallels have important implications. If they are accepted, then we need to revise the way we look at works such as *Phaedrus*. We

[76] For the shift to discussing rhetoric in *Phaedrus* as effecting a jolt on the reader see Ferrari (1987) 37, Werner (2007) 131–2.

[77] This could also be said of the space devoted to scene setting and topography, which some think unnecessarily large: either, with Ferrari (1987), we have to view the passages as thematically central to an extent we are perhaps not expecting, or we can regard the emphasis they are given as a way of upsetting our assumptions about which parts of a work are of most value.

[78] Cf. Mackenzie (1982).

should be less tempted to see them as anomalies or isolated problem cases. Instead, we should think of a spectrum of instances of the structural principles I have identified. Some works, to be sure, are more extreme, but they are only intensifying the same basic principles: they are not a totally different type of case. And it is here that the type of response encouraged by these structural patterns becomes important. In *Phaedrus*, they are employed in such a way as to threaten our ability to perceive the work as a unified whole. In *Meno*, they do not do this, but—as I hope to have brought out—they do still disrupt our reading experience, producing surprise and shock, uncertainty and confusion, discomfort and frustration, and disorientation. In doing this, they are markedly centrifugal in effect,[79] pulling against the unity of the work. It is not that we cannot make good sense of the work as a coherent unit, but its structural features ensure that the process is more difficult and involves a greater contribution by us. It looks to me, therefore, as though Plato is consciously striving for an impulse towards disunity in *all* his works, as a way of encouraging a certain type of response in the reader—a more active engagement. If this is so, we should not be trying to explain away the problematic features of a dialogue, but should recognize that their disturbing character is central to their inclusion: they are *meant* to challenge and unsettle us, and we are meant to struggle sometimes to find a coherent interpretation of a work. The extent to which they do this is a measure of their success, not their failure. Plato is working with conventions of unity in mind, but he is consciously subverting them: for radical changes in direction, dead ends, contradictions, and episodes of disproportionate length would not disturb us unless they ran contrary to what we expect.

So much for the continuities between 'unified' and 'disunified' works; there is still the question of why some works strike us as more structurally challenging than others. Here, we can note developments in structural patterns across 'early', 'middle', and 'late' works. 'Early' works tend to conform to a large extent with our expectations about unity; they have a strong dramatic and conversational structure, and the disturbing patterns I identified, although they certainly have an impact on the way we read, do not pose a

[79] The terminology is Heath's: see Heath (1989c) *passim*, first introduced at p.5.

serious challenge to our ability to see each work as a unit. Dead ends, especially of the smaller kind, are extremely common; but these works are too short to allow for large-scale changes of subject or shifts in mode, and for the same reason additive structure and lack of signposting are less disorientating. In 'middle' and 'late' works, however, there is a more challenging approach to structure—indeed, all the problem dialogues at which I glanced at the start of the chapter are among this group. There tends to be less emphasis (particularly in 'late' works) on conversational and dramatic unity, which creates such a strong impression of coherence in many 'early' works. And the unsettling patterns intensify in impact. For example, there is an increase in the extremity of the changes in direction, as illustrated in *Phaedrus*, *Parmenides*, and *Politicus*. These become more severe, less well signposted, and less easily read as natural thematic progressions. Dead ends are now increasingly used in combination with other features, with even more demanding effect. They may be used to trigger a shift into a new—and often more profound and more constructive—phase of reflection (as for example at the end of *Republic* I, or at the start of the discussion of being and not-being in *Sophist*).[80] Alternatively, they may be placed after a very challenging and extended section of discussion, such as the Many–One method in *Philebus*. Non-directed structure becomes more unsettling in longer works—as 'middle' and 'late' works tend to be—and in 'later' works is compounded by cases of disproportionate length, a technique that really comes into its own here. Iterative structure, while present across the spectrum of dialogues, is intensified in some 'late' works by being combined with the beginning or ending of the dialogue midway through a conversation (as in *Philebus* or *Sophist*): that way, the continuation of the iterations beyond the end of the dialogue is foreshadowed even more directly.

The increasing extremity of the structural effects in these works makes them less accessible and less initially satisfying than 'earlier' ones. At times, it can seem that an entirely different set of concerns and presuppositions underlies their composition—as indeed we may feel when we move from 'early' to 'late' styles of dialectic. Yet this

[80] Though this pattern occurs throughout the corpus (see McPherran (2003) and Miller (1986), there is an increasing sophistication in the handling of dead ends and the developments they introduce as we progress through the dialogues.

need not be the case: it could just as well be that Plato, in structuring *all* the dialogues, is aiming to prompt a similar type of involvement in the reader, and that the changing tactics are part of the way that the dialogues provide a changing learning context suitable to learners of different stages of advancement, adapting their discourse to the soul of the receiver. 'Early' dialogues avoid the alienating effect that severe disunity could produce in someone just starting out on the philosophical process, while using tactics such as dead ends and iterative structure to increase the philosophical value of the reader's response. By 'later' dialogues, the structural techniques challenge the reader far more strongly, requiring her to do more work in interpretation, to show more perseverance, self-motivation, and enthusiasm, and to possess a more developed understanding of why grappling with apparent disunity is of philosophical value to her—and why therefore it is worth persevering.[81]

Going further, we might even say that Plato is challenging our notions of the appropriate place for unity in a philosophical work, and in the enterprise of learning more generally. Traditionally, unity is sought within a work itself, in the satisfying integration of its different parts. What I have been trying to bring out is that all Platonic dialogues tend towards disunity on this level, so that the reader has to make a great deal of input before she can reach a stable interpretation of a work and see it as a coherent unit. Complete unity, that is, is not something that exists *in the work*, but has to be created *by the reader* on the basis of a longer process of reflection, so that the unity she eventually finds belongs, in an important sense, to her, not to the work. There are direct parallels here with the process of acquiring knowledge, which—as we saw at the start of the chapter—the dialogues repeatedly link with the ability to perceive unity in apparent disunity. Think, for example, of the single definition that captures the essence of many instances; the one Form that corresponds to many particulars; the connection of the Good with unity. In *Phaedrus* itself, the dialectician, Socrates says, must be able to discern the single structure among the many (265d–266c).[82] This involves a shift in

[81] Cf. Rowe (1995a) 3 on *Politicus*: 'the degree of tedium which we feel at the pedestrian speed with which the stranger sometimes moves will (or so he suggests) be in inverse proportion to our devotion to philosophy.'

[82] Cf. Krentz (1983) 40, Sayre (1995) 79–82. See also ch.4 n68 on coherence and order, closely related issues.

focus, for the learner must realize that the imperfect particulars of the everyday world are unable in themselves to offer knowledge and that she needs to look to the purer and simpler realities of the intelligible realm. In addition, as we saw earlier, it involves an adjustment in vision; it takes time and practice for the learner to be able to discern unity amidst the confusing multiplicity of particulars. Plato's handling of the structure of the dialogues encourages us to approach them in the same spirit. The dialogues' 'imperfections' indicate that perfect unity, connected as it is with completeness and secure understanding, is something that in fact *cannot* belong to a written work, just as it cannot belong to any object in the everyday world. It can only be created by the reader through a longer process of reflection; and what matters is not the form of a work, but our ability to make sense of it through our own effort.[83]

By using the structural features of his works to prompt the reader, in her engagement with a dialogue, to embark on something of the 'unifying' process she must undertake when seeking understanding amidst the particulars of the everyday world, Plato is on one level providing the reader with practice, in the aesthetic arena, of skills that are philosophically important. In a similar way, Socrates' sample definitions intend to familiarize Meno with the conventions of Socratic definition, and the analysis of the angler in *Sophist* provides practice in collection and division. At the same time, he is using disunified structure as a way of prompting us to embark on a process of wider reflection and to make initial steps on the path to acquiring knowledge itself.[84] In so far as the structure of a work encourages independent thought, self-motivation, and ongoing reflection, and discourages us from relying on anything that is said in the work as knowledge, it of course contributes to our philosophical development. By reflecting on the ideas and problems a dialogue contains as we try to make sense of it—whether rhetoric and love are complementary parts of the philosophical life, for example, whether writing can have philosophical value, whether Socrates' two speeches are in fact

[83] Cf. Welliver (1977) 6–7 on the apparent disunity of *Timaeus-Critias*. Clay (1987) develops a complementary approach to Plato's corpus as a whole; cf. also Griswold (1999), Gonzalez (1998) 145. Cf. Dewald (1997) 80–1 for the idea that structural patterns in Herodotus are left intentionally open as a way of reflecting the difficulty—for both author and reader—of attaining knowledge of events that have occurred; and the consequent importance of rereading.

[84] Cf. Ferrari (1987) 230.

incompatible—we are in fact beginning the process of analysis that is a crucial part of acquiring understanding.[85]

Phaedrus, as we saw at the start of the chapter, likens a well-structured composition to a living creature. The image places a central emphasis on the correct arrangement of the parts of the body: they must fit together with each other by 'necessity' to create an appropriate 'living' whole, in such a way that they cannot be rearranged without detriment. In the same way, issues of order and appropriate 'fit' have been at the heart of my discussion of structure in this chapter. If the parts of *Phaedrus* or *Meno* were rearranged so as to bring related material together, to remove contradictions, or to eliminate dead ends, the attendant impact on the reader would be lost. As such, though they may sometimes at first strike us as uneasy in structure, Plato's works approach the 'living creature' in Socrates' characterization of a successful composition.

The imagery of life Socrates uses is itself, I think, significant, resonating as it does with language used elsewhere in the discussion of spoken and written discourse which forms the context to Socrates' short reflection on unity. There, written works are presented, rather, as *lacking* life: Socrates compares written works to paintings, which appear to be alive, yet when asked a question maintain an unresponsive silence (275d); Phaedrus then adds that they are images of the 'living and breathing discourse of the person who knows' (276a8). But despite their limitations, written works are capable of engendering living discourse; for though lifeless themselves, they can sow a fertile seed, from which more discourse grows in the soul (276e–277a). The dialogues' careful yet unusual approach to structure, I suggest, is one way in which they encourage a 'live' dialogue with their receiver, and sow the seeds of further living discourse in us. For the arrangement of material within the dialogues encourages a more reflective and attentive kind of reading by producing effects such as shock, confusion, and disorientation in the receiver, by leaving the reader with puzzles which she cannot solve from within the text, and by thereby propelling her into independent reflection which is based on, but goes beyond, the process of reading. Far from finding it surprising that Plato should

[85] Cf. Notomi (1999) 224–30, suggesting that if we do not make a unity out of the judgements we reach, we are like sophists who rest content with a series of appearances, not knowledge; and Moes (2000) 159–61.

reflect on unity in so structurally challenging a work, we should appreciate how appropriate his comments are. They illuminate the importance of structural oddities in achieving the philosophically valuable type of discourse Socrates describes; and they constitute, in themselves, one of the puzzles which stimulates the reader's productive engagement.[86]

[86] Cf. Mackenzie (1982).

7

Plot and Action: Process vs. Resolution

7.1. PLATO'S DIALOGUES: CLASSICAL PLOT?

Echecrates: Were you with Socrates yourself, Phaedo, on that day on which he drank poison in prison, or did you hear about it from someone else?

Phaedo: I was there myself, Echecrates.

Echecrates: So what did the man say before his death? And how did he die? For I would gladly hear, for nowadays none of the Phliasian citizens travels to Athens at all, and no stranger has come from there for a long time, who was able to relate to us anything definite about these things, except that he drank poison and died. He was able to tell us about none of the other things.

Phaedo, 57a1–b3

In these opening lines of *Phaedo*, Echecrates begs his companion, Phaedo, for an account of Socrates' final hours. He indicates that the topic has been widely discussed, passing from person to person and town to town, and his questions convey that he, in turn, is eager to hear. He also wishes to ascertain the credentials of Phaedo's account—whether it is based on his own experience or on what he has heard from others. Echecrates has already heard the outline of the story, the poisoning and death, but his comments highlight the difference between this rough overview and a definite or clear (σαφές 57b1) account of the sort he seeks. In short, Socrates' final hours have attained something of the status of a legend, and Echecrates is concerned that the version he receives should be an accurate one.

This exchange forms part of the frame dialogue which introduces Phaedo's account of Socrates' death and his preceding conversation with his companions. By including such an introduction to the work, a dialogue enclosing a dialogue, Plato offers us a familiar warning to be alert to the status of the account we are about to encounter and careful in our approach to it as receivers.[1] Yet at the same time, he uses it to present the death of Socrates as a truly great story: one with wide-reaching fame, which people are impatient to hear. Indeed, the introduction invites us to regard Phaedo's account in its entirety—the tale of Socrates' final moments together with the myth of the nature of the earth and the discussion of the immortality of the soul that precedes it—as a narrative of sorts.

When approached as philosophical writing, the dialogues' use of narrative is one of their most striking features. The texts abound with engaging and memorable narratives of various kinds, which allow Plato to lend his works some of the power of literary genres such as tragedy and epic, and to connect philosophical issues with people (often 'real-life' individuals) and their lives.[2] But Plato's use of stories goes further than this. It is well recognized that the stories we tell, as individuals and societies, are crucial to the way in which we make sense of the world and think about ourselves. They form powerful tools for imposing order on our lives and the world around us, giving them meaning and shape. They offer engaging ways of looking at things, and encourage us to situate ourselves in relation to the narratives they present.[3] As such, stories are a crucial part of the cultural and religious traditions of many societies, and ancient Greece is no exception.[4] Quite apart from the private exchange of stories, gossip, and anecdote, storytelling was a public and competitive enterprise, central to civic life. It played a key part in political debate and the pleading of cases. Mythical stories of men, heroes, and gods were central to the way the Greeks thought about and interacted with their gods. Comedy, tragedy, and epic were all performed at large-scale public occasions; tragedy in particular, with its reworkings of traditional myths, has been viewed as an important arena for the interrogation and negotiation of Athenian values.[5] Traditional education, too, was

[1] On the contribution of narrated proems and scene setting passages to the reader's approach to a dialogue, see Morgan (2003) and (2004), Halperin (1992), Clay (1992) and (2000), McCabe (1996) and (2000) 8–10, Nightingale (1993), Belfiore (1984), Tarrant (1996), Hyland (1981) ch.1.

[2] Frede (1992a).

[3] See e.g. Cupitt (1991) ix–x and *passim*, Brooks (1984) 3–7.

[4] See esp. Buxton (1994).

[5] See e.g. Goldhill (1986), Pelling (1997a) and (2000) 164–88. The ability of tragedians to bring out the relevance of mythical stories to the lives of their receivers is crucial here: see e.g. Pelling (1997b), (1997c) esp. 228–9.

based on the stories of myth and literature.[6] It is generally accepted that Plato aimed to challenge the place of myth and literature in education and social acculturation, and it seems likely that his handling of stories was part of the way in which he aimed to do this.[7]

There is undoubtedly something unusual about Plato's stories. Though the dialogues abound with narratives,[8] they do not contain *plots*[9] of the sort we find in tragedy and Homeric epic. It is a commonplace of Platonic criticism, moreover, that conversational exchanges make up the real action of the dialogues, taking the place of the more tangible events we find in many other genres.[10] In previous chapters, I have suggested that Plato also asks us to look beyond the conversation itself to a deeper level of action, the philosophical ideas and arguments that form the dialogues' most fundamental stories. In fact, Plato's handling of events is often hard to evaluate: we seem to be presented with so many different types of event—potential and actual, past and future, 'real' and conversational, philosophical and human, worldly and otherworldly, individual and general—that it becomes hard to determine which are the most significant and how they fit into a story or plot. In this chapter, I want to gain a sharper picture of Plato's (distinctive) practice in this area and how this affects the way we engage with stories, both those in the dialogues and those in our lives. As I hope will emerge, we do not have to make a choice about which are the most significant events: they are all important, and what is interesting is the way in which Plato uses each type of event to deepen our understanding of the others.

[6] See e.g. Hobbs (2000) 175, Kerferd (1981) 37, 40–1, Cribiore (2001) esp. 192–205; also Morgan (1998) 9–21 for an overview of education in classical Greece, with a robust attitude towards the evidence for the study of particular authors.

[7] Cf. *R.*377b ff. Hobbs (2000) 65–6 (and *passim*) has interesting comments on the importance of narrative for the dialogues' presentation of role models, especially Socrates. I address the role of Socrates in ch.4; my concerns here will be slightly different.

[8] These should be distinguished from a work's 'story' in the technical sense I have been using the term: see ch.5 n55. Additional stories contained within the main story may be termed embedded narratives: see De Jong *et al.* (2004) xv–xvi.

[9] Cf. Bakhtin (1981) 22. Plot is difficult to define. Following Lowe (2000), I shall regard it as the 'affective determination of a reader's modelling of a story' (266) through its presentation in the narrative. As such it cuts across story and narrative levels. Cf. Brooks (1984) esp. 13–14, 37, 48.

[10] E.g. Ferrari (1989) 145. For plot in the dialogues as 'the doings and sayings . . . of all the characters from the opening scene to the end of the dialogue', see Press (1993b) 120–1.

At the heart of my approach, then, is an attention to the different sorts of events and stories that are at work in the dialogues; and in a moment I shall survey these directly. But first I am going to look briefly at a sophisticated approach to story and plot in Plato's dialogues suggested by N. J. Lowe. Lowe emphasizes the philosophical stories underlying the conversational ones, and so his approach can, at first sight, seem similar to mine. But while my inclination is to treat the different types of stories as co-existent and mutually enriching, Lowe juxtaposes them. My reservations will take us to the heart of the issues.

The emphasis of Lowe's book, *Classical Plot and the Invention of Western Narrative*, is, as its title suggests, on classical plots of the sort we find in Homeric epic, fifth-century tragedy, New Comedy, and the Greek novel, and which are characterized by elegance, economy, and efficiency.[11] But Lowe also glances at various 'unclassical plots', including the dialogue form.[12] He notes that Plato's dialogues do have something rather close to a traditional plot structure. They contain a closed list of speakers, and attend to characterization and motivation. The state of relations between the participants changes dynamically (we are, of course, familiar with plots that consist primarily of acts of communication, and where the central happenings are changes in characters' mental states: Virginia Woolf's *Mrs Dalloway* is a famous modern example). They also invite the reader to develop an understanding of how the conversation will proceed, producing powerful effects of delay, suspense, and resolution. But notwithstanding, Lowe argues, there are some fundamental differences. In works of classical plot, there is always some outward event or action to which the exchange of views ultimately connects and without which they would be senseless, whereas in the dialogues, he thinks, this is not the case. Beliefs, knowledge, immortality, and so forth are the ultimate topics of conversation. And it is the dialectical processes—the development of arguments—not the interaction between characters that ultimately produce the dynamic effects of delay, suspense, and resolution: these would be apparent even if the arguments alone were presented. Plato is exploiting a structural analogy between narrative and dialectic, and in doing so, he is communicating that philosophy is as powerful as storytelling. But, Lowe suggests, what we have is *plot-like* structure, not classical plot.

[11] Lowe (2000), esp. x–xi and 61–78.

[12] Lowe (2000) 93–6.

Lowe's analogy between dialectical structure and plot structure is, I think, an important and powerful one, and his account tries to do justice to the unusual character of the dialogues' plots. But there are points at which I diverge from him. First, I would like to refine our understanding of the philosophical stories with which Plato is ultimately concerned. Lowe lays a great deal of emphasis on dialectical structure, and it is the progression of arguments he appears to have in mind. Yet this is only one type of philosophical story contained within the dialogues. The works also ask us to look beyond arguments to the ideas and insights with which they grapple, in ways that I hope will become clearer in what follows. Moreover, in my view Lowe underestimates the importance of elements of classical plot—in particular the handling of character and outward happenings—for the way in which the dialogues direct our attention towards underlying philosophical issues. Plato is not, as Lowe seems to suggest, *replacing* these with philosophical (in his terms, dialectical) plot; he is rather introducing philosophical plot as an *additional* layer.

To begin with, Lowe proposes that the structural dynamics would be 'equally apparent if the arguments alone were presented, stripped of these dramatizing elements [character and setting], in a continuous, impersonal tract'.[13] Yet I hope that my observations in previous chapters have shown how distant Plato's arguments are from the sort we would find in impersonal tracts. As I brought out in chapter 5, interlocutors do not abide by formal rules of dialectical exchange in the Aristotelian sense; and logical soundness is frequently not the basis on which arguments are evaluated. Moreover, as I highlighted in chapters 1–4, the progress of the conversation depends as much on participants' particular attitudes and responses to what is said as on its logical content. Neither the impasse reached with the paradox of inquiry in *Meno*, nor the later introduction of the hypothetical method, for example, make full sense when abstracted from Meno's personality and Socrates' dialectical strategy in dealing with him. As readers, we need to reach a more impersonal understanding of the ideas interlocutors discuss, but we have to do so *through* considering their idiosyncrasies and personal agendas—a process which of course alerts us to our own limitations as learners. Similarly, an interlocutor's expression of his feelings about an argument—Euthyphro's

[13] Lowe (2000) 95.

frustration in the Daedalus passage (*Euthyphr.*11be) or Socrates' misgivings after his first speech in *Phaedrus* (241d–243d)—are, as I brought out in chapter 6, an important part of how Plato manages the pacing and structure of a dialogue, and therefore the reader's response. In consequence, the plot-like effects Lowe notices are not dependent on argumentative or logical structure in a narrow sense, as he suggests, but on a broader type of dialectical progression; and this is closely connected with the affective element both in the depiction of conversations themselves and in the reader's response.

Indeed, as Lowe himself notices,[14] the dialogues' dialectical developments sometimes bear striking resemblance to tragic patterns of discovery and reversal, revenge and punishment. An interlocutor's perception that the beliefs on which he has been grounding his life are mistaken bears some relation to Oedipus' calamitous realizations, and the vanquishing of an arrogant interlocutor can be viewed as punishment and reversal. If the events of a Platonic conversation potentially have as much impact on the lives of interlocutors as the tragic plots that they resemble, I see no reason why they should be regarded as any less real. To argue that the dialogues do not contain plots because they are based on *philosophical* discovery is to ignore the central relevance that dialectical happenings can have to a person's life.[15]

This brings us to my second point, which is that Lowe, in my view, underplays the importance of what he terms 'outward events' in Plato's conversations, such as the prisonhouse setting and death of Socrates in *Phaedo*. Scene setting is a matter of narrative convenience, he thinks, and outward events are not the true topic of the conversations.[16] Now, conversational exchanges—not setting—are what provide all Plato's dialogues with their most basic sense of coherence and unity. Moreover, I agree with Lowe that outward events are not the only topic of conversation in a dialogue, and do in part act as a way of

[14] Cf. Heath (1989a) 161–2, Gifford (2001).

[15] For other points of connection with Greek tragedy, see e.g. Rutherford (1995) 11–12, 166–8, Nightingale (1995) esp. 60–92, Clay (1975) and (2000) 141–9, Nussbaum (1986) esp. 122–35. Arieti (1991) attempts to interpret the dialogues as drama. On the relationship between the dialogues and Old Comedy, see Nightingale (1995) 172–92, Clay (2000) 141–9 and (1975). In addition to their comic elements, we might link the self-reflectiveness of the Platonic dialogues with the metatheatrical reflection of an Aristophanic parabasis: see Kahn (1983) 104. On metatheatricality in Aristophanes, see Revermann (2006).

[16] Lowe (2000) 95.

introducing—and making accessible—more abstract issues. But, nevertheless, the setting *does* have a significant impact on our understanding of issues such as immortality, knowledge, and the soul, because it brings out their centrality to people's lives: Socrates', his friends', and also our own. The thrust of the dialogues, in other words, is *practical*,[17] and by minimizing their connection with real characters and events, Lowe is in danger of obscuring this central preoccupation.

There is in fact a range of ways in which the dialogues link themselves with 'outward events'. To begin with, there are what I shall term *situational stories*: the events that provide the immediate context to the conversation, and the personal and interpersonal developments that occur during its course. In *Republic*, for example, this involves the meeting of the interlocutors at the Piraeus and the initiation of the conversation at Cephalus' house, as well as the interlocutors' shifting attitudes towards each other and the discussion itself, as it progresses.

Second (often closely linked with situational stories both in the works themselves and in the commentary of critics), there are the *life stories* of characters.[18] These may belong to characters actually participating in the conversation (e.g. Socrates) or others alluded to (e.g. Themistocles, Aristides, Pericles, and Thucydides at *Meno* 93b–94d), and they may be past, present, or potential.

Third, many dialogues contain *schematic representations of types of life*, such as the sketches of types of city and individual in *Republic* VIII–IX or the Eleatic Stranger's representation of the contemplative man and his counterpart at *Theaetetus* 172c–177c. This category might seem to be rather different in type from the previous two—and indeed it is, for it deals with general story patterns rather than narratives associated with specific individuals. But these are story patterns nonetheless and, as we shall see, they form an important source of narrative within Plato's works. Having said that, such passages do often evoke particular individuals (thus the generalized presentation of prisoners in the *Republic*'s Cave image recalls Socrates); but they are general in emphasis.

[17] This is well brought out by Frede (1992a). For Socratic philosophizing as aiming to change interlocutors' lives, see e.g. Kahn (1996) xiv–xv, Nehamas (1999b) 116, Cooper (1999c) 77; also (in ancient philosophy generally) Annas (1993). Cf. ch.2 section 2.1.

[18] I am not suggesting that the dialogues were composed to produce 'vignettes of Socratic biography' (an approach rejected at Vlastos (1994) 125); rather, that Plato presents us with life stories of characters including Socrates as a way of shaping our learning experience.

Fourth, we sometimes find *otherworldly stories*, such as Socrates' vision of the soul's existence before birth and its acquaintance with Forms in *Phaedrus*. These passages are narrative in form, and they deal with entities (such as the soul), settings (the underworld, the heavens), and times (before birth, after death) that are removed from the everyday. Again, they may overlap with other stories—an otherworldly narrative may be populated with actual characters and may also evoke generalized types of life—but they do nevertheless constitute an important group in themselves.

These different types of story are exactly the sort that, in another genre, might form the basis of a classical plot. The *Oresteia*, for example, zooms in on the changing relationships between a small group of characters over a short time (the homecoming of Agamemnon, his murder, and his children's revenge), yet it also evokes the events preceding the episode (the events at Troy and the fate of the house of Atreus) as well as the longer life stories of participants (Agamemnon, Iphigenia, Orestes, Clytemnestra). Moreover, the divine dimension to the trilogy, and in particular the role of the furies and the eventual intervention of Athena, give us a strong sense of an otherworldly story that extends beyond and intersects with the human events we witness. Yet, as Lowe has tried to bring out, Plato's handling of stories does strike us as significantly different from this. Can we reach a more satisfactory account of his practice?

In what follows, I propose that we can best explain the unusual quality of Plato's plots not by maintaining that he is uninterested in outward events, but by attending carefully to the way he handles them. In section 7.2, I offer a brief analysis of what is distinctive about the dialogues in this area, before backing up these synoptic observations with a more detailed look at *Laches*, *Republic*, and *Sophist* (sections 7.3–7.5). Finally, in section 7.6, I explore the implications of all this for the engagement of the reader and our understanding of the philosophical process itself.

7.2. UNCLASSICAL PLOT: PROLIFERATION, FRAGMENTATION, AND IRRESOLUTION

What, then, are the key tendencies in Plato's handling of his stories? First, there is an emphasis on *irresolution*, most apparent in the situational stories. Often, we just do not know what the upshot of the conversation is: whether Socrates has made any headway with Meno, whether Thrasymachus is at all persuaded—or even, as in *Philebus* or *Sophist*, how the conversation actually ends. There is frequently also ambiguity in the handling of a character's later life and actions. Commentators debate whether Euthyphro continues with his prosecution of his father or not;[19] and the future of characters like Protarchus is left tantalizingly uncertain. In all works, the plot separates off a set of events from those before and after it in an artificial manner, creating a coherent unit from an ongoing progression of events.[20] But the dialogues go out of their way to stress the continuity of the events they present with earlier and later ones, without allowing us enough insight into the larger picture to achieve a satisfying sense of resolution. The conversations we witness, Plato emphasizes, are snapshots in time, and cannot be understood without reference to the larger stories of which they form a part.

In addition, references to situational stories and characters' life stories are (as is often noted) usually concentrated at the start and end of a work, and are thereby *marginalized* within the work's overall construction. Of course, this is not the case without exception. Sometimes references to a character's life are included *allusively*, as, for example, the life of Socrates is evoked by *Republic*'s Cave image and by the threats of Callicles in *Gorgias*. This means that insights into the life of an interlocutor emerge, but they are not made the direct and primary focus, in the way that the earlier lives of Agamemnon and Orestes are in the *Oresteia*. In addition, the dialogues do make direct references to the situational stories and the lives of interlocutors at other points during their course. But here, they are usually fleeting and isolated, so that we are given only *fragmentary* insights.

In fact, even stories introduced directly in the opening and closing portions of a work are often treated fragmentarily, in that they touch on individual episodes in a character's life only (Ion's rhapsodic displays, for example, or Euthyphro's prosecution of his father and his activity as a religious expert). But at other points, the dialogues are even more inclined to evoke a story briefly, and then move on: think of Socrates' youthful endeavours to investigate the causes of things in

[19] See Beversluis (2000) 180–4 and McPherran (2003) 32–5; also Burnet (1924) 2.

[20] Rood (1998) 35 puts the point well: there is 'no natural way of cutting up the continuum of history'.

Phaedo; his earlier unhappy attempts to travel the long road of philosophy in *Philebus*; his own prosecution in *Euthyphro*; the future conversations with Lysias and Isocrates foreshadowed at the end of *Phaedrus*, and with Anytus at the end of *Meno*. If we move away from participants, examples multiply. To select just a handful from *Meno*, we have the story of Daedalus; the lives of Themistocles, Aristides, Pericles, and Thucydides and their sons; the story of the soul before birth; Socrates' meeting with priests and priestesses; and Teiresias' existence in the underworld. Of course, all works hint at stories that they do not develop. But the examples I have drawn from *Meno* occur at significant points within the work, and so impress themselves upon the reader's attention: we need to reflect on them to an extent to make sense of the speech or argument that is being put forward, and so we cannot just pass them by as unimportant details. Yet they are briefly and tantalizingly introduced: they invite us to imagine contexts, progressions, and connections, and they offer new resolutions, new areas of reflection, and new parallels, but they do not develop them for us. And a single dialogue will frequently contain a range of such moments. The effect is kaleidoscopic and, if we try to reflect on and draw out them all, almost dizzying.

This brings us to my final point, which is that it is not uncommon for a dialogue to evoke a range—sometimes a confusingly large one—of stories. In a classically plotted work, though there may be many narrative strands whose connection is not initially clear, they are generally drawn together into a coherent story as part of the working out of the plot. In Plato, however, this is not always so. In *Laches*, for example, the life stories of Nicias and Laches, Socrates, Lysimachus, Melesias, and their fathers, are all evoked. But they are not linked as part of a continuous story in the way that the lives of the successive generations of the house of Atreus are in the *Oresteia*; nor do they lead towards an ever-clearer and more definite denouement. Instead, they form a range of patterns of life, as a backdrop for the choice of life facing Lysimachus' and Melesias' sons. A similar effect is often created by the inclusion of otherworldly narratives and narrative paradigms such as *Republic*'s Cave image: these frequently are not introduced with specific reference to familiar characters (as the otherworldly themes in *Oresteia* and *Odyssey* are, for example), but are developed impersonally, and their connection with other narrative strands is left opaque. The principle is one of *proliferation* and *disunification*, rather than close-knit coherence; and the reader is left with a bewildering selection of different story patterns, which the work does not tie together for her.

In giving his dialogues these features, Plato is manipulating the elements of classical plot to create distinctive effects, and the key to understanding his strategy, I think, is the importance placed on *conversation*. Each dialogue evokes a range of stories of increasing scope—the events immediately preceding and succeeding the conversation, the life of specific characters, general patterns of life, and (sometimes) the events that lie beyond this world. In contrast to these, a conversation is a tiny event. Yet Plato chooses to focus on—and to structure his works around—the space occupied by the conversation within these larger stories. In narratological terms, one might think of this as a huge 'stretch' or 'slowdown': in relation to the larger story patterns evoked, the amount of space the dialogues devote to their conversations is hugely exaggerated.[21] The larger story patterns are still present, but they are treated in a tangential, marginal, and indirect way, and are given less sustained and structured treatment than we might expect.

One obvious effect of this is to guide our perception of the place of a Socratic conversation within the larger stories. For many interlocutors, a Socratic conversation does not bring about momentous changes in their lives—it turns out, that is, to be the tiny event which, in terms of its duration, it should be, when viewed from the perspective of their whole life. Yet Plato's tactics root us firmly in the present of the conversation, refusing to let us bypass its significance. This helps us to see the larger stories from the point of view of the conversation, and suggests that the conversation has the potential to influence their outcome—not in itself, in the way that tragedies often present the events of a single day as decisively determining the shape of their players' futures, but by helping to turn an interlocutor towards a life of *ongoing* philosophical conversation. The conversations represent, the suggestion is, moments at which the course of an interlocutor's life *could* have taken a different path, developed according to a different pattern, and progressed to a different otherworldly narrative—even if an interlocutor does not take his opportunity.

A second effect is an apparent inversion of the values of the classical plot. As construed by Lowe, classical plots are characterized by elegance, economy, and efficiency; they aim at a unified structure,

[21] Cf. the space devoted to speeches in Thucydides' account of the Peloponnesian War.

a coherent line of development, and a satisfying conclusion.[22] In Plato's dialogues, by contrast, we have an almost unruly wealth of different stories that are fragmentary, disconnected, marginalized, and often left unresolved. Of course, these stories point towards conclusion, but not in a definite way: there are numerous different ways in which we *could* project the continuation of the narrative strands and draw them together, but the dialogues refuse to do this for us. This lack of conclusiveness breeds the tension and suspense of an unfinished story. It invites us to think hard about how the stories *ought* to be concluded, the principles upon which we are drawing our conclusions, and the factors on which different conclusions would depend—thereby ensuring an active cognitive involvement that guides us, as we shall see, towards reflection on the deeper philosophical issues raised by the works. As it does so, it places the *reader herself* in the position of choice. Because Plato's approach makes it hard for us to avoid thinking about the different possibilities and lines of continuation, we come in a sense to be in the position of currently making these decisions ourselves—that is, actively involved in reflection and choice about our *own* lives, rather than detached observers.

Let us now put more flesh on the bones of this brief outline by looking at three dialogues in turn. In doing so, I shall try to bring out some of the developments that occur in this area, as in others, as we move from 'early' to 'middle' and 'late' works.

7.3. *LACHES*[23]

I have concentrated so far on the ways in which Plato's works depart from the conventions of classical plot. Nevertheless, there are a number of dialogues that are not hard to make sense of from that perspective, and *Laches* is among them. Conversational exchanges give the work a clear sense of structure (Lysimachus' opening question about the best way to educate his and Melesias' sons is followed

[22] D. Fowler (1997) 4 notes the connection between closed endings and classical works, though prefers to see a dialectic between open and closed elements even in such works.

[23] For detailed discussion of *Laches*, with attention to literary issues, see Stokes (1986) 36–113, Rutherford (1995) 83–7, von Reden and Goldhill (1999).

by a series of attempts at answering it) and they are bound up with a strong situational story. Laches and Nicias have just been taken to see a display of fighting in armour by Lysimachus and Melesias, who are concerned that if they do not offer their sons the correct education at this pivotal point in their development, they will have unremarkable lives like their fathers, rather than reaching the heights of accomplishment of their grandfathers. The dialogue explores what Laches, Nicias, and Socrates—whom the generals introduce as an additional authority—have to say, but ends without an answer. Instead, Socrates and Lysimachus arrange to meet the next day to continue the investigation. As well as helping us to view the conversational exchanges as part of a single whole, the context and interpersonal developments give the work a strong sense of progression and forward movement, of the sort Lowe associates with classical plot.

Even so, however, there are some interesting features in the dialogue's handling of its stories—not least the situational story—which pave the way for the more radical effects we find in 'later' works. Lysimachus, desiring to know how best to educate his son, consults Laches and Nicias, but the generals do not offer clear-cut advice on practical educational measures quite as he imagined.[24] Not only do the two disagree; they introduce Socrates, who, while refusing to take up a position of pre-eminence, nevertheless scrutinizes the views of the generals, revealing that they are not beyond the educational process, as Lysimachus has assumed. In other words, Socrates inverts the interpersonal dynamic: the generals, it now seems, need to seek education rather than educating others, and this creates some friction and annoyance between them.[25] However, it is left very unclear how they will respond in the longer term. Do they regard Socrates' teaching as an annoyance or as a help, as Nicias initially claims (187e6–188c2)? Will they be spurred on to further thought, or revert to their authoritative role when Socrates is not there? Significantly, the dialogue refuses us definite answers, returning to Lysimachus at the close.

Similar ambiguities surround the relationship between Socrates and Lysimachus. Initially, Lysimachus claims that their fathers were

[24] Cf. Beversluis (2000) 114 who terms the situation in which Lysimachus finds himself 'Kafkaesque'; also Stokes (1986) 40.

[25] Cf. Beversluis (2000) 126–32 who draws out the importance of these feelings for the progression of the conversation. Kahn (1996) 151 suggests that the prestige of the interlocutors adds to the dramatic interest of the debate.

close friends, and proposes rekindling the friendship between their houses (180e1–181c7) in a pattern of traditional, well-to-do social interaction. But as the dialogue progresses, we gain insight into another, more philosophical, sort of companionship: Socratic conversation, in which interlocutors examine each other and attempt to understand how they should live. This is the sort, Nicias claims (187e6–188c2), to which Socrates always reverts, and also the sort Socrates apparently intends to pursue when he meets Lysimachus the next day. Lysimachus, though, has only been involved in the present conversation as a spectator, and seems to seek a teacher who will give him straightforward answers; the extent to which he envisages engaging in active philosophical companionship is rather unclear. Again, by leaving the story unfinished, Plato asks us to imagine for ourselves how Lysimachus might—and should—act, and why.

A similar thing is true, on a larger scale, of the life stories evoked by the dialogue.[26] In his opening speech, Lysimachus suggests that his own and Melesias' have been unremarkable (*ἡμέτερα δ' αὐτῶν ἔργα οὐδέτερος ἔχει λέγειν*, 179c5–6) and this is borne out in what we know of them.[27] Their fathers, though, led lives of achievement (*ἡμῶν γὰρ ἑκάτερος περὶ τοῦ ἑαυτοῦ πατρὸς πολλὰ καὶ καλὰ ἔργα ἔχει λέγειν*, 179c2–3), and Lysimachus and Melesias hope that their sons, named Aristides and Thucydides after their grandfathers, will live up to their names. Though few further details are offered—Plato's approach here is highly allusive and fragmentary, and relies on us to supply the relevant information[28]—it is likely that Plato's original readers would have been familiar with these men. Melesias' father, Thucydides, was a prominent rival of Pericles (though later ostracized) and fought at Marathon.[29] Lysimachus' father Aristides, known as 'the just', also had a prominent political and military career, and was a byword for upright and honourable behaviour. As for their younger namesakes, Thucydides had, so far as we know, an unremarkable career.[30] Aristides, despite a promising start as a student, in the end came to no

[26] See Nails (2002) for details of the lives of the interlocutors.

[27] Nails (2002) 194, 198.

[28] This is not something that we can simply avoid: Lysimachus' and Melesias' concern that their sons will turn out like them rather than their grandfathers makes little sense unless we think about the life stories of the four men—yet the dialogue only hints at these.

[29] Though this is debated: see Nails (2002) 290–1.

[30] See Nails (2002) 292.

good.[31] If we are aware of this, as Plato's original readers might have been, it adds poignancy to the portrayal of these young men. But, at the point the dialogue is taking place, their futures are as yet undetermined. They could, as Lysimachus fears, continue in the unremarkable pattern of their fathers, or revert to the greater accomplishments of their grandfathers. In this regard, their situation evokes the undecided future of any young person.

When Lysimachus requests the help of Nicias and Laches, this implicitly invites us to think, in turn, about their credentials. Since both were well-known generals—Nicias particularly famous for his role in the ill-fated Sicilian expedition that ultimately resulted in the defeat of the Athenian fleet and his death at the hands of the Syracusans, Laches for his pro-Spartan policy and death in battle—this is partly automatic.[32] But, in addition, some of the details of the arguments appear to evoke their lives.[33] In particular, the reference to prophets in the examination of Nicias (195e8–196a3; cf. 198d1–199a3) and his concern with the need for foresight about fearful things (194e11–195a1) recall the Sicilian expedition. Similarly, Laches' emphasis on standing one's ground in battle (190e4–6) recalls his failure to do so at Delium and at Mantinaea where he met his death, and his admiration of Sparta (182e5–183b7) recalls his positive attitude to peace with Sparta. By evoking these life stories, Plato provides us with further patterns to think about and evaluate. But as before, he offers us only fragmentary allusions to isolated—though key—moments in these lives, relying on the reader's input to construct fuller life stories.[34]

Then there is the life of Socrates. At 181a7–b4, his bravery at Delium is mentioned, which, for Laches and Nicias, makes him a worthy representative of the aristocratic standards they espouse.[35] But as the reader is aware, his life can also be seen as a narrative that is in stark conflict with traditional values, and though this is not evoked heavily in the dialogue, his approach to the conversation implicitly rejects traditional methods of education. In other words, his presence points towards another set of values, though what would be involved

[31] Cf. *Tht.*150e–151a; Nails (2002) 49–50.

[32] Cf. Stokes (1986) 38, Gifford (2001) 43.

[33] Kahn (1996) 170, Rutherford (1995) 86, O'Brien (1971) 308–9, Gifford (2001) 48–51.

[34] For the incomplete treatment of characters' backgrounds and motives in the opening scene, see Stokes (1986) 39.

[35] Cf. Stokes (1986) 39.

in them—and to what they might lead Socrates—is only lightly touched upon.

Laches, then, for all the accessibility of its plot, illustrates many of the principles I outlined in section 7.2. Its treatment of life stories is fragmentary, so that we gain only fleeting insights into significant moments, and it often proceeds by allusion, so that the reader has to make significant input for herself—a tendency which we will see magnified in *Republic* and *Sophist*. It is the proliferation and irresolution of stories, however, that is most striking.

First, this emphasizes the *practical* implications of the conversation.[36] This is implicit anyhow in the way that the discussion constantly turns to actual or implied narratives for illustration: the young men in battle in Nicias' initial speech (182a5–b4); the story of the armoured fighter on board the ship in Laches' speech (183c8–184a7); the references at 191ac to the Scythians, the conduct of Aeneas at Troy and the Spartans at Plataea; and the sketches used to illustrate situations which do and do not involve courage from 192e. All these emphasize that the inquiry is not abstract, but directly rooted in behaviour. But the point is made even more powerfully by the evocation of life stories stretching beyond the present conversation. It is frequently observed that by foreshadowing the *actual* fates of characters, Plato adds resonance, urgency, and seriousness to the discussion in hand.[37] Here, Nicias' ultimate fate at Sicily adds poignancy to his failure to take Socratic conversation seriously enough, and our knowledge of the ultimate fate of Lysimachus' and Melesias' sons undercuts Lysimachus' apparent enthusiasm for Socratic conversation.[38] But in fact Plato does more than this. For he avoids spelling out how the life stories of participants—particularly the young sons, but also Nicias and Laches—*did* in fact end. And by presenting us with a range of patterns of life, in the life stories of Lysimachus and Melesias, the elder Thucydides and Aristides, and Socrates, he hints at a number of alternative ways in which they *could* potentially end. In this way, Plato discourages us from taking characters' life stories for granted, viewing the present conversation as a minor episode in a life largely determined by other factors. Rather, he encourages us to view their futures as still open to change and influence, and the present

[36] Cf. Kahn (1996) 153–4, Stokes (1986) 40–1.

[37] E.g. Gifford (2001), Rutherford (1995), esp. 86, 95–6, 167–8, 248–51.

[38] See esp. Gifford (2001) 48–51.

conversation as a moment of choice, which has the potential to alter the entire outcome of their lives and which is filled with significance and tension. As with tragic plots, we may know the eventual outcome, but it is the manner in which the players reach the endpoint that becomes filled with interest.

Second, by evoking a range of life stories, the dialogue invites us to think about the various possibilities open to its characters—and to us too. Though, in this work, Plato is still providing us with particular stories rather than generalized patterns, they are treated as representing different types of life, some of which we may not have considered. Lysimachus, Melesias, their fathers Aristides and Thucydides, Nicias, and Laches, all represent different varieties of the traditional aristocratic ideal, while Socrates—though also an intensely individual figure—stands for a type of life opposed to the social establishment. Similarly, Socrates' interactions with Laches and Nicias, and with Lysimachus, set up two general models of interaction: the traditional and the Socratic.[39] Indeed, there is something of a move within the dialogue towards presenting the issues under debate in universally applicable terms. At 185e1–6 Socrates says that their enquiry is one about souls, which we possess as much as the people actually participating in the dialogue, and Nicias' and Laches' exchange about the nature of Socratic conversation at 187e–189c implies that the inquiry is one which can make us *all* take thought for our lives. This tendency towards generalization is not pronounced in *Laches*, but it invites us to think about the issues and options in a more analytical and ordered way, and to relate them to ourselves, rather than just to the interlocutors. It will become more important when we turn to *Republic* and *Sophist*.

Plato's handling of life stories also enables him to suggest further implications of an individual's choice of life. The fact that the inquiry into Lysimachus' and Melesias' sons is played out against the background of their and their fathers' lives makes it a matter of the future of their entire houses. The picture Lysimachus paints is of degeneration that needs to be checked: the question is whether the sons will continue the decline or bring a return to former glory, and of course the patterns of education and familial interaction which might bring this about. Moreover, given the public prominence of the families in question, this is bound up with the future of the city itself. The terms

[39] See Kahn (1996) 152 on the tension between Socratic and traditional conceptions of excellence here.

in which education is discussed—the reference to the new prominence of educators such as the fighters in armour, the importance of battle and leadership—reinforce the public connection; it surfaces at 180a7–181b4, too, where it is said that if everyone had fought like Socrates at Delium, the fate of the city would have been rather different. In this way, Plato's technique unobtrusively draws us into reflection on what makes a good family or a good city, as well as what makes a good individual life—issues which will of course preoccupy him more overtly in works like *Republic*.

The proliferation and irresolution of stories, then, is a way of stimulating a personal response in the reader, it directs her towards reflection on the deeper philosophical issues that the dialogue raises. And like the allusive and fragmentary handling of stories, it is also a way of challenging and stretching her on a cognitive level. By including such a wealth of stories, the work challenges us to draw them together—to link the lives of individuals with one another, with the city, and with the current conversation—so that we can understand them as parts of a single unified story, rather than as disconnected fragments.[40] Yet we should not overstate the case. *Laches* is a short work, so drawing the threads together is not such a complex process. We are dealing primarily with the lives of people in this world. And the interpersonal dynamic, which makes the conversation accessible and lively, is kept to the fore.[41] We can see how Plato is adapting traditional event structures to achieve slightly unusual effects, but at this stage, he is only paving the way for the more radical demands on the reader made in *Republic* and *Sophist*.[42]

7.4. *REPUBLIC*

Plato's *Republic* immediately strikes the reader as more complex, in terms of its stories, than *Laches*. Like *Laches*, the work is given unity

[40] Cf. O'Brien (1971) 303 for the disunity of ideas in *Laches*, though he does not connect this with story patterns as I do.

[41] Nightingale (2002a) 232 makes similar points, though in terms of Plato's adoption of realistic or eikastic (as opposed to fantastic) representation in 'early' works: this is another dimension to the changes Plato introduces in different types of dialogue.

[42] Otherworldly stories are rare in 'early' dialogues and do not appear in *Laches*.

by the development of the conversation itself, but there is a lot more going on besides. And whereas in *Laches*, the additional stories deal primarily with the lives of familiar individuals in this world, *Republic* takes us much further out of our comfort zone. Let us start by reviewing the different types of story in turn.

Rather like the opening of *Laches*, *Republic* I offers us a well-defined situational story.[43] Socrates narrates how Polemarchus and some companions stopped him on his way back from the Piraeus and persuaded him to stay for discussion and for a horseback torch race later on. Once at Cephalus' house, Socrates begins to converse with his host. They have not met for some time, it emerges, though Cephalus encourages Socrates to visit more often, and they have rather different approaches to conversation. Cephalus is expecting an anecdotal chat, but Socrates soon draws him into a discussion of justice—at which point the old man departs, leaving his son, Polemarchus, to continue the argument. This opening setting raises the question of the relationship Socrates will establish with his interlocutors, both within the dialogue and beyond it. Will they engage seriously in philosophical debate or just withdraw? Will this become a regular way of life or remain an intermittent diversion? These questions become more pointed once Thrasymachus bursts aggressively in on the conversation, then becomes discomforted and unwilling, later withdraws his full participation, and finally at the end of book I abandons the argument—only for it to be renewed by Glaucon and Adeimantus, with whom Socrates has a warmer and closer relationship. And then there is the interested presence of others listening, some of whom are named, some not, whose response to the conversation is noted at points throughout the work. All this gives us an idea of the attitudes of Socrates' different interlocutors, and invites us to see the conversational exchanges that follow as developments of the relationships sketched here. As in *Laches*, moreover, it provides us with an accessible and familiar way of making sense of the conversation.

Book I also gives us insight into the lives of some of the characters. In his initial exchanges with Socrates, Cephalus describes the habits he keeps now he is getting older, the importance he attaches to paying what he owes and performing external duties such as sacrifice, and

[43] For detailed discussion, including Plato's representation of his interlocutors, see Blondell (2002) 165–89, Gifford (2001) 52–97, Ferrari (2003b), Annas (1981) 16–58, Beversluis (2000) 185–244, Lycos (1987).

the value he places on money as an ingredient in the good life. For some, Cephalus represents the virtues of the ordinary man. But for others, he is an epitome of the morally complacent traditionalist, concerned with material goods and eager to avoid discomfort at any cost. And in Socrates' counter-example to Cephalus' idea that justice comprises paying one's debts—the madman to whom one should not return arms (331c)—critics have detected a barbed reference to the family's business manufacturing weapons. As a lucrative and potentially morally dubious business, the allusion undercuts Cephalus' professed commitment to the philosophical life.[44] Similarly, the definition offered by Polemarchus, who is presented as heir to Cephalus' wealth as well as to his values and his argument, that justice is helping one's friends and harming one's enemies, has been thought ironically to recall his behaviour in the Athenian civil war and his fate at the hands of the Thirty.[45] Equally striking are the numerous references to the life and particularly the trial of Socrates, both here and throughout the work: the reference to persuasion and compulsion in Polemarchus' opening attempt to waylay him (327c4–14), then to the new celebrations of the goddess Bendis (327a2–3, 328a1–3); the Ship of state image which presents the philosopher as someone who is misunderstood and despised by the masses; and the Cave image, in which the anger and violence of the prisoners towards their liberator recalls the attitude of the Athenians towards Socrates.[46] As in *Laches*, these allusions bring out the practical relevance of the discussion, as well as tying it into a familiar framework of events.

In addition, *Republic* also contains a wealth of schematic representations of life, and this is where we start to move away from *Laches*. In book I, Thrasymachus supports his equation of injustice with happiness by describing a tyrant (343b–344c), and at the start of book II Glaucon uses the story of Gyges and his ring—a paradigm of injustice unpunished—in reintroducing Thrasymachus' argument. But it is Socrates who employs such generalized stories most frequently. In books VIII–IX he offers descriptions of democratic, oligarchic, and tyrannical men and cities, bringing out their unhappiness in contrast with the just man, so as to balance and outweigh Thrasymachus' and

[44] Gifford (2001). For negative assessments of Cephalus, see Annas (1981) and Blondell (2002). Beversluis (2000) is more positive.

[45] Gifford (2001). Blondell (2002) 174–7 offers a more favourable verdict.

[46] See Burnyeat (1997a), Clay (1992); cf. also Clay (2000) 33–40.

Glaucon's earlier portraits. In addition, we have the Cave image, the Ship of state, and the myth of Er, all of which provide allegorical representations of different types of life. But most obvious of all are Socrates' analyses of the just soul and city, which illuminate the underlying structure of justice in the two entities and which dominate Socrates' account of justice and consequently the construction of the work.

Finally, there is the otherworldly dimension. This is most evident in the myth of Er, which deals directly with life after death. However, it is also, in a sense, implicit in the Cave image, in so far as that presents us with a descent to an underworld-like realm and an ascent to places not reached by many humans, and deals with our insight into realities that lie beyond this world (as does the Ship image). Indeed, commentators have detected katabatic references in the descent to the Piraeus described in the work's very first words,[47] which would make the whole conversation a kind of journey into an otherworldly realm.

The first point to make here, already familiar from *Laches*, is that stories dealing with specific individuals are not resolved within the dialogue. Book I sets up a dramatic situational story, and as the dialogue progresses, we do gain further insights into its development—the pacification of Thrasymachus;[48] the ongoing enthusiasm and participation of Polemarchus,[49] which marks him out as something of a convert; the perseverance of Glaucon and Adeimantus. But these references tail off dramatically. After Glaucon's and Adeimantus' challenge in book II, whole books pass without comment on the feelings and responses of interlocutors. The close of the work also leaves us unsure how the relationships explored in book I continue:[50] the myth of Er ends with Socrates' words, yet there is no indication as to how the interlocutors respond, or how the gathering disperses. The life stories of the interlocutors, too, reach no definite resolution. Futures are alluded to, not played out, and the situational narrative, with its refusal to move beyond the happenings of the

[47] Burnyeat (1997a) 5–7, Clay (1992), Rutherford (1995) 216–17, Segal (1978) 323–4; cf. also Rutherford (1992) 155–6 on *Protagoras*.

[48] 498c9–d4.

[49] 449b1–6.

[50] Rutherford (2002) 256 notes that, despite the elaborate scene setting, the party can never have got to see the torch race, which indicates how far the dialogue cuts loose from its original anchorage.

individual conversation, encourages us, as in *Laches*, to think of those life stories as still in motion, still open to change and choice.

Moreover, *Republic* simply contains a very large range of stories. Not only does the situational story remain unresolved, but as we progress through the work, more and more narratives are evoked. Besides those discussed above, there are small-scale narratives, such as the allusion to the castration of Ouranos by Cronos at 377e–378a or the making of a statue at 420cd, which add to the effect of a proliferation of stories. Many of the dialogue's narratives are not explicitly linked with the people and setting to which we were first introduced, and they frequently involve looking at our lives in a different way—from a more generalized perspective, or a different point in reality. As with *Laches*, it is not that we *cannot* see links between the different strands introduced—in what follows I hope to show one way of doing this. However, the work does not draw them to a unified conclusion for us, as we might anticipate in a classically plotted work, but leaves us to do so for ourselves. And it should already be apparent how much more demanding a process this is here than in *Laches*.

The interplay of individual and general becomes even more interesting when we think about the distribution of the different types of story within the dialogue. References to the situational story and the life stories of interlocutors are concentrated in book I (which serves as an introduction to the whole work) and the start of book II, and so, in my earlier terminology, they are given a marginal place within the work. Now, this observation is in itself nothing new. Many critics have observed that Plato concentrates 'scene setting'[51] passages at the start of a work, before plunging into 'pure philosophy'. However, this is only half the picture. The situational story and the life stories of interlocutors are firmly tied to individuals: they are concrete, deal with particular people, and are concerned with life in this world. And after the opening of book II, stories of this type do indeed tail off. But they are replaced by a *different type* of story: more abstract, generalized, and otherworldly ones, such as the account of the ideal city, the different types of men, the Cave, Ship, and the myth of Er.[52] We do not have a decline in stories altogether.

[51] I continue to use this rather unhappy term for want of an obvious alternative; Ferrari (1987), esp. 1 n1, attempts to inject life into the metaphor.

[52] Roochnik (2003) 93–110, offering a different reading of this development, suggests that after the analytical style of the earlier books, in *Republic* VIII–X Plato moves to a narrative style, as required to give an adequate understanding of the soul.

This shift has various effects on the reader. It gives us a deeper and broader perspective from which to evaluate individual characters' lives, widening the range of things we might think relevant to evaluating them (one's soul, life after death, one's relationship with wider reality). It encourages us to approach them in a more analytical, detached, and objective way, and to move from thinking about what became or will become of particular men, to what lies behind different types of life. One important element here is the provision of generalized *patterns* of life, which provide a conceptual framework for our reflection and guide us towards thinking about general principles, not specific details. Another is the evocation of a wider picture of reality against which individual lives can be seen—most obviously here, the Forms. By indicating how the different lives fit into wider reality, Plato encourages us to look at them from a different—and, the dialogues suggest, more real—perspective, and helps us to move outside the narrow and blinkered viewpoint from which we have so far been proceeding. Attaining such a perspective is, of course, the ultimate goal of the knowledgeable person: his task (in the language of *Republic* at least) is to turn his vision from the particular things of this world to unchanging realities; once achieved, this enables him to see his life in this world for what it really is. By organizing a shift from particular to abstract in his stories, Plato mirrors this progression, and helps his reader to attain the accompanying change of perspective as she moves through the work.[53]

It is worth emphasizing how closely this shift is linked to the change in style from book II. As critics have often noticed, this new phase of the argument is marked by a more cooperative and constructive dialectical style, which contrasts with the adversarial mode of book I.[54] And it is at exactly this point that Socrates introduces one of the dialogue's most sustained and striking schematic stories: the account of the ideal city. This suggests to me that such stories—which we did not find in *Laches* at all—should be connected with a more sophisticated philosophical approach and a more advanced learner. If so, this offers a different angle on Socrates' somewhat unexpected

[53] On the shift towards an abstract perspective in *Republic*, see Burnyeat (1992). There are illuminating comments also at Rutherford (2002) and Nightingale (2002a) 234–44, who discusses the development using the terminology of fantastic *mimesis* and Bakhtinian chronotopes. McCabe (1996) sees a similar progression within *Parmenides*.

[54] See ch.5.

introduction of the city–soul analogy at this point. To the extent that critics address this question directly, they usually treat the analogy as a way of elucidating the three parts of the soul and bringing out the structural similarity of justice in city and soul.[55] But, as a more general and abstract story, it is also a means of guiding the reader to a more advanced type of reflection and a truer perspective.

There is a danger of over-simplification here, though. Two of the dialogue's major sources of allusions to the life of Socrates, it will be objected, are the Cave and Ship images, yet neither occurs at the start of the work. Similarly, the descriptions of the various defective persons and constitutions in books VIII–IX resonate with the picture of 'real life' politics sketched in the opening book.[56] In other words, the link I have drawn between the start of the work and specific or individual stories is too strict. What we do have, however, is a change in the *nature* of the allusions to particular events and individuals after the opening of the work.[57] The Ship, for example, at the same time as evoking the misunderstanding of Socrates by the masses, presents a paradigmatic image of the philosopher and generalizes his fate. It offers an account of why philosophers are so treated: they are in touch with higher realities which the masses cannot perceive, and are therefore thought to be mad, useless, even vicious. In doing so, it allows us to reach a new understanding of the individuals with whom the dialogue has been dealing: those like the philosopher (Socrates) and those like the masses (perhaps people like Thrasymachus).

By encouraging us to take this approach, Plato also opens up and magnifies the presence of choice in the individual and particular stories. This is not only because the general perspective helps us to think about the different options available to characters. For in addition, many of the generalized stories themselves contain implied choices. We can choose between the life of the ship's crew and its helmsman, for example, or between the prisoners who stay in the Cave and those who ascend to the light. The description of the democratic, timocratic, and tyrannical lives offers us a series of

[55] See e.g. Lear (1992), Annas (1981) 72–9, Cross and Woozley (1964) 75–8. Williams (1973) is a classic treatment.

[56] One might also object that we do find generalized depictions of types of life towards the start of the work: Thrasymachus' tyrant (343b1–344c8) and Gyges (359b6–360d7). However, these essentially function as examples to back up interlocutors' arguments. Only later in the work do such passages acquire central importance.

[57] Cf. Rutherford (2002) 256.

options. Finally, Er has choice as its central theme:[58] once dead, we have to choose our next life, and the choice we make then is dependent on the life we lead now.

This final point of choice is, on one level, the most important moment in the work. The development of stories within the dialogue involves, as I have suggested, a cognitive progression: as we move through the work, we are prompted to think about individual lives from an increasingly sophisticated perspective, and are required to make sense of more numerous, and more wide-ranging, stories. But it is also a dramatic progression.[59] The Ship and Cave are moving and powerful images in their own right, but reasonably short and compact. The account of the ideal city, while introduced in book IV, only reaches its highpoint with the descriptions of the different types of city and soul in books VIII and IX. An extended passage that stretches over two books, this culminates in the depiction of the tyrant, which is the conclusion of the moral argument so far, as Socrates announces with something of a fanfare at 580ac. But it is book X, with the myth of Er, which provides the stories of the work with their real climax.[60] Bringing a different perspective on justice that sits uneasily with the emphasis of the rest of the work, it is challenging to make sense of.[61] And as the most sustained piece of non-argumentative writing in the dialogue, in the higher literary style characteristic of Platonic myth, it engages us at a more intensely affective level. It reinforces all the tendencies we have been noticing towards the abstract, while at the same time bringing us back to the specific decisions that individuals—including ourselves—have to take about their lives. And as we think about the options available to the figures presented, their moment of choice is in some sense transferred to us, in as much as, by thinking about those options alongside them, we are enacting the choice in our own lives. But now, we can reflect on it more consciously and with a deeper understanding than we would have had when first embarking upon the work.

[58] Cf. Annas (1981) 351–2 and Harte (2010).

[59] Roochnik (2003) 4–5, 95, suggests that books VIII–X represent the climax of the work.

[60] If so, the book ought not to be seen as the coda it often is: see ch.6 n4.

[61] Annas (1981) 335 sets out the problems; at 349–53 she offers an unfavourable verdict on the myth as an ending to the work. For discussion and more positive appraisal, see Rutherford (1995) 214–16.

7.5. SOPHIST

Republic and *Laches*, for all their divergences from classical plot, do at least present us with stories that are accessible. Most importantly, they start by sketching a situational context that we can understand in terms of classical plot—even if Plato does not develop it as such. *Sophist* is rather different. Indeed, the minimal attention devoted to providing a situational story for the conversation or to evoking the life stories of characters is one of the features of the dialogue that will stand out most to someone approaching it fresh from 'early' and 'middle' works. The dialogue opens by mentioning an agreement made by the interlocutors on the previous day to meet again today, bringing the Eleatic Stranger as well (216a1–4, usually taken to be a reference to *Theaetetus*);[62] and at 217a7–217b9, we learn that in an earlier conversation the other interlocutors had asked the Eleatic Stranger the same question Socrates now poses him—how philosophical men are regarded in his country—and that he was unwilling to answer. But we are offered no more than this, and the dialogue closes without returning to the situational context.[63] Similarly, we are given only limited insight into the relationship between interlocutors, such a focus of drama in many dialogues. At the start, to be sure, there is a brief debate over the type of discussion the Eleatic Stranger will engage in with his interlocutor. Is he a god of refutation (*θεὸς . . . τις ἐλεγκτικός* 216b6), Socrates wonders, raising the possibility that he will adopt a disputatious style—though Theodorus replies that he is more reasonable (*μετριώτερος*) than this. Then Socrates asks him whether he prefers question-and-answer dialectic or lengthy exposition (217c3–5), and he opts for the former—though many have detected a covert preference for the latter in his apparently didactic[64] style. But from then on, these questions—on the discursive surface of the dialogue at least—take rather a back seat.

Nor do we find vivid portraits of interlocutors and dense allusions to their life stories, another hallmark of many 'early' and 'middle' dialogues. The Eleatic Stranger is an enigma; all that we are really told

[62] E.g. Lane (1998) 7, Notomi (1999) 20, Blondell (2002) 314.

[63] Some think that 217a4 foreshadows future discussions of the statesman (represented in *Statesman*) and philosopher (in an uncompleted dialogue); but the allusion is covert. See e.g. Blondell (2002) 314–15, Lane (1998) 6–7.

[64] I reject this characterization of 'late' dialectic in ch.5.

about him is that he comes from Elea, is a follower of Zeno and Parmenides, and has engaged in philosophical investigation extensively before.[65] We likewise learn little about Theaetetus, aside from his virtuous character and philosophical promise.[66] There are, it is true, a few scattered references to previous episodes in the lives of participants: Socrates' recommendation of Theaetetus as a discussion partner (217d4–7) suggests he has observed him in discussion before; we are told that Theaetetus has conversed with the Eleatic Stranger on a previous occasion (218a1–2); Socrates and the Eleatic Stranger have both participated in or witnessed discussions involving Parmenides (217c5–7, possibly referring to *Parmenides*, 237a3–9); and there is the previous day's conversation (216a1–2). But these references really are fragmentary in the fullest sense: they give us no fuller sense of the person's life, or of a story moving towards a resolution.[67]

References to individual characters, then, are marginalized to an extent we have not seen before. They are introduced so lightly, and in such a fragmentary way, that they can hardly be said to make up *stories*: it is not simply the case, as we saw in *Laches* and *Republic*, that the stories are left unresolved. This development is closely connected with others discussed in previous chapters—most obviously, the increasingly austere dialectical style and the altered handling of characterization. Just as those changes reflect the increasing philosophical development of *interlocutors*, the same is true here. Little attention *needs* to be focused on the development of the relationship between interlocutor and questioner now, because they can be relied upon to interact in a productive way. Similarly, discussion no longer needs to take its starting point from interlocutors' own lives and actions, since they can now approach problems in a more abstract and analytical way.

In addition, these changes have a significant impact on the experience of the *reader*. Most obviously, they make the work less accessible. By reducing the contextual setting for the conversation and the role of interaction between interlocutors in its progression, Plato deprives us of an obvious 'way in'. He forces us to focus on the dialectical exchanges and prevents us from relying on the characters' stories to

[65] Esp. *Sph.*216a1–4.

[66] On the characterization of the Eleatic Stranger and Theaetetus, see esp. Blondell (2002); also ch.4.

[67] Some critics detect references to Socrates' life and trial in the dialogue: e.g. Notomi (1999) 20–1, 32, Rosen (1983) 23–4, 62–6, 324–5. Blondell (2002) 386–90 vigorously argues against making these central to our interpretation of the work.

bring out the interest and relevance of the conversation, instead asking us to do the work of engaging with it for ourselves.

In addition, the changes make it harder for us to see the conversation as a discrete unit. Open closure[68] is a feature of most Platonic dialogues; we are always invited to see the conversation as incomplete, to revisit it, and to start philosophizing for ourselves. *Sophist* however, goes out of its way to present itself as an episode in a longer and more complex process of discussion. Throughout the dialogue, various apparently satisfactory definitions of the sophist are reached—but each time another aspect of his nature is subsequently uncovered, revealing the previous definition as partial or flawed. The dialogue ends with another of these. There are some closural markers here,[69] but in many ways the definition seems no different from any other. The interlocutors do not disperse or comment about having finished the discussion; there is no return to the situational context, and nothing to indicate that the conversation is actually stopping.[70] It feels as though the conversation could just go on again, as it has every time before; to put it another way, it is as if the camera has stopped filming but the conversation stretches on into the future regardless. The technique encourages us to see ourselves as overhearing part of a longer process of investigation, and this reinforces the need for us to carry on philosophizing much more effectively than when a dialogue's conversation actually comes to an end—albeit an unsatisfactory one.

This tactic becomes particularly interesting when we think about *Sophist*'s rare flashes of insight into the *past* lives of the participants. For whereas in many other dialogues, these refer to outward actions and events, here they are heavily preoccupied with conversations—those involving Socrates and Parmenides, the Eleatic Stranger and Parmenides, the Eleatic Stranger and the other interlocutors, Socrates and Theaetetus. Even the present conversation is treated as a continuation

[68] See e.g. Fowler (1989), esp. 79: 'A work . . . which leaves questions unanswered will be "open" to different interpretations, and may leave the reader feeling that where the work stops is not really The End.'

[69] *σχεδὸν ἤδη* 268c2, *συμπλέξαντες ἀπὸ τελευτῆς ἐπ' ἀρχήν* 268c6, *τἀληθέστατα . . . ἐρεῖ* 268d4.

[70] Cf. Dorter (1994) 16. This ties in with the structural irresolution that, I suggested in ch.6, is a feature of 'later' works. Compare Burnyeat (1997a) 18–19 on *Philebus*, though he suggests that the work is unique in this. On false closure in the dialogues, see Rutherford (1995) 214; and, on closure generally, Roberts *et al.* (1997), esp. D. Fowler (1997).

of the previous day's discussion. This, combined with the fact that these references are so fragmentary, creates the effect of a web of conversations surrounding the present one. The past and the future—and the lives of the characters—are presented as a series of conversations parallel to the dialogue itself. By drawing us into a world of conversation in this way, Plato suggests its importance within life and encourages us to see things from the perspective of philosophical discussion. Though this is, of course, a crucial point in *Laches* and *Republic*, it is made here in a much more radical fashion: conversation is not now just an important event, which intersects more familiar stories connected with external events, as it often is in 'early' and 'middle' dialogues. In *Sophist*, conversation has ousted those other stories from view altogether.

If attention is directed away from the individual and particular in *Sophist*, however, it is refocused on the general, intensifying the development we noticed in moving from *Laches* to *Republic*. In *Sophist*, the goal of the conversation, pursued through division, is to separate out the sophist's life from others; to this end we are constantly confronted with different types of life analysed to show what makes them distinctive, covering the whole spectrum of human activity from merchandizing and retailing to varieties of the 'intellectual' life. The dialogue becomes a catalogue of different patterns of life, and they overshadow other types of story. As in *Republic*, this brings out the importance of recognizing the patterns underlying individual lives—the need to avoid becoming bound up in the specifics of individuals and their fates, instead considering the underlying reasons why lives take the form they do. But here the point is more demandingly made. To begin with, the dialogue presents us with such an overwhelming number of patterns of life that the task of drawing them together into a coherent picture is daunting: the shift to the general has been used not to provide a simplified way of looking at different types of lives, as one might argue that it is in *Republic*, but to maximize the sifting and sorting the reader has to do. Second, there is the abruptness and decisiveness of the shift from particular to general. Whereas *Laches* and *Republic* move gradually from the particular to the general, progressively deepening our understanding of what is at stake in the individual narratives, here Plato simply avoids the particular. This is a challenging tactic: it deprives the reader of the familiar and accessible reference points provided by individual stories, and it forces her to take an analytic approach. It also assumes that she will be able to connect the general with the particular for herself—to see how the general patterns relate to the Eleatic Stranger, to Theaetetus, and to her own life.

In addition, there is a shift in the way the dialogue *presents* its patterns of life. In *Republic*, many of these are themselves absorbing and exciting stories, which are accessible and engaging for the reader; and a few of *Sophist*'s patterns, such as the two ways of purifying the soul of ignorance discussed at 229b–231b, are indeed painted in some detail. The rougher path, used by fathers on their sons, is based on admonition, whereas the smoother path involves questioning and contradiction, designed to make a person gentle towards others but angry towards himself. Similar is 233d–234e, where the Eleatic Stranger describes how the sophist, like a painter, can deceive children into thinking that they see real things not likenesses, and only when they get older do they painfully realize their mistake. At these points, the level of detail allows the portrait to expand into a story: the Eleatic Stranger offers realistic descriptions of experiences we can imagine people undergoing. But for much of the time, division produces a classification of lives without these narrative touches. The definition reached at 223b is typical: here we are told that the sophist hunts tame animals, privately, for pay, and claims to give education—a classification which gives a fair amount of detail on the supposed activities of this creature, and could lend itself to a more narrative treatment, but in fact takes a summary, analytic style.[71]

But the emphasis on story, so important in 'early' and 'middle' works, does not disappear entirely—it resurfaces on the level of the conversation itself.[72] For the process of dialectical exchange in which Theaetetus and the Eleatic Stranger are engaging, while deprived of almost any connection with external events, is at the same time presented metaphorically in these terms. To begin with, images of hunt

[71] On the 'tenselessness' of division, see Lane (1998) 115–16. Similarly, *Sophist* does not contain any extended otherworldly stories, though the Eleatic Stranger does situate some patterns of life within a wider picture of reality; e.g. suggesting that the sophistic art is not based on true knowledge but appearance, and cannot really put one in touch with realities (234be).

[72] On the narrative conducted at the level of imagery in Lucretius' *De Rerum Natura*, see Gale (1994) 122–4. The *Politicus* myth is another counter-example to the pattern I have been outlining; however, that myth is notoriously uncomfortable to read and hard to interpret, and falls into something of a different class from the engaging myths of the 'middle' works.

and search are used to describe the attempts of the Eleatic Stranger and Theaetetus to define the sophist: they hunt him, yet cannot grasp hold of him; they cast a net to catch him; he is many-headed; they take breathers before renewing their attempts; and they try new paths. The Eleatic Stranger talks of a battle between gods and giants, in which the giants drag things down to earth, grasping rocks and trees with their hands, and the gods defend themselves using weapons from the invisible world (246ac). At 247c he refers to the intransigent among the giants as the dragon's teeth sown by Cadmus. At 252c, self-refutation is described as having an enemy within one's own family and as giving forth speech from within oneself like Eurycles, a famous ventriloquist. Earlier, at 242c–243a, he characterizes theories put forward by Parmenides and others as stories told to children (242c8–9), involving war, marriage, child-bearing, friendship, and enmity. Even more striking, though, is the presentation of Parmenides: refuting him, the Stranger says, will be parricide (241d3–7).[73]

In these images, dialectical events become external happenings of the most dramatic and active sort. Some of them, moreover, are developed so as to form sequences that tend towards resolution—particularly the hunting[74] of the sophist and the killing of Parmenides—unlike other stories in the dialogue. The use of metaphors and images drawn from real life to describe conversation is of course not new in the dialogues. However, it is unusual for these to be so prominent, sustained, and colourful that they overshadow a dialogue's other stories. Again, we do not just have a conversation intersecting a range of external stories; rather, the conversation has become the most 'real' of the stories presented.

On one level, this simply adds drama to the argumentative progression. Plato's language invites us to view dialectical activity in terms of familiar and well-defined narratives, giving vividness to what might otherwise seem an impersonal discussion and foreclosing a neutral or unthinking response in the reader. But it also has an important impact on the way we view conversation itself. By blurring the boundary between life and conversation, it emphasizes the central position conversation ought to have in life. It is as though conversation—as

[73] See McCabe (2000) 60–6.

[74] Metaphors of hunting are a common way of presenting dialectical activity (in Plato and beyond: see Fowler (2000c) 210); but here they are more sustained and evoke an extended narrative of hunt and escape.

the most 'real' and dramatic story in the dialogue—is in fact the true focus of drama and interest in our lives, even that it is what determines real life. The implication is that one cannot have a conversation, reach a conclusion, and then make a contradictory decision in one's life, for to take a certain direction in conversation *is* to take a certain direction in one's life. Similarly, the skills and endurances which one needs in conversation are the same as those needed in life, so that the one equips you for the other. To participate productively in discussion is not therefore something separate from or tangential to one's real life: it can and should be central to it. This is of course a point Plato is often thought to make by linking Socrates' conversations so closely with the lives of his interlocutors in dialogues like *Laches*. Here he makes it even more elegantly and economically, and in a way that gives the reader no option but to focus on the conversation.

7.6. RESOLUTION VS. REPETITION: GETTING CAUGHT IN THE MIDDLE

It should be apparent, by now, how much more demanding *Sophist* is than *Republic* or *Laches*. Whereas they move away from the principles of classical plot gradually, using familiar stories to draw us in before guiding our response down more challenging paths, *Sophist* represents a complete departure from classical plot. We have to deal with fragments of stories, a proliferation of generalized portraits that defies easy comprehension, and a metaphorical conversational narrative that is often more vivid than the other stories. The particular has been replaced by the abstract, and the amount of material for the reader to analyse is overwhelming. The stories—to the extent that they can even be so termed—are not brought explicitly into connection with each other, and none reaches a satisfying resolution. If stories are a means through which material can be made familiar and accessible to the receiver, in *Sophist* Plato seems to be striving for precisely the opposite effect.

But for all the changes in the way *Sophist* handles plot and story in comparison with *Laches* and *Republic*, there are—I hope to have shown—continuities lurking beneath the apparent differences. We are in fact dealing with an ascent of difficulty, and a progressive use of techniques, across the different types of work. And as in the other areas we have looked at, the changes guide the reader towards greater advancement. At each stage, she has to engage in increasingly sophisticated and demanding types of reflection: more analytical, more abstract, more generalized, and wider-ranging. She has to focus more directly on the arguments and the underlying philosophical narratives they imply. She also has to do more to motivate herself to engage with the works, rather than relying on familiar stories as an easy way in to the conversation.

Accordingly, the disappearance of individual stories of the sort we associate with the situational contexts of *Laches* and *Republic* does not need to signal a decline in Plato's literary powers in 'later' works or a move to a more didactic mode, as some critics claim. Like changes in the handling of character and argument discussed in previous chapters, this trend should be connected with developments in the way the reader is engaged. Nor should we accept the related claim that passages of scene setting in 'earlier' works are there to add dramatic and literary interest, but contribute little philosophically.[75] *Laches* has suffered particularly badly, with critics complaining that its dramatic prologue lasts until section 189 or 190, thereby taking up around half the work[76]—though other works have received such treatment too. Not only do these passages contain material directly relevant to the philosophical issues that the dialogues ask us to reflect on, they are also crucial to the way that Plato draws the reader into a less familiar type of story and a more productive type of engagement. There is no simple distinction here between 'early' and 'late' dialogues.

A further point of continuity and development relates to the emphasis placed on conversation by the different dialogues. Earlier in the chapter, I suggested that many 'early' and 'middle' dialogues evoke the type of stories we find in classical plots but accentuate the place of conversation within them, so that the broader stories are somewhat excluded. Conversation absorbs most of a dialogue, and we are encouraged to see it as representing a moment of choice. But the dialogues also emphasize the value of conversation in a subtler way, by extending

[75] This widespread view is challenged by Ferrari (1987), Clay (1992), Burnyeat (1997a), Rutherford (1995) and (1988), and (with a different approach) Sedley (1999b), esp. 134–40.

[76] E.g. Kahn (1996) 151, who thinks that the prologue introduces not just *Laches*, but a group of 'threshold dialogues'; also Kahn (1986), Santas (1996) 23, Sharples (1985) 15, Beversluis (2000) 116–17 (at 131 he also terms the return to Lysimachus at the close 'post-elenctic chit-chat').

the time and energy the reader spends within the moment of the conversation. The irresolution of stories prevents the reader reaching a point of rest and resolution easily, instead leaving her to turn over different possible outcomes in her mind. The wealth of material to evaluate draws the reader into repetitive and deepening reflection, as she tries to make sense of the proliferating, disunified stories. Their allusive and fragmented handling requires her to make significant input if she is to see them as sustained narratives. In other words, the reader is effectively drawn into an ongoing process of reflection triggered by the stories introduced during the conversation, and is discouraged from moving beyond the present conversation to a point of resolution. In this way, the handling of the stories *enacts* the importance conversation is accorded on the works' discursive level, by extending the amount of time and effort the reader has to spend on reflection. We come to understand how important conversation and reflection are by being encouraged to engage in them more seriously and at greater length.

The same, I think, is true of *Sophist*—though in a more radical way. The dialogue is uncompromising in the importance it attaches to conversation: conversation is the 'real' action now, and more familiar stories are largely excluded. There is, moreover, much more work for the reader to do, in engaging with a wealth of inaccessibly presented patterns of life, making sense of them and relating them to her own life—and this ensures that she spends even more time in the present of the conversation. Significantly, too, the element of development in the stories themselves has receded, and instead we are often presented with 'static' analyses that do not invite forward movement towards resolution. It is as though the stories themselves—in addition to their handling—are now reflecting the importance of remaining in the present rather than rushing forward to conclusion.

This is crucial, to begin with, for the character of the reader's engagement with the texts. In the last chapter, I suggested that the structuring of the dialogues tends towards repetition and circularity, halting and rereading, so that the reader is constantly being asked to stop, reconsider her ideas, and revisit earlier questions; the same tendencies are, I think, present in Plato's handling of plot. Classical plot appears to involve progress: it develops and moves forwards towards resolution. Yet when we look at the shape of many of the stories with which Plato presents us, we may reflect that they involve progress that is rather too fast. Laches and Nicias, Aristides and

Thucydides, and Polemarchus and Thrasymachus would all have benefited by spending more time on Socratic conversation, rather than abandoning it, forgetting it, and moving onwards unreflectively in their lives. By gesturing towards classical plot, Plato creates an impulse towards forward movement in his readers, generating energy and engagement as we desire to reach resolution.[77] Yet he prevents us from moving onwards as quickly and as unadvisedly as his interlocutors, by offering us stories that do not allow easy and swift resolution, but force us to halt, reflect, and weigh up alternatives. The energy that would naturally be challenged into progression is re-channelled into iterative reflection. To put it another way, Plato shapes plots that do not allow us to move towards the end, but keep us permanently caught in the present—for this is an important part of the way that we can actually make philosophical progress.[78]

By evoking, yet ultimately rejecting, classical plot, Plato is able to generate a more committed and involved response in his readers than if he had cut it out altogether. The desire to reach an endpoint is of course one of the key elements in dialectical virtue, as I explored in chapter 3. In this case, this desire is channelled directly into more careful scrutiny of the arguments and ideas put forward themselves. However, it is also closely connected with the other two key elements in dialectical virtue: self-reflectiveness and practice. By preventing us from moving onwards and away from the moment of reflection, Plato provides us with greater opportunity for engaging in extended dialectical activity and thereby developing our dialectical skills through practice, both the intellectual qualities needed to engage productively with philosophical puzzles, and the qualities of endurance, patience, and resource necessary for ongoing progress. In doing so, he is also helping us to reflect on ourselves. Repeated, sometimes frustrating, engagement with the difficulties of a dialogue is likely to prompt greater self-awareness and self-examination than an easy and quick read through. And the very fact that, as readers, we are being discouraged from moving onwards as quickly—and as unproductively—as characters in classical

[77] On narrative desire, see Brooks (1984) esp. 37–61.

[78] Dunn (1997) 108–11 is very interesting here, with Bakhtin (1981) 3–40. In analysing open closure in Euripides' *Heracles*, Dunn draws on Bakhtin's analysis of novel-like genres as focusing on the present rather than moving onwards to a resolution. Bakhtin classes the Socratic dialogue among novel-like genres (Bakhtin (1981) 21–2); and the significance with which he invests the present as a point of choice and potential fits well with the analysis of Plato I have been developing.

plots prompts us to think about the qualities that they lack, and to consider how we ourselves match up to them.[79]

All this has implications, too, for the way in which we think of the philosophical process itself. Throughout this study, I have emphasized the importance of philosophical *progression*, whereby the learner moves from a point of ignorance towards greater understanding and virtue. I think that this kind of linear movement is also an important element in the dialogues' presentation of philosophizing, surfacing as it does in various of their images for the learning process: the journey up out of the Cave in *Republic*, for instance, or up to the surface of the world in *Phaedo*. But pause, repetition, and circularity are important too, both in the dialogues' handling of their stories (my focus so far), and also in those stories themselves—not least those representing the learning process. Of course, pausing can take a negative form, indicating stagnation and inertia, of the sort we see in the sluggish horse of *Apology*, the prisoners of the Cave, or the people who live beneath the surface of the earth in the *Phaedo* myth. Similarly, there is the regression of interlocutors who return to their former ways, of an ideal constitution that degenerates with time, of a golden age that is followed by decline. But pausing and repetition can also take positive forms. Circular movement is central to both reincarnation and recollection, as described in *Meno* as well as in *Phaedrus*' account of the soul. The philosopher has to return to the Cave to assist with the ideal city and the prisoners' education. In *Timaeus*, even thought and perception involve the continuous movement of the revolutions in our heads.[80] If this is so, then Socrates' apparent motionlessness as he waits lost in thought outside Agathon's house at *Symposium* 174d–175c in fact represents movement of a more profound and productive sort than his companions' more obvious energy and activity.[81]

The importance of pausing, repetition, and circularity on these levels reflects, I believe, its fundamental importance in the philosophical

[79] The points I make here relate to *how* Plato's stories get us to think, rather than *what* they get us to think. The question of the *type* of knowledge stories offer us is important too: Cupitt (1991) xi.

[80] 43c–44d, 47bc, 90bd. See Sedley (1999a) 316–19.

[81] Cf. Aristotle *Nicomachean Ethics* X.6–7 on *eudaimonia* as activity (ἐνέργεια) in accordance with virtue, and contemplation as the highest form of such activity. Cf. Sedley (1999a), though with an emphasis on godlikeness, not motion. On the complex relationship between rest and motion in *Sophist*, see Reeve (1985). On productive repetition in the dialogues, see Morgan (2007).

process itself, alongside linear progression. Pausing, though it arrests forward movement, may be full of action and movement of a different kind—repetition and iteration. Repetition can be a way of deepening understanding, and out of apparent regression may come true progression. That is, progress is not a matter of straightforward linear movement, but of repeated attempts through which we gradually gain deeper understanding. Process is crucial here, for repetition encourages us to think about the *manner* in which we engage in philosophizing, and it is only if we do so in a productive way that repetition can lead us to progression.[82]

All of this also has implications for the way we think about our own activity as readers. It suggests that if a dialogue is to have the positive impact on our lives that it could, then we cannot just pass through it, reading it once, but have to make a more sustained effort to engage with it. Though we may feel, as we read, that we can never reach the end of the question, or the end of the dialogue, this is the point: it is part of the way that the dialogue produces in us a more productive type of reflection, and in consequence a more effective response to the questions it raises.

If this is true, then we can see a philosophical motivation for Plato's move away from classical plot. If real progress, as I am suggesting, is based not on linear forward movement, but on iterative, re-evaluative activity, then by abandoning the progressive shape of classical plot, Plato is not arresting our development. He is rather suggesting an *alternative model* of development, based on repetition and circularity. This, in turn, brings us back to the point from which I began this chapter: Plato's engagement with—and attempt to distance himself from—genres such as tragedy and epic. These genres' use of classical plot, I observed earlier, is likely to be connected with Plato's own adoption of a different approach. I do not mean that Plato jettisoned one of their characteristic features as a superficial way of differentiating his own works. On the contrary, works like *Laches* go out of their way to emphasize their affinities with classical plot before introducing less familiar techniques; and Plato adopts the power of stories, both in the ways I have considered in this chapter, and in his representation of Socrates, discussed in chapter 4. But I do think we can see classical plot as one (among others) of the things about these genres that might

[82] This ties in well with the idea, often thought to emerge from the dialogues, that philosophical activity is an end and a mode of life in itself.

have troubled Plato at a deeper level, because of the power of stories to engage and involve their receivers, and draw them into a forceful—but ultimately damaging—forward movement. Here, I hope to have shown that Plato is not simply, as he is sometimes portrayed,[83] rejecting the importance of the story in exposition and reflection in favour of a non-narrative, timeless response to the world. Rather, his unusual handling of stories is part of the way that he sought to avoid the problematic effects of the types of writing he criticizes and to foster a more productive type of engagement, while still taking advantage of the power of stories to communicate in an affectively engaging way.

[83] E.g. Cupitt (1991) x–xi, 4–8, who argues for the importance of stories as a way of expressing understanding; cf. Buxton (1999). This polarizing approach to Plato is called into question by Rowe (1999), Murray (1999), and Gill (1993).

8

Reading, Learning, and Acting: Becoming Active Receivers

8.1. THE READER'S PROGRESS

This study has been an attempt to explore and to substantiate the familiar claim that Plato's readers engage in a dialogue with his texts parallel to the dialogue of interlocutors within them. I argued, in Part I, that the activity of Plato's readers is similar in kind and in value to that of his interlocutors, in that it constitutes a form of learning; Part II has been an attempt to explore the analogy, by looking at various ways in which the dialogues shape the reader's response.

A central strand in the study has been an exploration of what the dialogues suggest learning involves, in terms of the experiences that the learner must undergo in progressing towards understanding. Drawing parallels between interlocutors and readers, I argued that learning, as the dialogues present it, has four central features. It must involve the individual's own effort and participation, but also requires a second figure to trigger the learning process and ensure that the learner is exposed to stimuli appropriate to his stage of development. The learner's engagement must be cognitive-affective in character; and it involves a range of specific experiences, including discomfort, frustration, anger, confusion, disbelief, and a desire to flee. These experiences, I argued, are not wholly negative in significance, for they indicate that a learner is engaged in a way that involves his self. Indeed 'middle' and 'late' interlocutors continue to feel such impulses, though they are now able to deal with them more constructively. In fact, I suggested, it is helpful to regard the three types of interlocutors as representing different stages on the path to dialectical virtue: 'late' interlocutors do not find learning easier, but they now have the skills and virtues to cope with its challenges independently and productively. Acquiring dialectical virtue is a long and difficult process, and learners need motivation, self-examination, and self-awareness, together with plenty of practice. It is a competency that one acquires and refines over time, like other virtues and civic skills; and it is inseparable from a learner's progression towards knowledge and understanding. When viewed this way, knowledge is not something that can simply be acquired, once and for all; bound up as it is with the practice of dialectical virtue, it is an ongoing and unending project. Socratic conversation provides interlocutors with the context and stimuli they need, at each stage of their progress, to develop the elements in dialectical virtue.

Turning to the reader, my exploration of the dialogues' handling of character, argumentation, structure, and plot will, I hope, have made it plausible that they foster similar experiences in us. Reading the dialogues is confusing and disorienting; it may at points be tiresome, even uncomfortable, so we feel like giving up; it sometimes causes annoyance and antagonism. Yet it also draws us in, encouraging us to work though these responses towards a more positive engagement. Each aspect of the dialogues I have considered does this in its own way; irony and enigma are central to the perplexing handling of Socrates' character, for example, while departures from the order of logical demonstration are key to the engaging effect of Plato's arguments. But there has been one common thread: a tendency towards irresolution and uncertainty. The dialogues do not, in any area, provide us with answers—about what to make of Socrates or his and others' arguments, about what to regard as the ideas emerging from a work or even its true subject, about how to evaluate what individuals say or the way they lead their lives. For all the apparently dogmatic assertions of characters, the dialogues refuse us this kind of certainty—and this is crucial to their ability to prompt productive experiences in us. They point towards knowledge and resolution, yet deny them, and this impels us towards engagement and personal reflection.

Of course, the idea that the dialogues avoid presenting doctrine in an authoritarian way is not new. But I have been emphasizing the value of what they do *instead*, which is—if I am right—to encourage the reader to respond, like interlocutors, in a cognitive-affective way that can contribute to her progress towards dialectical virtue. The function of Socratic conversation in its changing guises, I suggested, is to provide interlocutors with the context and stimuli they need, at each stage of development, to progress to the next. In the same way, Plato's texts, like the discussion leader in face-to-face conversation, provide the reader with stimuli that trigger necessary responses in her. Her task is to work through the negative elements in those responses, analysing herself and her reactions, and practising to acquire more productive ones. Here the relationship between text and reader—and particularly the presentation of interlocutors—is especially important. For whereas in face-to-face discussion, the interlocutors can urge each other on and criticize each other's responses, there is a much greater danger that the reader, without such interaction, will disengage and turn away. By presenting us with interlocutors as imperfect images of ourselves and our efforts, the dialogues help us to think about how we need to respond and they assist us in analysing ourselves, generating an internal dialogue that can take the place of the dialogue within the text between respondent and discussion leader. If this is the case, then it should inform our idea of what the reader is doing, and achieving, in reading. The notion of a dialogue between text and reader is not a loose metaphor, but describes an active interaction that parallels the interaction between interlocutor and discussion leader, and enables the reader to engage in reading more productively and to work towards dialectical virtue as she reads. As we do so we develop, simultaneously, our competency both as readers and as learners.

This has interesting implications for how we think about reading, both in the dialogues and elsewhere. For those approaching a work with their eyes on the ideas it contains, the reading experience may not be at the forefront of their attention. Nor may they reflect much on what constitutes good reading—beyond detailed and accurate attention to ideas presented. Throughout my study, however, I have placed the reader at the centre of my interpretation; more particularly, I have been developing an approach based on what Louise Rosenblatt has termed aesthetic reading, whereby the *quality* of our reading experience, rather than any information we extract from a work, is what is taken to be of value. I have reflected already on the nature of the experiences generated by reading the dialogues. But important too are the *patterns of reading* encouraged. In preceding chapters, I have stressed the role of moving backwards and forwards through the text, stopping and starting, revising and rereading. It is very hard for us to read *through* the texts, to a stable point of interpretation; instead they encourage an iterative movement, whereby reading shades into reflection. This is central to the ability of the texts to encourage independent, ongoing philosophizing. It also means that we may need to revise our ideas about what good reading of the dialogues involves. We should not, I think, blame ourselves if we find ourselves often stopping in frustration or returning to an earlier point, baffled by unexpected twists and turns. This is how the works mean to engage us, and these experiences are part of our own progression towards dialectical virtue. Nor should we lead others—particularly those we teach—to regard linear reading as a productive way of engaging with the works. Reading can have value, and can be practised more or less well: this in itself should be a focus of attention among those who study and teach Plato's dialogues.[1]

Accordingly, the reader is at the heart of the learning interaction that takes place as she engages with the text. In this interaction, it is the reader's progress that matters: her dialogue with the text is pivotal—in the language of reader-response theorists—not simply to the creation of the work's meaning, but also to its value. The reader's engagement and development *makes* the work part of a dynamic interaction and, in consequence, can be seen as part of the work itself. The text is there for her sake, and only reaches its full potential and realization when it can contribute to her learning.

This becomes particularly clear when we look at developments between 'early', 'middle', and 'late' works. These, I have argued, present increasing challenges to interlocutors as they develop in dialectical virtue. A similar development occurs as the *reader* progresses through the different types of work—or so at least has been one major strand in my argument. The changes in style between 'early' and 'late' works do not, as is often thought, need to reflect changes in Plato's approach to philosophical interaction. Rather, they provide the reader with changing stimuli to spur her on to further development in dialectical virtue. At each stage, the cognitive tests are greater, but so too are the demands on her virtue—her ability to persevere, to motivate herself, and to analyse where she is going wrong. 'Early' works engage the reader in an obvious way—it is easy to see how they are interactive in intent. It is less so with 'later' works: drama and characterization fade; the style is more austere;

[1] On reading the dialogues, cf. Ferrari (1997), Sayre (1995) esp. 197–232, Roochnik (1995) esp. 133–51.

there is little by way of classical plot. The reader has to work harder, and make more effort, if she is to engage fully. However, this does not mean that the interactive element has disappeared: the works are just less central in initiating that activity. The focus of drama and activity is now with the *reader*, since she is now more responsible for driving the interaction and making the text a live part of her progression towards learning. Her ability to do this is an index of her increasing dialectical virtue.

This has implications for our approach to Plato's corpus, and I have suggested that we should see the three groups of dialogues as written with early-stage, intermediate-stage, and advanced-stage interlocutors in mind. To get the most out of 'later' works, we need already to have reached a certain stage of development; conversely, 'later' works invite responses appropriate to someone who has reached an advanced point in dialectical virtue. We should see the shape of the corpus from the point of view of the reader, in other words, not Plato: 'earlier' works prepare us for, and teach us how to respond to, 'later' ones. This approach sits naturally, I think, with the idea that the overall shape of the corpus was envisaged at a relatively early stage in its composition: for the idea of a progression from early-stage to advanced-stage learning is embedded, I hope to have shown, in the composition of all the dialogues. However, I would like to emphasize that I am only suggesting that the overall conception of what *learning* involves—the progression through different stages, the need for different stimuli and challenges, and for the development of skills and virtues—was conceived from the start. As I have been emphasizing throughout, this does not commit us to the view that dialogues were composed in a certain order, or that the different types of dialogue need to correspond to particular stages in Plato's career. And I am certainly not suggesting that the details of the corpus—the composition of specific dialogues, the development of certain ideas—were worked out in advance. This is a much stronger, and to my mind, much less plausible, viewpoint than the one I am suggesting, which allows development and flexibility within a very broad outline.

If we return to the interaction between reader and text, what emerges is a picture not of a *static* level of interaction between reader and text—as, on reader-response theory, the reader constantly plays a part in constructing the text's meaning—but of increasing activity, responsibility, and development on the part of the reader. Ultimately, the progression from 'early' to 'late' works is about the reader's development towards dialectical virtue: Plato's texts act as a stimulus to the reader's own reflection, thereby *enacting* the dialogues' emphasis on independent effort and inquiry. The dialogues invite such a development, and their 'story' is only fully realized if a reader engages with them in this way. To put it another way, the reader is essential to the plot of the works—both individually and as a corpus. Even in the most austerely plotless and characterless works, her personal development provides a strand of drama along more classical lines.[2]

In fostering the reader's progress in this way, the dialogues become an arena for the personal and philosophical development of the reader which is parallel to that offered to interlocutors by Socratic conversation. It has long been recognized that Socrates' rules of discussion—which underpin his entire dialectical approach—are designed to mark out his conversational practice as different from, and superior to, that of his rivals. In chapters 1 and 2, I tried to further our understanding of this difference by suggesting that Socrates' rules are part of his attempt to foster a cognitive-affective type of involvement in his interlocutors. By now, we can see that a similar set of distinctive features underpins the composition of the dialogues and this, as I suggested in chapter 2, offers us a way of reconciling the dialogues' concerns about literature with Plato's own literary practice. For although the dialogues may at first seem to resemble other genres, in fact they are differentiated by Plato's handling of a range of literary techniques. Their stories manipulate the conventions of classic plot to encourage productive circularity; their handling of structure places the reader's reflective activity at the heart of creating unity from disunity; and their presentation of character encourages critical distance rather than emotional identification. In each case, the dialogues take their starting point from familiar forms and features, yet handle them in such a way as to encourage a response of a fundamentally different kind from the emotional reaction Plato associates with poetry: a distinctive, cognitive-affective response that can contribute to the reader's progress in learning.

[2] Cf. Gale (1994) 124–6, Fowler (2000c), and Conte (1994) xxi on the reader's development as part of the plot in Lucretius' *De Rerum Natura*. Also Nehamas (1998) 47 on readers almost becoming characters in Plato's fictions; and Klein (1965) 6–9 on our reaction as part of the dialogues.

Once we see this, we can appreciate that Plato is not straightforwardly rejecting the literature he criticizes. Nor is he directly transposing literary techniques into a new setting or harnessing their power for philosophical ends. Rather, he is using them as a backdrop for defining and creating a literature of his own distinctive type. The forms and patterns he cultivates are so extensive and fundamental that they become bound up with our understanding of the works as a genre. In consequence, they serve a similar purpose to the rules which define Socratic conversation, because they ensure that Platonic dialogue, by its very nature and generic identity, tends to produce a cognitive-affective response. At a time when the medium of writing literacy was growing in prominence alongside oral methods of communication,[3] Plato is carving out two parallel and complementary arenas for the practice of cognitive-affective learning—Socratic conversation and Platonic dialogue. The dialogues are always pointing towards conversation, but even while doing so, they allow reading the dialogues, a newly forged type of philosophical literature, to play a valuable role in our progression towards understanding and virtue.

As well as expressing the full centrality of the reader to the strategy of the dialogues, such an approach allows us to take a positive view of the dialogues' relationship with the reader. Many interpreters feel that Plato is pessimistic about people's potential to change and improve: he presents a vision of what life might ideally be like, but balances it against a recognition of what, given human nature and society, is actually possible. To me, however, there would seem little point in Plato producing so many works dedicated to learning and inquiry if this were wholly true. Focusing on the reader offers us a way out of this dilemma—and here Lucretius' *De Rerum Natura*, another famously pessimistic work, offers an interesting parallel. Lucretius' poem ends abruptly with a description of the plague at Athens and an emotive evocation of the fear of death, a conclusion that many interpreters have thought casts doubt on the ability of Epicureanism to provide a successful way of dealing with the horrors of life. Peta Fowler, however, questions this interpretation,[4] instead treating the poem's ending as a challenge to the reader. Only a philosophically advanced reader, she suggests, will be able to respond to such a bleak picture in the spirit of Epicurean belief, calmly and tranquilly; yet

[3] See ch.1 section 1.1.

[4] P. G. Fowler (1997); cf. Gale (1994) 124–6.

only with such a response is the work really 'completed'. For by responding in an appropriate way, the reader demonstrates that she has fully absorbed the principles of Epicureanism and completed the journey of learning that the poem invites her to undertake. In other words, the power to bring completion and success to Lucretius' poem lies with his reader. A similar power, I suggest, lies with Plato's reader. Though the dialogues, in their portrayal of interlocutors, often seem to offer a pessimistic picture of human potential, the *reader* still has the ability to respond productively. If she does, then she has successfully risen to the challenge presented by the work, and her learning process gives the dialogues a fuller completion and a more meaningful success.

8.2. DIALECTICAL VIRTUE, CIVIC VIRTUE

My focus so far has been on individual learners; yet in Plato, no less than in Lucretius, we are encouraged to see individuals against the backdrop of their society. Most of Plato's dialogues are set in the city; they frequently put civic affairs at the heart of the interlocutors' conversations; and we are encouraged, as we have seen in previous chapters, to connect interlocutors' words with their lives and actions. Most prominently, of course, Socrates' trial and death at the hands of the Athenians is a motif running throughout the corpus, reminding us of the link between enquiry and civic affairs in Socrates' approach to and practice of the philosophical life. However, for many interpreters, Plato's disappointment at the political events of his time, not least the Athenians' reception of Socrates, led to a retreat into philosophy and a passionate rejection of the practice of politics. Physically, this is represented in the seclusion of the Academy; and in the dialogues, it is not hard to find passages which seem to signal disillusion with the conduct of civic and political affairs, or denounce those at the forefront of civic life, from sophists and poets to orators and political leaders. Moreover, the philosopher is often presented as striving for a world of eternal truths which takes his attention from the imperfections of everyday affairs: *Republic*'s philosopher must ascend from the Cave, *Phaedo*'s truth-seeker must separate himself from the life of the body, and *Phaedrus*' philosophical lover leaves behind earthly desire, devoting himself to the objects of true beauty.

A passage in *Theaetetus* articulates particularly clearly the notion of pure contemplation as a philosopher's ideal:

> *These men, to begin with, from when they are young, do not know the way to the market-place, nor where the court-room is, nor the council-chamber, nor any other place of assembly for the city; and they do not hear discussion about laws and decrees, or see them when they are inscribed; and the rivalries of associations after public offices, and meetings, and banquets, and revels with chorus girls—not even their dreams bring them close to doing such things... for he does not keep away from them for the sake of reputation, but really it is only his body that is situated and lives in the city, and his mind, considering all these things trifling and of no account, disdains them... investigating the complete nature of every one of the things that exist as a whole, never letting itself come down to any of the things close by.*
>
> *Theaetetus*, 173c–174a

Here, Socrates is contrasting the philosopher,[5] whose sights are set on the realities beyond the everyday world, with speakers in the law courts, whom he has just described. The latter, stunted and turned from truth by the constraints of their environment, find themselves in perplexity when confronted by the philosopher's questions; and conversely the philosopher, when he must appear in a law court, becomes an object of ridicule. The life of contemplation as a philosophical ideal is a significant strand running through the dialogues;[6] and these, accordingly, have sometimes been characterized as constructing a space for philosophical development which is in opposition to, and separate from, the political world Plato rejected.[7]

Yet at the same time, the energy of the dialogues' engagement with political and civic affairs is hard to ignore. Far from turning their attention away from the everyday world, Plato's works encourage us to examine the everyday morality of a Cephalus and the credentials of such public figures as Protagoras, Gorgias, and Alcibiades. They take us to the law courts, the symposium, the gymnasium, and gatherings at private houses; and they prompt us to view the poetry and rhetoric

[5] Socrates specifies that he is talking about the leaders among the philosophers at *Tht.*173c7–9; Sedley (2004) 67 argues that Socrates does not wholly identify with this ideal, because of his god-given mission to act as a midwife to his fellow citizens.

[6] See Sedley (2004) esp. 62–86.

[7] See e.g. Nightingale (1995), Goldhill (2008b), Greenwood (2008), von Reden and Goldhill (1999), Barber (1996).

which were central to civic life and education with a critical eye. Both indirectly and directly, discussion leaders attempt to engage with respondents' opinions and actions in matters of public relevance; and though failure is often the outcome, we are invited to view political engagement—and the attempt to work towards a better state of communal affairs—as an integral part of the philosophical project as it is portrayed in the dialogues. In recent years, moreover, critics have started to explore the dialogues' constructive engagement with the civic and political, and in particular with democracy.[8] Illuminating work has explored how Plato uses democratic concepts, such as frank speaking and being an active audience member, as a framework for articulating his philosophical project.[9] Conversely, critics have suggested that Plato presents philosophy as pointing the way towards a refined version of democracy, one in which a commitment to democratic features remains but where civic engagement is guided by philosophical truth.[10] If so, we may prefer to view the dialogues' polemical criticisms of civic and political life not as a complete rejection of the political, but as an attempt to put forward their own competing model of productive civic activity: one that unites a sense of political responsibility with philosophical understanding and dialectical virtue.

In articulating Plato's complex engagement with political discourse, von Reden and Goldhill draw on the notion of *theoria*, a term with both civic and philosophical resonances.[11] In civic terms, *theoria* encompasses the official duties of an ambassador as well as the varied circumstances—such as the assembly, law courts, and theatre—in which a citizen would act as a judging spectator in a democratic context.[12] To be an audience member on such occasions

[8] E.g. Goldhill and Osborne (1999), Euben (1996), Monoson (2000). Cf. also Cohen (2002), Burnyeat (2009).

[9] Monoson (2000), also von Reden and Goldhill (1999).

[10] Barber (1996) argues that, by looking to truth, the dialogues' version of political discourse departs from core democratic principles. Euben (1996) presents the dialogues as offering a critique, not a rejection, of democracy; cf. Monoson (2000).

[11] Goldhill (1999), von Reden and Goldhill (1999). Cf. Monoson (2000)'s development of the dialogues' treatment of being an audience member at a public festival, or a *theates*; also Osborne (2007b).

[12] For the connection of *theoria* with the terms *theoros*, an ambassador to the games or to an oracle, and *theates*, an audience member at a civic festival, see Monoson (2000) 206. Goldhill (1999) withholds judgement on the etymological connection between *theoria*/*theates*.

was a political act, and the activity of the evaluating spectator was an integral part of the practice of democracy. Yet at the same time, the term evokes key Platonic preoccupations: the dialogues' emphasis on self-scrutiny—a person's directing of their gaze towards themselves—as the basis for all learning, and the connection they often make between knowing and seeing, where the philosopher becomes ultimately a spectator of eternal realities. At *Meno* 81c5–7, for instance, Socrates declares that 'since the soul is immortal and has been born many times, and has seen all the things both here and in the underworld, there is nothing that it has not learned' (῞Ατε οὖν ἡ ψυχὴ ἀθάνατός τε οὖσα καὶ πολλάκις γεγονυῖα, καὶ ἑωρακυῖα καὶ τὰ ἐνθάδε καὶ τὰ ἐν ῞Αιδου καὶ πάντα χρήματα, οὐκ ἔστιν ὅτι οὐ μεμάθηκεν); in *Phaedrus*, Socrates describes how before birth the soul sees true realities as it stands at the rim of heaven;[13] and the prisoners in the Cave in *Republic* are led into a lighter world where they can see many more things.[14]

A *theoros* or *theates* in the Socratic mould, uniting these two resonances, would look to himself in making civic decisions, and would rely on self-scrutiny to guide his engagement in public procedures. He would thereby avoid the type of unthinking activity Plato associates with democracy, while preserving the importance of individual evaluation and decision-making; and his decisions would be informed, ultimately, by his vision of true realities, which would allow him to see things from a truer perspective and against a broader backdrop than others. In short, civic *theoria* would be grounded in philosophical *theoria*, and a citizen's successful fulfilment of his civic duties would parallel his productive engagement in the philosophical process. As a philosophical spectator, he would unite civic participation and responsibility with dialectical understanding and virtue.

The notion of *theoria* also resonates with the dialogues' concern over receivership among both interlocutors and readers, and as we noted in previous chapters, the dialogues frequently frame the activities of discussion and reception in terms which imply civic engagement. Evoking both Socrates' trial and his strikingly contented approach to death, *Phaedo* foregrounds the civic and the personal importance of the way in which we arrive at our opinions; and in this dialogue, the process of putting forward and responding to an

[13] *Phdr.*247a–248c. [14] *R.*514a–517c.

assertion is likened to scrutinising a case in court.[15] When faced by an argument put forward by Simmias and Cebes, Socrates says:

> *'For I think you mean that it is necessary for me to defend myself against these things, as if in a law court.'*
>
> *'Absolutely', said Simmias.*
>
> *'Come then', he said, 'I will try to defend myself more convincingly to you than I did to the judges.'*
>
> *Phaedo*, 63b

Likewise, in responding to the conversation between Socrates and his companions which Phaedo is narrating to Echecrates, these two more distant receivers are presented as judging the arguments for themselves in turn:

> *All of us, after listening as they spoke, were uncomfortable, as we said later to each other; for after we had been thoroughly convinced by the previous account, they seemed to throw us into confusion again and to cast us into distrust, not only with regard to the words spoken before, but also with regard to things that would be said in the future, in case we were not worthy judges of anything or these matters were beyond belief.*
>
> *Echecrates: By the gods, Phaedo, I sympathise with you; for after I myself have listened to you, it occurs to me to say such a thing: What argument shall we now believe? For the account which Socrates put forward was very credible, and now it has fallen into discredit.*
>
> *Phaedo*, 88cd

In these passages, the judicial language underscores the responsibility of the person putting forward a viewpoint: he must provide reasons to convince his listeners—reasons of sufficient strength to convince a jury in court—and he must be prepared to bring counter-arguments in response to their objections. Those receiving an assertion have a responsibility too, of responding critically and robustly, to ensure they only accept an idea when there are secure grounds for doing so.

Similarly, in *Theaetetus*, also set against the backdrop of Socrates' imminent court case, the activity of interlocutors is presented in comparable terms. At the start, Socrates raises the possibility that Theodorus' answers may make him liable to an action for false witness (ἔνοχος τοῖς ψευδομαρτυρίοις 148b5), and he urges Theaetetus not to draw back from the discussion on the grounds that Theodorus was jesting in putting him forward, otherwise Theodorus will have to

[15] Cf. ch.1 n8.

testify under oath (ἀναγκασθῇ μαρτυρεῖν 145c4). Later, at 154d, the idea of false witness resurfaces when, alluding to Euripides' *Hippolytus*, Socrates reminds his respondent to answer what he really thinks—if he is to avoid swearing with his tongue but not his mind. At 150c, Socrates attributes to his midwife's art the power of testing (βασανίζειν 150c1) a man and his opinions through questioning, so as to discriminate between what is true and what is false; and later he asks Theaetetus for proof (τεκμήριον 158b9, c4) that they are awake, and not dreaming.

One effect of *Theaetetus*' judicial references is to remind us of the shared purpose of philosophizing and the law courts: the pursuit of truth and the ability to distinguish what is real from what is false. The backdrop of Socrates' trial underscores the significance of the courts' faulty decisions and the importance of striving for a situation in which the decisions of jurors can be founded on truth. At the same time, the contrast Socrates draws, in his central digression, between the philosopher and the stunted public speaker, suggests just how limited the law courts were in actually being able to do so. But when viewed as part of the dialogue's engagement with the idea of judgement, in its philosophical and civic forms, Socrates' portrayal in that passage of the segregated life of the philosopher does not, I think, point the reader towards disengagement from philosophical and civic affairs. Through its application of the language of the law courts to the activity of interlocutors and receivers, the dialogue encourages us to see the development of personal understanding and virtue as a contribution to a wider social good. It reminds us that being a receiver is a political act, and that there is a wider, civic dimension to the skills we develop as readers. It asks us to view our philosophical engagement as akin to that of citizens or jurors, as a process of active engagement in which our personal judgements are formed. It also prompts us to apply our philosophical standards of discrimination to the civic activity of being a juror, encouraging us to insist, for all the limitations of the context, on the same high standards for accepting what has been said. We are being trained, we might say, to become better civic receivers—through being philosophically informed ones—than Socrates' original jurors, while also recognizing that achieving perfection in this may be unattainable in the imperfect world of the everyday.

In fact, the dialectical qualities we have considered throughout this study are, at once, social and civic qualities as well. Accordingly, the reader's development is at the same time part of her civic development and her cultivation of personal philosophical understanding. To begin with, by presenting philosophical progress as the development of virtue, the dialogues cast what could have seemed an isolated intellectual pursuit in terms readily comprehensible within a civic framework: the hard work, practice, and habituation which go with the development of virtue make the journey towards knowledge seem more accessible, without underplaying its difficulty. At the same time, the language of virtue implies that a reader's achievements in the dialectical sphere may be applicable to other areas of her life. Plato's texts confuse and frustrate us, I have argued, to the point of discomfort; they force us to make positive efforts of endurance and self-examination to continue reading; and they ask us to develop self-motivation in the face of ever-increasing challenges. Likewise they offer ample opportunity, over an extended programme of reading, for habituation in appropriate patterns of response. All these qualities are as relevant to the public and political sphere as they are to the dialectical, as Plato reminds us in portraying a Socrates whose endurance and steadfastness in facing his prosecution are mirrored by his tenacity and endurance in discussion.

Scrutiny and self-scrutiny, moreover, are as important to the reader's development as they are to that of the *theoros* or *theates*. The dialogues invite her to develop her own critical perspective and they place personal choice and independent decision-making at the heart of her development: we are encouraged to evaluate and judge things for ourselves, rather than taking our ideas on anyone else's authority. Plato's texts present us with figures who reflect ourselves and our efforts, thereby helping us to analyse our own traits and responses, and fostering a self-knowledge that has the potential to inform our decisions. Likewise, they encourage the reader to be a wary judge of character, forestalling a straightforward or automatic response to any interlocutor, even one who—like Socrates—may seem a positive role model. By inviting such a critical outlook, which is based on cautious and detailed evaluation, the dialogues furnish the reader with the ability to be a more careful judge of those she meets outside the dialogues, for instance, in the assembly or law courts. In consequence, this combined attention to the reader's evaluation of herself and of others is a civic, as well as a dialectical, virtue.

This raises the question of the transferability of what we gain through reading to other areas of our life—whether philosophical conversation or practical action. Does the fact that we undergo experiences and gain skills in a 'literary' arena mean that we cannot use them in other contexts? If so, the value of reading may seem somewhat limited. Yet it is worth noting here how closely the dialogues suggest conversation and action are connected—a link that as modern readers we do not take for granted. As commentators have long noted, Plato seems to think that Socratic conversation, if properly carried out, will have direct implications for interlocutors' lives and actions. And, as I pointed out in chapter 1, the lines between being a participant in conversation, an onlooker, and a receiver are very fluid. We should not, then, approach the dialogues thinking of reading as distinct from conversation and life, despite our modern inclinations to do so: developing skills and virtues in a dialectical arena may, the dialogues suggest, help us to evaluate ourselves and act with endurance and commitment in conversation and practical action as well as in reading. We will have to adapt our virtues according to the context, but possessing the basic skills will surely make this easier. By training us in dialectical virtue, the dialogues prepare us to act with parallel responsibility in a social context.

If this is accepted, then as well as pointing towards a refined version of civic engagement, the dialogues take a step towards enacting it; for through the patterns of response they encourage in us as readers, they are not preparing us, as the solitary activity of reading perhaps implies, to be detached onlookers, but for the active civic involvement their conversations portray. Far from turning their back on the possibility of positive engagement in political life, therefore, the dialogues help their readers to become productive citizens as well as better learners. Just as the dialogues delineate an arena for a distinctive type of education and a distinctive type of literary engagement (or so I have argued), in the same way, we might say they mark out a context for working towards civic engagement and responsibility of a particular type: one that draws on dialectical virtue and philosophical understanding to inform active, reflective participation.

8.3. THE MYTH OF *PHAEDO*: FROM READING TO ACTING

I would like to draw to a close by considering these general issues in connection with a final passage, *Phaedo*'s myth of the 'real world'.

Following a discussion of the immortality of the soul and immediately preceding the dialogue's closing account of the death of Socrates, the myth recounts the journey of souls through the underworld. Socrates describes the initial stages of the journey, before describing the regions of the earth, both its surface and its underground areas. Finally, we return to the fate of the souls and learn the regions to which good and bad souls are assigned. A passage filled, in turn, with images of horror and incredible beauty, the myth seems to remove us from the realities of our world to a fantastical landscape. At the same time, its mythical form seems to diverge from the dialectical mode of the earlier part of the discussion and to plunge us into a literary world which may strike us as an appropriation, by Plato, of the powers of poetry in the service of philosophy. In both content and form, therefore, the passage may strike us as a singular departure from the type of engagement which, I have argued, the dialogues make central to our development as learners and citizens. Yet despite this, I think we can make sense of the myth on both these counts within the framework I have set out in this study.

The role of myths[16] within Plato's dialogues has long troubled interpreters. As extended passages of narration they depart from the dialogues' dominant dramatic form; they take us into unfamiliar realms elaborated with great imaginative colour; and they are presented in more highly charged language. In short, they seem more *literary* or *poetical* than other parts of the works.[17] One traditional line of interpretation has been to regard Plato's myths as separate from the philosophical content of the dialogues. Through literary means, it is said, they appeal to our emotions, investing the philosophical life with an attraction without which the dialectical parts of the dialogues would fail to change our behaviour.[18] For some,[19] even,

[16] Plato's myths are notoriously hard to define: see Morgan (2000) 156–61, Rutherford (1995) 172.

[17] McCabe (1994) 162–3 and (1992) pose the problems very clearly. For discussion of trends in interpretation, and an approach to the interweaving of myth and philosophy different from the one developed here, see Partenie (2009a), esp. Partenie (2009b).

[18] Cf. Janaway (1995) 160; Rutherford (1995) 175; Edelstein (1949) 474, 477; Stewart (1905), esp. 1–76. Stewart thinks that the myths evoke a Transcendental Feeling, an effect associated with poetry, though with philosophical significance too. In this respect his approach has affinities with mine, although I differ from his analysis of the nature of the reader's aesthetic/affective response.

[19] Bostock (1986) and Gallop (1975) are striking examples.

they are literary ornament that may be omitted from serious consideration of the works. Such a viewpoint, however, though it acknowledges the myths' literary texture, fails to take account of the philosophical ideas and arguments they contain and presuppose. We should, as Annas maintains,[20] analyse these ideas and arguments both for themselves and in relation to those expressed elsewhere in a work. Kathryn Morgan has argued,[21] moreover, that the juxtaposition of *muthos* with *logos* is crucial in highlighting issues of philosophical method and communication: the fragility of language, the difficulty of communicating knowledge, the importance of methodological awareness. On readings of this type, the myths—like other parts of the works—aim to engage the reader on an intellectual level.[22] But although such work is, of necessity, alert to the differences between mythical and dialectical elements of the dialogues, it is at core 'non-aesthetic',[23] in that it focuses on the ideas that emerge from the myths. Unlike an 'aesthetic' approach, it does not place the experience of reading—which to many seems what is particularly striking about Plato's myths—at the centre of its analysis. My approach is different again. Though both the above interpretations contain important insights, both in my view go wrong in treating the 'cognitive' and 'emotional' aspects of a learner's response as separate. In line with the interpretation developed throughout this study, I think that Plato's myths, like other parts of the dialogues, do not engage us purely 'emotionally' or purely 'intellectually', but instead invite a cognitive-affective response.

In considering *Phaedo*'s myth, we should note, to begin with, how unusual a narrative this is. Despite commonly being treated as straightforward 'stories',[24] Plato's myths are not narratives as we often think of them, as dominated by an action sequence and with a clear plot or storyline. In fact, descriptive passages replace action as the focus of attention and interest in the *Phaedo* myth. The account of the regions of the earth takes up the bulk of the account (109a–113c), halting the narrative of the fates of the different types of soul; this creates an episodic feel, with the myth falling into discrete sections,

[20] Annas (1982a). Cf. also McCabe (1992), Mackenzie (1981) 225–39.
[21] Morgan (2000), esp. ch. 6–7.
[22] See also Nussbaum (1986), esp. 131–4 and Rowe (1993) 4, 10–11.
[23] See ch.2 section 2.2. [24] See e.g. Buxton (1994) 17, 179–81.

the connections between which are left implicit. In addition, the concentration of detail and emotive vocabulary in the descriptive sections contrasts with the compressed, summary style in which the fates of different souls are narrated. The account of the surface of the earth, for example, is highly aspirational: filled with comparatives of height, light, purity, and beauty, it is set against the suggestion that our own life in the hollows is defective—a life of weakness, disease, and corrosion. As inhabitants of the hollows, it is implied, we are in a state of imperfection, assimilating ourselves to fishes, ants, or frogs, rather than realizing our true human potential by living on the surface. By contrast, the underworld is a place of darkness and horror, full of violent and confusing processes. Liquid oscillates and waves up and down (112b2); the third river falls into a vast region burning with a great fire (113a7–8); and from the Pyriphlegethon streams of lava belch forth offshoots (113b5–6). Throughout both sections, the earth is described in terms reminiscent of a living thing: its pulsation is at some length likened to breathing (112b ff.); it is adorned (κεκοσμῆσθαι 110e7), its parts are in proportion (110de) like those of a body, and it is untouched by ugliness or disease (110e6–7); and the rivers of the underworld coil like serpents (112d7). The impression given is that the fate of the souls is one aspect of this larger cosmic drama. By making the descriptive passages so absorbing, Plato ensures that both reason and emotion are involved in our response to the text, and because the passages that engage us most on an emotive level are also those that aim to increase our understanding of the true nature of the world, the two aspects of our response are drawn together, thereby encouraging a response with both cognitive and affective dimensions. Here, acquiring cognitive insight *is* what involves the reader on an emotional level.

By contrast, the narrative sections of the myth, relating to the fate of different souls, effectively become a frame for the lengthy central description. It is not that nothing happens in *Phaedo*'s myth, but rather that the emphasis is not on action. The account is concerned with the judgement of souls after death, which is a paradigm of something that happens to everyone: a typical or timeless happening, rather than a unique set of events tied to particular individuals, like the murder of Agamemnon or the death of Hector, which, for all their potential relevance to our own lives, are highly specific happenings. Accordingly, the events do not have an absolute temporal placing (as opposed to a relative one, such as 'after someone dies' or 'before they are born'): they are possible happenings for all time. By downplaying traditional narrative interest in favour of description in this way, the myth prevents us being unthinkingly drawn into the logic of the story and implicitly accepting the picture of the world it presupposes. Instead, Plato makes the context or background for the action—which contains insights crucial for our ability to make sense of that action—break in on, and overshadow, the action sequence. In doing so, he forces us into a more reflective mode and emphasizes the importance of understanding the meaning and significance of events, rather than becoming involved in them for their own sake.

Moreover, *Phaedo*'s myth lacks classic character interest. There is an absence of characterized figures, and in particular of direct or indirect speech attributed to them. Instead, we are confronted with shadowy figures of the souls of the dead; and to the extent that these are given life, it is of a very generic sort. Thus Socrates presents one group of souls as 'bad' by specifying some of the misdeeds particular souls have performed; however, the effect of this is not to create a group of highly individualized characters, but rather to conjure up a hazily defined category of unworthy lives. In part, this helps defuse conventional dramatic and narrative interest, which traditionally revolves around character and action. Simultaneously, it focuses the reader's attention on situations rather than characters. Thus the shadowy souls evoke the situation of a person after death and, in particular, the judgement he undergoes, while the people/living things that rise to the real world draw attention to the possibility of experiencing this higher level of reality. In this way, the figures of the myth become vehicles through which situations of universal relevance are drawn to our attention and their possibilities explored. By divorcing issues from particular characters, Plato refuses the reader the refuge of imagining someone else in the situation he wants her to regard as of central importance for her own life, and encourages her to apply the situation evoked to herself, as someone who could fill the place of the shadowy figure: we are in a sense 'drawn in' to the narrative like a character.

In addition, *Phaedo*'s mythical narrative is distinctive for its striking emphasis on bringing out the *perspective* from which things are being seen and the way they would strike our *vision*.[25] The

[25] Cf. Nightingale (2002a) 238.

emphasis on vision, like the abandonment of classical plot, adds a rational edge to our involvement, and discourages us from immersing ourselves in an 'emotional' way. We are encouraged, initially, to imagine the journey or path a soul travels through the underworld: πορείας (107d5, repeated emphatically at 107e5) is the first word before the introduction of the myth proper, and in the following lines, our attention is directed towards the guidance of the soul and the places to which it is conveyed. Emphasis is added by the allusion to Aeschylus' presentation of the underworld: Socrates challenges the idea that the path is simple, and encourages us to think of it as containing many forks and windings (σχίσεις τε καὶ τριόδους 108a4). He then reinforces the effect by recounting the stages in the souls' progressions: the soul that loves the body hovers around the visible world and is forcibly led away by its guardian, and when it reaches the same place as the other souls, it is shunned and wanders in isolation, before arriving at its fitting habitation (πρέπουσαν οἴκησιν 108c2); the journey of a pure soul is much smoother, and in the end it also comes to inhabit a proper dwelling (τόπον προσήκοντα 108c5). The passage abounds with words of leading and following; of places and paths; and of making one's way. Imagining the soul's passage through such a complex topography becomes, in this myth, our entry point into thinking about the underworld and our fate after death.

These emphatic references to place at the close of the initial passage provide a bridge to Socrates' description of the 'wonderful regions of the earth' (108c6). Here, visualization becomes even more important, due to the way we are encouraged to 'view' the hollows and the surface of the earth from different perspectives. First, we are asked to regard our attitude to our world as analogous to that of a person living in the sea who mistakenly thinks he sees what is above its surface; then Socrates pictures someone reaching the surface of the air of our world, sticking his head above it like a fish, and seeing how much more beautiful things are there. We are thus prompted to build up an imaginative picture of underwater and above water, the hollows and the real earth, and, to fill in the details, Socrates provides a wealth of information about how they would strike our *vision*. The real world looks like a patchwork of colours, 'far brighter and purer' than ours—white, purple, gold, and silver; the water-filled hollows gleam amidst the other colours, creating the appearance of a wholly multicoloured surface; the stones are all like our jewels, though more beautiful still; decay has not corrupted the appearance of things. Beauty, colour, brightness, appearance, and seeing occur as leitmotifs throughout the passage, and the insistence on vision is also kept up by the mention of how people who live on the real earth see it: at 111a3–4 we are told that it is a sight to make those blessed who look upon it, and at 111c1–3 we learn that they see the sun and the stars as they really are, and in all other ways their blessedness is in accord with this. Following this passage, the description of the rivers of the underworld has in places a precision reminiscent of scientific description, and the detail with which the paths of the rivers are reported again encourages us to build up an image of their complex meanderings in our mind.

The emphasis on vision here is striking in the extent to which it dominates the narration.[26] The vivid visual descriptions make what is described *immediate*: the directness and colour of the visual presentation makes it easy for us to enter imaginatively into the world of the myth, an important first step towards properly appreciating the insights it contains. It also makes those insights exciting, bringing them close to us—at least for the time we are reading—in a way that enables us to regard them as significant for our own lives.[27] At the same time, the emphasis on vision recalls the connection the dialogues often make between seeing and knowing. By regarding ourselves as 'seeing' what we are told about in the myth, therefore, we are encouraged to think of ourselves as learning something new, and the technique adds a rational edge to our approach: by getting us to conceive of our attitude towards the narration on rational and reflective lines, Plato forestalls a purely emotional response. This tendency is reinforced due to the *type* of visual perspective the myth prompts us to adopt, which might be described as panoramic or holistic. That is, the visual details presented go towards building up an entire picture, which has a degree of logicality and illuminates the patterns in things. For example, as we read, we have to form a picture of the relation of the paths travelled by good and bad souls at the start of the myth, the different regions of the earth, and in particular the complex weavings of rivers and lakes; this requires concentration and 'distance' of a type incompatible with the emotional 'immersion' in a narrative that Plato

[26] Bacchylides 3.23–62, a narrative packed with vivid images and colour contrasts, which serve to add vividness and excitement to an essentially action-based account, provides an interesting comparison.

[27] Such imaginative engagement/projection is sometimes regarded as a way non-philosophical works have ethical value, though one Plato ignores. E.g. Nussbaum (1990) 45–9, Janaway (1995) 197–201.

criticizes in other literature. Rather than being immersed in individual details one by one, therefore, we are forced to take a more detached stance, as we try to make sense of the information Socrates provides. As we do so, we are in a sense building up an alternative vision of the world upon which, ultimately, to base our ideas and actions.

For all that they venture into unfamiliar territory, however, Plato's myths are closely integrated into their context. The *Phaedo* myth is preceded by dialectical argument, which encourages us to approach it critically and reflectively,[28] and dialectical elements within the passage further emphasize its similarity to other parts of the work. For instance, we find interruptions by Simmias, the formal addressee (e.g. 108d1–3, 108e3, 109a8, 110b3–4). There is open interrogation of alternative views about the paths to the underworld (107e–108a). The account is divided up neatly into clearly flagged sections (e.g. 111c, 112e, 113d), and within the sections, there is frequently an argumentative progression. At 108a1–2, for example, after his rejection of Telephus' view about the paths to the underworld, Socrates states, 'I think the path is neither simple nor single', following this up with his reasons, presented in two consecutive '*γάρ*' clauses, and then a reference to the earthly rites from which one of his conclusions is drawn (*τεκμαιρόμενος λέγω* 108a6). Socrates uses numbered points (108e4 ff.); analogies (between sea creatures and men 109c–110a, between the earth and coloured balls 110bc); precisely phrased comparisons (e.g. 111b1–2 'what the air is to us, the ether is to them'); and the language of reasoning and belief (e.g. *φαίνεταί μοι εἶναι* 108a2, *αἰτία* 112b1, *πέπεισμαι* 108e1).

Moreover, viewing myths as distinct from the rest of their dialogue also conceals their affinities with other statements of belief—*logoi*—offered in dialectical conversation, including definitions, speeches, extended metaphorical accounts (e.g. *Republic*'s Sun, Lane, and Cave), stories, and parables (e.g. the tale of Theuth and Thamus in *Phaedrus*). Myths, as is commonly noted, are frequently accompanied by reflection on the speaker's authority, the provenance and truth-value of the account, and the proper way of responding to it, as well as by description of the actual responses of participants and onlookers—and so are the other types of *logoi* I have mentioned. In *Phaedo*, for

[28] Cf. Macleod (1983) 52–67 on the relationship between Thucydides' speeches and their context as inviting our critical scrutiny.

instance, Socrates draws attention to the authority on which he bases his account,[29] telling us that he is recounting 'what is said' (λέγεται 107d4–5) rather than something that he himself has seen, attributing details of his accounts to Homer and the poets respectively on two occasions (112a, 113c), and referring to his account as a *muthos* on two occasions (110b1, 114d8). At the close of his account, he distances himself from the details of what he has just said, claiming that it would not be fitting for a man of sense to affirm them, though stressing his belief that this or something like it is true (114d). These parallels suggest that we see myths as another type of account, with a similar value and function in learning as the others. The inclusion of these features encourages us to respond reflectively and self-consciously, with an awareness of the appropriateness of our responses, when engaging with all types of account—myths not least. Indeed, the myths' often flamboyant handling of themes of receivership and quality could be a way of foregrounding the importance of such issues in dealing with all accounts, not just lengthy and poetic ones.

All this should encourage us, I think, to question the idea that myths invite a response that is purely emotional in character: though it achieves the effect in different ways, *Phaedo*'s myth—like other elements in the dialogue—invites us to engage, as reflective yet committed receivers, in a way that is at the same time cognitive and affective. Yet we are still left to question why Plato should have chosen to introduce an account of this particular type at this specific point in his dialogue: an account that takes our eye away from the everyday world and that, in some senses, undoubtedly diverges in character from its context. On one level, its stylistic qualities—the change in perspective and linguistic register, the use of narrative, image, and symbol—contribute to the ways, explored in previous chapters, in which the dialogues unsettle and challenge us, prompting a fully engaged and reflective response.[30] But in addition, we need to return to ideas about the *dialectical need* of interlocutors and readers developed earlier in this book, where I suggested that learners require stimuli appropriate

[29] Nightingale (2002b).

[30] Cf. Nightingale (2002a), Rutherford (2002). These differences also mean that reconciling what is said in myths with other parts of the works is more complicated—and engaging—than critics like Annas suggest. On the ability of images to help us learn, see Tecuşan (1992); and on the myths' symbolic form, Smith (1986).

to their stage of development and explained changing approaches to dialectic, characterization, plot, and structure with reference to the changing needs of increasingly advanced learners.

The dialogues' inclusion of myth alongside other types of *logoi* is, I believe, another facet of their responsiveness to dialectical need. In *Phaedo*, Socrates introduces his myth at the end of an extended discussion of the immortality of the soul, which provides the backdrop to Socrates' impending death. Socrates expresses his conviction that the soul survives death and one of his discussion partners, Cebes, states his agreement, but another, Simmias, still has doubts. Socrates recommends a careful examination of their argument and its starting points—further dialectical discussion, at another time, that is—yet he chooses to supplement his advice by offering his account of the soul's journey after death, and his comments as he brings it to a close (114c–115a) indicate that his intention has been to reinforce his listeners' conviction in the conclusions of the earlier argument. In this instance, the mythical account is introduced in response to a crisis or difficulty in the conversation, in case it can bring about progress that the dialectical discussion alone has not managed; as such, it responds to Simmias' dialectical need—as well as that of any reader who remains unconvinced. The need is a pressing one. Not only is Socrates soon to lose the opportunity to converse with Simmias at greater length himself and to revisit the first principles of the argument as he recommends, but in addition, Simmias, along with Socrates' other companions and Plato's readers, is about to witness Socrates' death. For Socrates' cheerful calm to make sense, it is vital for us to appreciate the philosophical outlook that underlies his approach and actions.

The myth helps us to do this in two closely connected ways. First, it engages us at a different level of belief. It presents a vision of the world in a forceful way, which challenges our ideas at a deep, all-encompassing, and highly aspirational level, not in the piecemeal way characteristic of dialectic. As such, it compels us to contemplate our opinions from a larger-scale and more holistic perspective[31]—though one that will also require further reflection on the details. It allows us, in other words, to see how individual beliefs can combine to form a view of the world which may have a radical effect on a person's

[31] Cf. Nightingale (2002a) 236–7.

outlook and behaviour. Second, the myth invites us to engage with its ideas in a more direct and affectively involved way, and to inhabit the picture presented and experience it as if we are ourselves committed to it—if only temporarily. By evoking a more immediately involved response, the myth forecloses the possibility that we will depart completely disengaged from the learning process—without registering that there might be a more appealing way of seeing the world, or having our ideas upset in any way. This responds to the most fundamental dialectical need of a reader: the need to be sufficiently engaged when she finishes reading for there to be some chance that the learning process will continue—at a point when she, like Simmias, is perhaps just about to break away disillusioned.

When viewed in this light, Socrates' myth is not the fantastical flight of fancy it may at first seem. It is, first of all, a means of offering us a more profound insight into Socrates' beliefs and behaviour as a philosopher and a citizen. By being juxtaposed with Plato's account of Socrates' death, it indicates the basis for Socrates' uncompromising demeanour as he faces death, and also for the actions that have defined his unusual life. The final section of the dialogue therefore complements the generality of the myth by providing a specific illustration[32] and deepens our sense of what commitment to such a vision of life would mean, in both emotional and practical terms. As such, it indicates how philosophy can shape the way a person lives, and underscores the profoundly civic resonance of Socrates' philosophical activity. Far from being an isolated vision, that is, it shows us in powerful terms the connection of the private and philosophical with the public and political.

At the same time, Socrates invites his receivers to adopt this viewpoint as the basis for their own lives and actions, thereby potentially contributing in a more direct way to their civic development. As he says to Crito shortly after drawing his account to a close, 'if you neglect yourselves and refuse to live in the tracks laid by our discussions both now and at a previous time . . . you will achieve nothing further' (115b8–c1). Although little dramatic action is directly represented in the *Phaedo* myth, a powerful dramatic motif, of decision and choice, is nevertheless implied. On one level, it is present in the idea that a soul's fate in the underworld is a product of the choices it

[32] Burnet (1911) 143.

made during life—the thought which introduces the myth—hinting at past decisions lying behind the current situation of the souls we encounter. On another, it surfaces in the contrast between our hollows and the real world above. The real world, it is implied, can be reached even in this life, if we make sufficient effort: weakness, slowness, and delusion are what prevent us; if we had the strength, we could reach it like a bird flying aloft or a fish swimming up to the air (109c2–110a1). This makes good sense if we regard the real world as representing the world of the Forms, which we can, with difficulty, access in this life by directing our gaze away from the sensible world. In addition, the earth's surface is the place where good souls live after death. It thus serves a dual function, mapping the life we opt to live now directly on to our fate after death.

The motif of choice is further underscored by the aspirational language applied to the real world, which, as I commented earlier, encourages us to identify with those who rise to the surface, rather than the ants and frogs in the hollows. The target of this rhetorically charged presentation is not the figures of the myth—their choices have already been made—but the reader, whose choice still lies in the present and future. The reader, therefore, is encouraged to regard herself as 'deciding' or 'choosing' as she reads, and to take responsibility for her future. Her response to the situation evoked by the myth thereby becomes the dramatic focus of the narrative, transforming her from a vicariously concerned onlooker to a person whose involvement is crucial to the resolution of the implied drama. This is the point of Socrates' concluding remark at 114c6–9, where he indicates that what is important about his narration is its impact on the way Simmias (and everyone else) lives: 'But, Simmias, because of these things which we have set out, it is necessary to make every effort to acquire virtue and wisdom in life; for the prize is fine and the hope is great' (*τούτων δὴ ἕνεκα χρὴ ὧν διεληλύθαμεν, ὦ Σιμμία, πᾶν ποιεῖν ὥστε ἀρετῆς καὶ φρονήσεως ἐν τῷ βίῳ μετασχεῖν· καλὸν γὰρ τὸ ἆθλον καὶ ἡ ἐλπὶς μεγάλη*).

Phaedo's myth cannot itself transform the way we live, for the beliefs it offers us are not yet grounded in our own thought. For true progress, an agent needs to develop a cognitive-affective engagement with the right way to live, and this can only happen through extended philosophical activity, not reading alone: as we have seen, the dialogues constantly ask us to see our literary experiences for what they are; and they constantly point towards, and attempt to generate, further investigation that can confirm, reject, or qualify the ideas and insights they themselves present. Yet in offering the reader an immediate and affectively charged engagement with Socrates' vision, the dialogue gives her a taste of what it would be like to hold a new basic belief in such a way that it informed her view of her whole life. In doing so, it shows us, in a sense, what we are aiming for in philosophizing, and gives us an understanding of what it would be like to be in that state.[33] Though her reaction has not been grounded and confirmed as it needs to be, the reader is engaged in the right sort of way, and this is something we could not gain through a description alone. In such a case, we might say, the process of reading functions as a weaker analogue of true philosophical activity, in that it achieves (to a less satisfactory degree) what real-life philosophical activity aims at, thereby helping the reader along the path to virtue.

Plato's development of the dialogue form, it has been suggested, may in part have been a response to a crisis of confidence in public methods of debate and an anxiety about citizens' mode of engaging in public affairs[34]—a matter in which, as we have seen, receivership is of central importance. As Cleon puts it, in his address to the Athenians in Thucydides' account of the Mytilenian debate:

> *'You have become regular speech-goers (θεαταί), and as for action, you merely listen to accounts of it; if something is to be done in the future you estimate the possibilities by hearing a good speech on the subject, and as for the past you rely not so much on the facts which you have seen with your own eyes as on what you have heard about them in some clever piece of verbal criticism... You are simply victims of your own pleasure in listening, and are more like an audience (θεαταῖς) sitting at the feet of a professional lecturer than a parliament discussing matters of state'.*
>
> Thucydides, *Peloponnesian War*, 3.38.4–7, trans. Warner (1954)

A *theoros* or *theates* is both a receiver and an actor; yet in Cleon's analysis, the Athenians' approach to looking and listening is such that it undermines a healthy basis for action. The two aspects of *theoria* have become separate, and are in conflict. For the philosophical *theoros*, by contrast, this is not the case: he is someone who, in a civic context, is an observer and a receiver, and who also has the

33 Cf. Press (1995) on Plato's dialogues as enactments.
34 Osborne (2007b).

wider vision, the self-motivation, and the self-discipline to make independent decisions and to act on them. Being a productive receiver, therefore, is an active accomplishment, and a political one. By training us to become good receivers, as I have argued that the dialogues do, Plato's texts make a direct contribution to our ability to contribute productively in civic life; and by establishing themselves as an arena for the development of active receivers, they are fully engaged with the political concerns of the time.

Despite initial impressions, *Phaedo*, I suggest, prompts us to become such active receivers. The picture of reality the myth presents to our 'vision' offers us the motivation to choose a philosophical life; and the myth's handling of character, action, and the motif of choice directs our attention towards ourselves, encouraging us to take responsibility for our own decisions and actions. Straight afterwards, Plato's closing account of the death of Socrates brings us back to the real world, and to the realities of civic choice and action. As Plato makes plain, the emotions evoked by Socrates' death are a challenge for his companions as much as for Socrates himself; at a further remove, they challenge a reader's ability to respond appropriately to Socrates' death. In doing so, the dialogue tests and develops the reader's dialectical virtue, giving her an idea of what it means to apply philosophical insights to a situation of both personal and civic relevance. While pointing her beyond the text to the world of civic action, therefore, the dialogue also prepares her for the challenges she will face, in learning and in life. As such, while reading can never, as *Phaedrus* emphasizes, itself be sufficient for philosophical progress, the dialogue helps its reader to bridge the gap between receiving and acting, supporting her progression towards philosophical and civic virtue.

References

Ackrill, J. L. (1997a) *Essays on Plato and Aristotle*. Oxford.

——(1997b) 'In defence of Platonic division' in Ackrill (1997a), 93–109.

Adam, J. (1890) *Plato:* Euthyphro. Cambridge.

——(1938) *The* Republic *of Plato*. Cambridge.

Adler, M. J. (ed.) (1984) *The Paideia Program: An Educational Syllabus*. London and New York.

Andiç, M. (1997) 'Commentary on Matthews', *Proceedings of the Boston Area Colloquium in Ancient Philosophy* 13, 56–68.

Annas, J. (1981) *An Introduction to Plato's* Republic. Oxford.

——(1982a) 'Plato's myths of judgement', *Phronesis* 27, 119–43.

——(1982b) 'Plato on the triviality of literature' in Moravcsik and Temko (eds) (1982), 1–28.

——(1992) 'Plato the sceptic' in Klagge and Smith (eds) (1992), 43–72.

——(1993) *The Morality of Happiness*. Oxford.

——(1999) *Platonic Ethics, Old and New*. Ithaca and London.

——(2002) 'What are Plato's "middle" dialogues in the middle of?' in Annas and Rowe (eds) (2002), 1–23.

Annas, J. and Rowe, C. (eds) (2002) *New Perspectives on Plato, Modern and Ancient*. Cambridge, MA and London.

Annas, J. and Waterfield, R. (1995) *Plato:* Statesman. Cambridge.

Anton, J. P. and Kustas, G. L. (eds) (1971) *Essays on Ancient Greek Philosophy*. Albany.

Arieti, J. A. (1991) *Interpreting Plato: The Dialogues as Drama*. Lanham, MD.

——(1993) 'Plato's philosophical *Antiope*: the *Gorgias*' in Press (ed.) (1993a), 197–214.

——(1995) 'How to read a Platonic dialogue' in Gonzalez (ed.) (1995a), 119–32.

Asmis, E. (1992) 'Plato on poetic creativity' in Kraut (ed.) (1992a), 338–64.

Atherton, C. (1988) 'Hand over fist: the failure of Stoic rhetoric', *Classical Quarterly* 38, 392–427.

Ausland, H. W. (1997) 'On reading Plato mimetically', *The American Journal of Philosophy* 118, 371–416.

——(2000) 'Who speaks for whom in the *Timaeus–Critias*?' in Press (ed.) (2000a), 183–98.

Bakhtin, M. M. (1981) *The Dialogic Imagination: Four Essays*, edited by M. Holquist and translated by C. Emerson and M. Holquist. Austin.

Baragwanath, E. (2008) *Motivation and Narrative in Herodotus*. Oxford.

Barber, B. R. (1996) 'Misreading democracy: Peter Euben and the *Gorgias*' in Ober and Hedrick (eds) (1996), 361–75.

Barker, A. (1976) 'The digression in the "Theaetetus"', *Journal of the History of Philosophy* 14, 457–62.

Barker, A. and Warner, M. (eds) (1992a) *The Language of the Cave*. Edmonton.

——(1992b) 'Introduction' in Barker and Warner (eds) (1992a), 1–11.

Barnes, J. (1969) 'Aristotle's theory of demonstration', *Phronesis* 14, 123–52.

——(1981) 'Proof and the syllogism' in Berti (ed.) (1981), 17–59.

——(1993) *Aristotle:* Posterior Analytics. Oxford.

——(ed.) (1984) *The Complete Works of Aristotle: The Revised Oxford Translation*. Princeton and Guildford.

Barthes, R. (1975) *S/Z*, translated by Richard Miller. London.

Bedu-Addo, J. T. (1984) 'Recollection and the argument "from a hypothesis" in Plato's *Meno*', *Journal of Hellenic Studies* 104, 1–14.

Belfiore, E. (1980) '*Elenchus, Epode*, and magic: Socrates as silenus', *Phoenix* 34, 128–37.

——(1984) 'Dialectic with the reader in Plato's *Symposium*', *Maia* 36, 137–49.

Benitez, E. (2000) 'Cowardice, moral philosophy, and saying what you think' in Press (ed.) (2000a), 83–98.

Benson, H. H. (1995) 'The dissolution of the problem of the elenchus', *Oxford Studies in Ancient Philosophy* 13, 45–112.

——(2000) *Socratic Wisdom: The Model of Knowledge in Plato's Early Dialogues*. New York and Oxford.

——(2003) 'Review of "Turning toward philosophy: literary and dramatic aspects in Plato's dialogues." Jill Gordon', *Philosophy and Phenomenological Research* 66, 743–5.

——(ed.) (2006) *A Companion to Plato*. Blackwell, Oxford.

Berti, E. (ed.) (1981) *Aristotle on Science: the* Posterior Analytics. Padova.

Beversluis, J. (2000) *Cross-Examining Socrates: A Defense of the Interlocutors in Plato's Early Dialogues*. Cambridge.

——(2006) 'A defence of dogmatism in the Interpretation of Plato', *Oxford Studies in Ancient Philosophy* 31, 85–111.

Blank, D. (1993) 'The arousal of emotion in Plato's dialogues', *Classical Quarterly* 43, 428–39.

Blondell, R. (2000) 'Letting Plato speak for himself: character and method in the *Republic*' in Press (ed.) (2000a), 127–46.

——(2002) *The Play of Character in Plato's Dialogues*. Cambridge.

——(2003) 'The man with no name: Socrates and the visitor from Elea' in Michelini (ed.) (2003a), 247–66.

——(2005) 'From fleece to fabric: weaving culture in Plato's *Statesman*', *Oxford Studies in Ancient Philosophy* 28, 23–75.

Bluck, R. S. (1975) *Plato's* Sophist. Manchester.

Blundell, M. W. (1989) *Helping Friends and Harming Enemies. A Study in Sophocles and Greek Ethics.* Cambridge.

——(1992) 'Character and meaning in Plato's *Hippias Minor*' in Klagge and Smith (eds) (1992), 131–72.

Bobonich, C. (1996) 'Reading the *Laws*' in Gill and McCabe (eds) (1996), 249–82.

Bonjour, L. and Sosa, E. (2003) *Epistemic Justification. Internalism vs. Externalism. Foundations vs. Virtues.* Malden, MA and Oxford.

Booth, W. C. (1961) *The Rhetoric of Fiction.* Chicago.

——(1974) *A Rhetoric of Irony.* Chicago.

Bostock, D. (1986) *Plato's* Phaedo. Oxford.

——(1988) *Plato's* Theaetetus. Oxford.

Brandwood, L. (1990) *The Chronology of Plato's Dialogues.* Cambridge.

Branham, R. B. (ed.) (2002) *Bakhtin and the Classics.* Illinois.

Brickhouse, T. C. and Smith, N. D. (1994) *Plato's Socrates.* Oxford and New York.

——(2002) 'The Socratic elenchos?' in Scott (ed.) (2002), 145–57.

Brooks, P. (1984) *Reading for the Plot: Design and Intention in Narrative.* Oxford and New York.

Brouwer, R. (2002) 'Sagehood and the Stoics', *Oxford Studies in Ancient Philosophy* 23, 181–224.

Brown, L. (1998) 'Innovation and continuity: the battle of gods and giants, *Sophist* 245–249' in Gentzler (ed.) (1998), 181–207.

Brumbaugh, R. S. (1988) 'Digression and dialogue: the seventh letter and Plato's literary form' in Griswold (ed.) (1988a), 84–92.

Brunschwig, J. and Nussbaum, M. (eds) (1993) *Passions and Perceptions.* Cambridge.

Burger, R. (1980) *Plato's* Phaedrus*: A Defense of a Philosophic Art of Writing.* University, Alabama.

Burges, G. (1865–77) *The Works of Plato: A New and Literal Version, Chiefly from the Text of Stallbaum, Vol VI.* London.

Burnet, J. (1911) *Plato's Phaedo.* Oxford.

——(1924) *Plato's* Euthyphro, Apology of Socrates *and* Crito. *Edited with Notes.* Oxford.

Burnyeat, M. F. (1977) 'Socratic midwifery, Platonic inspiration', *Bulletin of the Institute of Classical Studies* 24, 7–16.

——(1980a) 'Aristotle on learning to be good' in Rorty (ed.) (1980), 69–92.

——(1980b) 'Socrates and the jury: paradoxes in Plato's distinction between knowledge and true belief', *Proceedings of the Aristotelian Society, Supplementary Volume* 54, 173–91.

——(1981) 'Aristotle on understanding knowledge' in Berti (ed.) (1981), 97–139.

——(1985) 'Sphinx without a secret', *New York Review of Books* 32, 30–6.

Burnyeat, M. F. (1990) *The* Theaetetus *of Plato*. Indianapolis and Cambridge.

——(1992) 'Utopia and fantasy: the practicability of Plato's ideally just city' in Hopkins and Savile (eds) (1992), 175–87.

——(1997a) 'First words: a valedictory lecture', *Proceedings of the Cambridge Philological Society* 43, 1–20.

——(1997b) 'The impiety of Socrates', *Ancient Philosophy* 17, 1–12.

——(2009) 'Eikos muthos' in Partenie (ed.) (2009a), 167–86.

Buxton, R. (1994) *Imaginary Greece. The Contexts of Mythology*. Cambridge.

——(ed.) (1999) *From Myth to Reason? Studies in the Development of Greek Thought*. Oxford.

Calef, S. W. (1995) 'Piety and the unity of virtue in *Euthyphro* 11E–14C', *Oxford Studies in Ancient Philosophy* 13, 1–25.

Campbell, L. (1973) *The* Sophistes *and* Politicus *of Plato*. New York.

Carone, G. R. (2001) 'Akrasia in the *Republic*: does Plato change his mind?', *Oxford Studies in Ancient Philosophy* 20, 107–48.

——(2004) 'Calculating machines or leaky jars? The moral psychology of Plato's *Gorgias*', *Oxford Studies in Ancient Philosophy* 26, 55–96.

Carpenter, M. and Polansky, R. M. (2002) 'Variety of Socratic elenchi' in Scott (ed.) (2002), 89–100.

Cassam, Q. (ed.) (1994) *Self-Knowledge*. Oxford.

Cavini, W. (1995) 'Naming and argument: diaeretic logic in Plato's *Statesman*' in Rowe (ed.) (1995b), 123–38.

Chappell, T. D. J. (1993) 'The virtues of Thrasymachus', *Phronesis* 38, 1–17.

Chatman, S. (1986) 'Characters and narrators: filter, center, slant, and interest-focus', *Poetics Today* 7, 189–204.

——(1990) *Coming to Terms: The Rhetoric of Narrative in Fiction and Film*. Ithaca.

Clay, D. (1972) 'Socrates' mulishness and heroism', *Phronesis* 17, 53–60.

——(1975) 'The tragic and comic poet of the *Symposium*', *Arion* 2, 238–61.

——(1983) *Lucretius and Epicurus*. Ithaca and London.

——(1987) 'Gaps in the "universe" of the Platonic dialogues', *Proceedings of the Boston Area Colloquium in Ancient Philosophy* 3, 131–57.

——(1988) 'Reading the *Republic*' in Griswold (ed.) (1988a), 19–33.

——(1992) 'Plato's first words' in Dunn and Cole (eds) (1992), 113–30.

——(1994) 'The origins of the Socratic dialogue' in Vander Waerdt (ed.) (1994), 23–47.

——(2000) *Platonic Questions: Dialogues with the Silent Philosopher*. University Park, PA.

Cohen, J. R. (2002) 'Philosophy is education is politics: the dramatic interlude in the *Protagoras*', *Ancient Philosophy* 22, 1–20.

Cohen, S. M. (1973) 'Plato's method of division' in Moravcsik (1973a), 181–91.

Cohen, S. M. and Keyt, D. (1992) 'Analysing Plato's arguments: Plato and Platonism' in Klagge and Smith (eds) (1992), 173–200.

Conte, G. B. (1986) *The Rhetoric of Imitation: Genre and Poetic Memory in Virgil and Other Latin Poets*. Ithaca, NY and London.

——(1994) *Genres and Readers: Lucretius, Love Elegy, Pliny's Encyclopaedia*. Baltimore and London.

Cooper, J. M. (1999a) *Reason and Emotion: Essays on Ancient Moral Psychology and Ethical Theory*. Princeton.

——(1999b) 'Socrates and Plato in Plato's *Gorgias*' in Cooper (1999a), 29–75.

——(1999c) 'The unity of virtue' in Cooper (1999a), 76–117.

Cornford, F. M. (1941) *The* Republic *of Plato*. Oxford.

Coventry, L. (1990) 'The role of the interlocutor in Plato's dialogues: theory and practice' in Pelling (ed.) (1990a), 174–96.

Cribiore, R. (2001) *Gymnastics of the Mind: Greek Education in Hellenistic and Roman Egypt*. Princeton and Oxford.

Crombie, I. M. (1994) 'Socratic definition' in Day (ed.) (1994), 172–207.

Cross, R. C. and Woozley, A. D. (1964) *Plato's* Republic: *A Philosophical Commentary*. London.

Cupitt, D. (1991) *What is a Story?* London.

Davidson, D. (1994) 'Plato's philosopher' in Irwin and Nussbaum (eds) (1994), 179–94.

Davis, T. F. and Womack, K. (2002) *Formalist Criticism and Reader-Response Theory*. Basingstoke.

Day, J. M. (ed.) (1994) *Plato's* Meno *in Focus*. London.

De Jong, I. J. F. (2001) *A Narratological Commentary on the* Odyssey. Cambridge.

——(2004) 'Introduction: narratological theory on narrators, narratees, and narratives' in De Jong, Nunlist, and Bowie (eds) (2004), 1–10.

De Jong, I. J. F. and Nunlist, R. (eds) (2007) *Time in Ancient Greek Literature: Studies in Ancient Greek Narrative, Volume Two*. Leiden and Boston.

De Jong, I. J. F., Nunlist, R., and Bowie, A. (eds) (2004) *Narrators, Narratees and Narratives in Ancient Greek Literature: Studies in Ancient Greek Narrative*. Leiden.

De Jong, I. J. F. and Sullivan, J. P. (eds) (1994) *Modern Critical Theory and Classical Literature*. Leiden.

De Romilly, J. (1975) *Magic and Rhetoric in Ancient Greece*. Cambridge, MA and London.

De Vries, G. J. (1969) *A Commentary on the* Phaedrus *of Plato*. Amsterdam.

Depew, M. and Obbink, D. (eds) (2000) *Matrices of Genre: Authors, Canons and Society*. Cambridge, MA and London.

Derrida, J. (1981a) *Dissemination*, translated by B. Johnson. London.

——(1981b) 'Plato's pharmacy' in Derrida (1981a), 61–171.

Desjardins, R. (1988) 'Why dialogues? Plato's serious play' in Griswold (ed.) (1988a), 110–25.
——(1990) *The Rational Enterprise: Logos in Plato's* Theaetetus. Albany.
Dewald, C. (1997) 'Wanton kings, pickled heroes, and gnomic founding fathers: strategies of meaning at the end of Herodotus' *Histories*' in Roberts, Dunn, and Fowler (eds) (1997), 62–82.
Dickoff, J. and James, P. (1976) 'Sophistry and generation: in response to Turbayne and Sichel' in Simmons (ed.) (1976), 153–8.
Dillon, J. (1999) 'A case-study in commentary: the neoplatonic exegesis of the *Prooimia* of Plato's dialogues' in Most (ed.) (1999), 206–22.
Dodds, E. R. (1959) *Plato:* Gorgias. Oxford.
Doherty, L. (2001) 'The snares of the *Odyssey*: a feminist and narratological reading' in Harrison (ed.) (2001a), 117–33.
Dorion, L. A. (1995) *Aristote: Les Refutations Sophistiques.* Paris and Quebec.
Dorter, K. (1994) *Form and Good in Plato's Eleatic Dialogues: The* Parmenides, Theaetetus, Sophist, *and* Statesman. Berkeley and London.
Douglas, M. (2007) *Thinking in Circles. An Essay on Ring Composition.* New Haven and London.
Dunn, F. M. (1997) 'Ends and means in Euripides' *Heracles*' in Roberts, Dunn, and Fowler (eds) (1997), 83–111.
Dunn, F. M. and Cole, T. (eds) (1992) *Beginnings in Classical Literature.* Cambridge.
Eagleton, T. (1996) *Literary Theory: An Introduction. Second Edition.* Oxford.
Easterling, P. E. (1990) 'Constructing character in Greek tragedy' in Pelling (ed.) (1990a), 83–99.
Edelstein, L. (1949) 'The function of the myth in Plato's philosophy', *Journal of the History of Ideas* 10, 463–81.
Edmunds, L. (2001) *Intertextuality and the Reading of Roman Poetry.* Baltimore and London.
Edwards, M. W. (1991) *The* Iliad*: A Commentary. Volume V: Books 17–20.* Cambridge.
Emlyn-Jones, C. (1991) *Plato:* Euthyphro. *Text, with Introduction, Commentary and Vocabulary.* London.
Euben, P. J. (1996) 'Reading democracy: "Socratic" dialogues and the political education of democratic citizens' in Ober and Hedrick (eds) (1996), 327–59.
Everson, S. (1998) 'The incoherence of Thrasymachus', *Oxford Studies in Ancient Philosophy* 16, 99–131.
——(ed.) (1990) *Cambridge Companions to Ancient Thought I: Epistemology.* Cambridge.

Falkner, T. M., Felson, N. and Konstan, D. (eds) (1999) *Contextualizing Classics: Ideology, Performance, Dialogue. Essays in Honor of John J. Peradotto*. Lanham, MD.
Farness, J. (2003) 'Glaucon's couch, or mimesis and the art of the *Republic*' in Michelini (ed.) (2003a), 99–121.
Ferrari, G. R. F. (1987) *Listening to the Cicadas: A study of Plato's* Phaedrus. Cambridge.
——(1989) 'Plato and poetry' in Kennedy (ed.) (1989), 92–148.
——(1997) 'Strauss's Plato', *Arion* 5.2, 36–65.
——(2003a) 'Comments on Nightingale and Szlezák' in Michelini (ed.) (2003a), 241–5.
——(2003b) *City and Soul in Plato's* Republic. Sankt Augustin.
Fine, G. J. (1979) 'Knowledge and *Logos* in the *Theaetetus*', *Philosophical Review* 88, 366–97.
——(1990) 'Knowledge and belief in *Republic* V–VII' in Everson (ed.) (1990), 85–115.
——(ed.) (1999) *Plato 2: Ethics, Politics, Religion, and the Soul*. Oxford.
Fish, S. E. (1967) *Surprised by Sin: The Reader in* Paradise Lost. London and New York.
——(1970) 'Literature in the reader: affective stylistics', *New Literary History* 2.1, 123–62.
——(1989) *Doing What Comes Naturally: Change, Rhetoric, and the Practice of Theory in Literary and Legal Studies*. Oxford.
Ford, A. (2008) 'The beginnings of dialogue: Socratic discourse and fourth century prose', in Goldhill (ed.) (2008), 29–44.
Fowler, D. P. (1989) 'First thoughts on closure: problems and prospects', *Materiali e discussioni per l'analisi dei testi classici* 22, 75–122.
——(1997) 'Second thoughts on closure' in Roberts, Dunn, and Fowler (eds) (1997), 3–22.
——(2000a) *Roman Constructions: Readings in Postmodern Latin*. Oxford.
——(2000b) 'Postmodernism, romantic irony, and classical closure' in Fowler (2000a), 5–33.
——(2000c) 'The didactic plot' in Depew and Obbink (eds) (2000), 205–19.
Fowler, D. P. and Fowler, P. G. (1996) 'Literary theory and classical studies' in Hornblower and Spawforth (eds) (1996), 871–5.
Fowler, P. G. (1997) 'Lucretian conclusions' in Roberts, Dunn, and Fowler (eds) (1997), 112–38.
Frede, D. (1989) 'The soul's silent dialogue: a non-aporetic reading of the *Theaetetus*', *Proceedings of the Cambridge Philological Society* 35, 20–49.
——(1996) 'The hedonist's conversion: the role of Socrates in the *Philebus*' in Gill and McCabe (eds) (1996), 213–48.
Frede, M. (1992a) 'Plato's arguments and the dialogue form' in Klagge and Smith (eds) (1992), 201–19.

Frede, M. (1992b) 'The *Sophist* on false statements' in Kraut (ed.) (1992a), 397–424.

——(1996) 'The literary form of the *Sophist*' in Gill and McCabe (eds) (1996), 135–51.

Furley, W. D. (1985) 'The figure of Euthyphro in Plato's dialogue', *Phronesis* 30, 201–8.

Gale, M. R. (1994) *Myth and Poetry in Lucretius*. Cambridge.

Gallop, D. (1975) *Plato:* Phaedo. Oxford.

——(2003) 'The rhetoric of philosophy: Socrates' swan-song' in Michelini (ed.) (2003a), 313–32.

Gardner, F. Cairns, J., and Lawton, D. (eds) (2000) *Education for Values: Morals, Ethics and Citizenship in Contemporary Teaching*. London.

Gentzler, J. (ed.) (1998) *Method in Ancient Philosophy*. Oxford.

Gerson, L. P. (2000) 'Plato *Absconditus*' in Press (ed.) (2000a), 201–10.

Gibson, R. K. and Kraus, C. S. (eds) (2002) *The Classical Commentary: Histories, Practices and Theory*. Leiden.

Gifford, M. (2001) 'Dramatic dialectic in *Republic* Book 1', *Oxford Studies in Ancient Philosophy* 20, 35–106.

Gill, C. (1988) 'Review of H. R. Scodel, "Diaeresis and myth in Plato's *Statesman*"', *Classical Review* 38, 225–6.

——(1990) 'The character-personality distinction' in Pelling (ed.) (1990a), 1–31.

——(1992) 'Dogmatic dialectic in *Phaedrus* 276–7?' in Rossetti (ed.) (1992), 156–72.

——(1993) 'Plato on falsehood—not fiction' in Gill and Wiseman (eds) (1993), 38–87.

——(1995) 'Rethinking constitutionalism in *Statesman* 291–303' in Rowe (1995b) (ed.), 292–365.

——(1996a) *Personality in Greek Epic, Tragedy, and Philosophy: The Self in Dialogue*. Oxford.

——(1996b) 'Afterword: dialectic and the dialogue form in late Plato' in Gill and McCabe (eds) (1996), 283–311.

——(2001) 'Speaking up for Plato's interlocutors: a discussion of J. Beverluis, *Cross-examining Socrates*', *Oxford Studies in Ancient Philosophy* 20, 297–321.

——(2002) 'Dialectic and the dialogue form' in Annas and Rowe (eds) (2002), 145–71.

——(2006) 'The Platonic dialogue' in Gill and Pellegrin (eds) (2006), 136–50.

Gill, C. and McCabe, M. M. (eds) (1996) *Form and Argument in Late Plato*. Oxford.

Gill, C. and Wiseman, T. P. (eds) (1993) *Lies and Fiction in the Ancient World*. Exeter.

Gill, M. L. (1996) 'Introduction' in Gill and Ryan (eds) (1996), 1–116.

Gill, M. L. and Pellegrin, P. (eds) (2006) *A Companion to Ancient Philosophy*. Blackwell, Oxford.

Gill, M. L. and Ryan, P. (eds) (1996) Plato: *Parmenides*. Indianapolis.

Goldhill, S. (1986) *Reading Greek Tragedy*. Cambridge.

——(1990) 'Character and action, representational and reading: Greek tragedy and its critics' in Pelling (ed.) (1990a), 100–27.

——(1999) 'Programme notes' in Goldhill and Osborne (eds) (1999), 1–29.

——(2002) *The Invention of Prose*. Oxford.

——(ed.) (2008a) *The End of Dialogue in Antiquity*. Cambridge.

——(2008b) 'Introduction: why don't Christians do dialogue?' in Goldhill (ed.) (2008a) 1–11.

Goldhill, S. and Osborne, R. (eds) (1999) *Performance Culture and Athenian Democracy*. Cambridge.

Gonzalez, F. J. (ed.) (1995a) *The Third Way: New Directions in Platonic Studies*. Lanham, MD.

——(1995b) 'Introduction: a short history of Platonic interpretation and the "third way"' in Gonzalez (ed.) (1995a), 1–22.

——(1995c) 'Self-knowledge, practical knowledge, and insight: Plato's dialectic and the dialogue form' in Gonzalez (ed.) (1995a), 155–87.

——(1998) *Dialectic and Dialogue: Plato's Practice of Philosophical Inquiry*. Evanston, IL.

——(2000) 'The Eleatic Stranger: his master's voice?' in Press (ed.) (2000a), 161–81.

——(2002) 'The Socratic elenchus as constructive protreptic' in Scott (ed.) (2002), 161–82.

——(2003) 'How to read a Platonic prologue: *Lysis* 203a–207d' in Michelini (ed.) (2003a), 15–44.

Gordon, J. (1999) *Turning Toward Philosophy: Literary Device and Dramatic Structure in Plato's Dialogues*. University Park, PA.

Gould, J. (1992) 'Plato and performance' in Barker and Warner (eds) (1992a), 13–25.

Greenwood, E. (2008) 'Fictions of dialogue in Thucydides' in Goldhill (ed.) (2008a), 15–28.

Griswold, C. L. (1986) *Self-Knowledge in Plato's* Phaedrus. New Haven and London.

——(ed.) (1988a) *Platonic Writings, Platonic Readings*. New York and London.

——(1988b) 'Preface' in Griswold (ed.) (1988a), ix–xvii.

——(1988c) 'Introduction' in Griswold (ed.) (1988a), 1–15.

——(1988d) 'Plato's metaphilosophy: why Plato wrote dialogues' in Griswold (ed.) (1988a), 143–67.

——(1999) '*E Pluribus Unum?* On the Platonic "Corpus"', *Ancient Philosophy* 19, 361–97.

Griswold, C. L. (2002) 'Comments on Kahn' in Annas and Rowe (eds) (2002), 129–44.
Guthrie, W. K. C. (1975) *A History of Greek Philosophy, Vol. IV*. Cambridge.
——(1976) 'Rhetoric and philosophy: the unity of the *Phaedrus*' in Simmons (ed.) (1976), 117–24.
——(1978) *A History of Greek Philosophy, Vol. V*. Cambridge.
Hackforth, R. (1952) *Plato's* Phaedrus, *Translated with Introduction and Commentary*. Cambridge.
Hadot, P. (1995) *Philosophy as a Way of Life: Spiritual Exercises from Socrates to Foucault*, edited with introduction by A. I. Davidson and translated by M. Chase. Oxford.
Halliwell, S. (1988) *Plato:* Republic *10*. Warminster.
——(1990) 'Traditional Greek conceptions of character' in Pelling (ed.) (1990a), 32–59.
——(1991) 'Review of "Heath (M.) Unity in Greek poetics"', *Journal of Hellenic Studies* 111, 230–1.
Halperin, D. M. (1992) 'Plato and the erotics of narrativity', in Klagge and Smith (eds) (1992), 93–129.
Hardie, P. (1993) *The Epic Successors of Virgil: A Study in the Dynamics of Tradition*. Cambridge.
——(1997) 'Closure in Latin epic' in Roberts, Dunn, and Fowler (eds) (1997), 139–62.
Harris, W. V. (1989) *Ancient Literacy*. Cambridge, MA and London.
Harrison, S. J. (ed.) (1999a) *Oxford Readings in the Roman Novel*. Oxford.
——(1999b) 'Introduction: twentieth-century scholarship on the Roman novel' in Harrison (ed.) (1999a), xi–xxxix.
——(ed.) (2001a) *Texts, Ideas and the Classics: Scholarship, Theory and Classical Literature*. Oxford.
——(2001b) 'General introduction: working together' in Harrison (ed.) (2001a), 1–18.
Hart, R. and Tejera, V. (eds) (1997) *Plato's Dialogues and the Dialogical Approach*. New York.
Harte, V. (2002) *Plato on Parts and Wholes: The Metaphysics of Structure*. Oxford.
——(2010) '*Republic* X and the role of the audience in art', *Oxford Studies in Ancient Philosophy* 38, 69–96.
Havelock, E. A. (1963) *Preface to Plato*. Oxford.
Heath, M. (1989a) 'The unity of Plato's *Phaedrus*', *Oxford Studies in Ancient Philosophy* 7, 151–73.
——(1989b) 'The unity of the *Phaedrus*: a postscript', *Oxford Studies in Ancient Philosophy* 7, 189–91.
——(1989c) *Unity in Greek Poetics*. Oxford.

Helmbold, W. C. and Holter, W. B. (1952) 'The unity of the *Phaedrus*', *University of California Publications in Classical Philology* 14, 387–417.

Hershbell, J. P. (1995) 'Reflections on the orality and literacy of Plato's dialogues' in Gonzalez (ed.) (1995a), 25–39.

Hinds, S. (1998) *Allusion and Intertext: Dynamics of Appropriation in Roman Poetry*. Cambridge.

Hobbs, A. (2000) *Plato and the Hero: Courage, Manliness and the Impersonal Good*. Cambridge.

Holub, R. C. (1984) *Reception Theory: A Critical Introduction*. London.

Hopkins, J. and Savile, A. (eds) (1992) *Psychoanalysis, Mind and Art: Perspectives on Richard Wollheim*. Oxford.

Hornblower, S. and Spawforth, A. (eds) (1996) *The Oxford Classical Dictionary. Third Edition*. Oxford.

Howland, J. (1991) 'Re-reading Plato: the problem of Platonic chronology', *Phoenix* 45, 189–214.

——(2003) 'Plato's political writing and the cultivation of souls' in Michelini (ed.) (2003a), 77–98.

Hyland, D. A. (1981) *The Virtue of Philosophy: An Interpretation of Plato's* Charmides. Athens, Ohio.

——(1995) *Finitude and Transcendence in the Platonic Dialogues*. Albany.

Ierodiakonou, K. (ed.) (1999) *Topics in Stoic Philosophy*. Oxford.

Inwood, B. (2005) *Reading Seneca: Stoic Philosophy at Rome*. Oxford.

Irwin, T. H. (1986) 'Coercion and objectivity in Plato's dialectic', *Revue Internationale de Philosophie* 156, 49–74.

——(1988a) *Aristotle's First Principles*. Oxford.

——(1988b) 'Socrates and the tragic hero' in Pucci, P. (ed.) (1988), 55–83.

——(1995) *Plato's Ethics*. New York and Oxford.

——(1996) 'Art and philosophy in Plato's dialogues', *Phronesis* 41, 335–50.

——(1998) 'Common sense and Socratic method' in Gentzler (ed.) (1998), 29–66.

Irwin, T. H. and Nussbaum, M. C. (eds) (1994) *Virtue, Love, and Form: Essays in Memory of Gregory Vlastos*. Edmonton.

Iser, W. (1974) *The Implied Reader: Patterns of Communication in Prose Fiction from Bunyan to Beckett*. Baltimore and London.

——(1978) *The Act of Reading: A Theory of Aesthetic Response*. Baltimore and London.

Janaway, C. (1995) *Images of Excellence. Plato's Critique of the Arts*. Oxford.

Jauss, H. R. (1982a) *Toward an Aesthetic of Reception*, translated by Timothy Bahti. Minneapolis.

——(1982b) 'Literary history as a challenge to literary theory' in Jauss (1982a), 3–45.

Joseph, H. W. B. (1935) *Essays in Ancient and Modern Philosophy*. Oxford.

Judson, L. and Karasmanis, V. (eds) (2006) *Remembering Socrates: Philosophical Essays*. Oxford.

Kahn, C. H. (1983) 'Drama and dialectic in Plato's *Gorgias*', *Oxford Studies in Ancient Philosophy* 1, 75–121.

——(1986) 'Plato's methodology in the *Laches*', *Revue Internationale de Philosophie* 156, 7–21.

——(1996) *Plato and the Socratic Dialogue. The Philosophical Use of a Literary Form*. Cambridge.

——(2002) 'On Platonic chronology' in Annas and Rowe (eds) (2002), 93–127.

——(2003) 'On the philosophical autonomy of a Platonic dialogue: the case of recollection' in Michelini (ed.) (2003a), 299–312.

Kamtekar, R. (2006) 'Speaking with the same voice as reason: personification in Plato's psychology', *Oxford Studies in Ancient Philosophy* 31, 167–202.

Karasmanis, V. (1988) 'Plato's *Republic*: the line and the Cave', *Apeiron* 21, 147–71.

Kennedy, G. A. (ed.) (1989) *The Cambridge History of Literary Criticism, Vol. I: Classical Criticism*. Cambridge.

Kerferd, G. B. (1947) 'The doctrine of Thrasymachus in Plato's *Republic*', *Durham University Journal* 9, 19–27.

——(1964) 'Thrasymachus and justice: a reply', *Phronesis* 9, 12–16.

——(1981) *The Sophistic Movement*. Cambridge.

King, J. (1987) 'Elenchus, self-blame and the Socratic paradox', *Review of Metaphysics* 41, 105–26.

Klagge, J. C. and Smith, N. D. (eds) (1992) *Methods of Interpreting Plato and His Dialogues. Oxford Studies in Ancient Philosophy, Supplementary Volume*. Oxford.

Klein, J. (1965) *A Commentary on Plato's* Meno. Chapel Hill.

Knox, P. and Foss, C. (eds) (1998) *Style and Tradition: Studies in Honour of Wendell Clausen*. Stuttgart and Leipzig.

Kosman, A. (1987) 'Commentary on Teloh', *Proceedings of the Boston Area Colloquium in Ancient Philosophy* 2, 39–43.

Kraus, C. S. (1998) 'Repetition and empire in the *Ad Urbe Condita*' in Knox and Foss (eds) (1998), 264–83.

Kraut, R. (1983) 'Comments on Gregory Vlastos, "The Socratic elenchus"', *Oxford Studies in Ancient Philosophy* 1, 59–70.

——(ed.) (1992a) *Cambridge Companion to Plato*. Cambridge.

——(1992b) 'Introduction to the study of Plato' in Kraut (ed.) (1992a), 1–50.

Krentz, A. A. (1983) 'Dramatic form and philosophical content in Plato's dialogues', *Philosophy and Literature* 7, 32–47.

Laird, A. (1999) *Powers of Expression, Expressions of Power: Speech Presentation and Latin Literature*. Oxford.

Lane, M. S. (1998) *Method and Politics in Plato's* Statesman. Cambridge.

——(2006) 'The evolution of *Eirōneia* in classical Greek texts: why Socratic *Eirōneia* is not Socratic irony', *Oxford Studies in Ancient Philosophy* 31, 49–83.

Lear, J. (1992) 'Inside and outside the *Republic*', *Phronesis* 27, 184–215.

Lebeck, A. (1972) 'The central myth of Plato's *Phaedrus*', *Greek, Roman and Byzantine Studies* 13, 267–90.

Ledger, G. R. (1989) *Re-Counting Plato: A Computer Analysis of Plato's Style.* Oxford.

Lee, E. N., Mourelatos, A. P. D., and Rorty, R. N. (eds) (1973) *Exegesis and Argument: Studies in Greek Philosophy Presented to Gregory Vlastos.* Assen.

Lesher, J. H. (2002) 'Parmenidean elenchos' in Scott (ed.) (2002), 19–35.

Lloyd, G. E. R. (1979) *Magic, Reason and Experience: Studies in the Origin and Development of Greek Science.* Cambridge.

Long, A. (2007) 'The form of Plato's *Republic*' in Osborne (ed.) (2007), 224–41.

——(2008) 'Plato's dialogues and a common rationale for dialogue form' in Goldhill (ed.) (2008), 45–59.

Long, A. A. (1996a) *Stoic Studies.* Cambridge.

——(1996b) 'Socrates in Hellenistic philosophy' in Long (1996a), 1–34.

——(1996c) 'Dialectic and the Stoic sage' in Long (1996a), 85–106.

——(1998) 'Plato's apologies and Socrates in the *Theaetetus*' in Gentzler (ed.) (1998), 113–36.

Lorenz, H. (2006) *The Brute Within: Appetitive Desire in Plato and Aristotle.* Oxford.

Louden, R. B. and Schollmeier, P. (eds) (1996) *The Greeks and Us: Essays in Honor of Arthur W. H. Adkins.* Chicago and London.

Lowe, N. J. (2000) *The Classical Plot and the Invention of Western Narrative.* Cambridge.

Lycos, K. (1987) *Plato on Justice and Power: Reading Book I of Plato's* Republic. Albany.

Mackay, E. A. (ed.) (1999) *Signs of Orality: The Oral Tradition and its Influence on the Greek and Roman World.* Leiden.

Mackenzie, M. M. (1981) *Plato on Punishment.* Berkeley and London.

——(1982) 'Paradox in Plato's *Phaedrus*', *Proceedings of the Cambridge Philological Society* 28, 64–76.

——(1986) 'Putting the *Cratylus* in its place', *Classical Quarterly* 36, 124–50.

——(1988a) 'The virtues of Socratic ignorance', *Classical Quarterly* 38, 331–50.

——(1988b) 'Impasse and explanation: from the *Lysis* to the *Phaedo*', *Archiv für Geschichte der Philosophie* 70, 15–45.

Macleod, C. (1983) *Collected Essays.* Oxford.

Malcolm, N. (1971) *Problems of Mind: Descartes to Wittgenstein.* London.

Mann, W. R. (2006) 'Plato in Tubingen', *Oxford Studies in Ancient Philosophy* 31, 349–400.

Mansfeld, J. (1994) *Prolegomena: Questions to be Answered Before the Study of an Author, or a Text*. Leiden.

——(1995) 'Insight by hindsight: intentional unclarity in Pre-Socratic proems', *Bulletin of the Institute of Classical Studies* 40, 225–32.

Martindale, C. (1993) *Redeeming the Text: Latin Poetry and the Hermeneutics of Reception*. Cambridge.

——(1996) 'Reception' in Hornblower and Spawforth (eds) (1996), 1294–5.

Matthews, G. B. (1997) 'The career of perplexity in Plato', *Proceedings of the Boston Area Colloquium in Ancient Philosophy* 13, 35–55.

——(1999) *Socratic Perplexity and the Nature of Philosophy*. Oxford.

May, H. E. (1997) 'Socratic ignorance and the therapeutic aim of the elenchus' in McPherran (ed.) (1997), 37–50.

McCabe, M. M. (1992) 'Myth, allegory and argument in Plato' in Barker and Warner (eds) (1992a), 47–67.

——(1994) *Plato's Individuals*. Princeton.

——(1996) 'Unity in the *Parmenides*: the unity of the *Parmenides*' in Gill and McCabe (eds) (1996), 5–47.

——(2000) *Plato and his Predecessors. The Dramatisation of Reason*. Cambridge.

——(2006) 'Form and the Platonic dialogues' in Benson (ed.) (2006), 39–54.

McKim, R. (1988) 'Shame and truth in Plato's *Gorgias*' in Griswold (ed.) (1988a), 34–48.

McPherran, M. L. (1985) 'Socratic piety in the *Euthyphro*', *Journal of the History of Philosophy* 23, 283–309.

——(ed.) (1997) *Wisdom, Ignorance and Virtue: New Essays in Socratic Studies*. Edmonton.

——(2003) 'The aporetic interlude and fifth elenchus of Plato's *Euthyphro*', *Oxford Studies in Ancient Philosophy* 25, 1–37.

Michelini, A. N. (ed.) (2003a) *Plato as Author: The Rhetoric of Philosophy*. Leiden and Boston.

——(2003b) 'Plato's Socratic Mask' in Michelini (ed.) (2003a), 45–65.

Miller, M. (1980) *The Philosopher in Plato's* Statesman. The Hague.

——(1986) *Plato's* Parmenides*: The Conversion of the Soul*. Princeton and Guildford.

——(1987) 'Commentary on Clay', *Proceedings of the Boston Area Colloquium in Ancient Philosophy* 3, 158–64.

——(1999) 'Platonic mimesis' in Falkner, Felson, and Konstan (eds) (1999), 253–66.

Mitsis, P. (1993) 'Committing philosophy on the reader: didactic coercion and reader autonomy in *De Rerum Natura*' in Schiesaro, Mitsis, and Clay (eds) (1993), 111–28.

Moes, M. (2000) *Plato's Dialogue Form and the Care of the Soul*. New York.
Moline, J. (1981) *Plato's Theory of Understanding*. Madison.
Monoson, S. S. (2000) *Plato's Democratic Entanglements: Athenian Politics and the Practice of Philosophy*. Princeton.
Moravcsik, J. M. E. (ed.) (1973a) *Patterns in Plato's Thought*. Dordrecht.
——(1973b) 'Plato's method of division' in Moravcsik (1973a), 158–80.
——(1973c) 'The anatomy of Plato's divisions' in Lee, Mourelatos, and Rorty (eds) (1973), 324–48.
——and Temko, P. (eds) (1982) *Plato on Beauty, Wisdom and the Arts*. Totowa, NJ.
Moreau, J. (1968) 'Aristote et la dialectique platonicienne' in Owen (ed.) (1968a), 80–90.
Morgan, K. A. (2000) *Myth and Philosophy from the Pre-Socratics to Plato*. Cambridge.
——(2002) 'Comments on Gill' in Annas and Rowe (eds) (2002), 173–87.
——(2003) 'Plato's dream: philosophy and fiction in the *Theaetetus*' in Panayotakis, Zimmerman, and Keulen (eds) (2003), 101–13.
——(2004) 'Plato' in De Jong, Nunlist, and Bowie (eds) (2004), 357–76.
——(2007) 'Plato' in De Jong and Nunlist (eds) (2007) 345–68.
Morgan, T. (1998) *Literate Education in the Hellenistic and Roman Worlds*. Cambridge.
Mossman, J. (1995) *Wild Justice: A Study of Euripides'* Hecuba. Oxford.
Most, G. W. (ed.) (1999) *Commentaries-Kommentare*. Gottingen.
Murray, P. (1999) 'What is a *Muthos* for Plato?' in Buxton (ed.) (1999), 251–62.
Nails, D. (1995) *Agora, Academy, and the Conduct of Philosophy*. Dordrecht and London.
——(2000) 'Mouthpiece schmouthpiece' in Press (ed.) (2000a), 15–26.
——(2002) *The People of Plato: A Prosopography of Plato and Other Socratics*. Indianapolis.
Nehamas, A. (1998) *The Art of Living: Socratic Reflections from Plato to Foucault*. Berkeley and London.
——(1999a) *Virtues of Authenticity: Essays on Plato and Socrates*. Princeton.
——(1999b) 'Eristic, antilogic, sophistic, dialectic: Plato's demarcation of philosophy from sophistry' in Nehamas (1999a), 108–22.
——(1999c) '*Epistēmē* and *Logos* in Plato's later thought' in Nehamas (1999a), 224–48.
Nicholson, P. P. (1974) 'Unravelling Thrasymachus' Argument in *The Republic*', *Phronesis* 19, 210–32.
Nightingale, A. W. (1993) 'The folly of praise: Plato's critique of encomiastic discourse in the *Lysis* and *Symposium*', *Classical Quarterly* 43, 112–30.
——(1995) *Genres in Dialogue. Plato and the Construct of Philosophy*. Cambridge.

Nightingale, A. W. (2000) 'Sages, sophists and philosophers: Greek wisdom literature' in Taplin (ed.) (2000), 156–91.
——(2002a) 'Distant views: "realistic" and "fantastic" mimesis in Plato' in Annas and Rowe (eds) (2002), 227–47.
——(2002b) 'Towards an ecological eschatology: Plato and Bakhtin on other worlds and times' in Brahman (ed.) (2002), 220–49.
——(2003) 'Subtext and subterfuge in Plato's *Cratylus*' in Michelini (ed.) (2003a), 223–40.
Nimis, S. A. (1999) 'Ring-composition and linearity in Homer' in Mackay (ed.) (1999), 65–78.
Notomi, N. (1999) *The Unity of Plato's* Sophist: *Between the* Sophist *and the* Philosopher. Cambridge.
Nussbaum, M. C. (1980) 'Aristophanes and Socrates on learning practical wisdom', *Yale Classical Studies* 26, 43–97.
——(1986) *The Fragility of Goodness: Luck and Ethics in Greek Tragedy and Philosophy*. Cambridge.
——(1990) *Love's Knowledge: Essays on Philosophy and Literature*. New York and Oxford.
——(2001) *Upheavals of Thought: The Intelligence of Emotions*. Cambridge.
O'Brien, M. J. (1971) 'The unity of the *Laches*' in Anton and Kustas (eds) (1971), 303–15.
Ober, J. and Hedrick, C. (eds) (1996) *Demokratia: A Conversation on Democracies, Ancient and Modern*. Princeton.
Osborne, R. (ed.) (2007a) *Debating the Athenian Cultural Revolution: Art, Literature, Philosophy and Politics, 430–380 BC*. Cambridge.
——(2007b) 'Tracing cultural revolution in classical Athens' in Osborne (ed.) (2007a), 1–26.
Ostenfeld, E. (2000) 'Who speaks for Plato? Everyone!' in Press (ed.) (2000a), 211–20.
Owen, G. E. L. (ed.) (1968a) *Aristotle on Dialectic: The* Topics. Oxford.
——(1968b) 'Dialectic and eristic in the treatment of the Forms' in Owen (ed.) (1968a), 103–25.
Page, C. (1990) 'The unjust treatment of Polemarchus', *History of Philosophy Quarterly* 7, 243–67.
Panayotakis, S., Zimmerman, M., and Keulen, W. (eds) (2003) *The Ancient Novel and Beyond*. Leiden.
Partenie, C. (ed.) (2009a) *Plato's Myths*. Cambridge.
——(2009b) 'Introduction' in Partenie (ed.) (2009a), 1–27.
Patterson, R. (1987) 'Plato on philosophic character', *Journal of the History of Philosophy* 25, 325–50.
Pelling, C. B. R. (ed.) (1990a) *Characterization and Individuality in Greek Literature*. Oxford.

——(1990b) 'Childhood and personality in Greek biography' in Pelling (ed.) (1990a), 213–44.

——(1990c) 'Conclusion' in Pelling (ed.) (1990a), 245–62.

——(ed.) (1997a) *Greek Tragedy and the Historian*. Oxford.

——(1997b) 'Aeschylus' *Persae* and history' in Pelling (ed.) (1997a), 1–19.

——(1997c) 'Conclusion' in Pelling (ed.) (1997a), 213–35.

——(2000) *Literary Texts and the Greek Historian*. London and New York.

Penner, T. (1992) 'Socrates and the early dialogues' in Kraut (ed.) (1992a), 121–69.

Philip, J. A. (1970) 'The Platonic corpus', *Phoenix* 24, 296–308.

Pickard-Cambridge, W. A. (1984a) *Sophistical Refutations*, translated in Barnes (ed.) (1984), 278–314.

——(1984b) *Topics*, translated in Barnes (ed.) (1984), 167–277.

Politis, V. (2006) '*Aporia* and searching in early Plato' in Judson and Karasmanis (eds) (2006), 88–109.

Press, G. A. (1993a) *Plato's Dialogues: New Studies and Interpretations*. Lanham, MD.

——(1993b) 'Principles of dramatic and non-dogmatic Plato interpretation' in Press (1993a), 107–27.

——(1995) 'Plato's dialogues as enactments' in Gonzalez (ed.) (1995a), 133–152.

——(1996) 'The state of the question in the study of Plato', *The Southern Journal of Philosophy* 34, 507–32.

——(2000a) *Who Speaks for Plato? Studies in Platonic Anonymity*. Lanham, MD and Oxford.

——(2000b) 'Introduction' in Press (ed.) (2000a), 1–11.

——(2000c) 'The logic of attributing characters' views to Plato' in Press (ed.) (2000a), 27–38.

Prior, W. J. (ed.) (1996) *Socrates: Critical Assessments, Volume IV*. London.

——(2006) 'The portrait of Socrates in Plato's *Symposium*', *Oxford Studies in Ancient Philosophy* 31, 137–66.

Pucci, P. (ed.) (1988) *Language and the Tragic Hero: Essays on Greek Tragedy in Honor of Gordon M. Kirkwood*. Atlanta.

Reeve, C. D. C. (1985) 'Motion, rest, and dialectic in the *Sophist*', *Archiv für Geschichte der Philosophie* 67, 47–64.

——(1988) *Philosopher-Kings: The Argument of Plato's* Republic. Princeton.

Reis, B. (1999) *Der Platoniker Albinos und sein sogenannter Prologos. Prolegomena, Uberlieferungsgeschichte, kritische Edition und Ubersetzung*. Wiesbaden.

Renaud, F. (2002) 'Humbling as upbringing: the ethical dimension of the elenchus in the *Lysis*' in Scott (ed.) (2002), 183–98.

Revermann, M. (2006) *Comic Business: Theatricality, Dramatic Technique and Performance Contexts of Aristophanic Comedy*. Oxford.

Reynolds, N. B. (1988) *Interpreting Plato's* Euthyphro *and* Meno. Provo, Utah.

Robb, K. (1993) '*Asebeia* and *Sunousia*: the issues behind the indictment of Socrates' in Press (ed.) (1993a), 77–106.

——(1994) *Literacy and Paideia in Ancient Greece*. New York and Oxford.

——(1997) 'Orality, literacy and the dialogue form' in Hart and Tejera (eds) (1997) 29–64.

Roberts, D. H., Dunn, F. M., and Fowler, D. (eds) (1997) *Classical Closure: Reading the End in Greek and Latin Literature*. Princeton.

Robinson, R. (1953) *Plato's Earlier Dialectic*. Oxford.

Romilly, J. de (1975) *Magic and Rhetoric in Ancient Greece*. Cambridge, MA and London.

Roochnik, D. (1995) 'Socratic ignorance as complex irony: a critique of Gregory Vlastos', *Arethusa* 28, 39–52.

——(2003) *Beautiful City: The Dialectical Character of Plato's Republic*. Ithaca and London.

Rood, T. (1998) *Thucydides: Narrative and Explanation*. Oxford.

Rorty, A. O. (ed.) (1980) *Essays on Aristotle's* Ethics. Berkeley and London.

——(ed.) (1996) *Essays on Aristotle's* Rhetoric. Berkeley and London.

Rosen, S. (1983) *Plato's* Sophist: *The Drama of Original and Image*. New Haven and London.

Rosenblatt, L. M. (1978) *The Reader, the Text, the Poem: The Transactional Theory of the Literary Work*. Carbondale.

Ross, J. (2005) 'Shame, pleasure and the divided soul', *Oxford Studies in Ancient Philosophy* 29, 137–70.

Ross, W. D. (ed.) (1928) *The Works of Aristotle*, Vol. I. Oxford.

Rossetti, L. (ed.) (1992) *Understanding the* Phaedrus. Sankt Augustin.

Rowe, C. J. (1984) *Plato*. Brighton.

——(1986a) *Plato*: Phaedrus. Warminster.

——(1986b) 'The argument and structure of Plato's *Phaedrus*', *Proceedings of the Cambridge Philological Society* 32, 106–25.

——(1989) 'The unity of the *Phaedrus*: a reply to Heath', *Oxford Studies in Ancient Philosophy* 7, 175–88.

——(1993) *Plato*: Phaedo. Cambridge.

——(1995a) *Plato*: Statesman. Warminster.

——(ed.) (1995b) *Reading the* Statesman. Sankt Augustin.

——(1996) 'The *Politicus*: structure and form' in Gill and McCabe (eds) (1996), 153–78.

——(1999) 'Myth, history, and dialectic in Plato's *Republic* and *Timaeus–Critias*' in Buxton (ed.) (1999), 263–78.

——(2002) 'Handling a philosophical text' in Gibson and Kraus (eds) (2002), 295–318.

——(2006) 'The literary and philosophical style of the *Republic*' in Santas (2006), 7–24.

——(2007) *Plato and the Art of Philosophical Writing*. Cambridge.

Rutherford, R. B. (1988) 'Plato and lit. crit.', *Phronesis* 33, 216–24.

——(1992) 'Unifying the *Protagoras*' in Barker and Warner (eds) (1992a), 133–56.

——(1995) *The Art of Plato: Ten Essays in Platonic Interpretation*. London.

——(2002) 'Comments on Nightingale' in Annas and Rowe (eds) (2002), 249–62.

Ryle, G. (1966) *Plato's Progress*. Cambridge.

——(1968) 'Dialectic in the Academy' in Owen (ed.) (1968a), 69–79.

Santas, G. (1996) 'Socrates at work on virtue and knowledge in Plato's *Laches*' in Prior (ed.) (1996), 23–45.

——(ed.) (2006) *The Blackwell Guide to Plato's* Republic. Malden, MA and Oxford.

Sayre, K. M. (1988) 'Plato's dialogues in light of the *Seventh Letter*' in Griswold (ed.) (1988a), 93–109.

——(1992) 'A maieutic view of five late dialogues' in Klagge and Smith (eds) (1992), 221–43.

——(1995) *Plato's Literary Garden: How to Read a Platonic Dialogue*. Notre Dame, IN and London.

Schiesaro, A., Mitsis, P., and Clay, J. S. (eds) (1993) *Mega nepios: il destinatario nell'epos didascalico*. Pisa.

Schmid, W. T. (2002) 'Socratic dialectic in the *Charmides*' in Scott (ed.) (2002), 235–51.

Schofield, M. (1996) 'Likeness and likenesses in the *Parmenides*' in Gill and McCabe (eds) (1996), 49–77.

——(2007) 'Metaspeleology' in Scott (ed.) (2007), 216–31.

Scodel, H. R. (1987) *Diaeresis and Myth in Plato's* Statesman. Gottingen.

Scolnicov, S. (1976) 'Three aspects of Plato's philosophy of learning and instruction' in Simmons (ed.) (1976), 50–62.

——(1988) *Plato's Metaphysics of Education*. London.

Scott, D. (1995) *Recollection and Experience: Plato's Theory of Learning and its Successors*. Cambridge.

——(1999) 'Platonic pessimism and moral education', *Oxford Studies in Ancient Philosophy* 17, 15–36.

——(ed.) (2007) *Maieusis: Essays on Ancient Philosophy in Honour of Myles Burnyeat*. Oxford.

Scott, G. A. (ed.) (2002) *Does Socrates Have a Method? Rethinking the Elenchus in Plato's Dialogues and Beyond*. University Park, PA.

Scott, G. A. and Welton, W. A. (2000) 'Eros as messenger in Diotima's teaching' in Press (ed.) (2000a), 147–59.

Sedley, D. (1989) 'Teleology and myth in the *Phaedo*', *Proceedings of the Boston Area Colloquium in Ancient Philosophy* 5, 359–83.
——(1993) 'Chrysippus on psychological causality' in Brunschwig and Nussbaum (eds) (1993), 313–33.
——(1995) 'The dramatis personae of Plato's *Phaedo*' in Smiley (ed.) (1995), 3–26.
——(1996) 'Three Platonist interpretations of the *Theaetetus*' in Gill and McCabe (eds) (1996), 79–103.
——(1999a) 'The ideal of godlikeness' in Fine (ed.) (1999), 309–28.
——(1999b) 'The Stoic–Platonist debate on *kathêkonta*' in Ierodiakonou (ed.) (1999), 128–52.
——(2002) 'Socratic irony in the Platonist commentators' in Annas and Rowe (eds) (2002), 37–57.
——(2003) *Plato's* Cratylus. Cambridge.
——(2004) *The Midwife of Platonism: Text and Subtext in Plato's* Theaetetus. Oxford.
——(2009) 'Myth, punishment and politics in the *Gorgias*' in Partenie (ed.) (2009) 51–75.
Seeskin, K. (1984) 'Review of M. H. Mitchell, Jr., "The philosopher in Plato's *Statesman*"', *Ancient Philosophy* 4, 234–7.
——(1987) *Dialogue and Discovery: A Study in Socratic Method.* Albany.
Segal, C. (1978) '"The myth was saved": reflections on Homer and the mythology of Plato's *Republic*', *Hermes* 106, 315–36.
——(1994) 'Foreword: literary history as literary theory' in Conte (1994), vii–xv.
Sharples, R. W. (1985) *Plato*: Meno. Warminster.
Sheffield, F. C. C. (2001) 'Psychic pregnancy and Platonic epistemology', *Oxford Studies in Ancient Philosophy* 20, 1–33.
Sichel, B. A. (1976) 'Is Socrates a sophist?' in Simmons (ed.) (1976), 141–52.
Silk, M. (1990) 'The people of Aristophanes' in Pelling (ed.) (1990a), 150–73.
——(2001) 'Pindar meets Plato: theory, language, value and the classics' in Harrison (ed.) (2001a), 26–45.
Simmons, G. C. (ed.) (1976) *Paideia: Special Plato Issue.* Buffalo and Brockport.
Skemp, J. B. (1942) *The Theory of Motion in Plato's Later Dialogues.* Cambridge.
——(1952) *Plato's* Statesman. London.
Slater, N. W. (1990) *Reading Petronius.* Baltimore and London.
Slings, S. R. (1981) *A Commentary on the Platonic* Clitophon. Amsterdam.
Sluiter, I. (1999) 'Commentaries and the didactic tradition' in Most (ed.) (1999), 173–205.

Smiley, T. J. (ed.) (1995) *Philosophical Dialogues: Plato, Hume, Wittgenstein.* Oxford.
Smith, J. E. (1986) 'Plato's use of myth in the education of philosophic man', *Phoenix* 40, 20–34.
Smith, N. D. (1997) 'How the prisoners in Plato's Cave are "like us"', *Proceedings of the Boston Area Colloquium in Ancient Philosophy* 13, 187–204.
Sprague, R. K. (1962) *Plato's Use of Fallacy: A Study of the* Euthydemus *and Some Other Dialogues.* London.
Stauffer, D. (2006) *The Unity of Plato's* Gorgias: *Rhetoric, Justice, and the Philosophic Life.* Cambridge.
Sternberg, M. (1978) *Expositional Modes and Temporal Ordering in Fiction.* Baltimore and London.
Sternfeld, R. and Zyskind, H. (1976) 'Plato's *Meno* 89c: "Virtue is knowledge": a hypothesis?' *Phronesis* 21, 130–4.
——(1977) 'Plato's *Meno* 86e–87a: the geometrical illustration of the argument by hypothesis', *Phronesis* 22, 206–11.
Stewart, J. A. (1905) *The Myths of Plato.* London.
Stokes, M. C. (1986) *Plato's Socratic Conversations: Drama and Dialectic in Three Dialogues.* London.
——(1992) 'Plato and the sightlovers of the *Republic*' in Barker and Warner (eds) (1992a), 103–32.
Strang, C. (1986) 'Plato's analogy of the Cave', *Oxford Studies in Ancient Philosophy* 4, 19–34.
Suleiman, S. R. (1980) 'Introduction: varieties of audience-oriented criticism' in Suleiman and Crosman (eds) (1980), 3–45.
Suleiman, S. R. and Crosman, I. (eds) (1980) *The Reader in the Text: Essays on Audience and Interpretation.* Princeton.
Sullivan, J. P. (1994) 'Introduction' in De Jong and Sullivan (eds) (1994), 1–26.
Szlezák, T. A. (1985) *Platon und die Schriftlichkeit der Philosophie.* Berlin.
——(1999) *Reading Plato*, translated by G. Zanker. London.
Taplin, O. (1971) 'Significant actions in Sophocles' *Philoctetes*', *Greek, Roman and Byzantine Studies* 12, 25–44.
——(ed.) (2000) *Literature in the Greek and Roman Worlds: A New Perspective.* New York.
Tarrant, H. (1993) *Thrasyllan Platonism.* Ithaca and London.
——(1996) 'Orality and Plato's narrative dialogues' in Worthington (ed.) (1996), 129–47.
——(2000a) 'Where Plato speaks: reflections on an ancient debate' in Press (ed.) (2000a), 67–80.
——(2000b) *Plato's First Interpreters.* London.

Tarrant, H. (2002) '*Elenchos* and *Exetasis*: capturing the purpose of Socratic interrogation' in Scott (ed.) (2002), 61–77.
Taylor, A. E. (1961) *Plato: The* Sophist *and the* Statesman. London.
Taylor, C. C. W. (1982) 'The end of the *Euthyphro*', *Phronesis* 27, 109–18.
——(2006) 'Socrates the sophist' in Judson and Karasmanis (eds) (2006), 157–68.
Tecuşan, M. (1992) 'Speaking about the unspeakable: Plato's use of imagery' in Barker and Warner (eds) (1992a), 69–87.
Teloh, H. (1986) *Socratic Education in Plato's Early Dialogues*. Notre Dame, IN.
——(1987) 'The importance of interlocutors' characters in Plato's early dialogues', *Proceedings of the Boston Area Colloquium in Ancient Philosophy* 2, 25–38.
Thesleff, H. (1982) *Studies in Platonic Chronology*. Helsinki.
——(2000) 'The philosopher conducting dialectic' in Press (ed.) (2000a), 53–66.
Thomas, R. (1992) *Literacy and Orality in Ancient Greece*. Cambridge.
Tompkins, J. P. (ed.) (1980a) *Reader-Response Criticism: From Formalism to Post-Structuralism*. Baltimore.
——(1980b) 'An introduction to reader-response criticism' in Tompkins (ed.) (1980a), ix–xxvi.
Vander Waerdt, P. A. (ed.) (1994) *The Socratic Movement*. Ithaca and London.
Vasiliou, I. (1999) 'Conditional irony in the Socratic dialogues', *Classical Quarterly* 49, 456–72.
Versényi, L. (1982) *Holiness and Justice: An Interpretation of Plato's* Euthyphro. Washington, DC.
Vlastos, G. (1983) 'The Socratic elenchus', *Oxford Studies in Ancient Philosophy* 1, 27–58.
——(1991) *Socrates: Ironist and Moral Philosopher*. Cambridge.
——(1994) *Socratic Studies*. Cambridge.
Volk, K. (2002) *The Poetics of Latin Didactic: Lucretius, Vergil, Ovid, Manilius*. Oxford.
Von Reden, S. and Goldhill, S. (1999) 'Plato and the performance of dialogue' in Goldhill and Osborne (eds) (1999), 257–89.
Wardy, R. (1996) 'Mighty is the truth and it shall prevail?' in Rorty (ed.) (1996), 56–87.
Warner, R. (1954) *Thucydides: The Peloponnesian War, Translated with an Introduction and Notes by M. I. Finley*. Harmondsworth.
Warren, J. (2010) 'Plato on the pleasures and pains of knowing', *Oxford Studies in Ancient Philosophy* 39, 1–32.
Waugh, J. (1995) 'Neither published nor perished: the dialogues as speech not text' in Gonzalez (ed.) (1995a), 61–77.

Weingartner, R. H. (1973) *The Unity of the Platonic Dialogue: The* Cratylus, *The* Protogoras, *The* Parmenides. Indianapolis.

Weiss, R. (2001) *Virtue in the Cave: Moral Inquiry in Plato's* Meno. Oxford.

Welliver, W. (1977) *Character, Plot and Thought in Plato's* Timaeus-Critias. Leiden.

Werner, D. (2007) 'Plato's *Phaedrus* and the problem of unity', *Oxford Studies in Ancient Philosophy* 32, 91–137.

West, E. J. M. (1995) 'Plato's audiences, or how Plato replies to the fifth-century intellectual mistrust of letters' in Gonzalez (ed.) (1995a), 41–60.

White, J. B. (1996) 'Plato's *Crito*: the authority of law and philosophy' in Louden and Schollmeier (eds) (1996), 97–133.

White, N. P. (1979) *A Companion to Plato's* Republic. Oxford.

——(1993) *Plato*: Sophist. Indianapolis and Cambridge.

Wians, W. (1989) 'Aristotle, demonstration, and teaching', *Ancient Philosophy* 9, 245–53.

Wilamowitz-Moellendorff, T. von (1917) *Die Dramatische Technik des Sophokles*. Berlin.

Wilberding, J. (2004) 'Prisoners and puppeteers in the Cave', *Oxford Studies in Ancient Philosophy* 27, 117–39.

Wilkes, K. V. (1994) 'Conclusions in the *Meno*' in Day (ed.) (1994), 208–20.

Williams, B. (1973) 'The analogy of city and soul in Plato's *Republic*' in Lee, Mourelatos, and Rorty (eds) (1973), 196–206.

Williamson, T. (2000) *Knowledge and its Limits*. Oxford.

Wolfsdorf, D. (1998) 'The historical reader of Plato's *Protagoras*', *Classical Quarterly* 48, 126–33.

——(2004) 'Interpreting Plato's early dialogues', *Oxford Studies in Ancient Philosophy* 27, 15–40.

Woodman, T. and Powell, J. (eds) (1992a) *Author and Audience in Latin Literature*. Cambridge.

——(1992b) 'Epilogue' in Woodman and Powell (eds) (1992a), 204–15.

Woodruff, P. (1988) 'Reply to Ronald Polansky' in Griswold (ed.) (1988a), 210–14.

Worthington, I. (ed.) (1996) *Voice into Text: Orality and Literacy in Ancient Greece*. Leiden.

Young, C. M. (1994) 'Plato and computer dating', *Oxford Studies in Ancient Philosophy* 12, 227–50.

Zagzebski, L. T. (1996) *Virtues of the Mind: An Inquiry into the Nature of Virtue and the Ethical Foundations of Knowledge*. Cambridge.

Zanker, P. (1995) *The Mask of Socrates: The Image of the Intellectual in Antiquity*, translated by Alan Shapiro. Berkeley and Oxford.

Zuckert, C. (2003) 'Comments on Howland, Farness and Ausland: new readings of Plato's *Republic*' in Michelini (ed.) (2003a), 145–51.

General Index

Index of Works